Family Communication

Cohesion and Change

Kathleen M. Galvin

Northwestern University

Bernard J. Brommel

Northeastern Illinois University

Scott, Foresman and Company

Glenview, Illinois

Dallas, Tex.   Oakland, N.J.   Palo Alto, Cal.   Tucker, Ga.   London, England

To my family: The Galvins, Wilkinsons, Nicholsens, and Sullivans, plus the special friends I consider as my family.

KMG

To my children: Michaela Ann, Brian, Debra, Brent, Brad, Blair; with thanks to Alice and Mary Frances Hanrahan and Wayne and Winifred Jones.

BJB

An Instructor's Manual for *Family Communication: Cohesion and Change* is available. It may be obtained through a Scott, Foresman representative or by writing to Speech Communication Editor, College Division, Scott, Foresman and Company, 1900 East Lake Avenue, Glenview, Illinois 60025.

Library of Congress Cataloging in Publication Data

Galvin, Kathleen M.
  Family communication.

  Bibliography: p. 291
  Includes index.
  1. Family. 2. Interpersonal communication.
I. Brommel, Bernard J., 1930–   II. Title.
HQ734.G19   306.8   81-9332
ISBN 0-673-15380-0   AACR2

Acknowledgments

Excerpts from *Family Worlds* by Robert D. Hess and Gerald Handel. Copyright ©
1959 by The University of Chicago. Reprinted by permission.

Virginia Satir, *Peoplemaking*. Palo Alto: Science and Behavior Books, Inc., 1972.

From "Circumplex Model of Marital and Family Systems: 1. Cohesion and
Adaptability Dimensions, Family Types, and Clinical Application" by David H.
Olson, Douglas H. Sprenkle, and Candyce Russell in *Family Process,* Vol. 18, No. 1,
March 1979. © 1979 by Family Process, Inc. Reprinted by permission.

From *Inside the Family* by David Kantor and William Lehr. Copyright © 1975 by
Jossey-Bass, Inc., Publishers. Reprinted by permission.

From *Social Penetration* by Irwin Altman and Dalmus Taylor. Copyright © 1973 by
Holt, Rinehart and Winston, Inc. Reprinted by permission of the authors.

From "Communication and Adjustment in Marriage" by Leslie Navran in *Family
Process,* Vol. 6, No. 2, September 1967, pp. 173–184. © 1967 by The Mental
Research Institute and The Family Institute. Reprinted by permission of Family
Process, Inc.

William W. Wilmot, *Dyadic Communication,* © 1979, 2/e, Addison-Wesley
Publishing Company, Inc., Chapter 1, pp. 10–11; Chapter 6, pp. 143 and 145.
Reprinted with permission.

From Salvador Minuchin, *Families and Family Therapy.* Reprinted by permission of
Harvard University Press, Cambridge, Massachusetts.

Reprinted from "Empirical and Theoretical Extensions of Self-Disclosure" by Shirley
Gilbert in *Explorations in Interpersonal Communication,* edited by Gerald R. Miller,
pp. 210, 211–212, © 1976 by Sage Publications, Inc., Beverly Hills, by permission of
the publisher.

Alton Barbour and Alvin A. Goldberg, *Interpersonal Communication: Teaching
Strategies and Resources.* Urbana, Illinois: ERIC Clearinghouse on Reading and
Communication Skills, 1974, p. 31.

From "Marital Conflict and Marital Intimacy" by Larry B. Feldman, *Family Process,*
Vol. 18, March 1979, p. 70. © 1979 Family Process, Inc. Reprinted by permission.

Reprinted from "The Sexual Role" by John Carlson in *Role Structure and Analysis of
the Family* by F. Ivan Nye, pp. 103, 105, © 1976 by Sage Publications, Inc., Beverly
Hills, by permission of the publisher.

From "Communication with Children: Toward a Healthy Construction of
Communication Roles" by Fern Johnson. Paper presented at the Central States
Speech Association Conference, April 14, 1978, Chicago, Illinois. Reprinted by
permission.

Thomas J. D'Zurilla and M. R. Goldfried, "Problem Solving and Behavior
Modification" in *Journal of Abnormal Psychology,* 78 (1971): 107–126.

"Fight Elements Chart" and excerpts based on pp. 162–165 in *The Intimate Enemy*
by Dr. George R. Bach and Peter Wyden. Copyright © 1968, 1969 by George R.
Bach and Peter Wyden. Reprinted by permission of William Morrow & Company.

Photo Credits

PREFACE

Family Communication: Cohesion and Change evolved in response to a need for a textbook which examines the family from a communication perspective. It is for students and teachers of family-related courses in communication, psychology, sociology, counseling, home economics, theology, and health. Historically, family interaction has received attention within a medical and therapeutic perspective. Only recently have scholars turned their attention to interaction within functional families, with the past decade witnessing growing interest in ordinary family interaction processes within all of the social sciences. Current scholarship is examining the role of communication in long-term relationships such as those found in marriages and families. This text addresses itself to an overview of these issues.

The basic premise of the book is that communication undergirds family functioning. Using a systems approach, we consider in depth the communication processes within the family and the extent to which communication affects and is affected by the family. The focus of the text is descriptive rather than prescriptive, because we believe that description provides the understanding necessary to the eventual development of valid prescriptions. We recognize the vast range of family types and life-styles. Within this diversity, however, we examine how family members typically perform what we consider to be primary family functions—regulating cohesion and adaptability—and secondary family functions—developing appropriate family images, themes, boundaries, and biosocial beliefs.

The first three chapters of the book establish the foundation for what follows by presenting basic communication concepts, a framework for analyzing family communication, an explanation of how specific family meanings develop, and the role of one's family-of-origin in establishing communication patterns. The remaining chapters explore communication issues related to basic family interaction: relationship development, intimacy, roles, power, conflict, developmental stages, and adjustment to unpredictable crises. The final chapters focus on the physical and temporal contexts for communication patterns and on approaches toward the improvement of family communication.

Throughout the book we rely on first-person examples and quotations gathered from our students, clients, colleagues, and our own families. These complement and expand upon the content, make direct applications of the ideas, and serve as a valuable resource in piquing students' interest and involvement in the issues. Thus, the book contains a combination of research and experience.

Many persons contributed to the completion of the work. Arthur Bochner, Temple University, and Merelyn Jacobs, Dartmouth College, shared their teaching materials with us and thus furthered our involvement in the family communication course. We received valuable feedback on manuscript drafts from Virginia Satir; Judy Goldberg, Arapahoe Community College; John Masterson, University of Miami; and Robert Ross and his students, University of Northern

Colorado. We are deeply indebted to Daniel Wackman, University of Minnesota, for his insight and suggestions, and to Edna Rogers-Millar for excellent, comprehensive, and constructive reviews that significantly shaped the final version.

Peggy Parsons, Gertrude Edelheit, Marcy Velick, and Jean Walsh typed the manuscript; Geri Staniec helped compile the index. Pamela Cooper provided organizational support while Charles Wilkinson supplied numerous examples from his family practice. Northeastern Illinois University provided Bernard Brommel with a faculty grant for research on this book.

We are grateful to the Scott, Foresman editorial staff: JoAnn Johnson for actively pursuing the project, Barbara Muller for her supportive encouragement and guidance through the writing stages, and Anita Portugal for directing us through the final stages as painlessly as possible. To our families we express our gratitude for their exceptional patience and moral support even when we wrote about them in these pages!

Finally, the book comes from our own commitment to and enthusiasm for teaching the family communication course. Unlike most other academic courses, students bring their own personal experiences to the course content and thus start with considerable insight and knowledge of the subject. The result is a variety of teaching and learning methods and experiences which continue to educate us, as well as the students, about how families function and what it means to be a member of a family.

Kathleen M. Galvin
Bernard J. Brommel

Contents

Introduction to Family Communication

For me communication plays a central role in the growth of family relationships. I grew up in a family in which people kept a great distance from each other both physically and emotionally. Even today my mother is the only person who communicates with everyone else. The rest of us seem to be strangers assuming the role of family members.

As I grew older I swore that my children would never feel that way about their family. My husband and I have worked very hard to stay close to each other and to provide physical and emotional closeness for the children. Over the years we have had some rough moments but we always took risks to share things with each other so that we could grow together and not apart. Our communication holds us together.

Family Communication. As you read these words you may think that this will be a totally new area of study, or you may respond that you have been talking to family members all your life and wonder what else there is to know about it. It is true that in this book we will be discussing a subject that each of you knows something about since you have spent years of your life functioning within a family. You may have spent those years trying to understand the other members and trying to be understood, or you may have spent the years feeling very connected to the other family members. Thus you have considerable experience with family communication. Yet since each of you has lived only in either one or a small number of families, your experience is limited, compared to the range of possible family experiences.

Within these pages we will present a framework for examining communication within families; by the end of the text you should be able to apply this model to an unknown family and eventually understand that family as a communication system. We also hope that you will apply what you learn to your own family or to the family you will eventually form, in order to improve communication among family members.

In order to illustrate many of the concepts, we will rely on situations related by our friends, students, and clients. You will find this material set off as a quotation and written in the first person. We hope these statements will motivate you to apply your own experiences to the material in order to understand it more completely. As you read this text, you should encounter some material that reminds you very specifically of your own family experiences and you should find other material which seems very different from your own background since people relate to each other very differently within what is called a "family."

As an introduction to the area of family communication, this chapter will discuss families and the communication process in general and the relationship between the two. Such a discussion will lead to a framework for understanding the rest of the book.

FAMILIES: DEFINITION AND BASIC PREMISES

We have been talking about families as if each of us has a similar understanding of what is meant by the term *family.* Traditionally families have been viewed according to consaguine, or blood ties, and according to conjugal, or marital ties. In keeping with this, Laing (1972) suggests that we identify, as families, "networks of people who live together over periods of time, who have ties of marriage and kinship to one another" (3). Emphasizing the generational aspects of families, Terkelsen (1980) suggests that a family is a "small social system made up of individuals related to each other by reason of strong reciprocal affections and loyalties, and comprising a permanent household (or cluster of households) that persists over years and decades" (23). In contemporary society family diversity abounds. One indication of the complexities of today's families may be found in the range of families interviewed by Jane Howard for her book *Families* (1978). Her subjects include: large extended blood-related families, formal communal groups, single parents, gay parents, and families of various races and economic situations. Even your authors represent two different family orientations. One of us grew up on an Iowa farm in a family of eight children, married, fathered six children, divorced, and is recently a new grandfather. The other grew up in New York City as an only child. After her parents died, she acquired an adopted family with three siblings. Currently she is married and raising three children, one of whom is adopted. Although our blood relatives are important to us, each of us has friends whom we consider to be members of our families.

Some of you may have grown up in a small family or a large family, an intergenerational household or a nuclear family. Your brothers and sisters may be blood-related, step, or adopted. Some of you may be single parents, step-parents, or foster parents. Whereas some of you may have experienced one long, committed marriage, others of you may have experienced divorce, death, desertion, and remarriages. No simple pattern exists.

When we use the term *family* in this book, we refer to a wide range of people-combinations that are encompassed within the following styles of family formations: the "natural" family, the single-parent family, the blended family, the extended family, and the couple without children (Satir, 1972, and Terkelsen, 1980). These are not discrete categories; some families may belong to more than one. A natural family consists of two parents and the children who are from the union of these parents. Thus blood ties and the original marriage bond characterize this type. Although this type is frequently thought of as the "typical" family, it no longer represents the vast majority of family types.

A single-parent family consists of one parent and one or more children. This formation may include: an unmarried woman or man and his or her off-spring; men and women without partners through death, divorce, or desertion, and the children who remain; single parents who have adopted or foster children.

The blended family style consists of two adults and their children, all of whom may not be from the union of those two parents. Families may be blended through the remarriage of adults whose spouses have left, a situation that brings the children into new family ties. Families may also be blended through the addition of adopted or foster children. Many of us have witnessed the common pattern in which a natural family becomes a single-parent family for a period of time after which it evolves into a blended family.

Although an extended family usually refers to that group of relatives living within the surrounding city or nearby area, it may be more narrowly understood as the addition of blood relatives to the everyday life of a parent-child unit. For example, this may take a cross-generational form including grandparents who live with a parent-child system or who take on exclusive parenting roles for grandchildren.

I grew up in an extended family. My great-grandparents were the dominant figures. Although there was no one living in the base household while I was growing up, many of the family members had lived with the dominant figures at one time or another. There were six different households in the neighborhood I grew up in. My great-grandmother, referred to as Mother, babysat for all the kids while our parents were at work.

There are also people who were informally adopted in my family. My mother and one of my cousins were raised by their grandmother even though their parents did not live there. In my family, no one is considered half or step. You are a member of the family and that is that. You have equal access to everything and are included in all family activities.

Another variation of the extended family may be viewed as the communal family, a couple or a group of people, some of whom are unrelated by blood, who share a commitment to each other, live together, and consider themselves to be a family. Formal examples of these family types are found in a kibbutz or in religious organizations, whereas other communal families are informally formed around friendship or common interests or commitments. Two families may share so many experiences that over time both sets of children and parents begin to think of each other as part of the "family."

Although we usually think of families as having children, couples without children have formed their own familial unit, as an outgrowth of their original families. These may include heterosexual or homosexual partners as long as the partners consider each other as family. These couple members serve as children to the previous generation at the same time each partner provides loyalty and affection to the other over years.

As we talk about families in this book, then, we will be taking a broad inclusive view; therefore if the members consider themselves to be a family we would accept their self-definition. Generally we will be referring to networks of people who live together over long periods of time bound by ties of marriage, blood, or commitment, legal or otherwise. Such a definition encompasses countless variations and numerous interaction patterns.

It is important to distinguish between two types of family experience—current families and families-of-origin. As you well know, families in combination beget families through the evolutionary cycles of coming together and separating. Thus each person may experience life in different families starting with his or her family-of-origin. *Family-of-origin* refers to the family or families in which a person is raised. The family you grew up in is your family-of-origin. Satir, noted family therapist, stresses the importance of the family-of-origin as "the main base against and around which most family blueprints are designed" (200). She suggests: "It is easy to duplicate in your family the same things that happened in your growing up. This is true whether your family was a nurturing or a troubled one" (200). As we will discover, family-of-origin experiences are crucial in the development of communication patterns in newly-formed or current families.

Another concept central to understanding the family is its systemic nature. Although the next chapter will explore in detail the family as a system, we can highlight the family's systemic process through this analogy.

If you walk up to a knothole in a fence and look through, you might see a strange sight. You see a man in a striped outfit and a funny peaked cap standing lackadaisically on the grass scratching his head. After a moment you see him lean forward intently, hands resting on his knees. This is followed by a quick look to the right, an excited start, and then a loud cheering noise. Your man looks very happy. After this he goes back to the initial relaxed position. A minute later he repeats the intent position and then leaps in the air, one arm raised, catches something, lands, and throws it. Then he throws down his hat and stomps on it in a rage. Finally he walks out of your line of vision. That's what you may witness. Viewed from the knothole the person may appear to be acting very strangely, but if a hole was cut in the fence large enough to allow your entire face to fit through it, you may discover that there are other people in similar outfits on the field, that a crowd is sitting in stands, and that a game of baseball is underway. Those seemingly strange behaviors appear much more understandable when seen within the context of the other persons surrounding the man you have been watching. (We acknowledge Miriam Reitz and Charles Kramer, Institute for Family Studies in Chicago, for developing this analogy.)

So too when observing a particular family member. When you see an individual, certain behaviors may appear strange or even bizarre, but if you understand the whole family context, your perceptions may change. Many individual's behaviors are more understandable when viewed within the context of the human systems in which they function, since the context provides the environment and the other people who influence the individual family member. Thus the environment and kinship serve as contexts for shaping familial systems.

Within a system the parts and the relationship between them form a whole; changes in one part will result in changes in the other parts. So too in families. Satir says it well (1972) when she describes a family as a mobile. Picture the mobile that hangs over a child's crib as having people instead of animals or sailboats on it. As events touch one member of the family, other family members reverberate in relationship to the change in the affected member. Thus if members of your family get a raise, flunk out of school, marry, or become ill, each of these events affects the surrounding family system to a greater or lesser extent depending on each person's current relationship with the specific individual. In Chapter 2 we will examine in detail the family as a system in order to understand how communication works within families.

As you move through this book you will encounter again and again the previous basic premises about the family: (1) Families may be considered as one of five types—the "natural," the single parent, the blended, the extended, and the couple without children; (2) The family-of-origin is influential in the development of the current family; (3) Viewing the family as a system is the most productive way to study families.

WHAT DO WE MEAN BY "COMMUNICATION"?

My sister and I have a long history of intimacy. Since early childhood, we have shared unique communication behavior. Our intimate name-calling is truly unique. Gail refers to me as "Sis," "K. C.," or "Coops." I, in return, call her "Kitten," "G. K.," or "Li'l Coops." As a result of doing many activities together, we acquired the duplex nickname of "The Coop Sisters." Occasionally, my mother refers to me by the name Loree. This is my middle name and the name of her grandmother whom she loved deeply. She is the only one who calls me this. "G. K." and I have always shared some type of personal jargon. This ritual began with our secret language of "witchtalk." "Witchtalk" meant saying the exact opposite of what one really meant. Now, in our current jargon, a romantic relationship is "official" only if one has been kissed by the male and "the bone" refers to a male who is sexually exciting. We also share a peculiar handshake which can be interpreted as meaning "I agree with you 100%" or "I can identify with you."

In this book we are exploring the family as an interaction system, concentrating on the mutual influence between communication and family development: (1) how communication patterns affect family relationships, and (2) how relationships among family members affect communication. In order to do this we have to examine the general communication process and then apply it to family situations. Within the framework of common cultural communication patterns, each family has the capacity to develop its own communication code based on the experiences of individual members and the collective family experience. Most of us develop our communication skills within the family context learning both the general cultural language and the specific familial communication code. Since most of us take our own backgrounds for granted, you may not be aware of the context your family provided for learning communication. For example, on a simple level, you may have learned "funny" words for familiar things such as "official" or "the bone"; on a deeper level you have learned particular ways to express feelings of affection or conflict. People in other families may have learned these things slightly differently.

The Communication Process

Communication may be viewed as a symbolic, transactional process, or to put it more simply, as the process of creating and sharing meanings. By saying that communication is *symbolic,* we mean that symbols are employed to transmit messages. Verbal behavior or words are the most commonly used symbols but the whole range of nonverbal behavior including facial expressions, eye contact, gestures, movement, body posture, appearance, and spatial distance may be used symbolically. Also, objects and ideas can be referents or symbols. Different families may use kisses, special food, toys, or poems as symbols of love. Although symbols allow us to share our thoughts on the widest range of possible subjects, the symbols must be mutually understood for the meanings to be shared. Witness the confusion in the following situation:

On a Sunday morning early in our marriage, my wife told me that every Sunday morning before the wedding she had coffee and peanuts to start the day off right. So, being a sensitive bridegroom I trotted off to the kitchen and returned with coffee and a handful of peanuts to meet the (rather unusual) request of my bride. After a full minute of hilarious laughter, she calmed down enough to inform me that she expected coffee and the newspaper with the "Peanuts" cartoon strip. I went away feeling like Charlie Brown. . . .

If meanings are not mutually shared, it is very difficult to communicate.

To say that communication is *transactional* means that when people communicate, they have a mutual impact on each other. In short, you do not originate communication. you participate in it (Watzlawick et al., 1967). Thus, in communicative relationships, all participants are both "affecting and being affected, even when one *appears* to be sending many more messages than the other" (Miller in Book [ed.] 1980, 12).

The transactional nature of communication also implies that it is more appropriately viewed from a relational perspective; within a systems perspective it becomes nonproductive to analyze each personality or each act separately because of the integrative nature of the system. Each personality and each communication act occurs within the context of a system and reflects the nature of those relationships:

My father and my brother had a very difficult relationship with each other for many years although each of them had an excellent relationship with everyone else in the family. Dan saw Dad as repressive and demanding although I would characterize him as serious and concerned. Dad saw Dan as careless and uncommitted although no one else saw him that way. Whenever they tried to talk to each other, each responded to the person he created and it was a continual battle.

In this example, knowing Dan or his father separately does not account for their conflictual behavior when they are together. Each influences the other's interaction. Each creates a context for the other and relates within the context. It is as if you say to another: "You are sensitive," or "You are repressive," or "You are shiftless," "And that's how I will relate to you." The content and style of the messages vary according to how each sees himself and how each predicts the other will react. As well as taking the environment or context into account, the transactional view stresses the importance of the communicator's perceptions and actions in determining the outcome of interactions.

Thus the relationship pattern, not one or another specific act, becomes the focal point. Our perception of one another and our subsequent behavior can actually change the behavior of the person we see. A mother who constantly praises her son for his thoughtfulness and sensitivity, who notices the good things in his efforts, may change her son's perception of himself and his subsequent behavior with her and with other people. On the other hand, a husband who constantly complains about or objects to his wife's parenting behavior may lower her self-esteem and change her subsequent behavior toward him and the children. Thus, in communication relationships, each person influences and is influenced by the other.

Wilmot (1975) summarizes the major points of the transactional approach to communication in the following way:

1. Communication is contextual.
2. Each participant simultaneously creates and interprets communication cues.
3. Each participant affects and is affected by the other.
4. In a communicative transaction, any variable can be seen as a stimulus or response, contingent on your point of view. (11)

To say that communication is a *process* "implies a continuous interaction of an indefinitely large number of variables with a concomitant, continuous change in the values taken by these variables" (Miller and Steinberg, 1975, 40). Thus, the communication process derives its complexity from the interactions of numerous factors that affect relationships and which vary in intensity over time. In the following chapters, we will analyze the countless internal and external factors that affect any family.

And finally, process implies change—the variables in a process and their relationship to each other change continuously (Miller and Steinberg, 41). Relationships, no matter how committed, change constantly and communication both affects and reflects these changes. The passage of time brings with it predictable and unpredictable crises which take their toll on family regularity and stability. Yet everyday moods, minor pleasures, or irritation can shift the communication behaviors on a day to day basis.

As each day passes family members subtly renegotiate their relationships. Today you may be in a bad mood and people adjust to that with you, tomorrow adaptations may be made around your brother's great report card. Next week a major job change may affect all your relationships. Over time whole families change as they pass through stages of growth; members are born, members age, members leave, members die. As you will see in the chapters on family development and change, communication patterns reflect these developments in family life.

As we said earlier, communication may be viewed as a symbolic, transactional process or a process of creating and sharing meanings. Let us now examine the ways in which meaning develops.

Meanings and Messages

How does a person gain a set of meanings? Basically our perceptions of the world, which affect our meanings and messages, result from our filter systems which reflect our past experiences and the current situation. You might say we have lenses or filters through which we view the world. This filter process involves physical, social, and individual factors (Bandler and Grinder, 1975, 8–12). These factors combine uniquely for each individual and determine how that person perceives and interacts with the world in general, and more specifically how he or she relates directly to the surrounding family system. Although this sounds like a very singular process, as we talk about communication events we must remember our transactional perspective. Each communicator constantly affects and is affected by the other, thus perceptions are occurring within the context of a relational system and are constantly influenced by that system.

Development of Meanings • Our physical state based on our human sensory systems—sight, hearing, touch, taste, and smell—constitutes the first set of filters. Our perceptions are also filtered through the social system or through the way we use language, our accepted ways of seeing things, and all the socially agreed-upon conventions that standardize parts of our world. We come to share some common meanings for our verbal and nonverbal symbols with those around us. We may share some very general experiences with many people we encounter and much more specific experiences with a smaller group of people. For example, with some persons we share only global experiences such as cultural background including language, geographic area, customs, beliefs, and attitudes. With others we may also share the specific and narrow experiences of living together in the house at 6945 Osceola Street and learning to understand each other's idiosyncrasies.

The social experience frames our world. For example, the language we speak limits the meanings we can ascertain. Eskimos have over twenty words for snow, therefore they have many more ways of perceiving this substance than most other Americans. The current pressure to use nonsexist language reflects a belief that women have formed less powerful images of themselves due to the emphasis on the masculine in pronouns and particular words. Yet although language affects our meanings, we are capable of broadening such perspectives by learning new languages, opening ourselves to new experiences.

Thus, the overall culture affects perceptions and meanings but the immediate groups to which one belongs exert a strong influence on an individual's perceptual set. The family, the school, the office, the friendship group, all provide contextual meaning and influence the way we give meaning to the sense data we receive. If giving a handmade gift at Christmas is considered a special sign of caring, a knitted Christmas stocking may be valued, but the most expensive necklace will not be perceived as having great value. Being a member of the Thurman family, a farmer, a square dance caller, a volunteer fireman, or a church elder provides context for giving meaning to the world for the individual and for a small segment of people who surround that person.

Although the physical and social systems provide the basic general filters, specific constraints upon an individual influence that person's meanings and his or her interpretation processes within the larger society. Individual constraints refer to all the representations we create for our meanings based on our own personal histories. Although some of us may have similar histories, each person develops a unique way of dealing with sensory information and, thus, an individual way of seeing the world and relating to others in it. Two members of the Thurman family may share being farmers, square dance callers, firemen, and church elders, yet they will respond differently to many situations. Witness the many brothers and sisters who disagree on the kind of family life they experienced together. One declares, "I had a very happy childhood" versus a sibling's statement, "I would never want to go through those years again." For each of us specific events and people affect our meanings—a creative third-grade teacher, a bad bout with pneumonia, the summers at our Aunt Mary's—all contribute to our response to the world yet all are influenced by others' responses.

My sister Diane was considered the "problem child" in our house. As far as experts can determine, her emotional difficulties stem from an unknown trauma when she was three, when they suggest she was rejected by my parents at a time when she needed love. The reality was that Diane functioned as a scapegoat for all of us. Although Diane and I are very close in age, we had different experiences in our family

> because of the way she perceived the family and was perceived by family members.

As family members we do share many similar perceptions with the other family members who have learned to see the world in similar ways to us.

When we talk about communication, we are dealing with symbolic acts to which we assign meaning through our transactions with the people around us. The meanings emerge through the use of symbolic acts as our interactions give us information on how to interpret the symbols. After each encounter with a person or object we become better able to deal with similar situations and our behavior takes on certain patterns. The greater the repetition, the greater the probability of the assigned meaning.

After you have functioned within a family system, you begin to become comfortable with your ability to handle the symbols, mainly because you are able to interpret the symbols on all levels and feel that you really understand them. As a child when you heard your mother yell "Johnny" or "Sara" or "Elizabeth-Marie," you were able to tell from her tone of voice just what to expect. Today, you can sit at dinner and hear your younger sister say, "I just hate that Ernie Johnson" and know that she's really falling in love.

Levels of Meaning and Metacommunication • Communication of meaning occurs on two levels: "Every communication has a content and a relationship aspect such that the latter clarifies the former and is, therefore, a metacommunication" (Watzlawick et al., 54). When two people are talking, each is relating information to the other but simultaneously each person is also "commenting" on another level on how the information should be understood (Littlejohn, 1978, 206). This simultaneous relationship-talk or metacommunication is often nonverbal. When a mother says, "When are you going to pick up those clothes?" she is asking an informational question, but there is another level of meaning. It is up to you to determine if, by her nonverbal tone, she is really questioning at what time of day you will remove the articles, or if she is telling you to get them out of there in the next thirty seconds.

One level of communication is often referred to as a content or report function, or that which conveys the data of communication, while the other level is called the relationship or command level, or the instruction about how to interpret the report level.

Metacommunication occurs when people choose to communicate about their communication: to give verbal or nonverbal instructions on how their actions should be taken. Such remarks as "I was only kidding," "This is important," or "Talking about this makes me uncomfortable" serve as signals to another on how to take certain comments as do facial expressions, gestures, or vocal tones. On a deeper level, many couples or family members have had to spend countless hours talking about the way they fight or the way they express affection.

> I married a woman who was like the farmer who explained his lack of expressed affection by saying, "I told you I loved you when I married

you. If I ever change my mind, I'll let you know." I grew up in a very loving household with demonstrative parents and when Elaine and I were first married, I thought that we must be having real problems since she never seemed to return my statements of affection. We had to have many long sessions on how affection is not to be taken for granted and how I needed to hear that she loved me.

Thus metacommunication, meaning verbal or nonverbal communication about communication, assumes great significance in relational situations.

Yet metacommunication may serve to confuse or distort the message. Although the verbal and nonverbal message should be congruent, or the metacommunication should clarify the original message, sometimes a person sends a mixed message in which he or she disqualifies the original message. For example, if the report and command aspects of a message contradict each other, the listener is left with confusion and often misinformation. "Oh, you two go ahead and have a good time, I'll be fine here by myself" can easily become a mixed message if the tone of voice indicates disappointment, if the facial expression displays depression, or if the subsequent words reflect something like "It never does any good to tell you anything different anyway." Thus, the metacommunication serves to disqualify the original message.

You may be able to see how this happens if you take expressions such as the following and envision them being spoken with sarcasm or disappointment: "I don't care" or "You be sure to have fun." Picture the following interchange in which a disqualifying comment negates the earlier statements.

Son: Are you sure you don't want to go?
Father: No, I'm fine.
Son: OK, see you later.
Father: See, you never want an old man ruining all your fun.

Such messages can be baffling and frustrating for other family members to deal with as they try to understand what is really being said.

I found that I sent mixed messages without being conscious of it. Often my small daughter would ask, "Are you happy, Mommy?" when she sensed a negative change in my mood. I found that I usually snapped something like "Yes, I'm fine," when clearly my tone of voice or face would indicate the opposite. After I caught myself doing this a few times, I resolved to be honest and to explain how I am feeling and why. It takes longer but it teaches her that negative feelings are OK.

Thus, metacommunication, as exemplified in positive and negative message patterns, remains an integral and vital part of every transactional communication. All messages include communication about communication.

For most people concerned with interpersonal communication, there is an underlying assumption about communication, namely, how people exchange messages influences the form and content of their relationship. As communication serves to shape the structure of the family system and the individuals involved, a family develops its own set of meanings.

Although we have used many family examples in describing the communication process, we have not explored the role of communication within the family. In the following section we will examine the role communication plays in forming, maintaining, and changing family systems as families perform core functions.

COMMUNICATION PATTERNS AND FAMILY FUNCTIONS

When you come into contact with another family, you have probably noticed how their communication differs from that of the families in which you have lived. Ways of relating, making decisions, sharing feelings, and handling conflict may vary slightly or greatly from your own personal experiences. Each family's unique message system serves to provide the means of dealing with the major functions which give shape to family life. In other words, communication serves to provide form and content to a family's life as members engage in family-related functions. We will examine two primary family functions and four supporting functions which both affect and are affected by communication.

Primary Functions

In their attempt to integrate the numerous concepts related to marital/ family interaction, Olson, Sprenkle, and Russell (1979) suggest that the conceptual clustering of these concepts ". . . reveals two significant dimensions of family behavior—cohesion and adaptability" (3). We will use these categories as underpinnings for understanding functions that affect and are affected by communication. From our perspective, two major family functions involve:

1. Establishing a pattern of cohesion, or separateness and connectedness;
2. Establishing a pattern of adaptability.

An examination of both of these will reveal their importance to family interaction.

Cohesion • From the moment you were born, you have been learning how to handle distance or closeness within your family system. You were taught directly or subtly how to be connected to, or separated from, other family members. Cohesion implies "the emotional bonding members have with one another and the degree of individual autonomy a person experiences in the family system" (Olson et al., 5). In other words, a family attempts to deal with a core issue of the extent to which physical or psychological intimacy will be encouraged or discouraged.

When I got married, I tried to reserve a psychological space that was just mine—something that would keep me from being so involved with my husband that I could not separate one from the other. I was afraid that if anything happened to him I would not be able to cope unless I could keep from sharing everything with him. Over the past five years of my marriage, I've changed my mind because I began to believe that I was only cheating the two of us out of the best relationship we could have. I realize that David is willing to love me as fully as possible so I've grown to take the risk to respond as fully as possible. It still frightens me.

The issue of cohesion has been identified by numerous scholars from various fields as central to the understanding of family life. Family researchers Kantor and Lehr (1976) view "distance regulation" as a major family function; family therapist Minuchin (1967) talks about "enmeshed and disengaged" families; sociologists Hess and Handel (1959) describe the family's need to "establish a pattern of separateness and connectedness." Other variations of the same theme abound (Olson et al., 7). Cohesion in a family affects and is affected by the communication among members. It is through communication that family members are able to develop and maintain or change their patterns of cohesion. A father may decide that it is inappropriate to continue the physical closeness he has experienced with his daughter now that she has become a teenager, and he may limit his touching or playful roughhousing. She may become angry, find new ways of being close, develop more outside friends, or attempt to force her father back into the old patterns. A husband may demand more intimacy from his wife as he ages. He may desire more serious conversation, make more sexual advances, share more of his feelings. His wife may ignore this new behavior or engage in more intimate behaviors on her part.

Families with extremely high cohesion are often referred to as "enmeshed," members who are so closely bonded that individuals experience little autonomy or fulfillment of personal needs and goals. "Disengaged" refers to families at the other end of the continuum in which members experience very little closeness or family solidarity, yet each member has high autonomy and individuality.

Disengaged Families	Cohesion	Enmeshed Families
←———————————	——————————————	———————————→
Low		High

Specific issues that we can use to examine the degree of family cohesion are "emotional bonding, independence, boundaries, time, space, friends, decision-making, and interests and recreation" (Olson et al., 6). Throughout the book, we will look at ways families deal with issues of coming together or staying apart and how they use communication in their attempt to reach their desired cohesion level.

Cohesion is not a static process, however. A family does not come together and stay there, as is evident from the previous examples. Hence, we must account for change within a family's life.

   Adaptability • When you think of the changes in your own family over the past five or ten years, you may be amazed at how different the systems and its members are at this point. Rather than existing as an unchanging entity, a family experiences change as it goes through its own developmental stages and as it deals with crises that arise in everyday life, such as adapting to the marriage or a job transfer of one of its members.

   When writing about family change, Olson et al. define adaptability as "the ability of a marital/family system to change its power structure, role relationships, and relationship rules in response to situational and developmental stress" (12). From our perspective of the family as a system, we can say that each human system has both stability-promoting processes (morphostasis) and change-promoting processes (morphogenesis) to maintain itself. Such systems need periods of stability and of change in order to function. Families that regularly experience extensive change may be considered chaotic—due to total unpredictability and stress they have little opportunity to develop relationships and establish common meanings. Rigidity characterizes families on the other extreme who constantly repress change and growth.

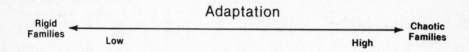

Family systems constantly restructure themselves as they pass through predictable developmental stages: marriage, pregnancy, birth, parenting, and the return to the original couple all represent major familial changes. Likewise when positive or negative stresses arise involving such issues as money, illness, or divorce, families must adapt.

My son and daughter-in-law adopted an older child and had to adapt their communication patterns to accommodate Shirley. Although lying was forbidden in their family when they adopted Shirley, they had to reassess this position because she had learned to lie for most of her life. My son and daughter-in-law had to learn to be more tolerant of this behavior, particularly when she first joined the family, or they would have had to send her back to the agency.

On a more global level the family as an institution has demonstrated its ability to adapt to societal developments. The social changes of the twentieth century necessitate a family system that both structurally and functionally is ". . . highly adaptive externally to the demands of other social institutions and internally to the needs of its own members . . ." (Vincent, 29). The many family types listed earlier stand as testimony to the adaptive capacity of the family.

Communication remains central to the adaptive function of a family. Any effective adaptation relies on shared meanings gained through the family message system. Through communication, families (1) make it clear to their members how much adaptation is allowed within the system, and (2) regulate the adaptive behaviors of their members and the system as a whole. Variables that affect this family function include: family power structure (assertiveness and control), negotiation styles, role relationships, and relationship rules and feedback (positive and negative). Olson et al. hypothesize that where there is a balance between change and stability within families there will be more mutually assertive communication styles, shared leadership, successful negotiation, role sharing, and open rule making and sharing (13).

Adapting the work of Olson et al., we can visualize the mutual interaction of adaptability and cohesion within families by placing them on an axis (see Figure 1-1a). By adding the extremes of cohesion (disengagement and enmeshment) and adaptability (rigidity and chaos), we can begin to picture where more or less functional families would appear on the axis (see Figure 1-1b).

The more central area represents balanced or moderate levels of adaptability and cohesion, seen as a highly functional communication pattern for individual and family development, although there may be instances when a different pattern could aid a family through a particular crisis. The outside areas represent the extremes of cohesion and adaptability, the less functional consistent communication pattern. Most families function short of the extremes.

In certain circumstances extremes may serve a purpose. If a family is faced with the loss of a member through death, a highly cohesive communication pattern may be critical for mourning purposes. In the following diagram (see Figure 1-2a), at the time of a family death, family members may find themselves at point *Y*, reflecting the strong cohesion as well as the great changes such a death created, and their communication would reflect this relatively extreme position. If, on the other hand, a teenager enters a severe acting-out period, a family may

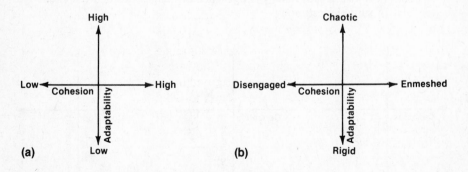

Figure 1-1   Family Cohesion/Adaptability Axis

find itself shifting from point X to point Z on the axis, as the adolescent demands greater freedom and less connectedness from the family and forces changes upon the system (see Figure 1-2b).

The following example may be graphed as moving through three family stages from *A-B-C* (see Figure 1-2c):

During one period of my childhood after my parents' divorce, my mother took a series of part-time jobs with variable hours, and my father left the state. My brother and I depended upon ourselves and the neighbors for whatever we needed. The family was very fragmented and due to money and health problems, we never knew what would happen from day to day (point *A*). After my mother seemed to straighten out her life a bit, we were able to do more things as a family and to get closer to each other again. Life was still pretty unpredictable (point *B*). Finally, my mother married again and we now live a very predictable life-style, but it has allowed us to get closer to each other again. We are a somewhat dull, but close family (point *C*).

Throughout the text we will relate the cohesive/adaptive framework to family communication behavior.

Supporting Functions

As we examine the role of communication within the cohesion/adaptability framework, we need to focus on additional family functions which contribute to the understanding of family communication processes. These functions, along with those of cohesion and adaptability, give shape to family life. Hess and Handel identify processes or family functions in which a family engages which interact with the development of its message system. Every family has to engage in the following activities:

1. Establish a satisfactory congruence of images through the exchange of suitable testimony.

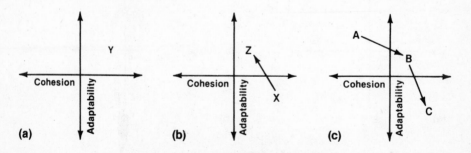

Figure 1-2 Application of Family Cohesion/Adaptability

2. Evolve modes of interaction into central family concerns or themes.
3. Establish the boundaries of the family's worlds or experiences.
4. Deal with significant biosocial issues of family life, as in the family's disposition to evolve definitions of male and female, and of older and younger.
5. Establish a pattern of separateness and connectedness.   (4)

Each of these processes deserves special attention. Since we consider the fifth process to be part of the cohesion function, discussed earlier, we will not develop it further here. Rather we will concern ourselves with the first four functions that support the family's efforts to regulate cohesion and adaptability.

Family Images • If you had to assign images, or mental pictures, to certain family members, what would they be? Would your father be a Teddy Bear who is warm, soft, and lovable? Would he be a milquetoast—reserved, shy, kind? Might he be a martinet—organized, military, distanced? Or would his image combine some of these qualities? Every family operates as an image-making mechanism. Each member develops an image of what the other family members are like and what the family unit is like; these images determine his or her interaction patterns toward the others. An image of a person is one's definition of that person as an object of one's own action or potential action. A person's image of his family embodies what is expected from it, and what is given to it, and how important it is (Hess and Handel, 7–8). Thus the image has both realistic and idealized components plus a transactional nature that reflects both the imagined and the imaginer. In his discussion of how people imagine their families, Laing presents the following client's perception:

> My family was like a flower. My mother was the centre and we were the petals. When I broke away, mother felt that she had lost an arm. They (sibs) still meet round her like that. Father never really comes into the family in that sense.   (6)

If two people's images of each other are congruent and consistent for a period of time, a predictable pattern of communication may emerge in which both may be comfortable. If a mother sees her son as a helpless and dependent creature, she may exhibit many protective behaviors such as keeping bad news from him or restraining him from taking physical chances. If the son's image of his mother is as a protector, the congruence of the images will allow harmonious communication, whereas if the child sees his mother as a jailer, conflict may emerge. If one child sees the mother as a jailer and the other sees her as an angel, the lack of consistent images held by family members may result in strong alliances among those with congruent images. Yet since complete consensus remains improbable and change remains inevitable, the patterns will never become totally predictable; but the level of congruence relates to the effectiveness of communication within the family.

Family Themes • As well as having images for the family and for every family member, each family shares themes—or takes positions in relationship to the outer world that affect every aspect of its functioning. A theme may be viewed as a pattern of feelings, motives, fantasies, and conventionalized understandings grouped around some locus of concern which has a particular form in the personalities of individual members (Hess and Handel, 11).

Themes represent a fundamental view of reality and a way of dealing with this view. Through its theme, a family responds to the question, "Who are we?" and "What do we do about it?" Sample theme issues which some families value include the following: physical security, strength, dependability, inclusion, and separation. To demonstrate the viability of themes in a family, we view them as statements which actualize the values more specifically:

1. We have responsibilities toward those less fortunate than we are.
2. It's hard to be a family without a man.
3. The only people you can depend on are the members of your family.
4. We are survivors.

Themes relate directly to family actions since themes affect the strategies for family functioning. Kantor and Lehr make a direct connection between themes and a family's cohesion and interaction patterns:

Themes give content to a family's strategic intentions, content around which family strategies take shape. Strategic themes, like the distance regulation patterns associated with them recur frequently throughout a family's life. Together, these strategic patterns and themes constitute a family's style of relating.   (57)

Such themes make a powerful impact on the development of relationships.

I grew up with a family theme related to success. Our real theme might be stated: "We must uphold the Roland name through our successes." Sub-themes would include "Rolands will do well in school," "Rolands do not quit," "Rolands play to win." As you can well imagine, this affected communication because when you did well you got lots of positive reactions, support, and praise. When you did not do well it was clear, particularly nonverbally, that you had disappointed the family. The best communication happened after you won something.

Living according to a theme necessitates the development of various patterns of behavior which affect (1) how members interact with the outside world, (2) how they interact with each other, and (3) how they develop personally. For example, a family system with the theme of "We have responsibilities toward those less fortunate than we are" might be a flexible system open to helping relationships with non-family members and may accept temporary family members who have problems, such as foster children. Yet, it may be difficult or impossible for such a family to accept help from an outside source because of its own self-definition as helper. Members may tend to put themselves and other family members second as they deal with outside problems. Following the classic line of the shoemaker's children without shoes, a mother who lives according to this theme may spend hours working at an adolescent drop-in center for the community and be unaware of the problems her own teenage children are having because of the outward focus of the family life. Young members may grow up learning to minimize their problems and may not have much experience express-ing painful feelings. Yet, they may learn to willingly self-sacrifice for those less fortunate and may be very attuned and empathetic to the needs of others.

Family themes may be complex and subtle. They may involve beliefs that are not immediately obvious. It is important to identify a family's main theme(s) in order to fully understand the communication behavior of the group members.

Boundaries • As well as developing images and themes, families create boundaries within which members are expected to function. Hess and Handel believe each family system sets up physical and psychological boundaries for dealing with the world—these determine for family members what parts of the outside world may be dealt with. Some boundaries are permeable, or allow movement across them, and others resist much movement across them. Certain families will permit or encourage their children to make many different kinds of friends, to explore alternative religious ideas, and to have access to new ideas through the media; such permeable boundaries permit new ideas, people, and values to enter the family. Conversely some families retain rigid control of their children's activities to prevent them from coming into contact with what the family considers "undesirable." Extremes of such behavior result in the creation of rigid boundaries around the family system.

Although we are close to our parents, my sister and I can do anything that most other young people in our area are allowed to do. My cousins from Greece live in a different world. They are not allowed to date even though they are 16 and 17. Their parents do not want them to go away to college and they will be expected to live at home until they are married. They constantly hear that "good Greek girls would not do that." There are far stricter boundaries on what they are al-lowed to experience than what I can do.

Yet no matter how set the boundaries are initially, they will vary according to the personalities of the members, the types of experiences to which members are exposed, and the freedom each member has to create his or her own value system.

Although the family unit system may set strong boundaries, the personal subsystems or interpersonal subsystems may test or reject these boundaries. A strong self-assured person may challenge rigid or stereotyped thinking about certain issues and reject the traditional boundaries set for him or her. An intensely emotional or sensitive child may comprehend things never imagined by other family members. This child may push far beyond the geographic limits or aspira-tional levels held by other family members. As the Kentucky mountain girl becomes an unmarried San Francisco novelist, she may have to cross most of the family's accepted boundaries regarding place, aspiration, and position. Such actions represent a threat to the family value system that stands as one guardian of their boundaries. This type of action may result in decreased meaningful communication as the gulf between the two worlds continues to widen.

Interpersonal subsystems create their own boundaries. For example, the marital subsystem represents a critical entity in the functioning of family life. In most families, husbands and wives share unique information and give each other special emotional and physical support. Children are not allowed to share in all aspects of the marital dyad. Many types of conflict may arise if the system's interpersonal boundaries, particularly the marital boundaries, are too permeable and children or others are expected to fulfill part of the spouse role. For example, troubled families, such as those with an alcoholic spouse, may experience shifts in the marital boundary. If an alcoholic husband cannot provide the interpersonal support needed by his wife, she may co-opt one of the children into the marital subsystem by expecting the child to act as an adult confidant and emotional support. When boundaries are inappropriately crossed, roles become confused and pain may result for all members.

Interpersonally testing or forcing boundaries may involve deep emotional conflicts which could be resolved through the increased growth of all family members or by the severing of bonds with specific members who eventually leave the system. Each of you has to have experienced resisting boundaries or having persons challenge your systems boundaries with positive or negative results. Your family relationships may have eventually become stronger or certain relationships may have suffered. Thus, the physical and psychological boundaries set by each family strongly influence the kinds of interpersonal communication that can occur within the system.

Biosocial Issues • All families operate in a larger sphere which provides conventionalized ways of coping with biosocial issues, but each family creates its own answers within the larger framework. Hess and Handel identify the following as included within biosocial issues: male and female identity, authority and power, shaping and influencing children, and children's rights (17–18).

Margaret and I are really working to define how we want to raise our son in today's society. It's harder to raise a boy today because society does not seem ready to give the boy as much leeway as it does to girls. We have spent hours discussing how to deal with Keith when he cries or plays with girls' toys or does things considered traditionally "feminine." As parents we have a major responsibility for helping a child establish his identity but it is a very complex issue.

All people are faced with sexual identity issues while growing up and/or while forming their own family systems, and raising their own children. Sexual identity and physical development issues affect styles of interaction and vice versa. A family that assigns responsibilities based on a member's sex operates differently than one which uses interest or preference as the basis for assigning responsibilities. If physical stature automatically determines duties and privileges, the interaction will be different than in a setting where physical development is only one factor among many by which privileges are awarded and duties are appropriate to males and females. For example, women will not swear or tell sexual jokes but they may express their emotions freely, an experience denied the male members.

Other value decisions in the social sphere relate to the use of power within the family structure. To what extent are leadership, decision making, and authority issues resolved according to traditional sex and role configurations? Families negotiate the use of power within the system and members may find themselves in the renegotiation process for much of their lives. The social sphere also involves attitudinal issues related to roles and responsibilities which may be exemplified in parent-child relationships. Parent-child interactions reflect the mutually-held attitudes. If a parent sees a child as a responsibility to be dispensed with at a given age, the interactions will be immensely different than if the parental attitude reflects a prolonged responsibility for his or her offspring, perhaps far beyond the years of adolescence. To what extent a child is permitted privacy, physical or psychological, also reflects a biosocial orientation.

The development of images, themes, boundaries, and responses to biosocial issues interact with the functions of cohesion and adaptability. Flexible families will experience greater variety in themes, images, boundaries, and responses to biosocial issues than will rigid ones who allow little adaptability. These responses also affect the family's acceptable level of cohesion. For example, a family with very fixed boundaries and themes related to total family dependence will develop extremely high cohesion in contrast to the family with themes of service or independence and flexible boundaries. This entire process rests with the communication behaviors of the family members. Communication, then, is the means by which families establish their patterns of cohesion and adaptability based at least partially on their interactions in the development of images, themes, boundaries, and responses to biosocial issues.

A FRAMEWORK FOR EXAMINING FAMILY COMMUNICATION

To analyze the family as a system, we could take numerous approaches such as looking at a family as an economic, a political, or a biological system. Since our concern lies with the interaction within and around the family, we will center on the communication aspects of the family system. We will look at the family according to a communication perspective, seeing it as "an organized, naturally occurring relational interaction system, usually occupying a common living space over an extended time period and possessing a confluence of interpersonal images which evolve through the exchange of messages over time" (Bochner, 1976, 382). More specifically, we will use the following framework for examining family communication:

WE VIEW THE FAMILY AS A SYSTEM IN WHICH COMMUNICATION REGULATES COHESION AND ADAPTABILITY BY A FLOW OF MESSAGE PATTERNS THROUGH A DEFINED NETWORK OF EVOLVING INTERDEPENDENT RELATIONSHIPS.

WE VIEW THE FAMILY AS A SYSTEM—
We see the family as a set of parts, or people, together with the relationship between them which form a complex whole: changes in one part will result in changes in other parts of the system. In short, family members are inextricably tied to each other and each member and the family as a whole reflects changes in one part of the system.

IN WHICH COMMUNICATION REGULATES COHESION AND ADAPTABILITY—
Communication, that symbolic, transactional process by which messages are exchanged, serves as the means by which families develop their capacities for closeness or separateness and flexibility. We believe that how people exchange messages influences the form and content of their relationship and that communication and families have a mutual impact on each other. Communication affects the way family members relate and family relationships affect the communication that occurs.

BY A FLOW OF MESSAGE PATTERNS THROUGH A DEFINED NETWORK—
Based on families-of-origin and other environmental sources, each family develops its own set of meanings which become predictable since family members interact with one another in the same manner over and over again. Such message patterns move through boundaries which define the relationships along specific paths or networks which determine who actually communicates with whom.

OF EVOLVING INTERDEPENDENT RELATIONSHIPS.
Family life is not static; both predictable or developmental changes and unpredictable changes or crises force some alteration upon the system. Thus, family relationships evolve over time as members join and leave the system and members become closer or farther apart from each other. Yet, due to the family's systemic nature, members remain interdependent or joined as they deal with relational issues of intimacy, conflict roles, power, and decision making.

The following diagram (Figure 1-3, p. 23) may help you to visualize these relationships.

Throughout the following chapters, we will examine the concepts mentioned in this framework in order to demonstrate the powerful role communication plays in family life.

Finally, let us forecast the type of family communication we will be discussing.

Historically, most of the literature on family interaction dealt with troubled or pathological families. Only recently has the "normal" or nonpathological

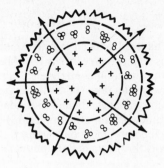

+ + + + + + +   Cohesion/Adaptation Variations

⟵————————————⟶   Message Patterns

————————————   Defined Network

⧉ ⬭ ⧉ ⬭ ⧉ ⬭ ⧉ ⬭   Evolving Interdependent Relationships

〰 〰 〰   Environment

Based on their levels of cohesion and adaptability, families develop message patterns which flow through a defined network of evolving interdependent relationships. All this occurs within the context of a specific environment.

Figure 1-3   Development of Family Meanings

family received much attention. And as you may imagine from our previous description of family formation, there is much unresolved controversy about what constitutes a "normal" family, leading family scholars to use the terms "functional" or "nonpathological," each of which still presents definitional problems. Yet in this text we will attempt to focus on communication within the nonpathological or functional family since this constitutes the major family experience for most people. Hopefully one myth this book will dispel is that there is "one right way to communicate within a family." Throughout the following pages you will encounter an infinite variety of descriptions of family life and communication behavior. Our purpose is to help you gain a better understanding of the dynamics of family communication, not to try to solve specific problems. Hence we will take a descriptive, rather than a prescriptive approach.

We hope there is some personal rather than just academic gain from reading these pages. Most of you come from the "functional" families which have their shares of pain and trouble as well as joy and intimacy. It is our hope that you will gain a new insight into the ordinary people with whom you share your lives.

CONCLUSION

In this chapter we have introduced our definition of family and our basic premise about the family as a system. We briefly described the process of communication and provided our position on communication patterns and family functions, including the primary functions of cohesion and adaptability and the supporting functions of family images, themes, boundaries, and biosocial issues. We concluded with our framework for studying family interaction. We view the family as a system in which communication regulates cohesion and adaptability by a flow of message patterns through a defined network of evolving interdependent relationships.

In order to get the most out of the following chapters, come prepared to bring your life experiences to them. Read the pages with your own family or other families in mind. You also may rely on literary families or families with which you have some passing acquaintance. By the end of the text you should be able to apply this framework to an unknown family and analyze it as a communication system. We also hope you choose to apply what you learn to your own family although it may be a difficult process at times.

Analyzing my own family has not been an easy process. As I began my entire soul cried out, "How do I begin to unravel the web of rules, roles, and strategies that make up our system?" I do not claim to have all possible answers, certainly my opinions and attitudes are different from those of the others in my family. I also do not claim to have all the answers to our problems. But I have tried to provide answers to my own confusion and to provide some synthesis to the change and crises that I have experienced. And I have grown from the process.

We have indeed grown from the process of writing this book. We hope you may also grow from the process of understanding family communication.

2

The Family as a System

The most graphic representation of the systemic qualities in our family occurred when my little sister was born. She was very ill for two years and my parents were always taking her to doctors and hospitals. Almost all their attention was focused on her. During this time the three younger boys had to adjust to a very different way of life, and they each responded in a different way. Greg just went crazy in school. He got into fights, never did his work, and almost had to repeat fifth grade. Doug, who was quiet to begin with, withdrew into a shell and just lived in his books. The world just went on around him and he didn't seem to notice. Brian tried to help in any way he could—just to get some extra attention from my parents. After Angela started to get stronger, my parents began to focus on the whole family again and slowly things started to shift back to the ways they were. Greg got straightened out and Brian relaxed. Doug still hides in his books some of the time but you can see that he has changed some. Things will never be exactly the way they were but you could see the effects of a crisis on a system because everyone was affected.

In the previous chapter we provided a brief description of communication within the family system—a perspective that will carry throughout the text. In order to understand the communication of particular family members, you need to be aware of the communication within the whole family since this often provides a context for understanding the messages of individual members. The opening example provides a dramatic and explicit indication of how the family operates systematically. Yet systemic patterns are often subtle and implicit with powerful effects. Nonverbal indications of displeasure, avoidance of issues, or ways of expressing affection may dramatically influence how members function. Unless you understand the context for the messages you may not understand the message. In order to understand communication within the family system, we will examine what a system is, how it works, and how this relates to family life.

Any system consists of a set of objects (parts) together with the relationship between them and their properties which form a complex and unitary whole. If one component of the system changes, the other parts will change in response to the original change. Systems may be closed or open. A closed system has no interchange with the environment; this concept applies mainly to physical elements, such as a machine which does not have life-sustaining qualities. An open system engages in interchange with the environment and is oriented toward growth; living or organic systems fit into this category. As we investigate a family system, we can begin with the properties that characterize human systems.

CHARACTERISTICS OF HUMAN SYSTEMS

Very simply stated any system consists of three elements: objects, attributes, and relationship among the objects within an environment (Littlejohn, 1978, 31). The objects are the parts, or members, of a system and may be quite easily understood as the family members in a familial system. The attributes are the qualities or properties of the system and its members. Thus a family or a person may have generalized family system attributes such as goals, energy, health, or ethnic heritage which are distinctive to them in terms of athletic goals, high energy, ill health, or Armenian heritage.

The relationship among system members applies directly to the relationships among family members—our major focus in the book. Such relationships are characterized by communication about acceptable levels of cohesion and adaptability at a given point in a family's life. An additional factor, environment, recognizes that systems are affected by their surroundings. Families do not exist in a vacuum—they exist within a time period, a culture, a community, and potentially countless other factors that influence their existence, such as a larger family system, or religious or educational organizations.

As you begin to read about the family as a system, you may resist some of the more technical terminology in this chapter because it will seem strange to look at a group of people in this way. It is hoped that this initial reaction leads eventually to valuing a systems approach to understand family functioning. Understanding the characteristics of a system as they are applied to families should aid you in analyzing family interaction, predicting future interactions, and creating meaningful changes within the system.

Specifically we will apply the following systems characteristics to families:

interdependence, wholeness, mutual influence/punctuation, patterns/rules, calibration/feedback, adaptation, openness, equifinality, information processing, and organizational complexity (Watzlawick, et al., 1967; Littlejohn, 1978; Kantor and Lehr, 1976).

⌊Interdependence⌋

Within any system, the parts are so interrelated as to be dependent on each other for their proper functioning. Thus this related dependence, or interdependence, becomes a critical factor when describing a system. For example, the regulatory powers of the human body provide you with protection against disease. When infection occurs, your white corpuscles multiply and rally to combat the invader and then diminish in numbers when the infection decreases.

One graphic way to picture the interdependence within your family system is to imagine yourself sneezing in two different locations. If you sneeze while sitting in a bus station you are likely to get no response from surrounding people, yet if you sneeze while sitting at the kitchen table you may hear, "God bless you," "Don't get sick before our vacation," "I hope you're not getting my cold." These comments typify the sense of connectedness characteristic of a human system.

The family, because of its powerful and long-lasting effect on its members, represents a highly interdependent type of system. Traditionally this interdependence was viewed as the means of maintaining a delicate balance among the system's parts, or members. Family therapist Jackson (1957) was one of the first to describe the process of family homeostasis or the mechanism of bringing a disturbed system back into balance. In Chapter 1 you encountered Satir's image of the family as a mobile in which members respond to changes in each other. As members respond to situations, certain other members may consciously or unconsciously shift to adjust to the quivering system. Current thinking suggests that families do not only seek balance, rather they move through evolutionary periods which affect all members.

Each of you may be able to pinpoint major or minor events in your own families which influenced all family members in some identifiable way. Examples in family therapy literature suggest that parents may use, or focus on, an acting-out child to keep them together, or the child may use the parents' overprotectiveness to keep him or her safely close to home (Hoffman, 1980, 54). Thus, interdependence becomes a powerful element in understanding family functioning. Since ". . . the behavior of every individual within the family is related to and dependent upon the behavior of all the others" (Watzlawick et al., 134).

Wholeness

"He's different. He's got more Connelly blood in him." This was my family's explanation for the fact that I did not behave the same way as the other members of the Dempsey clan. My father, uncles, and brothers were all known as athletic, hard-working, practical jokers who were the life of the party on any occasion. Although I think I have some sense of humor and can work hard, I was never very outgoing and always felt that I was disappointing people if I did not live up to the Dempsey image.

Every system, although it is made up of parts, results in an organic whole which may be viewed as such although the parts are still self-evident. Overall family images and themes reflect this wholistic quality. The Palmers, the McCarthys, or the Boyers have a life that characterizes the family as a whole, that is above and beyond the life of every family member. The Boyer family may be characterized as humorous, religious, warm, and strong—adjectives that do not necessarily apply to each member. Unique behaviors may be ascribed to the group that do not reflect certain individuals within the group. How would you characterize your family and how do you fit in that characterization?

A corollary to this sense of unity may be found in the life given to a family system through *synergy* or *non-summativity*. Have you ever had the experience of working with someone else and realizing that the two of you together could accomplish more than each of you working individually could do? When you consider an ongoing human system the parts, or the people, have importance, but once these parts become interrelated they may take on a life greater than their individual existences. In other words, the whole is greater than the sum of its parts. Non-summativity may be experienced when two or more people can generate energy greater than the sum of their individual efforts. History documents the amazing power of families which accomplished the impossible through their members' concerted efforts. For example, certain immigrant families rose to power and fame through the single-minded dedication of all members. Think about the accomplishments of your own family or other families you know and try to imagine such strength or willpower being exercised if each person acted as an isolated individual. In most cases you will conclude that the group spirit made the difference. Synergy or non-summativity accounts for the emergence of unique communication patterns between or among family members which seem to have a life of their own. Certain conflict or affection may become an inherent part of communication between various members. A certain cue may trigger whole patterns of behavior without individual persons being aware of it. Some of these specific communication patterns will be examined in Chapter 3.

Mutual Influence and Punctuation

When you function within an ongoing system, any single act serves both as a stimulus and as a response. *Mutual influence* implies that once a cycle of behavior starts, each behavioral act serves to trigger new behavior as well as to respond to previous behaviors. This transactional quality renders fruitless any attempts to label things as cause and effect. The following example may demonstrate this:The act of having an affair may be seen as a reaction to the husband's ignoring behavior and as a stimulus to the husband's attending behavior. Similarly, the act of staying home may be viewed as a reaction to the mother's depression and a stimulus or trigger to the mother's functional state. In most

	Pattern A		**Pattern B**

Pattern A

husband ignores wife

wife has an affair

husbands attends to wife
wife gives husband full
  attention
husband ignores wife

wife has an affair

husband attends to wife
wife gives husband full
  attention etc.

Pattern B

son stays away from
  home
mother becomes
  depressed
son stays home
mother becomes
  pleasant/functional
son stays away from
  home
mother becomes
  depressed
son stays home
mother becomes
  pleasant/functional
  etc.

families, many patterns of behavior emerge that soon have a life of their own, and it is fruitless to try and assign a cause to them because the behaviors are so intertwined with each other. The wholistic, synergistic nature of the system moves behaviors into a cycle.

Punctuation refers to the interruption or breaking into a sequence of behavior at intervals in order to give meaning to the behavior. It often involves suggesting "things started here." "Interaction sequences like word sequences . . . must be punctuated or grouped syntactically to make sense" (Littlejohn, 206). Behaviors are not just a chain, but rather as we just noted, they may serve stimulus and reaction functions. The previous patterns of behavior may be punctuated or interrupted in various ways. Communication breakdowns may occur when people punctuate the communication sequence differently, therefore assigning different meanings to the behaviors.

A son may say, "Our trouble started when my mother became depressed" whereas the mother may indicate that the family problems began when her son stayed away from home. Punctuating the cycle according to his suggestion would imply laying blame on the mother. If the cycle is punctuated according to the mother, the son would be at fault for the troubles of the family. The yes/no cycle could go on indefinitely. If we work from the cybernetic idea of circular causality within a system, it remains less important to try to punctuate the system and assign a beginning point than it does to look at the act as a sequence of patterns and try to understand this ongoing process without needing to say, "It really started here."

The best thing we learned in marriage counseling was to stop blaming each other and to start looking for a pattern of behavior that we could begin to control. For example, instead of screaming "you started it" if we get into a pattern of one-up one-down, I have learned to call him on the power play instead of whining, and he has learned to call me on whining and some heavy-handed moves.

Some families try to explain their difficulties by going back *x* number of years and saying, "It started when he took a job requiring travel" or "Things began to fall apart when my wife went back to work." The actions occurring since those blamed behaviors have so altered the system that the jobs in either case would not necessarily resolve the current issues since the system has long since readjusted. Only the current behavior, not the past, would be of value in analyzing the family's life and trying to note areas for change. Disagreement about how to punctuate the sequence of events is at the root of many family problems (Watzlawick et al., 1967, 56).

Patterns and Rules

How do you greet family members in the morning? How do you give and receive gifts in your family? How do you resolve family disputes? Although you may not be aware of it, you have learned to live within a relatively predictable pattern of interaction that characterizes your family system. All systems have repetitive cycles which help maintain their equilibrium and provide clues to their functioning. The importance of the system's patterns lies in their ability to put an act into context. The pattern provides data by which to understand isolated acts that may appear confusing or strange. For example, interaction patterns provide a means of assessing communication behaviors within a system because they provide the context for understanding specific or isolated behaviors. Taken as an isolated event, it may be hard to interpret acts such as Mike hits his brother, or Sally acts like a baby. Yet, if these isolated acts are viewed as part of a contextual pattern, they may begin to make sense. If the parental fighting and Mike's aggressive acts are related, you may discover patterns in which Mike's parents blame each other for his aggression or you may find that Mike feels guilty for his parents' anger and takes his feelings out on his brother. If every time her mother decides to let Sally do more on her own, Sally acts like a baby, the patterns may indicate Sally's unwillingness to take on more self-responsibility or the mother's pressure to find her own independence. Messages may be discovered through the patterns which the isolated behaviors cannot indicate.

All systems need some regularity and predictability to continue functioning. Patterns govern important aspects of life. Rules are relationship agreements which prescribe and limit a family member's behavior over time. They are redundancies at the relationship level. Families have rules that govern all areas of life including communication behavior. We will explore a family's communication rules in Chapter 3.

Calibration and Feedback

I am very conscious of how much pressure I could place on my eldest child because I remember that I was the eldest and served as the "ice-breaker" for the rest of the family. It was always such a big deal if I wanted to do anything different, but after I had done it, the others were able to follow along pretty quickly. I had all the battles and they got the rewards. I was always testing my limits and usually I got punished, but sometimes I was able to reach new freedoms and it made me feel as if I was finally growing up. As a parent I try to outguess some of my daughter's moves and try to foresee some of the times when the rules are not applicable anymore before we get into huge fights over them.

Traditionally the function of maintaining stability and predictability has been critical to the continuance of any system; such a function involves calibration. *Calibration* implies checking and rectifying a scale, and in the case of a family, it implies checking and rectifying, if necessary, the scale of permissible or acceptable behaviors. Hence a system engages in what is called "morphostasis" or an attempt to maintain the status quo. Let us explain this further.

All systems display a need for constancy within a defined range (Watzlawick et al., 147). Thus a system needs to maintain some type of standard that is reached by noting deviations from the norm and correcting the deviations if they become too significant. The thermostat represents the most commonly used example of a calibration process. Usually your home heating mechanism is set for a particular temperature, which allows a defined range of acceptable degrees. If the temperature drops below the lower acceptable level, the heat will kick on and the temperature will rise to within the acceptable range. The entire system may be "recalibrated" or set to a different temperature if the standard is changed through the use of feedback.

Systems generate negative and positive feedback but within systems language the terms are used differently than they are in everyday usage. Negative feedback implies constancy and serves to maintain the acceptable standard and to minimize change, whereas positive, or change-promoting, feedback results in recalibrating the system at a different level. No value is implied by the labels.

According to Olson et al. (1979), positive feedback provides the family system with "constructive system-enhancing behaviors that enable the system to grow, create, innovate, and change, i.e., system *morphogenesis*. Conversely, negative feedback attempts to maintain the status quo, i.e., system *morphostasis*" (11).

When your family rule has been developed over time, your family may be viewed as calibrated or "set" to regulate its behavior in conformity to the rule. If your family or an outside force alters the rule, the family is recalibrated in accordance with the new rule. The following example demonstrates this process: An unwritten family rule may be that the sick fourteen-year-old may not be allowed to hear the truth regarding his illness. This rule may keep any serious discussion of the young man's illness from him. If anyone should suggest that he has a blood disease, negative or constancy feedback in the form of a nonverbal sign or a change of subject may serve to keep him relatively uninformed. The family is "set" not to discuss the issue with him. Yet the rules may be changed and the system recalibrated through a variety of positive feedback mechanisms. If the young man guesses the severity of his illness, he may confront one or more

Today's families represent a wide range of combinations of people formed into systems of varying sizes and configurations. Living in one neighborhood there may be natural families, in which the children all have blood ties to both parents; blended families, reflecting both remarriage and adopted or foster children; and single parents with their children. There may also be couples who have chosen a childless life-style as opposed to extended families sharing the same or neighboring homes, some tied to each other by blood, others tied through commitment. Although each family may share system characteristics, they all contain a unique combination of persons.

family members and insist on the truth. Once the truth has been told he cannot return to his previous naive state and the system will now include some discussion of this illness. Another source of positive feedback may arise in the person of the doctor. The doctor may suggest that the young man's condition be discussed with him and may personally inform the young man or require the family to do so. Again the system would be recalibrated as family members mature and are considered able to handle certain information or experiences.

Recent thinking about family systems views the concept of calibration as mechanistic and narrow since it seems to suggest a static, error-activated process; given a deviation in the system, the mechanism receives negative feedback and brings itself back into line. In her discussion of change in family systems, Hoffman (1980) suggests that the functioning of living systems cannot be explained by the negative feedback view, maintaining:

> This point is dramatized by the step-wise, sudden leaps to new integrations characteristic of such systems, which are not only unpredictable, but irreversible. The conceptual emphasis is on self-organizing processes that reach toward new evolutionary stages rather than on processes that tend toward equilibrium.   (54)

In other words, families also experience change through leaps—as random and unpredictable forces propel members into new forms and experiences.

Thus we can put an evolutionary framework around the traditional calibration model which recognizes the attempt at maintaining the current system but which also accounts for the transformations which occur that change the original system dramatically. This will be further developed throughout the book in terms of the system's adaptive quality.

Adaptation

As we saw in our earlier discussion of adaptability in Chapter 1, human systems must change and restructure themselves in order to survive. As such, families constantly restructure themselves to cope with developmental and situational changes.

Historically, family theorists viewed the family as a primarily morphostatic system, one attempting to maintain stability or the status quo. Yet, "Viewing the family as solely maintenance-oriented . . . is restrictive and misleading" (Olson et al., 11). In keeping with a developmental approach which sees families as necessarily capable of change and adaptation, we stress the necessary relationship between morphostasis, maintaining the status quo, and morphogenesis, the growth-promoting process.

Openness

An open system, as opposed to a closed one, permits interchange with the surrounding environment. Whereas closed, mechanical systems do not need outside organisms and will break down if they encounter such organisms, human systems need interchange with elements and people in the environment in order to sustain themselves physically and psychologically. The family as a social system maintains an almost continuous interchange not only within the system but across the boundary between the inner environment and the outer environment (Kantor & Lehr, 10). This influence helps keep a family aware of its place in the larger scene. As a small child you may have depended entirely on your family for all your immediate needs but as you grew older you needed to interact with numerous nonfamily members in order to function in our society. For an entire family to function, such interchange with and adaptation to the environment remains critical. Most family members must interact with others for survival and to fulfill physical and psychological needs. Maintaining the bare necessities of life (food, clothes, and shelter) involves a functional relationship with the environment. Education and work provide additional sources of environmental contact, whereas friends, co-workers, and future spouses must be found outside the immediate family system and its narrow limits.

A young family member may encounter desirable or undesirable influences in an inspirational teacher, a delinquent companion, a mind-expanding book, or an R-rated movie, and such encounters may influence his or her behavior within the family. A family with no outside contact would lose its reproductive capacity and eventually its survival capacity in our world. These outside forces cause some changes in every family because of the feedback they provide to its members.

As a teacher who works with deaf children, I am aware that the feedback I give to a family about their child influences how the family feels about itself. For example, I have been able to demonstrate to parents that their children have the capacity for a full life and that they should not relate to their children primarily in terms of their deafness. I think I have helped some parents feel less guilty or depressed about having a handicapped child. A family that can accept a child's deafness provides a much more supportive atmosphere for the child.

Equifinality

An open adaptive system demonstrates *equifinality* or the ability to achieve a similar final state in many ways from many different starting points. Equifinality means that the same results may spring from different origins because it is determined by the nature of the organization (Watzlawick et al., 127). Two different families may achieve a similarly defined "good life" based on a particular income, education, and relationship level through incredibly diverse means. Each success story carves its own path but in doing so adapts to circumstances as it strives toward a goal. Three families may have a theme of "We have responsibilities to those less fortunate than us" and each may work toward their goal of living out such a theme differently by taking in foster children, raising money for overseas relief efforts, or achieving political power in order to aid the underprivileged.

Information Processing

Every system needs some mechanism by which the parts are inter-related. Within open systems, adaptation and change are made possible by the sophisticated information processing or message transmission capabilities. When we talk about human systems such as families, the information processing capacity merges with the communication process so that we are discussing a family's communication function. On the basis of their research in families, Kantor and Lehr assert that "the information processed by the family system is distance-regulation information" (12). Thus the major information processed by a family system contains the messages which regulate separateness/connectedness or cohesion. The concept of cohesion was introduced in Chapter 1, and Chapter 3 will further elaborate on messages and meanings so the topic will not be pursued at this point.

Organizational Complexity

Human systems are complex organizations. The primary reason for this is the existence of subsystems within a hierarchy. The system is therefore a series of levels of increasing complexity (Littlejohn, 32).

This type of system may be viewed through a family tree such as in the following model (Figure 2-1). This type of figure only provides a formal skeleton for a system. If you draw your family tree, you will only account for the formal relationships among people. This type of structure allows you to see the formalized relationships but does not indicate the quality of those relationships or the lines of communication between people.

The complexity of the family system may be seen through the subgroups or subsystems that exist within its boundaries. The family as a unit forms a system

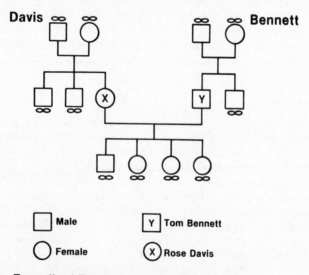

Figure 2-1 Formalized Family Relationships

comprised of individuals and the relationships between them. Each family unit or family system contains subsystems, specifically: (1) interpersonal subsystems, and (2) personal or psychobiological subsystems, which contribute to the family functioning. As we saw in our discussion of "wholeness," knowing the family system does not necessarily mean knowing the specific members or their relationships. Using the previous figure (Figure 2-1), we can say that to know the Bennett family is not to know totally Tom Bennett or Rose Bennett, nor is it to know Tom and Rose Bennett's particular interpersonal relationship.

Every family contains a number of small groups called interpersonal subgroups that are likely to be made up of two or three persons and the relationship between or among them. Even a three-person system becomes complicated by the interpersonal subsystems within it. A mother, daughter, and grandson triad represents three such subsystems—the mother and daughter, the daughter and her son, and the grandmother and grandson.

Thus each of the subsystems has to be considered in order to understand the functioning of the whole. Each subsystem has its own rules, boundaries, and unique characteristics. For example, Mom may never tease Janice but easily kids with Doug. Yet Dad may tease both of them very comfortably and be more affectionate with them than Mom is able to be. Mom and Doug may spend long hours talking about his future plans whereas Janice may choose not to discuss this with any immediate family members. Mom, Doug, and Janice may bind together to deal with problems resulting from Dad's poor health.

In most cases subgroups change membership over time. Yet certain subgroups may become so strong or tight that particular members either feel overwhelmed or powerless, or feel very left out. If the members only relate to specific other members, coalitions or alliances result.

The easiest pattern to envision occurs when two family members seem joined against the other one. Although such triangles exist in all families since the arrival of the first child creates the initial triangle, they only become problems if the alliances are always formed in the same way—if Mom and Rob always ally against Dad or if Mom and Dad always ally against Beatrice. In large families there may be several triangles operating. Satir (1972) calculates that a family of three has nine triangles whereas a family of ten has 376 (152–153).

I saw a dramatic example of a triangle growing up in a house where my Dad was an alcoholic. My mother and oldest brother formed this tight relationship against him, and almost against anyone else. They agreed on everything and my brother became my mother's protector. Even when Dad started to get on the wagon he could not break up that alliance, and I think that had something to do with the reason they got a divorce.

Coalitions or alliances may have positive or negative effects within families. Two or three family members objecting to another's insensitivity may have positive results. An older brother-younger brother alliance could result in the younger one entering a gang or raising his grades depending on the model he sees in the older male. Most of us have seen families where two children seem to have a permanent alliance against a third member, resulting in much anger or unhappiness for the "third wheel." As family systems grow larger, the complexity of the interpersonal subsystems develops accordingly. Using the Davis-Bennett family, the subsystems may be viewed in the following way to account for alliances that exist within the formal system (see Figure 2-2):

To further complicate the issue, a family system may be said to contain a third systemic level. Each family member represents his or her own personal or psychobiological system which is tied to, yet separate from, the family unit. The structure of a family includes the intrapsychic organization of its individual members (Hess and Handel, 1959, 3). Each member or personal subsystem contains unique biological and psychological characteristics. Throughout life the experiences encountered by each member differ from those of others in the family and continue to heighten the individuality of each of the members. Hess and Handel suggest that ". . . in his relationship in the family an individual member strives toward predictability or preferred experience, attempting to discover or create circumstances which fit his image of what the world around him should be—how it should respond to him and provide opportunity for expression of his own preference" (3). In short, no matter how much Ellen, Lisa, and Kurt Bennett may resemble each other, they are psychobiological entities who function partially in an independent manner. Thus the three levels of systems may be seen in Figure 2-3 (p. 39).

Throughout this chapter most of our examples apply to small family units but do not deal with larger extended families or blended systems. From our perspective, divorce or death do not dissolve family systems; rather they alter them. These altered systems may become involved in a second marriage necessitating the interweaving of three or more families into a remarried family system. The organizational complexity of such systems are often staggering as the systems and subsystems interweave to form a new whole.

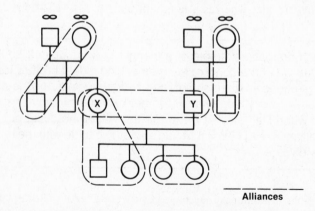

Alliances

Figure 2-2 Coalitions and Alliances within the Formal Family Structure

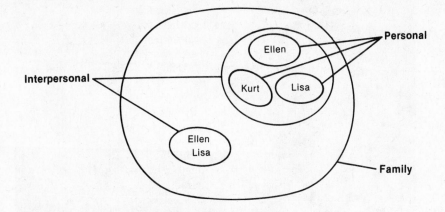

Figure 2-3 Levels of Family Systems

Although this chapter and its approach may appear technical, such a perspective may aid you in understanding some of the intricacies of family life. For example, being aware of the process of mutual influence may prevent you from the common trap of "finding the cause" as a way to deal with marital or family problems. Being sensitive about the existence of patterns and rules may allow you to see them where you might not have before. Knowing that families, as human systems, reach similar points in varying ways may encourage you to be comfortable with what appears different. Understanding the family as a system will alter the way you view families both academically and personally.

CONCLUSION

In this chapter we have applied a systems perspective to the family. We determined that a family system consists of members, the relationships among them, the family attributes and the members' attributes, and an environment in which the family functions. We examined the following systems characteristics as they apply to family life: interdependence, wholeness, mutual influence/punctuation, patterns/rules, calibration/feedback, adaptation, openness, equifinality, information processing, and organizational complexity.

We believe that a systems approach provides a valuable perspective from which to analyze family interaction. When viewed from this perspective, the focus shifts from individual member's behavior to the family as a whole, with its interdependent relationships and patterns which affect cohesion and adaptability. This perspective allows one to analyze specific behavior patterns in terms of the interpersonal context in which they occur and to understand their meanings in light of the entire family system. We now need to explain the role of communication within the family system. This will be done in the chapters to follow.

3

Family Meanings
and Communication Patterns

When my mother and her sisters grew up they lived in a very strict home. Before any girl could leave the house they had to tell my great-grandfather the password, "Dresses down, Panties up." If they went out with girls, all of them had to say it individually and if a boy was taking them out they had to make sure he heard it. We were not brought up that strictly but very often we will use that expression in kidding around and dates or visitors never know how to react. Our family has all kinds of secret messages that other people can never figure out.

When you think about your childhood, you will probably recall many messages that were special only to family members—ways of greeting, touching, arguing, caring, or teaching. In the previous chapter we examined the family as a system. Now we will examine the communication aspects of the family system. To do so we will look at the formation of family meanings, family communication patterns including rules and networks, and the role of the family-of-origin.

FORMATION OF FAMILY MEANINGS

In this text, we are assuming that *how* people exchange messages influences both the form and the content of their relationship. In other words ". . . how interactions proceed and are organized will at least partially determine the psychological and sociological characteristics of the system and its members" (Rogers-Millar, 1979, 21). Thus, communication not only serves as a simple transmission between people, but it serves to alter and shape the structure of the interpersonal system and the individuals within it. As a family system evolves, the communication among members will affect the continuously adapting form of the structure.

We are also assuming that communication serves to regulate cohesion among family members and this distance regulation function interacts with the family's adaptive processes. Over a period of time family members are able to develop meanings for each other. According to Hess and Handel (1959):

> On the basis of the meanings which the members have for one another, particular interpersonal ties evolve. The closeness between any two members, for example, or the distance between a group of three closely joined members and a fourth who is apart, derives from the interlocking meanings which obtain among them. (18–19)

In order to see this more closely, let's look at the behaviors of a couple as they begin to form a family system since the adult partners are the architects of most family systems. Family therapist Minuchin (1974) suggests that each young couple must undergo a process of mutual accommodation through which the couple "develops a set of patterned transaction—ways in which each spouse triggers and monitors the behavior of the other and is, in turn, influenced by the previous behavioral sequence. These transactional patterns form an invisible web of complementary demands that regulate many family situations" (17). In order to form a communication system, a couple is faced with a process of negotiating a set of common meanings through a process of mutual accommodation so that eventually the meanings for one are linked through conjoint action with those of the other. The actual negotiation process remains both subtle and complex.

A couple must make the accommodation that allows them to use mutually meaningful language. Certain general similarities in their physical and social processes assure certain generalized common meanings. Usually, the more similar the backgrounds, the more limited some of the negotiation processes. With the entire realm of verbal and nonverbal behavior available to them, they have to negotiate a set of common meanings which reflect their physical, social, but particularly their individual processes for viewing the world.

As this negotiation process continues and the marriage and family relationships develop, certain meanings expressed verbally and nonverbally within the relationship take on idiosyncratic dimensions. In their work on the development of interpersonal relationships, psychologists Altman and Taylor (1973) describe certain characteristics which appear in committed and close relationships. Among the characteristics of these developed relationship patterns are richness, efficiency, uniqueness, substitutability, pacing, openness, spontaneity, and evaluation (129). We can use these to examine certain aspects of the development of meaning within family systems.

Characteristics of Close Relationships

Richness refers to the ability of people in close relationships to have many ways of conveying the same thing. Siblings and spouses have many ways of sharing displeasure, delight, or other feelings. Nonverbal behaviors may not be appropriate for casual acquaintances. Affection may be shared in words, either teasing or serious, or may be shared through pats, hugs, kisses, etc. "I always thought it was neat that my father could pat my mother on the fanny or that she would sit on his lap in front of us kids." A relationship without richness remains in a very predictable and limited pattern of the "same old thing."

Efficiency in a relationship refers to accuracy, speed, and sensitivity in the transmission and receipt of communication. "In well-established interpersonal relationships, intended messages are transmitted and understood rapidly, accurately, and with great sensitivity" (Altman and Taylor, 131). Family shorthand abounds in which the meaningful raised eyebrow conveys more than fifty related words while the expression "I don't want another Cape Hatteras" conjures up countless images of bad weather, sick kids, poor camping conditions, and loud arguments. Only members of the family group can code and decode messages with this efficiency.

Within my family, problems that arise are approached with indifference or avoided. They are never faced head on and worked on due to a failure of family members to communicate their feelings in a real and meaningful way. If my mother senses something is bothering me, she will casually or indifferently ask what is wrong, usually when she is preparing dinner and I have just come in from work. I don't feel comfortable talking in this situation when her main concern is the food. Neither she nor I will push the subject. I will shrug off her efforts and although she seems bothered by my unwillingness to talk, she doesn't try to do anything else about it. Neither do I.

Highly developed relationships are characterized by the *uniqueness* or generation of unique or idiosyncratic message systems. Verbal expressions may take on new meanings, words may be created or used meaningfully in different contexts. Certain types of vocal tones, facial expressions or body movements may have unique meanings understood only by members of the system. If a family member claims a need for "puddling time," other members may willingly withdraw whereas a neighbor will not associate a raindrop pool with time to relax alone. In their study of the world of intimate talk and communication uniqueness, Hopper et al. (1981) report interviewing 112 cohabiting couples about their personal idioms. They report the eight functions of idioms: teasing insults, confrontations, expressions of affection, sexual invitation, sexual references and euphemisms, requests and routines, partner nicknames and names for other persons (28).

Substitutability refers to increased experience in a relationship leading to more ways becoming available to convey the same feelings in a substitute fashion. One need not wait for the last guest to leave after the party to convey anger through a yelling match because nonverbal signs such as a glance, "meaningful" silence, or a specific cast of the eyes will alert one spouse to the fact that the other is extremely angry.

Altman and Taylor suggest that these four characteristics of richness, uniqueness, efficiency, and substitutability probably overlap but that taken together they reflect the idea that the interpersonal development process:

> . . . involves interaction at multiple levels of functioning, that communication can be rich, varied and complex and that an increasing bond between people is associated with a better understanding of the meaning of transactions.   (132)

Pacing or *synchronization* refers to coordination and meshing of interpersonal actions as people work into mutual roles and act in complementary ways. "Whether it be in a superficial conversation or in lovemaking, the well developed relationship functions in a meshed fashion without verbal or physical stumbling" (Altman and Taylor, 133).

My mother and father have been married for 27 years and it's amazing to watch them function. One always seems to know what the other is doing and thinking and they work together beautifully, in the kitchen, in dealing with the children, and in general conversation. I would compare their relationship to a well-oiled machine but that sounds too cold. It's just that they appear in total harmony with each other.

The *openness* of a highly developed relationship implies verbal and nonverbal accessibility to each other. Family members may touch each other or share personal information in ways that do not exist in their other relationships. Yet it is not just more intimate interactions that characterizes the openness but ". . . also the ability of partners to engage in interaction more freely when barriers have been crossed . . . people move in and out of areas in a quick and facile way" (Altman and Taylor, 134). As relationships deepen a spontaneity grows in them. The informality and comfort of strong relationships allow one to break their patterns. "Movement across topical areas is facile and fluid, movement into intimate areas occurs readily and without hesitation or formality, and the relationship flows and changes direction constantly" (135). Quick or unexpected lovemaking, surprise trips, unpredictable comments, and changed plans all have their place as a couple develops a life together. Finally, such relationships involve the sharing of negative and positive judgments about one another. With the security that the relationship will not end if negative feelings are discussed, family members can express true feelings in hopes of finding resolution. Correspondingly, praise need not be viewed as "moving too fast" or threatening, resulting in the airing of positive feelings that might otherwise be unspoken.

Taken together these eight characteristics of developed relationships provide the backdrop for communication patterns that emerge within particular family systems. It should be clear that adaptability and cohesion are central to the development of such committed relationships; adaptation remains a core feature of efficiency, substitutability, pacing, and spontaneity while cohesion issues underlie the development of uniqueness, richness, openness, and evaluation. Yet threads of both dimensions run through the patchwork of characteristics comprising the developed relationship.

The security of such relationships, characterized by these factors, allows the widest range of interpersonal behaviors to occur and fosters the continued growth of the individuals and the relationship itself. Thus, each family develops, to some degree, particular message behaviors that are understood by members of the system. When one enters a new home as a guest, he or she has to try to adapt to the message systems within that environment. The fourteen-year-old daughter Linda may be referred to as "Nickel" (with a vague explanation of Wee Willie Winkie at its historical root); the baby may walk around carrying her "doe" which serves as a blanket and psychological comforter; Grandpa may continually refer to four-year-old Neal as the "heir to the throne"; and the hall closet may be known as the "pit." Such a visitor constantly makes decisions about the emotions behind the tone of voice that first calls "Matthew" and later "Matthew Noel Wilkinson." Although the father's manner may not appear to change, the visitor learns to respect the whispers of the other family members to "leave him alone right now—he's got that look in his face" since they are reading something unavailable to the untrained eye. "In" jokes and past references abound and the outsider finally begins to feel that he or she is getting a handle on things by knowing what it means to "pull a Louis stunt," "see the sky is high," or "have another graduation mess on our hands." Family members may scream and shout in ways that make the visitor most uncomfortable, but no one else appears bothered. On the other hand, the visitor may be hugged and kissed every time he or she arrives and leaves, which could be very pleasant or very disconcerting. Over time these behaviors form patterns that become predictable within each family.

Communication Among Married Couples • It seems appropriate at this point to present some information about how happily married couples report they are more likely to communicate. Twenty-four couples designated as "unhappy" were administered the Locke-Sabagh-Thomes Primary Communication Inventory and the Locke Marital Relationship Inventory. The results show marital adjustment to be positively correlated with the capacity to communicate (Navran, 1973, 183). In descending order of discriminatory power, happily marrieds differ from unhappily marrieds as follows:

They much more frequently talk over pleasant things that happen during the day.

They feel more frequently understood by their spouses; i.e. that their messages are getting across.

They discuss things which are shared interests.

They are less likely to break communication off or inhibit it by pouting.

They more often will talk with each other about personal problems.

They make more frequent use of words which have a private meaning for them.

They generally talk most things over together.

They are more sensitive to each other's feelings and make adjustments to take these into account when they speak.

They are more free to discuss intimate issues without restraint or embarrassment.

They are more able to tell what kind of day their spouses have had without asking.

They communicate nonverbally to a greater degree, via the exchange of glances.

In a similar study of 21 maritally satisfied couples and 21 maritally dissatisfied couples, Kahn (1970) reports the scores of satisfied and dissatisfied couples on the Marital Communication Scale indicated that "dissatisfied husbands and wives are particularly prone to misinterpreting each other's nonverbal signals" (455). For example, Kahn suggests the "dissatisfied husbands were clearly more inclined than the satisfied husbands to attribute negative connotations to their wives' attempts to communicate affection, happiness and playfulness."

In an attempt to distinguish between distressed and nondistressed couples Gottman et al. (1977) concluded that nonverbal behavior was an important key. They found that distressed couples were more likely to "express their feelings about a problem, to mindread, and to disagree, all with negative nonverbal behavior" (467–468). Thus the use of verbal and nonverbal messages and their eventual patterns plays a significant role in a family's existence. Yet, you will always find some exception to the norm—due to a systems equifinality, or ability to reach the same point differently, we will always have examples of the unique happily married couple that breaks all the rules.

FAMILY COMMUNICATION PATTERNS

As was mentioned in Chapter 2, every family system needs patterns to provide some order and predictability for system members. There are ways, times, places, and reasons to do things that make life functional for family members and serve to stabilize or bring equilibrium to the system. In this section we are concerned with two specific types of communication patterns: (1) communication rules, or the "oughts" that prescribe and limit communication; and (2) communication networks that determine the ways in which family members are able to communicate.

Family Communication Rules

In her moving book *Widow,* Lynn Caine (1974) describes the first months during which her husband had cancer and how neither of them would talk about the fact that he was going to die. There was an unwritten rule that the subject could not be raised. After he died, she lamented the fact that there was so much they could have shared had they been able to talk about what was uppermost on their minds. In their work on rule-based communication, Cronen, Pearce, and Harris (1979) suggest that rules exist in social situations because (1) social behavior has regularities even though individuals may act in unpredictable ways, (2) persons judge each other and hold each other accountable for their actions, and (3) persons perceive an "oughtness" or "expectedness" in their social actions. Ever since birth we have learned to adjust to social and personal regulations and we have expected others to do the same. We have lived in a world of rules for all kinds of behavior, including communication behavior. How do we learn these rules? Rules may be viewed as emergent or as givens depending on the circumstances. Rules may both emerge from repeated interaction patterns and structure ongoing behaviors because of their past occurrence. A couple may develop rules for conflict over a two-year period which remain as givens for future fights both for the members of the couple and for the children of that marriage. Whereas the couples experience the rules as emerging, the children receive them as givens, unless there is a change in the system. In actuality rules function as "working arrangements" that are always potentially changeable.

As was noted briefly in the previous chapter, every family has a set of relationship agreements or rules which prescribe and limit the behavior of family members. More specifically, every family has rules that govern communication behavior.

How Rules Develop • Each new family system develops its own set of relationship agreements as spouses create their own patterns. Some rules may be directly negotiated between or among family members, such as "when we have children we will always do *x* and never do *y*." But most rules emerge as a result of multiple interactions. After sharing certain common experiences over time, members of a system develop set ways of handling certain situations. Many family rules reflect the couple's original families' rules which, if not questioned, pass on from generation to generation. If spouses come from families with dissimilar rules, more overt negotiation will have to take place for the new system to reach a stable state.

Persons who form a system have to be sensitive to the relational consequences of their acts. Consider the difficulties if individuals with the following rules for conflict marry each other.

Person 1: In the context of a family argument, if very personal emotional disclosure is given, the other person should leave the room to consider it carefully and refrain from spontaneous response.

Person 2: In the context of a family argument, if a very personal emotional disclosure is given, the other person should respond with emotional supportiveness. To leave the room would indicate total rejection.

Person 1: In the context of family decision making, if money is being discussed, the final decision on how it is spent rests with the breadwinner.

Person 2: In the context of family decision making, if money is being discussed, the final decision on how it is spent rests with the couple, whether or not both work outside the home.

You can just imagine the negotiations that would have to occur in order for Person 1 and Person 2 to be comfortable with each other in a marriage where the communication patterns reflect both people.

Due to the transactional nature of communication within the system, the mutual influence process will result in new relational patterns. The following describes the process:

> No matter how well one knows the rules of communicator A, one cannot predict the logic of his/her communication with B without knowing B's rules and how they will mesh. The responsibility for good and bad communication is thus transactive with neither A or B alone deserving praise or blame.   (Cronen et al., 36)

Analysis of any rule-bound system requires an understanding of the mutual influence patterns within which the rules function.

My Mom's boyfriend has lived with us for two years and when he first arrived, it was really hard because he was very reserved and private. For about six months he was treated almost as a guest until it was clear he was going to stay. Once he started to become part of the system, you could almost see the rules start to shift. I think my younger brother Cary won him over first since he is very friendly and Mark seemed to do things with him. By now he's become more open and we have learned to respect some area of privacy he really seems to need.

Each family system determines its own hierarchy of rules. The Parsons and the Coopers may each have the rule that you share your troubles with the family first, but in the Parson family it is of primary concern whereas with the Coopers it is not at the top of the hierarchy. Once you learn the family rules, you then have to figure out the importance placed on each of them. Imagine trying to function in your family without a large number of rules. You would probably live in total chaos. Rules serve to provide predictability and stability in interactions and serve a socialization or teaching function for younger family members. If every time a "hot" topic, such as death or sex, arose, a family had to renegotiate each member's response to the subject, the uncertainty would hamper any important interaction. Predictable communication patterns allow a family to carry on its functional day-to-day interactions smoothly. Members know who to ask for lunch money, who to see about romantic problems, and from whom to request permission to use the car.

Once rules are established, changing them may be a complicated and time-consuming process unless the family has a flexible adaptation process. When a family rule has been developed over time, and members are accustomed to certain "acceptable" behaviors, the family can be viewed as calibrated or "set" to regulate its behavior in accordance with the rule limits. Rules function in terms of both positive and negative feedback although they are more likely to be thought of as negative feedback or limits rather than positive feedback or growth. These limits can be recalibrated unconsciously or consciously. For example, rules may be renegotiated as family members pass through certain developmental stages. A child of twelve may not be allowed to disagree with his parents' decisions but when he reaches seventeen, his parents may begin to listen to his arguments. This recalibration may not be a totally conscious process but one that evolves as the child matures toward adulthood. On the other hand, rules may be openly negotiated or changed as the result of various factors such as member dissatisfaction or feedback through parent-teacher conferences about what is acceptable. "Provide Michaela with more limits." "Encourage Patrick to state his own opinions."

As implied by the word, rules involve prescriptions. You may have lived with certain rules for so long without discussing them that the rules are unconscious but are adhered to as closely as if they were printed on your kitchen wall. Yet even a member of a family system may operate according to rules unknown to the others. A major source of couple conflict centers around breaking rules that one member of the pair may not even know exists. "You should know enough not to open my mail or listen to my phone calls." The more conscious the prescriptions, the greater the possibility of their renegotiation at appropriate times.

My wife and I were childhood sweethearts and our families were friends for years. When we married I figured that we would see most things the same way and never thought to talk about some of our differences. For example, I grew up learning that you never talk about your personal finances outside the immediate family and I would get really angry when my wife would talk about salaries or mortgages with our friends. After we were married about five years I really exploded one day and she was shocked. It never occurred to her that we should not talk about money. Since that time we've talked about many different "rules" and resolved some of the difficulties.

Once all parties involved know each others' rules they can negotiate; if only one person knows the rule, hurt feelings become inevitable.

Functions of Rules • Rules serve to set the limits for cohesion within a family. One may learn that everything is to be kept within the family, intimate physical and verbal behavior is expected and friends are to be kept at a distance. Or one may encounter a lack of concern for "protecting" family issues, suggestions that problems be taken elsewhere, and injunctions against anything but reserved physical interactions. By this point it should be clear that one's original family serves as the initial source of communication rules which are eventually brought to a new family system, consciously or unconsciously, and interrelated with a partner's rules. Let's explore this further by using three guidelines: what can be talked about, how it can be talked about, and who can be talked to about it (Satir, 1972, 98–99).

Most children are socialized into these rules by verbal and nonverbal cues. That first set of rules relates to what one is allowed to talk about. Can death be talked about in the family? Is sex discussed openly? Is a child allowed to know her father's salary? Are there special topics such as overweight, drinking, drugs, or certain relatives that are "off limits"? Most families have topics that are taboo, either all the time or under certain circumstances. Sometimes a family may openly agree not to raise a particular topic, but usually, family members realize a topic is inappropriate because of the verbal or nonverbal feedback they receive if they mention the subject.

My father left home when I was three years old, and neither my twin sister nor I was allowed to talk to my mother about him for fifteen years. When we turned eighteen, she finally shared with us the reasons she thinks he left. The topic was so painful for her that she had refused to discuss it for all those years. We quickly learned not to ask questions.

The previous example may be an extreme case, but most people have examples of less dramatic instances. Many people report that they were not allowed to talk about their parents' fights when they were growing up. If, after a fight, the children would ask, "What's the matter?" the answer was "nothing." Or if the question "What were you fighting about?" was raised, the response was, "We weren't fighting." Following is a less serious example:

Growing up, it was important that the man appear to be the provider in the family, so when my mother decided to go back to work, my parents decided that we would not tell the other relatives. Thus, I was told that, if any relative asked, I was to say that my mother did not work. This was our rule. The only problem was that my mother taught in the school I attended. Thus, I was faced with the following: "Oh, I hear your mother's gone back to teaching," to which I replied, "Not my mother. She doesn't work." When the next comment was, "Well, Mary says her nephew has your mother in class," I would reply, "Not my mother." So, every day I walked back and forth from school with my mother while maintaining my mother *did not* work. After about six months of this, my parents changed the communication rule to allow me to say that my mother was "helping out" in the school!

Although topics may not be restricted, many families restrict the feelings you can share within the system—especially if they are negative feelings. These may be totally denied. Emotions such as anger, sadness, or rage may be avoided at all costs and not shared with other family members.

Decision making often provides a fertile field for family rules. Does the system allow children to question parental decisions, or are they "the law" which cannot be challenged? In some families the inability to question decisions appears very clear, whereas in other cases, the same message is sent with subtlety.

While growing up, children may hear the words, "We're moving and that's final. I don't want to hear another word about it." Other families make room through their rules for family decision making through discussions, persuasion, or honest voting. In such cases all members are allowed to question the decision. We will analyze decision making in greater detail in Chapter 8.

Once the issue of "what you are allowed to talk about" has been considered, the next step is to consider "*how* you are allowed to talk about it." Within your family, can you talk about things directly, really level about feelings on a particular issue, or must you beat around the bush, or sneak in other ideas? For example, in some families with an alcoholic member, the other family members may say, "Daddy's not feeling well again," or "Mom's under the weather," but no one says, "Daddy drank too much," or "Mom is an alcoholic." There is a tacit agreement never to deal with the real issue. The same thing often occurs when someone dies. Children may learn that "Grandpa's gone to a better world," or "He passed away," but the reality of death is not discussed within the family system. Many couples have neglected drawing up a will, because they cannot find the way to talk directly to each other about the death of one of them. Parents have effectively prevented the treatment of their handicapped children by referring to them as "special" or "different" and ignoring the reality that they are retarded or hard of hearing. Older family members switched to a foreign language, if a touchy subject arose. Thus, the "how" may involve allusions to the topic or euphemisms for raising certain subjects. What strategies exist in your family? A pipe and slippers for Dad may be out of date, but each family has its own strategies for providing information to certain members. How does one gain a special favor from a parent? How does one ask for it? If there is bad news, how is it broken? How are pleasant surprises set up? How may anger be expressed?

These strategies may involve a change in the verbal and nonverbal communication behavior. A competent woman may suddenly lisp in a childish tone to express disapproval acceptably. Her husband may respond with corresponding parental behavior. A teenager may put her arms around her father's neck and he may dig the car keys out of his pocket. The reciprocal influence forms predictable patterns for disagreements.

Each of us has strategies for asking favors, receiving compliments, borrowing money, etc. and many of these strategies may involve changes in nonverbal behavior. "I always know something's up when my son puts his arm around my shoulder." Other aspects of the strategy may involve the timing of conversations. "Don't bother your father with that while he's eating," or the timing of a particular issue, "We won't explain to Bobby that he's adopted until he's seven years old."

"How" also involves the place for communication. Many married couples have agreed not to fight in the bedroom, to prevent the room from becoming associated with anger and conflict. Some families have a certain table or place in the kitchen, where the "real" talking gets done. For certain young people, the car serves as the place for really good conversations. In investigating a family's communication system, it is important to recognize the verbal and nonverbal strategies, as well as the issues of time and place, which indicate *how* members may talk about things.

The final issue remains, "Who are you allowed to talk to?" This may be exemplified by the following: "Don't tell Grandma, she'll have a stroke if she hears about it." "Do you think Jenny is old enough to understand about custody?"

   In some families, the rules for "who" are related to the age of the family members. While children are small, they may not hear much about family finances, but as they grow older they are brought into the discussion of how money is spent.

   You have probably experienced changes in rules as members of the family grew older and adaptation is made to developmental or situational events. Sometimes, unforeseen circumstances such as death or the breakup of a family move a child into a conversation circle that would have been denied otherwise. A fourteen-year-old in a single-parent family may discuss things with a parent that the other parent would usually have heard. A widow may discuss previously undisclosed financial matters with close relatives. Family myths about who can be talked to about what dictate the directions of many conversations. The whole issue of "Don't tell so and so—she can't take it" sets up the myths which may prevail for years. No one ever attempts to see if Grandma will be outraged, or Cousin Alice will be angry—it is just assumed and the communication proceeds accordingly.

When I was growing up, the family myth was that we could never talk about my Uncle, who died when I was eight, in front of my grandmother. We were told that "she just falls apart, if you mention his name." Last Christmas, I stopped over to see my grandmother, and we started to talk about things that happened when I was little, and somehow I accidentally mentioned my Uncle. This led into a discussion of my Uncle, and not only did my grandmother remain very composed, but she was glad to know that I remembered him so well. Obviously no one checked out the myth that arose around her initial mourning behavior.

   In order to fully appreciate the what, how, and who of family communication rules, it is necessary to analyze a system to see what rules are enforced. The following set of communication rules were developed by a young woman who analyzed her family's rules thoroughly. Among the general rules she isolated the communication rules with which she was raised.

Children don't talk back to their parents.
You are respectful at all times.
Tell the truth at all times.
You are polite at all times.
You do not fight.
Don't talk about our family's worth or goals.
Don't swear.
Tell all school-related problems to mother.
Do not discuss sex.
Don't discuss politics or religion.

Follow orders from authority figures.
Don't talk about Sandy's relationship with her boyfriend Mark.
Don't ask for money from Dad unless it is an absolute emergency.
You kiss or hug only on special occasions.
Family deaths aren't discussed.
Aunt Grace's marriage isn't discussed.
Mother's pregnancy at marriage isn't admitted.

The author of these rules discovered she had learned not to talk about anything important. The issues of what, how, and who provide one way for looking at basic issues in communication rules.

Rules may also be affected by cultural or ethnic backgrounds. In discussing problems in doing therapy with multi-generational Irish families, Pearce suggests the interview ". . . may be frustrated by everyone clamming up. This is because there are particularly strong rules about telling unflattering tales across generational and sexual lines . . ." ("Understanding the Irish Culture," 1980, 1). Each ethnic or cultural group may have its own rules.

Metarules • On top of everything else there are rules about rules, or *metarules.* As Laing (1972) aptly states, "There are rules against seeing the rules, and hence against seeing all the issues that arise from complying with or breaking them" (106). When a couple does not make a will, because of the difficulty of dealing with death, there may also be a rule that they do not talk about their rules about ignoring death. Laing goes so far as to suggest the following pattern may develop. Rule A: Don't. Rule A_1: Rule A does not exist. Rule A_2: Rule A_1 does not exist (113). The following thoughtful analysis of the rules in one young woman's family indicates this meta level of rule-bound behavior:

Sex may be a topic that is never mentioned and so becomes one of those topics you should forget. In order to forget it, you must make the rule saying you can't mention the rule that forbids the discussion of sex. In this way you can pretend it isn't forbidden and that deep levels of communication actually exist.

So, if I can't discuss my love life at the dinner table, I have to first acknowledge that rule. Then I must make a rule saying that I will not confront my parents with the rule against sex, since they have already gone through the forgetting process. In this way our communication about sex, if it exists at all, becomes entangled in an intricate system of rules that work only when everyone abides by them . . . which we usually do.

Perceiving the rules of our own system becomes very difficult because often we are not used to thinking about the basic rules, much less the rules about those rules. We live our lives in patterns with limited attention given to most of the patterns.

Breaking the rules may result in the creation of a new set since the system may recalibrate itself to accept more variety of behavior. Old patterns may be shifted. For example, "I have broken the rule about not discussing sex by openly discussing my living arrangement with my mother. She is now completely vulnerable, because she can no longer use the familiar pattern of communication. My action has completely upset the communication balance in our family." Yet the new system may be more open and flexible as a result.

The process of forming new systems through marriage or remarriage provides fertile ground for renegotiating existing rules and requires adaptation skills. For example, the rules become even more complicated in blended families, where people come together having learned sets of communication rules in other systems. When widowed or divorced persons remarry, they may involve each of their immediate families in a large recalibration process as the new family system is formed.

Although rules serve the practical function of getting us from day to day without renegotiating every interaction, they can stifle countless interactions unless we remain aware of their function and become flexible to changing the rules. Communication rules serve to influence the communication networks that develop in families.

Family Communication Networks

Through communication members of a family organize themselves into some kind of a group. Over time families develop communication networks to deal with the general issue of cohesion or separateness-connectedness and with specific issues such as carrying out instructions, organizing activities, regulating time and space, sharing resources. Family adaptability may be seen through the degree of flexibility in forming and reforming networks. Families with high adaptability and flexible rules may use a wide variety of network arrangements; families with low adaptability and rigid rules may continuously use the same networks for all concerns.

By definition a *network* determines the flow of messages back and forth from one family member to one or more other members or significant others outside the family. Feedback operates in all networks as individual family members regulate the directions of messages up, down, or across the lines of the network (Mortensen, 1972, 322). The direction of this flow of messages may be horizontal as when one sister wants to find out something, she asks another sister, who in turn may ask another brother, or when parents and children sit down and work out problems together. In such cases all persons have an equal say and status or role differences are minimized. The communication becomes vertical when real or imagined power differences are reflected in the interaction. For example, although the Turner children may share in many family decisions, they know that certain things are not negotiable. Mrs. Turner sets curfew and limits on the car which means she hands down information on these topics in a vertical manner.

These networks become a vital part of the decision-making process and relate to the power dynamics operating within the family. Certain networks facilitate dominance while others promote more shared communication. Networks also play an integral part in maintaining the roles and rules operating within the family system. Thus networks and rules have mutual influence—rules may dictate the use of certain networks; networks may create certain rule patterns.

To become aware of networks, observe the usual patterning of the verbal exchanges between members of a family. This processing of communication may be horizontal or vertical and fit into one of several networks: a chain, *Y,* wheel, circle, all-channel or completely connected. As you read this, try to determine which networks operate in your family:

There are eight girls in our family and over the years we have developed a specific pattern of requesting things from our parents. There are two different sets of four girls who seem to talk together and then the oldest of that group has to talk to Mom or Dad. It's like Gina tells Angel, she tells Celeste, Celeste tells me, and I talk to the folks. The other four girls have the same thing but somehow we never seem to cross over the lines. I guess part of this started when the older girls were assigned responsibility for certain younger ones.

The previous example demonstrates the *chain network.* It has a hierarchy built into it in that messages proceed up through the links or down from an authority source. Quite often a father or a mother control the chain network and pass out orders to children. For example, in male-dominated families the father may control the flow of messages on vital family issues. As in all of these networks there are times when the chain has definite advantages. All busy families tend to rely on a chain network when certain members cannot spend enough time together.

Sometimes chains tend to keep certain family members separated. If Annemarie always avoids dealing with her stepfather by communicating all her desires or concerns through her mother, she will remain very distant from her stepfather. People may obey the rules about who you cannot talk to directly about a subject by using a chain network.

In the chain network there can be a two-way exchange of information between all except the end members, who only have one member with whom to communicate (see Figure 3-1).

In the *Y* network messages are channeled through one person to one or more other family members. A housekeeper may receive messages from two working parents and relay them to their child. The same kind of network could function in a family where both parents work and all children are in school during the day. When school is out, the oldest child may take charge until one of the parents arrives home and then may serve as an assistant to the parents and relay messages to them from younger children. In blended families with a new stepparent, the natural parent may consciously or unconsciously set up a *Y* network, separating the stepparent from the children (see Figure 3-2). For example, such families have rules that only the biological parent can talk to the children on

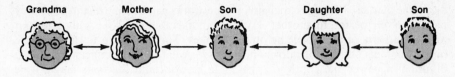

Figure 3-1 Chain Network

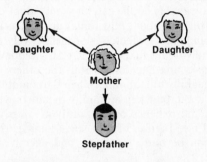

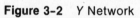

Figure 3-2 *Y* Network

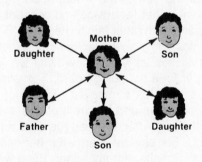

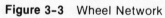

Figure 3-3 Wheel Network

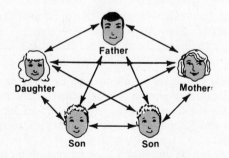

Figure 3-4 All-Channel Network

discipline matters. Messages in chain or *Y* networks can become distorted as they pass from one person to another. Each family member can selectively filter out or change parts of a message he or she dislikes. This may help to diffuse some family conflicts but the misinformation could escalate other conflicts. There is a diffusion of power and control in the circle network and decisions may not be quickly reached. Contacting all members and adapting ideas or adjusting complaints via feedback in this network takes time.

The wheel pattern depends upon one family member who channels all messages to other members. It can be quite autocratic if the control figure in the network operates that way. He or she can filter and adapt messages positively or negatively or enforce the rule about how things are said as they pass through the network. He or she can balance effectively or ineffectively tensions in the family system. The central individual's function may result in dominance or exhaustion. Since only one person communicates with all the others, this person becomes critical to the ongoing family functioning. When the communication load is heavy and concentrated, as it can be when all family members want to get off to work or school, the talents and patience of the family member in the wheel network will be severely taxed (see Figure 3-3). In some families the central member of the wheel network can be quite nurturing and effective in holding a family together.

My mother was the hub of the wheel in our family. When we were children, we went to her for advice and consent and expected her to settle our problems with other family members. She always knew what everyone was doing and how everyone felt. When we left home each of us children always let Mom know what we were doing and continued to use her for a sounding board. Each week, those of us who moved away, almost felt compelled to write or telephone. Mom digested the family news and let my brothers and sisters know what each of us was doing. After she died the six surviving children had no regular contacts. For several years after her death we had little contact except occasionally with my father. But it wasn't the same. With Dad communication is a one-way channel. He likes to hear from us but he never goes to the phone to call long distance (too tight) and letter writing just never appealed to him. Now seven years later we have formed a new subsystem in which four of us stay in contact with each other. One sister, Mary Alice, is the new hub.

The completely connected or all-channel network provides for two-way exchange between all family members. Communication can flow in all directions and effective decisions can be made because all members have an equal chance to discuss the issues and respond to them. This network provides for the maximum use of feedback.

All interaction can be direct and transactional. No other family member serves as a "go-between" and each can participate freely in the process of sharing information or deciding issues (see Figure 3-4). Yet if the rules say certain subjects should not be raised, access will have little effect. Although this network allows equal participation, it can be the most disorganized and chaotic since messages can flow in all directions. Each family member can compete for "air time" to ventilate his or her views. For this network to be successful in operation, the rules in the family have to provide for respecting each member's turn in communicating and remaining quiet to listen to each member's views. Listening to one another is a key way to avoid chaos in this network. Participants tend to express satisfaction with this network (Cronkhite, 1976, 63).

In families other networks are possible, including combinations under certain circumstances. The ends of the chain may link forming a circle; chains may lead toward the central figure in the wheel. Most families use some variety of networks as they progress through daily life. Special issues in a family may cause a family to change the usual network patterns and adopt new ones to solve the issue. In daily life a family, for example, may operate essentially in the chain and wheel network, but when vacations are planned the network used is all-channel.

The definition of networks includes the possibility that significant others outside the immediate family may have an influence upon the communication patterns within it if the boundaries are permeable. A *significant other* is a person who has an intimate relationship with one or more of the family members. This may be a grandparent, aunt or uncle, close family friend, lover, or fiancé of one of the children. The family member who has ties to a significant other outside the family may very well make decisions within the network that were determined by this relationship. When children leave home and form their own family networks, a parent may remain a significant other and influence the operation of the new network. Problems with in-laws arise often because the networks are intertwined and boundaries not established.

Family networks tend to change over time. As children grow up and increasingly take over the direction of their own lives, adaptive families often move from the chain or wheel network to the circle or all-channel. The wheel and chain networks facilitate order and discipline, but may no longer be needed when children become autonomous and capable of directing their own decision making. Parents may signal their recognition of these changes by permitting more issues to be discussed via a completely connected network.

As we saw in Chapter 2, subgroups and alliances may emerge within families—such connections interact with the family networks. The two people on one end of the chain may become very close and support each other in all situations. The key person in the Y formation may ally with another member and keep certain information from the others, or control certain information. Some family members may never relate directly as the parts of the network form small groups that support or relate to each other.

Thus the networks serve a very important function within families. They determine who talks to whom, who is included or excluded, who gets full or partial information, and who controls certain information. Yet the rules for what, how, and whom to communicate to exist within each style of network.

Before closing our discussion of the formation of meaning and message patterns, we need to consider one important source of input that influences each family's development of meaning.

Although we eventually learn our communication behavior by participating in numerous relationships, as was suggested in Chapter 1, our family-of-origin serves as the first and often as the most significant source of instruction in developing relationships. We learn how to regulate distance among members and how to adapt to developmental or situational aspects of family life through the communication within our family-of-origin. Hence it deserves special attention.

FAMILY-OF-ORIGIN ISSUES

"He's a Kaplan all right. He'll walk up and talk to anyone without a trace of shyness." "She's just like Aunt Lorraine—clams up and you can't get a thing out of her." "You know the Yogevs—always keeping the family secrets." These familiar sayings serve to perpetuate certain myths about how whole families relate. Yet they highlight the potential family-of-origin influence in communication patterns that form as new systems are created. When we use the term *family-of-origin* we are referring to the family or families in which a person is raised. Thus the family you grew up in is your family-of-origin. Many of you still live within your family-of-origin system whereas others of you have already formed new family systems.

Although the mutual accommodation and the development of common meanings with a marital relationship depend on the physical, social, and individual filters of each person, the family-of-origin background each spouse brings to the relationship remains a significant social influence. Although many of us may desire a family life different from the one we grew up in ". . . familiarity exerts a powerful pull. Most people will choose the familiar, even though uncomfortable, over the unfamiliar, even though it might be comfortable . . . People often work out marriages similar to their own parents' not because of heredity; they are simply following a family pattern" (Satir, 1972, 127).

Families-of-origin may provide blueprints for the communication of future generations. Initially, communication is learned in the home and throughout life the family setting provides a major testing ground for communication behavior. Each young person who leaves the family-of-origin to form a new system brings with him or her a set of conscious and unconscious ways of relating to people. The idiosyncrasies of the Andersons may be passed on to the Hanrahans, Galvins, and then to more Andersons and from there on to countless generations.

My mother said my grandmother referred to ice cream as 'I-box' when she was little, and my mother called it that for me, and I have taught it to my son. I hadn't thought about it for years, but it just came back when Steven was old enough to ask for it.

Just as the simple language terms travel across the generations, more significant attitudes and rule-bound behaviors move from a family-of-origin to a newly-emerging family system. For example, in their examination of male and female expressiveness, Balswick and Averett (1977) tested the following as one of their hypotheses: Persons whose parents were expressive to them will be more expressive. The authors report, "Our evidence suggests the expressive children come from expressive parents, or at the very least, from parents who are perceived as expressive" (126).

Rules on keeping things "in the family," or the acceptability of discussing certain subjects, and how to do so, may pass from generation to generation. These may be accompanied with understandings about how information should travel, or what networks should be used—such as a woman always serves as the "hub" of the wheel, or fathers always need a "buffer" from the children's demands.

Sometimes, the transition of such behavior is smooth because the other spouse has a similar background or does not resist the particular behavior. On the other hand, wide differences in family-of-origin behaviors can lead to communication breakdowns in the young couple's system. In the following example, a young wife describes the differences in nonverbal communication in her family-of-origin and that of her husband's:

It was not until I became closely involved with a second family that I even became conscious of the fact that the amount and type of contact can differ greatly.

Rarely, in Rob's home, will another person reach for someone else's hand, walk arm in arm, or kiss for no special reason; hugs are reserved for greetings and occasionally for comfort. Never have I witnessed the men touch each other at all, with the exception of a handshake. When people filter into the parlor to watch television (usually everyone views the program of their choice in their own room), one person will sit on the couch, the next on the floor, a third on a chair, and finally the last person is forced to sit on the couch. And *always* at the opposite end!

Touching, in my home, was a natural, everyday occurrence. Usually, the family breakfast began with good morning hugs and kisses. The men in the family, including relatives, also enjoyed physical contact. After meals, we often would sit on our parents' laps rocking, talking, and just relaxing. While watching television, we usually congregated on and around someone else as we sat facing the set. As adults, our behavior has altered somewhat, but physical closeness is still an integral part of our family functioning. No one would ever hesitate to cuddle up next to someone else, run their hands through another person's hair, or start tickling whoever happens to be in reaching distance.

The previous example graphically illustrates the extent to which each member of the couple was raised differently and how that can affect the communication behavior in the new system. When you consider your parents' marriage, or your own marriage, you can find either simple or very complex instances of this type of situation where the rules or networks affect how and what communication happens.

Changes in such a system depend on the nature of feedback within the system. Negative or constancy feedback that reinforces the status quo prevents change or adjustment. "If I don't say anything he'll grow out of it" or "That's just the way she is so I'll go along." Positive or change-promoting feedback forces the issue into the open in a risk-taking move that the situation can be changed. "I really need more affection from you" or "Let's cuddle." The context in which the family functions affects the type of communication and nature of instruction that exists. In discussing the attempts of Irish Americans to "gain respectability" in America, sociologist Andrew Greeley (1974) maintains three to four generations of people rejected their creative strain and taught their children and their children's children to live by two concerns: "Two favorite Irish American phrases summarize the almost pathetic quest for respectability: 'Who do you think you are' and 'What will people say' " (299). He strongly suggests that Irish American parents, aiming for respectability, consciously limited the creative communication of subsequent generations. Rather they instructed their offspring in appropriate upward-mobility behaviors. Cross-cultural differences in a couple's background may lead to strong conflicts as each plays out behaviors appropriate to his or her family-of-origin.

Unfortunately one of the biggest problems in our marriage comes from something that is very hard to change; my husband and I are from very different cultural backgrounds. He is from rural Central America and I grew up in Kansas City. I married him when I was 18 and he was 26 because I was pregnant and he has always treated me as a child even though we now have three children. When I say I would like to get a job, or I would like to have more freedom he gets upset. I want to be part of making decisions and I want to make more American friends. He gets angry because a "good wife" would not want that. I try to explain to him how I grew up but it sounds strange to him. We are both trying to live the way we grew up but because there are so many differences, it is very hard.

Such differences may never be resolved because of the strength of the family pattern or compromises may be found as the whole family is influenced by social forces.

Although the families-of-origin remain a primary force in influencing the development of a new system, other sources such as the media, educational and religious institutions, and significant others affect young people's ideas of how family life should be. Print and nonprint media are devoting much attention to the changing roles of men and women, facing many readers and viewers with alternative life-style possibilities. Next-door neighbors or extended family members and family friends may provide living models of various family forms. When we deal with roles in Chapter 6, we will examine the differences between role expectations and role performance, demonstrating how patterns can be very powerful unless they are actively rejected.

When you look at your current interpersonal behaviors, you may see reflections of your family-of-origin. If you have formed a new system you probably have experienced adjusting to behaviors that reflect your spouse's family-of-origin. You will adapt to that family's network and follow some (or all) of their rules. The family-of-origin issues influence all aspects of family communication and account for many of the communication patterns, rules, and networks you bring to a new relationship.

CONCLUSION

In this chapter we examined the formation of family meanings including the characteristics of developed relationships of richness, uniqueness, efficiency, substitutability, pacing, openness, spontaneity, and evaluation. These characteristics are reflected in the verbal and nonverbal behaviors with which family members negotiate a set of common meanings and develop their own unique message system. We also examined the patterns that family systems needed to provide order and predictability for their members, focusing specifically on communication rules and the networks by which messages are transmitted. Finally we looked at the role of the family-of-origin as a primary force in influencing the communication behavior of family members in current and future systems.

As we will see throughout this book, each family system develops its own communication meanings that may be either similar to or different from those of other family systems. Members learn the fundamentals of communication and relationship development in their families-of-origin and carry these learnings into all other aspects of their lives. Newly forming systems reflect, to some extent, the families-of-origin of the specific members.

Communication and the Development of Family Relationships

My wife and I started to get to know each other in a really strange way. We met at a college mixer and at the end I started to walk her home and we stopped on the way at the campus duck pond to sit and talk. We sat and talked until about six A.M. And we talked about the most amazing things. We shared about our backgrounds, values, wishes, fears. Donna is a very open person and since she was comfortable talking about these things, she made me comfortable sharing similar types of information. That was 16 years ago and we still are able to share all important aspects of our lives.

Each of you probably has similar special stories about the beginning of the very important friendships or romantic relationships in your life. Most of your reports would include the importance of *sharing* information, not just letting one person make all the effort, do all the talking, or take all the risks. Most couples would report that as their relationship developed, each of them engaged in an exchange process, a mutual effort and sharing, that led to the deepening of their relationship. Parents and children and siblings often report similar experiences as the children develop and are able to participate in the sharing process by choice.

In this chapter we will examine the communication dynamics involved in the process of developing relationships, specifically family relationships. The discussion will focus more directly on the development of adult family relationships since these involve more voluntary and conscious efforts; parent-child and sibling relationships also involve and depend upon mutual interaction and sharing but young children cannot make the same conscious choices about participating in the process of relationship development. In order to understand the relationship development process and its communication dynamics, we will look at: (1) social exchange as the basis for marital and family relationship development, (2) the stages of relational development and their application to marital and family life, and (3) the relational currencies used by various families to communicate affection and build relationships.

SOCIAL EXCHANGE IN FAMILIES

Although it doesn't sound "romantic," when I married for the second time, I looked for very different things in a husband. I looked for the ability to maintain a good job. I wanted someone who was kind and I didn't care if he was the most sexy and dashing person I knew. After six years with a flirtatious, playboy type, I knew that you couldn't eat charm and it didn't take care of you when things went wrong.

The basis of relationships may be viewed from numerous perspectives. Theorists such as Schutz, Goffman, and McCall and Simmons provide alternative ways of examining the human relational process. In this text we have chosen to focus on a social exchange approach. Unfortunately no one approach deals directly with family life, rather the focus is placed on adult-adult or parent-child relationships.

Social exchange theory examines the role of rewards and costs in the maintenance of relationships. Although it *doesn't* sound romantic, much of our interaction, especially in the family setting, depends on gaining a reward or profit from the relationship. In other words, people tend to perceive rewards from their relationships in order to remain in them unless they see no other possible alternatives. Thus, although some family relationships, specifically parent and small child, remain nonvoluntary, most ongoing familial relationships involve choice, allowing us to look at relationship development and maintenance through exchange theory.

Social exchange theory combines behavioristic psychology and economic theory. It assumes that interpersonal relationships are evaluated by the persons involved in terms of the value of the consequences of their interactions and that people engage in behavior only as long as the rewards for the behavior are greater than the costs. In lasting relationships, such as occur in families, members may forfeit immediate rewards in favor of some long-term gain. There may be a balancing of costs and rewards over time and no one given event is likely to cause a relationship to end. But, could this really apply to our romantic concept of marriage or family life? In 1952 Goffman suggested the practical approach to the marital relationships when he described marriage as a process by which a man sums up his attributes and suggests to a particular woman that hers are not so much better as to preclude a marriage.

Although in today's society either men or women may extend a marriage proposal, the underlying concept remains the same. Most people engage in some type of analytic process similar to economic theory as they evaluate important relationships. In his work *Sexual Bargaining,* Scanzoni (1972) suggests that "It is a general sociological principle that associations are formed and maintained on the basis of reciprocity-exchanged rewards and benefits. A love relationship is no exception" (51). He further asserts that ". . . the essence of the husband-wife relationship is based on the attainment of interests, or reward-seeking, which may be more accurately and fundamentally described as a reciprocal . . . type association" (32). A child-parent relationship is harder to view from this perspective until the child reaches an age where he or she can evaluate the costs and rewards of being actively involved in the relationship.

Rewards and Costs

Relationships may be thought of as involving costs and rewards, profit and loss. *Rewards* consist of anything that meets a person's needs, or the pleasures, satisfactions, and gratifications a person enjoys. Each of us has observed marriages in which we can't imagine why the people stay together and wonder what could be in it for each one. Yet rewards differ according to the person. Security may keep one person in a relationship, affection may hold another, and pride may maintain a third. Past good deeds and happy memories may cause others to stay and hope for a return of the "good old days." The greater the exchange of rewards, the more likely it is that the behaviors will be repeated.

On the one hand, a person may say, "It's better to put up with this rather than to be by myself or to try to get a job after 23 years." Or someone may say, "It's too painful to live this kind of life any longer. Anything would be better than this and I'm leaving." Thus *costs* are those factors that deter the repetition of a particular behavior. High costs may involve great physical, mental, or emotional effort. They make a behavior less likely to occur or be repeated. "I can no longer expend the energy it takes to live with a drug abuser. The price is too high."

My wife was an alcoholic and things got so bad that I was losing my contact with the children as well as with her. I would lie to the boys about their mother's drinking but they knew what was going on. Finally I realized that my marriage was a failure and the boys were drawing further and further away from both of us because we were living a big lie. Although the divorce was painful, it changed my relationship with the boys and we are able to have an open honest relationship in a relatively calm house.

Communication may serve as a means of exchanging certain rewards or costs or may itself serve as a reward or cost in certain relationships depending on the perception of the persons involved.

Rewards and costs will vary from person to person, and system to system. A girl may appreciate her stepmother because the older woman can introduce her to the world of make-up and stylish clothes. A great-grandmother may be rewarded by having a two-year-old to cuddle in her lap. A couple may find a marriage rewarding because their sex life is good, both can be independent, and both enjoy athletic activity. For one person a highly cohesive family may be rewarding whereas another may perceive such cohesion as stifling and label it a cost. Family themes may influence the perception of rewards and costs. A mother in a family with strong themes of dependence may find it costly to watch her son gain independence; in turn, the son may find the freedom rewarding and his mother's hovering a cost to be borne.

There are external (exogenous) and intrinsic (endogenous) determinants of rewards and costs (Thibaut and Kelley, 1959, 14). External determinants include a person's values, needs, skills, tools, and predispositions to anxiety that are carried along as one moves among the various relationships of life. These determinants may be linked to the family-of-origin of one or both spouses. The extent of rewards to be gained by two interacting persons will depend on their individual needs and values and how closely their mutual behaviors mesh with those values and needs. A person's rewards may come from his or her own behaviors in the presence of another, which in actuality could be attained alone (e.g., reading a book in presence of another). Or rewards may result from the other's behavior (teasing someone out of a bad mood). The latter type of reward derives directly from the other's behavior.

The internal or endogenous determinants of rewards and costs occur when the "specific values associated with a given item in A's repertoire depend on the particular item in B's repertoire with which, in the course of the interaction it is paired" (Thibaut and Kelley, 15). Specific needs elicit specific appropriate responses during mutual interactions; each has the capability to respond to the other's needs.

Thus, the paired set of specialized responses are intrinsic to the relationship and underscore the transactional quality of the relationship. If when Jim cries he needs to have someone hold him, and his friend Anne panics when he cries and tries to cheer him up, or talk him out of it, their behaviors are not paired. There is no intrinsic reward. Perhaps Anne does not have that holding behavior in her repertoire, perhaps she is incapable of sending that type of nonverbal message, particularly when dealing with men. Yet if Jim's brother Michael holds him when he cries, that relationship has an intrinsic determinant of reward for that situation. The reward for Jim is intrinsic because his needs can be met by behaviors in Michael's repertoire. Perhaps Michael also experiences a reward through being needed by Jim.

Relational Profit

The reward-cost issues also include the concept of *profit*. Profit emerges as a result of reward minus the cost. *(Profit = Reward − Cost)* You may measure the profit you derive from a relationship by subtracting the costs from the rewards you receive. Members of a particular family may find their relationships profitable as they subtract the costs of compliance and high expectations from the rewards of cohesion, support, and affection.

People may evaluate their relational profit subjectively in terms of two levels of comparison. Comparison Level or *CL* is a "standard by which the person evaluates the rewards and costs of a given relationship in terms of what he feels he deserves" (Thibaut and Kelley, 21). On the basis of past experiences, a person creates a standard against which to judge relationships. The Comparison Level is the neutral point between satisfaction and dissatisfaction on one's mental continuum for judging relationships. One would see relationships that fall above the *CL* as satisfactory and attractive and vice versa, those that fall below the *CL* are undesirable. One's *CL* may change as one experiences new relationships. After expectations or desires are fulfilled, the *CL* tends to be raised and higher satisfaction may be anticipated from that and future relationships.

I had never had a very good dating relationship until I met Janice and then I really learned what to expect in a close romantic relationship. Now that I realize what such a relationship could be, I cannot just date for the sake of going out. I really want another relationship with some of the things I shared with Janice.

CL alt or Comparison Level for Alternatives, can be defined as "the lowest level of outcomes a member will accept in the light of available alternative opportunities" (21). In other words, it is the standard one uses to decide whether to remain in, or leave, a specific relationship based on an analysis of available alternatives. A woman who remains in a marriage unhappily may believe there are no alternatives when her children are small but may leave the marital relationship when they are older due to her ability to be self-supporting or because she has found support in another relationship. A widower may remain extremely dependent on his daughter's family because he sees no alternative relationship from which he will receive emotional support. In applying *CL alt* to marriage, Scanzoni suggests, "When that point, *CL alt,* is reached by either or both partners, it represents the breaking point at which the reward-cost ratio is deemed too unfavorable to maintain the relationship any longer" (101). When the lower threshold is reached by either or both partners, it is then that dissolution, such as separation or divorce, becomes a possibility. Until *CL alt* is reached, any marriage ". . . is likely to continue simply because the reward-cost ratio is, at the least, 'barely tolerable,' and in some cases may even range into the 'acceptable,' or perhaps on into the 'very favorable' " (101).

In order for a mutual relationship to function adequately, the jointly experienced outcomes must occur above each person's *CL alt.* In marriage where one person's needs can only be fulfilled by negating the other's needs, major conflict will emerge. If you think about your own important relationship, you will realize that you try for optimum positive outcomes, i.e., you both try to reward each other at low cost.

In my first marriage we both tended to drain each other. We were very different and although we loved each other, it was always an effort to please the other person. Finally each of us lived such separate lives that it seemed silly to remain married. I have lived with a woman for three years now and things are entirely different. We are very similar in attitudes, interests, and beliefs and we work at trying to stay in touch with where the other person is. This relationship is much more rewarding for both of us than either of our previous marriages.

Thus, reciprocity becomes a critical factor in the maintenance of long-term intimate relationships. Each person must experience some rewards and profit for a relationship to continue.

In discussing romantic sharing Scanzoni says:

> If both parties define their inputs and rewards as "just," "beneficial," or "satisfactory," then the love relationship is quite likely to be maintained and to evolve into marriage. If one party does not feel that the cost-reward ratio is satisfactory to him, he (she) may cut back his inputs, thereby reducing the satisfactions of the other, and thus increasing the likelihood that the relationship will be terminated.   (51)

A further consideration in social exchange is the rule of distributive justice which suggests that investments, rewards, and costs should all be roughly comparable, or "If one's costs are higher, for example, one's rewards ought to be higher, so that the profits (rewards less costs) will be roughly equal among all the parties to the exchange" (McCall and Simmons, 1966, 154). The rule of distributive justice acknowledges an ideal of fairness in relationships ("The more I put in, the more I should get out."), and the goal of relationships with mutual profit ("We both get more out of this relationship than we put into it.").

Yet in long-term relationships, such as those found within a family, after the initial relationships have been firmly established, immediate reciprocity need not be equal in amount or kind. As relationships progress, inequality of rewards or costs may be tolerated or accepted on the assumption that the burdens or benefits will shift at a later time within the relationship. ". . . this reciprocity helps to account for marital stability because it sets up a chain of enduring obligations and repayments within a system of roles in which each role contains both rights and duties" (Scanzoni, 64). Knapp (1978) suggests that lovers and spouses are "less likely to expect a constant balance of rewards and costs because they anticipate that the favors given and received will average out during the course of their relationship" (30).

Up to this point we have been discussing voluntary relationships. Yet not all marital or family relationships have this quality. Circumstances may "require a person to remain in a relationship that he regards as unsatisfactory" (Thibaut and Kelley, 21).

Relationships are said to be nonvoluntary, and therefore below one's standard of satisfaction, when a person must remain in a relationship in which the outcomes are poor, or through which he or she is excluded from alternative relationships. Initially any family relationship involving young children has a nonvoluntary quality since the child did not choose to engage in such relationships and is excluded from alternative relationships. Also, other members of the system may not have desired a new child or sibling. Eventually as the young person matures, he or she begins to engage in the conscious process of analyzing the family relationships and may determine that whereas some are rewarding, others are not. Other members of the system make similar judgments about their relationships to this individual. A child who exists in a family that provides minimal rewards may eventually seek links to other families, if the system's boundaries permit such freedom, or may lower his *CL* in order to function within his system.

Factors such as children, religion, money, or illness may influence individuals to perceive their relationships as involuntary.

Of all the people I know, my aunt had the hardest life. She married an irresponsible man when she was very young and he left her when their son was eight years old. Although she was only 30 at the time, she refused to consider remarriage because she was Catholic and according to her, she had "married for life" and could not remarry as long as her former husband was alive. My cousin died when he was 16 and my aunt has lived the rest of her life alone. My heart aches every time I think of her.

No matter what factors are involved, certain people will not be able to act on their negative or high cost evaluations of their relationships because they consider themselves as nonvoluntary members of the relationship.

In keeping with our perspective of evolution and change in systems, we need to note that perceptions of rewards and costs change with time so that the reward of being a homemaker may eventually be perceived as a cost by a woman who eventually desires to return to work full-time. The original rewards coming from a dependent relationship may be perceived very differently ten years later. Likewise, actual costs and rewards in relationships change over time. The cost of relating to a bossy ten-year-old brother may eventually transform into the reward of finding a good listener in that same person ten years later. How often do siblings talk about becoming good friends once "everyone became adults"?

Thus people tend to seek optimum profits from their relationships, including familial ones, although those who are, or perceive themselves to be, in nonvoluntary relationships may not be able to exert control over their rewards and costs. Due to the subjectivity of what is considered a reward or cost, individuals or systems may differ in their perceptions of profit and loss, and over time may change their perceptions. Although we present this as a rather straightforward process, it is more subtle and complex than it may first appear. Persons may have unconscious or barely conscious reasons for valuing something as a reward; habits may dictate the continuation of long-held perceptions. The routines of daily life are not conducive to the minute scrutiny of each evolving relationship in terms of profit and loss; only under pressure or at sensitive moments may we revert to such analysis consciously.

In order to fully understand the role of costs and rewards in family life we need to consider the stages of relational development.

RELATIONAL DEVELOPMENT

The old saying, "You can choose your friends but you can't choose your relatives," suggests that many family relationships are involuntary and not likely to be as desirable as those of a chosen friendship. Yet as we saw earlier, many of these "involuntary" relationships develop into close friendships, typified by comments such as, "My daughter is becoming my best friend," or "My brother-in-law and I are very close to each other." Whether they be with friends or relatives, the relationships you consider deep or special do not just happen—they develop slowly over time and usually reflect mutual caring and trust as the result of both of you working on building the relationship. Since families are built upon, and incorporate, relationships, it becomes critical to examine the process of relationship development and the role of exchange in relationship growth.

Basically, "Our dyadic relationships with others progress through stages of initiation, maintenance, and dissolution" (Wilmot, 1979, 143). All relationships go through an initiation or orientation stage after which they end or move toward some type of ongoing maintenance. Eventually relationships face termination or dissolution as death, divorce, or separation takes its toll. We will consider relationship dissolution in a later chapter and concentrate now on building and maintaining relationships.

Social Penetration

Although there are many ways of looking at how relationships develop, we will use the social penetration process as our model and relate it to our previous discussion of social exchange. Psychologists Altman and Taylor (1973) present this model for understanding relationship development between any two persons regardless of the nature of their relationships. *Social penetration* refers to "(1) overt interpersonal behaviors which take place in social interaction and (2) internal subjective processes which precede, accompany, and follow overt exchange" (5). These authors hypothesize that interpersonal exchange gradually progresses from superficial, nonintimate areas to more intimate, deeper layers of the self; people assess interpersonal costs and rewards gained from the interaction, and the future development of the relationship depends on the quality and quantity of these rewards and costs (6). Wilmot describes the link between exchange theory and relationship development:

Proponents of exchange theory speculate that participants pass through the following relational stages: (1) sampling—searching out others who fit our needs and who reward us, (2) bargaining—working with one another to develop a relationship that is mutually satisfying to both, (3) commit-

ment—forming bonds between each other, and (4) institutionalization—
publicly affirming that the relationship has an ongoing status.   (145)

This process may be applied to all relationships including familial ones and may
be understood in terms of the communication that occurs between the relationship members that fosters relational growth or limitation.

Most new families develop from the members of a couple who come from
similar, although not identical family backgrounds, yet sometimes individuals
from very different backgrounds choose to marry. As the couple merges, new
relationships are developed between members of the two systems. When you
marry, you may acquire a mother-in-law, sister-in-law, new nephews, cousins, or
grandparents. Divorce and remarriage may give you new stepsisters or stepbroth-
ers, stepparents, stepchildren, and their relatives. Although they are somewhat
nonvoluntary, these adult relationships develop along the same lines as any
nonrelative friendship. Most likely you start sharing at very superficial levels and
assess the costs and rewards of pursuing a relationship further. For example, a
woman may choose not to pursue a relationship with a particular man because
he has custody of his three children and she does not wish to incur the costs of
becoming involved in such a system. Since the social penetration process assumes
direct effort and consciousness on the part of the persons involved, small children
do not fit as readily into this model. Yet as children grow older and can make
certain choices and exhibit particular behaviors, they may develop strong interpersonal relationships with siblings or related family members. Again we must
qualify our description of a straightforward process, reminding you of the unconscious and complex considerations that may affect relational development.

Carl Sandburg once said, "People are like onions, you uncover them a
layer at a time and sometimes you cry." This statement crystallizes Altman and
Taylor's position that interpersonal ties develop incrementally and that we discover other people or share ourselves by revealing the layers of our personality
through communication, and interpersonal exchange gradually progresses from
superficial, nonintimate areas to more intimate deeper layers of the self. In other
words, people gradually let others know them. They also maintain that "people
assess interpersonal rewards and costs, satisfaction and dissatisfaction, gained
from interaction with others, and that the advancement of the relationship is
heavily dependent on the amount and nature of the rewards and costs" (6). Thus,
people make judgments about the cost or reward of a current encounter and
predict the value of future interactions at the same or deeper levels.

Advocates of the social penetration theory propose an onionskin structure
which has depth and breadth dimensions that are uncovered as people share
central aspects of their personalities. The information people share may be characterized according to the topics they talk about, the breadth of the topic or the
number of things within a particular category, and the depth of the topic or its
connectedness to a person's self-concept. As a topic moves toward more depth
and is more connected to the core of one's personality, it is illustrated in Figure
4-1 as being closer to the center circle.

Some individuals may share information from all categories freely, others
will be more selective about the categories from which they disclose. Some will
openly share at great depth within categories whereas others will tend to remain
at superficial levels. Yet making statements about individuals is misleading since

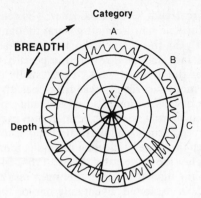

Category
A
BREADTH
B
X
Depth
C

Figure 4-1 Depth and Breadth of Information Related to Personality

each relationship, due to its transactional quality, may bring out various dimensions of the persons involved. Simply put, you may discuss serious concerns about war with your father because he reveals his deep feelings about aging with you; although you may never discuss such feelings about war with your brother, you may share deeply about family pressures because you reciprocate on that topic. You may never discuss any topic in depth with your sister because you get feedback that she is uncomfortable. The core areas are those that are usually shared later and more cautiously in a relationship.

Let's apply the following diagrams (Figures 4-2a and 4-2b) to a relationship between Ellen and Jack and see how their communication about certain topics may enhance or hinder relationship growth.

Whereas Jack and Ellen may share the shaded areas easily early in a relationship, if one or the other pushes for too much depth too quickly the

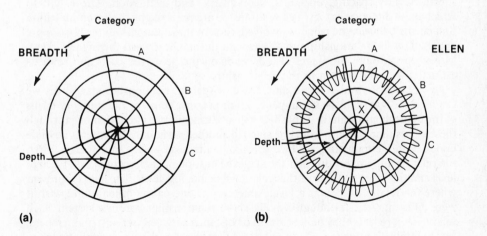

Category

BREADTH
A
B
Depth
C

(a)

Category

BREADTH
A
ELLEN
B
X
Depth
C

(b)

Figure 4-2 Application of Information Sharing

relationship will be threatened. Assume category *A* is religion. Although Ellen and Jack may be comfortable sharing some general thoughts on religion, if Ellen tries to share too early in the relationship the importance of prayer in her everyday life (issue *x*), Jack may be threatened, especially if Jack holds different views. No matter what the topic happens to be, usually one cannot jump into depth levels until the more superficial areas have been thoroughly covered.

As we noted in our discussion of social exchange, once a strong relationship is established, then sharing need not be so evenly paced. But, in the beginning, the timing is important since if a love relationship is to develop into a lasting mutual attachment then the "lovers' affection for and commitment to one another [must] expand at roughly the same pace" (Blau, 1964, 84–85). If one gives far more to the relationship than the other, this may result in feelings of being trapped, overwhelmed, or exploited. Eventually one or the other will probably end the relationship.

A number of theorists have hypothesized about the stages relationships go through and the role of communication in such movement. Wilmot talks broadly about relationship initiation, stabilization, and dissolution (143–168). Knapp has developed a ten-stage model with five stages of relationship development ranging from initiating to bonding and five stages of relationship dissolution ranging from differentiating to terminating. (17–26). He stresses that the movement through the stages is generally systematic and sequential, may be forward, backward, or occur within stages, yet it always is toward a new place (32). Such concepts keep us aware of the evolutionary nature of any relationships.

Stages of Relational Development

The stages we would like to examine in more detail are those proposed by Altman and Taylor which are an outgrowth of their understanding of the social penetration process. They propose a model of four stages, the movement through which is tied to the eight characteristics of a developed relationship discussed in Chapter 3. Just to remind you, these include: richness, uniqueness, efficiency, substitutability, pacing, openness, spontaneity, and evaluation. The extent to which these dimensions exist in a relationship are reflected by the communication that occurs between the persons involved; each of these dimensions becomes more apparent as the relationship moves through the stages toward the highest point. Movement through the stages also depends on the perceived costs and rewards estimated by each person in the relationship.

Let us look at Altman and Taylor's specific relationship stages. As we examine the stages in the social penetration process, think of the stages in terms of the model continuum in Table 4-1. You are much more likely to move through these stages than to jump from one stage to another, although the latter is possible under certain circumstances. Two specific points need to be remembered. First, the relationship moves through the stages. Thus, one person cannot be at a high level and the other member of that relationship at a low level. The levels represent where the relationship is at a given time even if one or the other would wish it were different. Also, although we talk about relationships within a system, each relationship reflects the connectedness or distance between two system members. For example, three sisters would not move through the stages as one relationship.

They would represent three separate dyadic relationships that may be very similar and have overlap, but the relationship belongs to a dyad.

Table 4-1 Stages of Relationship Development

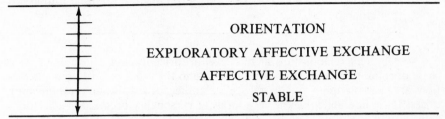

ORIENTATION

EXPLORATORY AFFECTIVE EXCHANGE

AFFECTIVE EXCHANGE

STABLE

Orientation Stage • The *orientation stage* represents the first meeting(s) when most people are on their best behavior. You can think of yourself meeting a new person and trying to make a good impression by attempting to avoid conflict or negative topics most of the time. You are not likely to be very free in the interaction because you do not know the other person well enough. Probably you will follow traditional social rules searching for common interests or mutual acquaintances as you discuss things at a superficial level. Reciprocity occurs around general information. Your nonverbals may be limited and restrained. You can't exchange knowing looks, in-jokes, or complete someone else's sentences. There are none of the characteristics of a developed relationship. For example, little uniqueness or efficiency exists for the two of you. In short, you are trying to reduce your uncertainty about the other person and to increase your predictability about future interactions.

Except for situations that involve babies or very small children, all family relationships started at this point although some previous information may have been known about "the other." Future in-laws may have eyed each other over an obligatory introductory dinner; future step-parents and step-children may have skirted around countless topics as they tried to be polite for "Mom's" or "Marcia's" sake. Future husbands and wives may have been co-workers or classmates who met at the watercooler or in geology class.

Exploratory Affective Exchange • The second stage, labeled *exploratory affective exchange,* represents that type of relationship characterized by casual acquaintances or friendly neighbors. By this point the relationship contains some richness. You are more willing to share opinions or feelings that are not too personal but that do reveal your beliefs or positions as disclosure increases. Although people are still cautious at this stage, more risk-taking is evident; certain topics move off the superficial level. You may risk giving or receiving some limited evaluations such as "You seem grumpy when you're tired." You are more likely to increase your accuracy in communication and to mutually understand catch-phrases or certain smiles or glances. Greater pacing exists between your verbal and nonverbal patterns. Spontaneity, both verbal and nonverbal, increases.

My father lives for sports and that's one of the few things we can really talk about. He doesn't know how to really share himself with another person, and when my sister tried to push him for a close relationship, she just got frustrated. I have learned not to expect too much of the relationship. We fish together and go to sporting events, and have a beer, but it's more like good buddies rather than a strong father-son relationship.

Although relationships at this level are friendly and enjoyable, no real sense of commitment exists. When you relate to the other person, your interactions are pleasant, but if you do not see each other for a while, no great difficulty arises. Little interaction at the core levels of personality occurs. Most relationships in our lives do not go beyond this second casual, exploratory stage.

Countless family relationships remain at this stage. Uncle Ned may be delightful and you enjoy seeing him, but you do not seek him out beyond the annual Christmas get-together. Siblings may find friends with whom they have stronger bonds, but, although the relationship may be pleasant, no real sense of sibling ties exists. Some parent-child or husband-wife relationships evolve to points of friendly acquaintances with little sense of commitment, although they may be in a different stage next year. Many nonvoluntary family relationships remain here because the related persons do not perceive rewards coming from more involved interactions.

Affective Exchange Stage • The third, or *affective exchange* level, is characterized by close friendships or courtship relationships in which people know each other well and have a fairly extensive history of association based on their reciprocity. This association may be built over a long period of time or through intense shorter meetings. By the time you are in this stage of a relationship, the interpersonal exchange may be more freewheeling and loose. You may be able to conflict over the superficial areas of topics and may be able to share positive and negative evaluations about certain aspects of each other without jeopardizing the entire relationship. For example, you may assume that if you say something negative, the other person will not slam down the phone and never talk to you again, although the other person may be hurt and you will both have to deal with that. By now the partners exhibit certain unique communication behaviors and high substitutability occurs. There are private references, shared in-jokes, mutually understood gestures or glances. Communication sensitivity increases. Comments such as "I always know when Neal is mad because he gets quiet and starts to concentrate on his pipe" can be made rather accurately. People around you may be able to tell you are close friends because of your open affection from touching to teasing. Although very intimate areas of personality may still remain closed, high levels of self-disclosure do occur and a strong trust is developing.

One of the most special aspects of these years is how my relationship with my daughter in college has developed into a friendship. Karen and I went through some rough times when she was in high school, but in the past two years we have developed a closeness I never thought possible. We can really sit down and share some very personal thoughts. I am learning to let her be an adult and have stopped trying to impose my way of life on her. I think because of that she is willing to tell me more about her life. There are certain parts of my life I may never be able to tell my daughter about, but it is such a pleasure to have an adult female friend who is also my child.

By the time a relationship reaches the affective exchange level, a real commitment exists and the relationship itself is likely to be a subject of conversation. You may hear remarks like these: "I really miss you when you go out of town" or "It's so good to know you; I can really talk to you." The relationship has become special for both partners.

Within families some relationships may exist at this level, at least for periods of time, although others will remain at lower areas of the continuum. As children grow old enough to make efforts at developing or maintaining relationships, they can participate more fully in the transactional process needed to reach the affective exchange level. Often such abilities are a reflection of the type of communication modeled by older members of the system. If a child sees parents or other family members able to communicate and share within a relationship at this level, and experiences this type of communication when interacting with them, he or she has a greater potential for developing the capacities necessary for participation in affective exchange levels of relationship.

Such levels of relationship are likely to occur in families with themes that support close interactions and interpersonal boundaries which permit extensive sharing. Families that value intense cohesion may find it difficult to permit close subgroups to form, while families that expect great distance provide few models for such close relationships. Since members of a relationship at the affective exchange level must adapt to each other based on their mutual perceptions, families that hold either very rigid or very chaotic positions on the adaptability issue provide a poor atmosphere for learning such adapting skills.

For many people this stage represents the highest relational level they will ever experience. They may not have the desire or opportunity to take further risks or to invest more energy than this level requires, or the other person may block such moves. Many marriages occur at the exploratory affective or affective exchange levels and people remain either satisfied or frustrated depending on the specific partner. For many people this level of intimacy remains sufficient.

Stable Stage • Finally, certain relationships enter the *stable stage*. This stage is characterized most often by successful marriages, committed friendships, or special familial relationships. Openness, richness, and spontaneity abound. In a relationship at this level, you are likely to experience your highest level of self-disclosure at that point in your life. Both negative and positive aspects of personality are shared and accepted between the partners. Effective communication occurs because the partners are very tuned-in to each other and really have learned to predict what the other might do or say.

At the stable level, communication is efficient, verbal and nonverbal cues are easily interchanged, and predictions are made with accuracy. In addition to verbal sharing, there is a freedom of access to each other's personal belongings that may not have been available before.

Yet even these unique relationships require much work if they are to be maintained. Partners who share a stable relationship are very aware of each other's needs, changes, and are willing to engage in intense risk-taking behavior to maintain those relationships.

After 26 years of marriage my parents seem to have an incredibly close relationship that I haven't seen in other people. They will hold hands very often. They share a great deal of common interest in music and will play together. They just can't get enough of each other. Life hasn't been all that easy for them either. My brother became seriously ill about eight years ago and had to be institutionalized. My father has had some serious illness and they've had some money problems. Yet they have coped with these things together and I think it increased their love. I can see them make efforts to please one another. My mother is always aware of my father's needs and moods and is constantly trying to imagine what will please him. Yet, he does the same for her. After all these years of living together they almost sound alike. They finish each other's sentences and seem to have a shorthand by which they understand each other. Someone even said they're beginning to look alike. I'm very grateful to them for what they have taught me about loving another person.

Such relationships usually require a high investment of time, energy, and sensitivity, but participants find great rewards from their interactions. Again, family themes, images, and boundaries influence the ability of a relationship to move to, or remain at, such an intense level of sharing. The participants have to reach mutually acceptable levels of adaptation and cohesion.

We are not suggesting that a relationship may actually follow the four stages easily and simply. Some relationships may speed through certain stages; others may remain at one stage for years. Other relationships may move up and down the levels as the partners' lives change. Relationships that proceed too quickly to core areas may have to retrace steps through lower stages.

Altman and Taylor suggest that the process can be reversed when considering the dissolution of a relationship. For example, a couple may have moved toward the stable stage before the birth of their children but attending to the children may have taken so much time and energy that the couple's relationship moves to the lower level of affective exchange. We will explore this issue further in Chapter 11.

There are close links between social exchange and the social penetration process. The greater the ratio of rewards to costs the more rapidly a relationship will move through the penetration process. Especially in the beginning, reciprocity will influence such movement; if a love relationship is to develop into a lasting mutual attachment, then the affection for and commitment to one another must grow at roughly the same pace until the relationship has been firmly established and inequality of costs and rewards are acceptable because of the perceived future reciprocity. Commitment lessens the need for constantly equal rewards.

Since Altman and Taylor's stages apply to all relationships, you should be able to see how they relate in your own life. As you grow older, you participate in and/or observe other family members moving up or down through the stages. Perhaps you developed a deep relationship with an older brother or sister as you grew into a young adult. Perhaps you watched parental or other relationships suffer and move down the stages. And as you analyze relationship movement through the stages you should have seen reciprocity and exchange processes at work. Such movement through the stages affects not only the participants in the specific relationship but all members of the systems to which these members are connected.

In his discussion of relationships in the future, Toffler (1971) raises the issue of expected relationship turnover and suggests family relationships are those expected to last longer than what he considers "medium duration relationships" (relationships with friends, neighbors, job associates, and co-members of voluntary organizations). He suggests "we expect ties with immediate family and to a lesser extent with other kin, to extend throughout the lifetime of the people involved" (100). However, people involved in long-term relationships cannot remain at a peak level of communication. Many relationships will never reach the affective exchange or stable level and those that do can expect to move downward at specific periods with the potential of developing more strongly in the future.

In order to complete our discussion of relationship development we will examine the relational currencies, or the means by which people communicate their feelings in order to avoid costs and gain rewards, and to enhance or block further relationship development.

RELATIONAL CURRENCIES

As we discussed in Chapter 3, all family members engage in an exchange of communication behaviors which have meaning for other family members. Thus a wife may cook beef stew to please her husband, a child may scream with delight at the sight of her parents' return, a grandfather may rock a grandchild for an hour while telling him stories of years gone by. Each of these instances represents an attempt to exchange affection, yet each message is unique to the people involved, and their response depends on the specific relationship. The husband may devour the stew or he may wish his wife would make lasagna; the parents may hug their daughter or tell her not to yell; the grandchild may "cuddle in" or struggle against staying put.

Such "communication behaviors that carry relationship meaning about the affection or caring dimension of human relationships" may be viewed as "relational currency" (Villard and Whipple, 1976). This concept is based on the premise that all relationships involve (1) an investment of time and/or money, (2) a trading of currencies, and (3) a degree of risk-taking. The currencies that are exchanged may be intimate or economic.

Intimate currencies relate to personal verbal and nonverbal ways of sending relationship messages. For example, one can smile, hug, engage in intercourse, and exchange secrets as ways of sharing affection. Thus physical or psychological identity is shared with another. The intimate currencies make a direct statement. The act is the message—a hug means "I'm glad to see you," or "I'm sorry you are leaving." Usually the sender's intent is clear and easily interpreted. Economic currencies may involve loaning money or possessions, doing favors, giving gifts, sharing things or time with one another. The economic currencies permit a greater range of interpretation. Exactly what is the message contained within the act of sending a bouquet of flowers? After a family quarrel, does the arrival of flowers mean "I'm sorry," or "Let's keep the peace," or "I still love you even if we don't agree on one issue"? The message may not be as direct as the message sent through a smile, hug, or words of endearment.

Although intimate or economic currencies may be exchanged with the best intentions, accurate interpretation occurs only when both parties agree upon the meaning of the act. Misunderstandings may be more frequent when two family systems attempt to blend into a new one. For example, in the man's family, gifts may be given often for no special occasion as ways of saying "I care." If the woman comes from a family where this was not practiced, she may be delighted to start a new tradition and give and receive gifts at nonspecial occasions, or she may have difficulty adapting to this type of relational message. She might think it is a waste of money to buy nonholiday gifts or she may never think to reciprocate on ordinary days, leaving her husband to feel unappreciated. Thus, if mutually shared norms for exchanging affection do not exist, family members need to negotiate about this type of communication if relational messages are to be received as they were intended. Such understanding is critical to the upward movement of relationships to the higher development stages characterized by accuracy and predictability. Also, if family members find themselves unable to exchange affection meaningfully there will be limited rewards to be gained from their interactions. There must be personal meaningfulness for all family members involved, either as a whole system or within the interpersonal subsystems. A closer examination of each currency type is in order.

Intimate Currency

The intimate currencies, or the sharing of one's physical and psychological self, may be experienced in a variety of ways. Perhaps the most important way of sharing oneself and maintaining a relationship involves *self-disclosure.* When a father takes the risk to share some of his fears about growing older with a teenage son, he is using a currency that has not been very acceptable for men until recently. Males, especially those in the father role, have traditionally been expected to refrain from sharing fears, concerns, or any other signs of weakness. Yet, as this father addresses his child, he gives of himself in a way that no other gift, favor, or affection display could accomplish. If the son misses the point of what is being said and shrugs it off, the currency has not been exchanged. If, on the other hand, his son acknowledges the risk and replies, "I'm glad you told me that. Now I understand some of the things that have been going on," or "It's nice to know that you can talk about those kinds of things," or nonverbally expresses his understanding, the currency of self-disclosure has been well exchanged and mutual rewards have been gained. Most marital relationships develop through the exchange of such messages, yet after the initial years, the addition of children and other circumstances may conspire to limit the sharing of innermost feelings and force them to rely on other currencies, such as gifts, to "stay in touch." The many hours of self-disclosure experienced during courtship may dwindle to one dinner out a month when the couple finds time to "really talk."

The value of *touch* varies between and within families. In certain homes tickling, hugging, affectionate wrestling, and cuddling are the rule of the day. On the other hand, many families reserve touch for special occasions and for punishment. Each growing family negotiates how touch will be used as a relational currency to indicate caring. Even different children have different levels of tolerance for physical touch, and communication with each person may have to be adapted. A mother may learn to give one child a great deal of physical affection and to tone down her responses to another child who does not respond in the same way. Yet, the sensitive family member can also distinguish the person who likes to be cuddled but who may be a little embarrassed to indicate such liking. Sometimes, the family touch pattern changes as children mature. For example, many affectionate fathers institute a "hands-off" policy when daughters reach puberty, a policy that often leaves them bewildered about what happened to the father who played, wrestled, and cuddled with them two years ago. Unless another intimate currency is substituted, the father-daughter relationship may deteriorate.

As an extension of physical touch, *sexuality* serves as an important intimate currency for exchanging affection between husband and wife. One spouse may consider sex to be the ultimate currency in married life and place a high value on sexual relations. This may include the expectations that sexual relations will be exclusive to the dyad, that sex will be engaged in only when both people are satisfied in the relationship and desire to have sex. If the other partner holds similar views, the sexual currency will be appropriately exchanged. Yet, if the other partner does not place the same value on the sexual act, finding it acceptable to have sexual relations outside the marriage, or expecting to have sexual relations at any time whether or not things are going well for the couple, these two people will have difficulty with the communication of affection through this currency.

Affect displays, which include verbal and nonverbal signs of liking, serve well as relational currency. Behaviors such as smiles, winks, and blown kisses all communicate caring. If a grandmother opens the front door and her three-year-old grandson jumps up and down, grins, and runs to meet her, she will receive his message of love. Compliments, direct statements of caring, requests for shared time or experiences all may contain affection messages. Traditionally affect displays have been the major relational currency for women rather than men since women have been encouraged to display their feelings through words or facial affect much more frequently. Villard and Whipple suggest that as a result:

> It is not uncommon for a woman to complain that her husband never shows any emotion and that she has difficulty determining what her spouse is thinking and how he is feeling. What she is actually complaining about is the absence of one of the feedback mechanisms by which she evaluated her own interaction in the relationship, her performance as a wife, and the degree of caring and satisfaction with the relationship displayed by the husband.   (151)

In effect, she may be feeling that her husband's lack of "affect" keeps her from gaining the support or sense of self she needs from the relationship.

Aggression may be considered as an intimate currency in certain families. When adults do not know how to express intimacy in positive ways, children may experience hitting, sarcasm, or belittling as the only means of parental contact. This recognition, although unpleasant, may indicate intimacy. Some people seem to be able to show caring only through verbal or physical aggression. Some conflictual couples may maintain their contact through screaming and yelling behaviors that may seem frightening to a visiting friend, but which have become part of the means of keeping contact within that family system. Such relationships have limited rewards and usually do not allow the kind of communication necessary for progressing to the higher stages of relationship development. Real difficulties arise when children raised in such a system marry and attempt to create a new system with someone raised in a home where the intimate currencies were positive touch and self-disclosure. The selection of the intimate currencies often reflect the communication rules in the family-of-origin.

All family members exchange intimate currency as a means of communication, but in his research with married couples, Villard found that wives were more likely to use intimate forms of behavior than husbands, although husbands and wives were not found to differ in their usage of economic forms of affection exchange.

Economic Currency

Although each family system exchanges both intimate and economic currencies, some systems rely heavily on the economic currency as a way of demonstrating caring. The economic currency involves sharing of physical resources or time. The most obvious type of economic currency involves sharing money. Some families have unspoken groundrules that one always tries to help out a relative, so loaning a cousin $500 is acceptable but loaning a friend $10 is not appropriate. Some family members "buy" affection by providing economic support for children or less wealthy relatives. Because money may be tied to an affection currency, some family groundrules state that all children must be treated alike so if one gets $10 the others must receive the same or its equivalent. For many couples money serves as a sign of how much trust or love exists in the relationship. Does money accrued before marriage become "our" money or does it remain in the individual member's control? For one couple, the wife's money served as her "power" in the relationship and her unwillingness to make it "joint" money indicated to her husband that she did not truly love or trust him. For him, a way of receiving love would be to share her wealth. In many families money stands as the symbol of the amount of love one family member feels for another.

Another type of economic currency involves *access rights* or the ability to give or receive physical things and time. Can any family member walk into another's closet and borrow a sweater? To what extent is one's toothbrush "sacred"? Who has access to the car keys? If a college student returns to her parents' home for a visit, does she feel as free to use the refrigerator or to invite people over as she used to? For some people one sign of caring involves the right to borrow or use another's things. In some families, immediate relatives are allowed rights to possessions whereas friends and acquaintances are not. Also, there may be rules by which things may be borrowed or used, such as "tell me if you took something," or "ask before you borrow something." As long as the communication rules are followed, this currency provides a way of telling another person that he or she is special. Many families set high expectations on access rights for family members and "outsiders" do not give or receive rights to any degree.

A more subtle form of access rights concerns the right to take another's time.

My doctor tells the story of sitting down with his grown son and reminiscing over things that happened as the son was growing up. At one point that son referred to the "time you fixed my bike" as "one of the most important points in our relationship." The doctor came home late from a hectic day with only enough time to change his clothes before he was to leave to be a guest of honor at a professional banquet. When he got to the driveway, his fourteen-year-old son was working on his bike and looking upset. As the father headed in to change, the son asked if he would help him with the bike since he had been working for two hours and couldn't fix it. The father replied that he had a meeting but the son pleaded for a few minutes of help. At that point, the doctor took off his jacket, sat down and worked for 45 minutes to fix the bike. He left a delighted son as he raced to change and arrive late at the banquet. Two days later the father had forgotten the incident but years later his son reminded him of the day he stopped and shared his time.

For the son, this right to ask for and receive his father's undivided attention represented a gift. The currency of time was well exchanged.

Although favors serve as economic currency, some people report doing a favor for another, only to discover it wasn't even noticed. Or, even worse, that the other person was upset by it. Favors serve as a type of currency that may be misunderstood or ignored unless both parties are sensitive to the efforts that are being made.

The sister who usually has a messy half of the room expects to hear a thank-you from her sibling after cleaning the place up, whereas the organized counterpart may just assume that's the way the room should look. Villard and Whipple state, "Usually the expenditure of time and energy needed to perform the favor is proportional to the amount of affection and caring felt for the person and value placed on the relationship" (152). The more rewarding the relationship, the greater the effort that will be made.

Gifts stand as a commonly used message symbol and it is up to the receiver and sender to negotiate the understanding of the message. A father appreciates the frayed, crayoned Valentine from his five-year-old; a young woman understands the message intended when her grandmother passes on the family Bible.

Sometimes family members rely on gifts as a substitute for love they are prevented from sharing. Some divorced parents feel forced to "buy" affection from the children they see infrequently by providing trips, sporting equipment, and other expensive presents as a way of showing caring since such caring cannot be displayed daily. Sometimes neither the parent nor the child value the "gift" currency greatly but feel compelled to use it since exchanging intimate currencies is almost impossible. No matter which currencies are used, their effectiveness depends on the ability of both people to share the same message or to assign the same personal meaning to the communication act. If this is not the case, they are dealing in mixed currencies.

Mixed Currencies

For some people, personal norms dictate that you give to others before you give to the family members. Many people have heard one parent say to another, "If you would stop worrying about so-and-so's health, and stop helping them, then you could start to do some of the same things around here and things would be a lot better." Often parents substitute money for access rights, yet their children do not value the monetary currency as greatly as they value the time. Eventually sad conversations may be held with young adults who say, "I just wanted you to be around." A more positive instance involves the man who gave up his second job because he realized it was more important for him to be home sharing with his family than providing them with an extra car or a better vacation. Each system sets its own priorities, deciding if it is important that similar values are placed on the subtle commodity of time.

Villard and Whipple suggest that "when one offers intimacy while another offers economics in any interpersonal relationship, more frequently than not, personal frustration, relational misunderstanding and quite often relational conflict" (160) will result. After interviewing married couples, Villard concluded that spouses with more similar affection exchange behaviors were more likely to report (a) high levels of perceived equity and (b) higher levels of relationship satisfaction, thus greater relationship reward. Interestingly, accuracy in predicting (i.e., understanding) how the other spouse used currencies does not raise equity or satisfaction levels. Just knowing that your husband sends love messages through flowers does not mean that you will be more positive toward this currency if you prefer intimate currencies. People who were very accurate at predicting how their spouse would respond to certain items still reported "low equity and low marital satisfaction if the couple was dissimilar in their affection behaviors" (Millar et al., 1978, 15). Unfortunately this finding, coupled with the finding that wives are more likely to use intimate currencies, suggests that "many marriages may be predisposed to unhappiness, unfulfillment, conflict and/or divorce because of socialized differences between men and women in how they share 'who they are' and how they manifest 'affection' " (15).

Mixed currencies can also lead to parent-child difficulties. If a child values and uses one type of currency and a parent values and uses another, attempts at sharing affection may result in frustration. Children may not feel as loved as they think their friends are because their parents do not engage in the intimate currencies of touch, affect displays, and self-disclosure found in other homes. Yet, the parents may not recognize, or be able to deal with, the value placed on the intimate acts by their children and continue to provide economic currency as their way of expressing affection.

My father never used affection, or intimate currencies, as a way of saying "I love you." He always gave big gifts to indicate caring during holidays and birthdays. As a child it was hard for me to feel loved since my father did not demonstrate affection by hugging me or playing with me the way my friends' fathers did. As I have become an adult I have been able to understand the gift-giving as my father's only real way of making contact. He came from a family that was not affectionate and he was unable to display any of the behaviors that came so easily to my mother or her relatives. Although I personally still value affection and self-disclosure as the most important signs of affection, I can make room for my father's way of expressing affection and I no longer get angry about what he is unable to do.

Villard found that couples with children who were being seen for emotional, behavioral, or adjustment problems were found to have "(a) the lowest overall affection scores (i.e., combining both economic and intimate forms) and (b) report the lowest level of intimate affection usage" (Millar et al., 15).

A family's levels of cohesion and adaptability interact with their communication of affection. Highly cohesive families may demand large amounts of affection displayed with regularity, whereas low cohesion families may not provide enough affection for certain members. Systems near the chaotic end of the adaptability continuum may change the type of currencies used and valued frequently while more rigid systems may require the consistent and exclusive use of a particular currency. Family themes may dictate the amount or type of currencies used. "The Hatfields will stick by each other through thick and thin" may set the expectation that family caring will be supported by providing money for hard-pressed members. Boundaries may establish which members or outsiders may receive the more personal types of affection.

Because the family system constantly evolves and changes, personal meanings placed on intimate or economic currencies will change over time. As relationships mature, members may change their ways of sharing affection because of new experience, pressures, or expectations. For example, certain biosocial beliefs about sex roles may hinder a man from displaying affection at first, but as he becomes comfortable as father and husband, he may be open to using more intimate currencies. Actual economic conditions will affect how certain economic currencies are exchanged. A lost job may result in fewer gifts but more favors within a family. Such changes will affect the levels of relationships attained by family members. For one subgroup a period of extensive exchange of intimate currencies may place them at a high relationship stage and provide them with mutual rewards. Circumstances may eventually limit this exchange and lower the rewards and the level of the relationship, at least for a period of time. Thus the communication of affection serves as a determining factor in relationship reward or satisfaction and in the levels of relationship reached.

CONCLUSION

In this chapter we examined family relationships and communication within the contexts of social exchange, relational development, and relational currencies. We described the role of the social exchange of costs and rewards in the decisions to begin, maintain, or terminate relationships. Such rewards and costs are unique to the individuals and may be exchanged unevenly over time as people store up future benefits or accrue additional benefits based on immediate need. We described the process of relational development and specifically detailed Altman and Taylor's stages of social penetration and the communication behaviors that may accompany levels of orientation, exploratory affective exchange, affective exchange, and stable stages. We examined in detail the relational currencies, both intimate and economic, used to communicate affection within relationships and discussed the difficulties that arise when mixed messages occur within a relationship. Finally, we tied these currencies to relationship development.

As was cautioned earlier in the chapter, the processes are more subtle and complex than they may first appear, especially when you try to apply them to your own family's life. Yet by beginning to understand the role that communication plays in relationship development, you can analyze certain familial situations more accurately and possibly avert or improve some painful family relationships.

5

Communication of Intimacy Within Families

I remember how I phoned my mother the second day of my flu and was really feeling the lack of the pampering I got when I was sick as a small child. I live 25 minutes away, but in just over half an hour my buzzer rang and there at the door was Mom loaded down with a new humidifier, a tray with flowers, homemade vegetable soup, and some magazines. We ate the soup together, she fluffed my pillows, and made me feel thoroughly loved. Her face, her arms, her whole being spoke of acceptance and warmth.

She was a very touching person. She spoke of her love through little gifts—a new potato peeler because she noticed that mine was rusty—through hugs and smiles, and through the time she took to listen and understand. She always took time to show her love.

Most family members experience special moments of closeness in which they feel good about themselves, about the other family members, and their connectedness to each other. In some families such moments are an everyday occurrence; in others they are very rare. Every family faces the question, "What extent of psychological or physical closeness is acceptable within our system at this time and how do we reach the acceptable level?" This is a question arising from a family's need to deal with the issue of cohesion. Many families target high goals but find themselves frustrated with the degree of closeness actually attained. The desire for closeness may be stymied by their communication which focuses on the everyday tasks of running a family which involves few interpersonal risks. Yet such communication does not serve to move relationships to higher stages of development or to maintain them at such levels.

In this chapter we will focus on the role of communication in developing intimacy among family members, thus allowing them to reach and function at higher levels of relationship development. We assume that such intimacy requires effort and risk-taking behaviors but that it provides rewards for the persons who choose to develop such closeness in their relationships. In order to explore intimacy and its development, we will look at intimacy and its growth through confirmation, self-disclosure, and sexual communication.

DEVELOPMENT OF INTIMACY

Every family has to engage in the kinds of communication that keeps the home running, the children fed, the clothes washed, the car gassed, and the bills paid. Life revolves around the patterns and routines that get us from day to day and communication must support such task-oriented interactions. Yet all families have the opportunity to provide their members with different kinds of communication experiences—including those which nurture the relationships involved. Such communication contributes to intimacy among family members.

Nurturing communication involves intimacy, or a special kind of interpersonal sharing. In his treatment of marital intimacy, family researcher Feldman (1979) suggests that marital intimacy involves the following characteristics: (1) a close, familiar, and usually affectionate or loving personal relationship; (2) detailed and deep knowledge and understanding arising from close personal connection or familiar experience; (3) sexual relations (70). With the exception of sexual relations this definition may be applied to all family relationships, implying that intimate family relationships involve caring, affectionate personal relationships and detailed knowledge and understanding of these significant people that can be gained only from close personal experience. Yet the way each family expresses its intimacy, if it does so, varies with each system and interpersonal subsystem.

As we discussed earlier, all relationships have implicit or explicit rules for intimacy which define the range of acceptable behaviors. Feldman states, "The level of acceptable (tolerable) intimacy in a marital relationship is determined by the complex process by which an interpersonal system is 'calibrated' or 'set' " (70). From his work with marital couples, Feldman hypothesizes that couples experience a patterned intimacy-conflict cycle. He suggests that when one member of a couple feels that the intimacy is becoming too great, he or she will initiate some type of conflictual behavior to decrease the amount of interpersonal intimacy.

The same concept may be applied to other family relationships. Each dyadic subgroup sets its limits for acceptable intimacy. Each two-person relationship sets its limits for acceptable intimacy. A small son and his mother may cuddle, tickle, kiss, and hug. The teenager and mother may share important events and exchange kisses on occasion. A husband and wife develop limits for acceptable and unacceptable sexual intimacy as well as for sharing feelings and showing affection.

As we noted in our discussion of relational currencies, what constitutes caring messages varies according to the perceptions of the persons involved. Although the "intimate currencies" discussed by Villard and Whipple (1976) may lead to family intimacy, so too, may the economic currencies. You may not consider sexual intercourse intimate, but discussing your desire for a child may be intensely intimate for you. Another person may consider sharing apparel, food, or personal belongings as a sign of intimacy. Each dyad has to work out a mutual understanding of desirable intimacy or conflicts will arise.

Although all humans seem to have intimacy needs—to be loved, held, touched, and nurtured, there may also be a fear of intimacy—a fear of being controlled by another, loved and left by another, possessed by another. The potential rewards of becoming intimately involved with one another must be balanced against the possible costs of such a relationship. Thus the needs and fears, rewards and costs, become calibrated as the balance of the intimacy scale is set, at least for a period of time.

Each familial system will be influenced by their overall themes, images, and boundaries which indicate some acceptable intimacy limits for family members. Family themes that stress verbal sharing, "There are no secrets in this family" or "All problems are discussed within and kept within our family" may promote honest disclosure if a sense of community and support exists, or they may promote individual secrets if such does not exist. Images of family members contribute to the development of intimacy; risks may be taken with someone viewed as a warm caregiver rather than with the person viewed as an unfeeling computer. Family boundaries will influence how much intimacy is shared among family subgroups and how much intimacy may be developed with those outside the immediate family. Biosocial beliefs enter into the issues of intimacy development since they may support or restrict the capacity of members in certain roles or power positions to develop certain levels of intimacy. A belief that a father has to remain slightly aloof from his children to be respected in his "head of the house" position will limit the level of intimacy he will reach with his children as long as that belief is maintained.

In the following pages we will examine certain communication behaviors that encourage the development of intimacy within marital and family systems. We will focus specifically on confirmation, self-disclosure, and sexual communication.

Confirmation

The basis for all relationships lies in the members' abilities to share meanings. We previously discussed relational currencies—communication behaviors that carry meaning about affection or caring dimensions of human relationships. At this point we would like to examine the use of these intimate and economic currencies to proceed beyond just maintaining a relationship; rather we need to understand how they provide mutual confirmation in relationships, leading to the development of a close, familiar loving relationship.

Confirming behaviors communicate acceptance of another human being as he or she is—thus giving value to the other's existence. Such behaviors are likely to be perceived as rewarding by the receiver. If you remember the distinction between the report and command, or content and relationship level in a message, you will remember that the relationship level comments on the bond between the people. In other words ". . . on the relationship level people do not communicate about facts outside their relationship, but offer each other definitions of that relationship and, by implication, of themselves" (Watzlawick, et al., 1967, 83–84). For example, you may communicate to another person, "This is how I see myself" and that person has the following options for response: to confirm you, to reject you, or to disconfirm you. Watzlawick et al. maintain that confirmation of one's self-view is critical to mental development and stability, stating, "We feel that what the existentialists refer to as the *encounter* belongs here, as well as any other form of increased awareness of self that comes about as the result of working out a relationship with another individual" (85).

Sieburg (1973) provides four criteria for confirming messages. A message may be perceived as confirming to the extent that it:

1. expresses recognition of the other's existence as an acting agent;
2. acknowledges the other's communication by responding to it relevantly;
3. is congruent with and accepting of the other's self-experience;
4. suggests a willingness on the part of the speaker to become involved with the other person.

Using just the four criteria listed above, can you see how confirming messages are sent to you, and by you? Who makes it clear that they value you? To whom do you try to send such relationship messages? Are these people members of your family?

In order to understand how confirming messages work, let's look at some underlying principles. In their summary of Sieburg's work on confirming behavior, Barbour and Goldberg (1974) present the following principles:

1. It is more confirming to be recognized as existing than to be treated as nonexisting.
2. Dialogue is more confirming than monologue.
3. Acceptance is more confirming than interpretation.
4. It is more confirming to be treated personally than impersonally. (31)

Let us examine each one individually:

1. It is more confirming to be recognized as existing than to be treated as nonexisting.

Sometimes in families certain members get the feeling they aren't there. People talk about them in front of them, people ignore or interrupt them, people misinterpret most of their actions, people refrain from affectionate physical contact. Such behaviors become costs for the receiver.

My sister and I live with our grandparents and she acts like my grandfather does not exist. She assumes that because he has one bad ear that he can't hear with the other one also. She will be eight feet away and complain about how he never gives her any money (false!) and how unfair he is. She tells my grandmother everything but she hardly talks to him. I know he's hurt by this but he doesn't say anything. For her it's as if he's part of the furniture.

Verbally you may confirm others by using their name, arguing with or supporting their ideas, acknowledging their presence. Comments such as "I missed you, I'm glad to see you" serve to confirm another verbally particularly when accompanied by congruent nonverbal messages. In their work on communication skills related to marital satisfaction, Boyd and Roach (1977) suggest a spouse's comments such as "I listen and attend when my spouse expresses a point of view" or "I make statements that tell my spouse that she (he) really counts with me" is characteristic of desirable behavior (541).

Nonverbal confirmation has more subtle but equal importance in signifying recognition. From earliest infancy, recognition serves as the basis for relationship. A child develops his or her earliest sense of recognition through touch. Montagu (1978) suggests:

It appears probable that for human beings tactile stimulation is of fundamental consequence for the development of healthy emotional or affectional relationships, that "licking" in its actual and its figurative sense, and love are closely connected; in short, that one learns to love not by instruction but by being loved. (28–29)

Yet in many families physical recognition through touch, eye contact, or gesture becomes tied to the communication rules which may restrict such interaction. In many families " . . . much of the truly satisfying, nurturing potential of affection among family members is not enjoyed because family rules about affection get mixed up with taboos about sex" (Satir, 1972, 104). This may be particularly difficult in families where the father suddenly refrains from physical contact with his newly adolescent daughter because he feels it may not be "safe." As we noted earlier, persons who come from very different backgrounds may find difficulty understanding the abundance of, or lack of, nonverbal messages from a spouse or in-law.

2. Dialogue is more confirming than monologue.

When family members say things in front of each other "without actually responding in an honest and spontaneous way to each other's ideas and feelings, their interaction might be described as a series of monologues rather than a dialogue" (Barbour and Goldberg, 31). Dialogue implies an interactive working involvement with the other. Husbands and wives, siblings, parents, and children must be able to share attitudes, beliefs, opinions, feelings, and work at resolving their differences. Comments such as "Because I said so," "You'll do it my way or not at all," or "That's the way it is and that's final" do not reflect a dialogical attitude, whereas "What do you think?" "How can we solve this?" "I'm upset with you, can we talk about it?" open the door to dialogue, and rewarding interactions. Boyd and Roach found comments such as "I 'check out' or ask for clarification so that I will understand my spouse's feelings and thoughts" and "I ask honest direct questions without hidden messages" associated with marital satisfaction (541).

Nonverbal dialogue occurs in families where hugs, kisses, and affect displays are mutually shared and enjoyed and where hugs of consolation or sorrow can be exchanged. Later in this chapter we will refer to monological or dialogical approaches to sexuality—or sexual involvement for one's own pleasure versus that of mutual satisfaction. From our perspective dialogical sexual expression provides confirmation within a relationship.

3. Acceptance is more confirming than interpretation.

My father thinks he knows me so well that he is constantly telling other people what I really meant. He'll say, "Oh, she wasn't really that upset" when I am furious about something. When I say I love Ellen, he says, "You like her a lot." He always hears what he wants to hear and most of the time he misunderstands what I actually said.

We show acceptance when "we respond to the statements of another person by genuinely trying to understand the thoughts and feelings he or she has expressed and by reflecting that understanding in our responses" (Barbour and Goldberg, 31). This may involve allowing ourselves to hear things we really don't want to hear and acknowledge that we understand. Although a mother may find it painful to hear that her son is leaving college because he has failing grades, she should not insist, "I understand. You just need some time to find yourself."

The nonverbal messages such as the wink, the smile, the barely perceptible nod that says "I agree" or "Keep up the good work" serve to reinforce and confirm another family member.

4. It is more confirming to be treated personally than impersonally.

How often have you revealed something to another person and had your feelings ignored? If you say, "I'm really worried about having a healthy baby," the confirming response would react to the feelings whereas a more impersonal response would note the statistics in having healthy babies and how you shouldn't worry. When people refer to us by labels when we are standing there, we feel impersonally treated. Remarks such as, "My wife, she likes country music too" appear strange when both members of the couple are present. Boyd and Roach include, "I allow her (him) to speak for herself (himself)" as indicative of communication leading toward marital satisfaction (541).

Impersonal responses are much more formal, contain fewer personal pronouns, and are more indirect than personal responses. When someone close to you seems to treat you exactly the way he or she treats most other people, you may not feel confirmed as special.

Although it seems like a silly complaint, I have asked my husband if there could be a type of endearment that is just ours. He is a very warm, affectionate man who treats all his friends and relatives as if they are very special. But when I hear him say "I love you" or call his mother and sisters "Darling" I feel that there isn't much special that is unique to us.

The role confirmation plays in developing intimate relationships cannot be overestimated. If such behaviors are viewed as rewarding and responded to with equivalent acts, a mutually rewarding relationship will result. For family members to move toward intimacy with each other, each person must feel accepted and cared for by the others. Children learn such behaviors by watching other family members and experiencing the confirmation and affection directed at them.

We can carry Montagu's comments a bit further if "one learns to love by being loved," then one learns to confirm by being confirmed, and to be affectionate by experiencing affection.

Self-Disclosure

I'm always fascinated by all the letters to the advice columnists about "Should I tell my spouse about . . . ?" and then they mention some secret. I will be married in eight months and although my fiancé and I have a very special relationship there are some things he does not know about me and, I imagine, he has some secrets too. I wonder about the value of total honesty especially when it could hurt the other person. There are some things I don't think I'd want to hear from him.

How free are you to express positive or negative feelings to your spouse, your children, or your parents? Has being honest fostered development of your family relationships or has it hindered the development of certain ones? Do you believe that spouses should reveal everything to each other? All these questions relate to the role of self-disclosure in your life.

Before we go further let us define self-disclosure. *Self-disclosure* occurs "when one person voluntarily tells another things about himself which the other is unlikely to discover from other sources" (Pearce and Sharp, 1973, 414). Thus it involves a willingness on the part of the informant and usually involves a risk since this information is private. As we discussed earlier, as people move from the orientation stage to higher levels of a relationship the process usually involves extensive mutual self-disclosure, which may be tied to reward/cost factors of past, present, or future relationships. We make predictions about how others will deal with our disclosures and usually attempt to build up a series of positive experiences before engaging in strong negative self-disclosure.

In her examination of family self-disclosure Gilbert (1976a) links self-disclosure to intimacy by defining intimacy as:

> . . . the depth of exchange, both verbally and/or nonverbally, between two persons and which implies a deep form of acceptance of the other as well as a commitment to the relationship.   (221)

Thus, high mutual self-disclosure is usually associated with voluntary relationships which have reached the affective exchange or stable exchange level and which are characterized by confirmation and affection. Yet, high levels of negative self-disclosure may occur in nonvoluntary relationships characterized by conflict and anger.

Traditionally self-disclosure has been considered desirable for fostering intimate communication within family systems. "The optimum in a marriage relationship . . . is a relationship between I and Thou, where each partner discloses himself without reserve" (Jourard, 1971, 46). "These couples who enjoy trust, who give trust to each other, probably are among the most fortunate people alive" (Lederer & Jackson, 1968, 109). Many current marriage enrichment programs support self-disclosing behavior (Galvin, 1978) as do popular texts on the subject of marital or parent-child interaction. Premarital counseling often focuses on revealing areas of feelings or information not yet shared by the couple. For example the 40-item Premarital Communication Inventory is used by teachers or counselors to foster sharing areas of difference, misunderstanding, or avoidance (Bienvenu, 1975, 68). Yet, as we shall see in the next section, some cautions about unrestrained self-disclosure also need consideration. In order to understand the importance of exchanging self-disclosure within the family system, we have to review some relevant research and examine the applicability of self-disclosure to developing family intimacy.

Much of the work in self-disclosure has been done through questionnaires and self-report forms rather than examining the actual behavior. Most of this has focused on the self-disclosing behavior of individuals and not on transactional processes. Unfortunately the questionnaire/self-report data gained from family members, usually couples, has not been linked to clinical material provided by family theorists and therapists. What family material exists focuses on marital couples or parent-child interactions; entire family systems have not received attention. Yet, with these concerns expressed, we can look at some of the findings and draw implication for family relationships.

Research on Self-Disclosure • Some generalizations can be made about self-disclosure that have bearing on family relationships but much of the original research in the area is under review due to more sophisticated follow-up studies. Characteristically women are considered to be higher self-disclosers than men (Jourard and Lasakow, 1958; Komarovsky, 1967; Gilbert and Whiteneck, 1976), yet Rosenfeld et al. (1979) maintain such a generalization is inaccurate, arguing that "psychological sex" (based on socialization) rather than "anatomical sex" needs to be considered (86). Recently researchers have begun to examine self-disclosure on the basis of male or female characteristics rather than sex, resulting in new ways of considering sex and self-disclosure. Thus role and socialization theories rather than biological theories may be applied to understanding self-disclosure. This explanation may account for some contradictions in the self-disclosure literature and needs to be kept in mind when referring to sexual self-disclosure differences in families.

In exploring the relationship between self-disclosure and marital satisfaction, Levinger and Senn (1967) found satisfied couples disclosed more than unsatisfied couples. However, unsatisfied couples disclosed more unpleasant feelings than satisfied couples. A later study found similar satisfaction directions plus a small correlation between spouses' disclosure levels; both partners tended to be either high or low disclosers (Burke, Weir, Harrison, 1976). When you consider your family experiences, you may discover that when you were least satisfied with certain relationships you tended to engage in more negative self-disclosure.

Family-of-origin issues, socioeconomic background, and expectations may influence self-disclosing behavior. Hurvitz and Komarovsky (1977) report a comparison of marital studies done with middle-class, high-school graduates in the Los Angeles area and a working-class urban community, called Glenton, where most couples did not complete high school. The middle-class respondents were more likely to view spouses as companions to each other with expectations of sharing activities, leisure time, and thoughts. Marriage, as seen by members of the Glenton community, was more likely to include sexual union, complementary duties, mutual devotion, but not friendship.

In the Glenton study Komarovsky found that two-thirds of the wives had at least one person apart from their husbands in whom they confided deeply personal experiences. In 35 percent of the cases the wife not only enjoyed such intimate friendships but shared some significant segment of her life more fully with her confidant than with her husband. In most of the cases the confidants were female and almost two-thirds were mothers or sisters of the wives. Thus, in this community, marital boundaries did not restrict the communication of private information to others, particularly among women in extended families.

The effect of age or length of marriage on spouse self-disclosure remains unclear since the content of the talk may vary over time (Waterman, 1979, 226–227). Parent-child disclosure has received some attention but, although the investigations have relied on nonclinic populations, most of the studies have involved self-report data. From her review research, Waterman suggests: "Most studies report mothers receive more self-disclosure than fathers but exceptions exist" (227). Though high-school girls tend to remain constant in self-disclosure to parents whereas boys show an overall decrease (Rivenbark, 1971, 38). Parents perceived as nurturing and supportive elicit more disclosure from children who find those encounters rewarding (Doster & Strickland, 1969, 382). In her study of families with adolescents, Abelman (1975) reports mutual self-disclosure exists mainly between parents and children of the same sex and adolescent self-disclosure correlates more highly with self-image than with parental self-disclosure (xii). Such a brief review only highlights certain issues but it indicates the complexity of a subject that some popular writers tend to treat simplistically as they opt for unrestrained "open" communication in family relationships.

Self-Disclosure and Relationship Satisfaction • In her work on self-disclosure and communication in families, Gilbert (1976a) raises practical issues which bear directly on exchanges within family systems. She cites conflicting reports on the effects of self-disclosure on relationships and raises the question ". . . what results can one expect from communicating very openly with other members of one's family?" (222). In order to answer this, she urges a consideration of differences including content (what is said about what topic), valence (positive or negative statement about the issue), and level (degree of intimacy of statement). She also suggests that self-esteem of members may affect self-disclosure in family relationships. Finally she hypothesizes that medium amounts of disclosure would be associated with higher family satisfaction than either high or low self-disclosure. In order to understand her hypotheses, we need to set some background.

The valence, or positive or negative position toward a particular issue, relates directly to how comments will be received.

> One of the most neglected areas of communication between partners, and the most important for a loving relationship, is disclosing positive feelings. When partners have been deeply moved by something, or touched by a tender observation that strikes a note of response in them, they should try to express it, to disclose it to the other and capture the moment before it is gone. With positive self-disclosures, that is, telling the good things you feel, husband and wife can open up the way for honesty in more critical areas of feelings and knowledge of each other.   (O'Neill and O'Neill, 1972, 111)

In their prescriptive guide to marriage, these authors support positive self-disclosure wholeheartedly while calling blunt or brutal honesty "indulgence in destructive or unnecessary criticism." They maintain "The marriage relationship gives you no license to make childish confessions of past misdeeds, or to turn your mate into a dumping ground for your personal guilts" (114). Rather one needs sensitive honesty related to the current situation. Such a popularized suggestion concurs with the findings in some studies reported earlier that higher self-disclosure levels are more characteristic of happily married couples, but that unhappily married couples are higher in disclosure of a negative valence. Families characterized by pleasant, content self-disclosure will be able to experience intimacy at higher levels more easily than those trying to discuss painful, negative-laden issues. For example, talking about a desire for continued sexual experimentation within a generally satisfactory relationship has much greater possibilities of leading to further intimacy than a revelation of severe sexual dissatisfaction within a relationship.

Satir (1972) views self-esteem as the basis for all positive communication within families. According to her, integrity, honesty, responsibility, compassion, and love all flow easily from high self-esteem persons because they feel they matter. Such people are willing to take risks whereas low self-esteem persons constantly feel they have to defend themselves. Satir places the responsibility for building self-esteem on families which have the almost exclusive responsibility for young children's esteem. "Every word, facial expression, gesture, or action on the part of the parent gives the child some message about his worth" (25). Abelman found that the self-disclosures of adolescents to their parents seemed more closely tied to their own self-esteem than to the amount of self-disclosure received from the parents. Gilbert supports the relationship between self-disclosure and esteem maintaining "Research literature relating self-disclosure to self-esteem, within the context of interaction in family systems, reveals that often people refrain from expressing their feelings because they are insecure about their marriage" (225). Since self-disclosure requires risk-taking, it appears more likely that persons who feel good about themselves would be more willing to take such risks, than persons who have low self-esteem.

Based on a review of self-disclosure research, Gilbert (1976b) suggests a curvilinear relationship between self-disclosure and satisfaction in the maintenance of relationships advocating that a moderate degree of disclosure appears to be most conducive to maintaining relationships over time (209). This position contrasts sharply with that of Jourard or Lederer and Jackson, who advocate full disclosure within relationships. The following diagrams (see Figure 5–1) will help you to visualize the differences. According to diagram A, as relationships become more disclosing, satisfaction moves from a growth pattern to a decline, whereas according to diagram B, increased self-disclosure is directly related to increased satisfaction. Let's look further at the underlying claims of each position. The research-based curvilinear view holds ". . . as disclosures accumulate through the history of a relationship and as the nature of the relationship itself changes, then the connection between disclosure and relational satisfaction reverses from a positive to a negative association . . . this is the way disclosure functions for most relationships" (Gilbert, 211). When you think of many of your friends or relatives, you may realize that you do not share the particularly negative aspects of

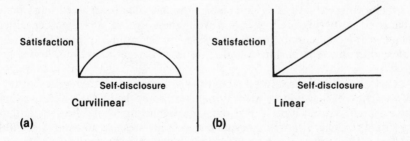

Satisfaction — Self-disclosure — Curvilinear — **(a)**

Satisfaction — Self-disclosure — Linear — **(b)**

Figure 5-1   Relationships Between Self-Disclosure and Satisfaction

yourself, or discuss theirs, because this may begin the decline of the relationship. Perhaps you have been in a relationship in which very unpleasant disclosures seemed to diminish or end the relationship. Family members may not have been able to cope with the negative information they received about themselves or other family members.

As a child I never fully understood what happened but there was a big change in the relationships in our house and there seemed to be a dark secret that no one would talk about. Fifteen years later I found out from my oldest brother that my father had a short affair with someone at the office and after it was over he told my mother. I guess she couldn't handle it because she always adored him and that changed their relationship for many years.

The linear point of view suggests that self-disclosure "may and should remain a positive source of relational satisfaction throughout the history of the relationship," clearly describes an "optimum state of affairs" rather than how things usually are (Gilbert, 211). Even Jourard indicates this is the ideal which is rarely achieved (46).

Yet the linear relationship, and its positive outcomes, may occur in special cases when mutual capacity to handle positive and negative deep self-disclosure exists. Such cases, though, are uncommon. Gilbert suggests a threefold process for understanding the potential linear relationship. In linear relationships the focus has to be placed on the effects that the *response of the other* has on the discloser. For such disclosure to exist in intimate relationships, it is hypothesized that both persons need (1) healthy selves, including high self-esteem, (2) a willingness to risk a commitment to the relationship and a willingness to push it to higher levels of intimacy, and (3) reciprocal confirmation, allowing "affective responses of acceptance and confirmation in its deepest form, of not only the disclosures but of the person making them" (212). The following diagram (Figure 5-2) presents the possible combination of approaches to self-disclosure and satisfaction found in the different types of relationships.

This diagram suggests that as relationships move from being non-intimate to intimate, the initial high positive self-disclosure shifts until, at the intimate level, negative self-disclosure gains in importance. In order to handle this and remain satisfied with the relationship, the individuals involved must both be characterized by high self-esteem, a willingness to risk, and high capacities for confirmation and commitment. If these capacities are not present, their satisfaction with the relationship will decline as the negative self-disclosure increases.

Since family life involves long-term involvements, during which people grow and change, it would be ideal if members could handle the negative and positive aspects of each other's development, permitting a total honesty within a supportive context. Yet, many negative self-disclosures are necessarily painful for one or both members of the relationship and each individual's capacity for,

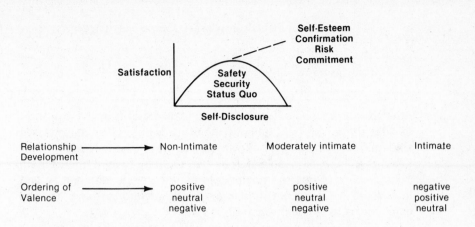

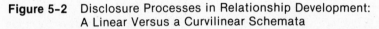

Relationship Development	⟶	Non-Intimate		Moderately intimate		Intimate

Ordering of Valence	⟶	positive neutral negative		positive neutral negative		negative positive neutral

Figure 5-2   Disclosure Processes in Relationship Development: A Linear Versus a Curvilinear Schemata

and willingness to endure pain, varies. Thus in many relationships high levels of self-disclosure result in low levels of satisfaction.

The Practice of Self-Disclosure • Now that we have talked about the research and thinking in the area of marital or family self-disclosure, we would like you to think about your family relationships according to the following general characteristics of self-disclosure.

1. Relatively few communication transactions involve high levels of disclosure
2. Self-disclosure usually occurs in dyads
3. In a dyad, self-disclosure is usually symmetrical or reciprocal
4. Self-disclosure occurs in the context of positive social relationships
5. Self-disclosure usually occurs incrementally
   (Pearce & Sharp, 1973, 416–421)

If you think about family relationships, according to Pearce and Sharp's generalizations, you can begin to see ways in which family systems tend to encourage or discourage self-disclosure.

1. Relatively few communication transactions involve high levels of self-disclosure.

If you remember our discussion of all the task-oriented communication that occurs in families in order to move them through the day, you can understand how little time or energy can be devoted to the nurturing type of communication which includes self-disclosure. Additionally, with the exception of new couples or newly blended families, there is not the need to spend much time revealing past history since family members have shared those issues over time. Hence, risk-taking communication is not likely to occur very frequently within family life, but certain developmental or external stresses may trigger extensive amounts.

2. Self-disclosure usually occurs in dyads.

After joining a Double Trouble group (parents of twins), Sam and I decided that we always dealt with the twins as just that—the twins. We seldom did anything with one without the other, and only really knew them as a team. Now on Saturdays we each try to take one of them to lunch or to the store—anything to get time alone with her. At first they didn't like it but now I think they look forward to some "special time" alone to talk with each of us.

If high levels of disclosure occur mainly in dyads, how often do two-person systems get to spend time together? How much time does a couple get together after the first child arrives? How often does a parent of four children get time alone with each of them? When does an 18-year-old sister spend time with her 11-year-old brother? Yet such time may be important for self-disclosure to develop.

3. In a dyad, self-disclosure is usually symmetrical or reciprocal.

If self-disclosure is reciprocal, it is more likely that parents provide the initial impetus and model for self-disclosing behavior. Yet this is not always the case. Television personality Phil Donahue makes this point well:

My kids have never really shared things with me. I guess I learned more about them by listening to them talk to *guests* who came to the house. I came to the conclusion that it was because their old man didn't share many feelings with them. I think that's a very common, pervasive, masculine thing, and one of the reasons is that *our* fathers weren't that open with *us.* ("TV's Top Interviewer," 1980, 12)

As children age they may begin to share in reciprocal ways with the adults in their lives depending on what they have experienced, just as the adults depend upon reciprocity to build their own relationships.

4. Self-disclosure occurs in the context of positive social relationships.

Families provide unique opportunities for self-disclosure because of the joint living experiences that may provide needed time and space for such talking. Yet the positive social relationships, including trust, may not exist. Parents may find that they have unwittingly halted the development of self-disclosure with a child because they discussed the child's concern with another adult, not recognizing the child's real desire for privacy. Unless people clearly discuss their perception of how private certain information is to them, another person may accidentally reveal the information and destroy the relationship.

My sister's big mouth almost blew my marriage sky-high because she had to break my trust. When Ginny and I had problems in my marriage I would talk to Margaret about them but I trusted that she would not tell anyone. Instead she told my mother who never liked Ginny much from the beginning. My mother started asking questions and making comments that made Ginny suspicious and it was finally clear that our problems were becoming a family issue. In order to save my marriage we dropped out of the family circle for almost two years and even now I am very careful not to talk about anything personal with my mother or sister.

If the trust level remains high, then those relatively few moments of high self-disclosure may occur without repercussions and over time the pattern of sharing develops within the family.

5. Self-disclosure usually occurs incrementally.

Families provide an appropriate setting for incremental self-disclosure. Shared time, space, and trust can foster relational growth over time and parental models can set the stage for the time when children are old enough to engage in such disclosure. Realistic relationships would include positive and negative self-disclosures over long periods of time which add to the depth of the relationships, although this may not always be the case.

We can hypothesize that self-disclosure bears a direct relationship to family levels of cohesion and adaptation. Extremely cohesive families may reject negative self-disclosure since it would threaten their connectedness, particularly if the family has a low capacity for adaptation. For example, a highly cohesive family with a theme of "We can only depend on each other" would resist negative disclosures that might threaten their security and cause internal conflict. Such a theme might be accompanied by rigid boundaries which would resist self-disclosures to outsiders.

Families with very low cohesion may tolerate negative self-disclosure but have difficulty with positive self-disclosure which might lead to greater cohesion. Families with moderate to high adaptation and cohesion capacities may cope relatively well with the effects of high levels of positive or negative levels of self-disclosure.

As you have discovered through these pages, self-disclosure represents a complicated, involved process which may result in intimacy when two people make the effort to mutually share with each other.

It's unfortunate but since our separation I have gotten to know each of our boys a little better. I now have long uninterrupted times with them, usually Saturday afternoon until Sunday evening and we spend a great deal of it sitting around and talking or going places and then talking over hot dogs or something. Before I only saw them with their mother and the two older girls and we never had much time alone. Rob and I will often sit up late after Eddie's in bed and talk about all kinds of things.

The capacities for confrontation and self-disclosure apply to all family members and contribute to meeting Feldman's first two criteria for intimacy, namely developing: (1) a close, familiar, and usually affectionate or loving personal relationship; (2) detailed and deep knowledge and understanding arising from close personal connection or familiar experience. Feldman's third criterion for sexual relations can only be applied to the marital couple within the family. Let us turn to this now.

Sexual Intimacy and Communication

I envy the freedom that young people seem to have these days to deal more directly with sexual issues. I married in the era when "nice people didn't discuss sex" even if they were married and the early years of marriage were very tense. We just pretended our sexual differences didn't exist and tried to live like they didn't matter. Now I hear the things my children can discuss and I feel cheated.

How would you describe sexual experience within the marital relationship? As a series of isolated encounters? As an integral part of the growing relationship? Do you see marital sexuality as restricted to "being good in bed"?

For most people the concept of sex within a marital relationship involves far more than just physical performance; it involves the partners' sexual identities, their background regarding sexual issues, their mutual perceptions of each others' needs, and the messages contained within sexual expression. All of these issues relate directly to communication particularly to confirming and disconfirming messages.

Feldman stresses the importance of sexual relations to marital intimacy, yet the quality of the sexual relationship affects, and is affected by, the other characteristics of intimacy—the affectionate/loving relationship and a deep detailed mutual knowledge of the two partners.

Within this section we will conceive of sexual behavior as a form of marital communication as well as a contributing factor in overall marital satisfaction. Sociologist Scoresby (1977) supports viewing sexual behavior as communication suggesting that sexual behavior is a profound source of meaning related to the many facets of the human personality. He maintains:

. . . sexual expression needs to consist of clear messages that effectively communicate the feelings of both partners. Sexual pleasure that is freely given, in an honest and mutually intimate way, can draw two people together into a loving and passionate bond that is continually strengthened, enhancing the marriage.   (45–46)

Socialization and Sexuality • The basis for a mutually intimate sexual relationship reflects the individual development of each of the partners. Clinical psychologist Greene (1970) believes an individual's sexuality remains closely intertwined with his or her intrapersonal, interpersonal, and environmental systems—systems that interlock yet vary in importance according to an individual's age. Greene states:

> The sexual feelings (intrapersonal) and behavior of a person are a reaction to the parental attitudes (interpersonal) in which he was raised. These attitudes, in turn, were handed down by their parents and were largely molded by broad cultural viewpoints specific to their social class (environmental forces).   (57)

Most of our sexual conduct is originally learned, coded, and performed on the basis of biosocial beliefs regarding gender identity, learned originally in our families-of-origin. Parents possess a set of gender-specific ideas about males and females which they learned and they observe "typical" behaviors of girls or boys of similar ages to their children. Based on these and other personal experiences, parents transmit a gender identity from earliest infancy, resulting in children establishing gender identities at a very young age. This identity is so strong that efforts to alter such socialization patterns must be presented to children before age three or they will have little impact (Gagnon, 1977, 68). For all of us our personal identities include sexual/gender identity as a core component which influences our later sexual experience. According to Gagnon:

> when we do begin having sex in our society, our beliefs about woman/man strongly influence whom we have sex with, what sexual things we do, where and when we will have sex, the reasons we agree, and the feelings we have.   (59)

Our overall sense of personal identity, with a core sexual identity is "a prerequisite for intimacy in marriage and sexual relationship" and is also "strengthened and affirmed by experiences of interacting constructively with a person of the complementary sex" (Clinebell & Clinebell, 1970, 138). Sexual experience contains powerful confirming or disconfirming messages.

Much of this learning about sexuality takes place within the rule-bound context of each family. If you remember back to an earlier discussion of communication rules, you will recall that most of them are negative directives—"Do not _____." Often communication around sexual issues remains indirect, resulting in confusion, misinformation, or heightened curiosity. If you try to remember how your sexuality was explained to you, you may remember much mystery and confusion as you tried to sort things out. If your genitals were talked about, how were they talked about? What attitudes did you pick up regarding your gender and sexuality?

I can see my sister trying to deal with having her first son and not being too sure how to deal with his sexuality. Last week Teddy, who is three, went to the bathroom and after a while my sister called to him, "What are you doing?" He yelled back, "Nothing" to which she replied, "Well, cut it out and get out here." If this is a typical pattern, Teddy may be in for some real confusion about what she is really trying to say.

Messages, such as in the above example, communicate concern or displeasure but the issue remains hidden. These veiled messages often continue through adolescence and into adulthood. According to Satir:

> . . . most families employ the rule, "Don't enjoy sex—yours or anyone else's—in any form." The common beginning for this rule is the denial of the genitals except as necessary nasty objects. "Keep them clean and out of sight and touch. Use them only when necessary and sparingly at that." (105)

In many families the marital boundary remains so tight around the area of sexuality that children never see their parents as sexual beings—no playful swats, no hugging, no tickling occurs in view of the children. Yet in other families the marital boundary is so diffuse that children encounter incestuous behaviors as they are co-opted into spousal roles.

The family represents the first but not the only source of sexual information. As children mature they gain additional information about sexuality from peers, church, school, and the media. When you look back over your childhood and adolescence, what were your major sources of sexual information? What attitudes were communicated to you about your own sexuality? What could have improved the messages you received?

As an individual embarks upon sexual experiences, his or her sexual identity influences the encounters, as does the partner's sexual identity. Open communication becomes critical for both individuals since a good sexual relationship depends on what is satisfying to each partner. Based on his or her personal experiences each individual:

> . . . evolves a unique set of needs that have to be met if satisfying sexual feelings are to result. In a sense these needs, these factors, might be considered prerequisites to pleasure: our term for them is the sexual value system. At the baseline, it includes all the considerations—the time, the place, the mood, the words used, the gestures made, the thousand-and-one little signals that a man and woman give each other without language— that the individual requires in order to respond emotionally, to let feelings come to the surface. (Masters and Johnson, 1975, 42)

Yet such understanding comes only through a combination of self-disclosure and sensitivity as spouses reveal their needs and desires while learning to give pleasure to another. In other words, we can distinguish between monological and dialogical sex—the former being sexual experiences in which one or both partners "talk to themselves" or attempt to satisfy only personal needs. Dialogical sex would be characterized by mutual concern and sharing of pleasure (Wilkinson, 1979).

Yet often the "rules" of childhood remain to stultify the adult sexual experience, preventing husbands and wives from communicating freely about or through their sexual encounters. The following statements vividly portray the euphemistic language so characteristic of even long-term marriages:

> Consider the kinds of talk that occur before intercourse in most households. In some the husband or wife may say, "Let's go do it," but such directness is rare. What usually happens is that the husband may say, "I think I will take a shower." What that really says is "I am going to be clean for you." The wife then says, "I will be upstairs in a few minutes." That is a "yes." Or she says, "I am too tired today; I have a headache; I have been to the hairdresser; the kids might wake up." These are all "no." A man will say, "I am tired; I have to get up early in the morning; I have some reading to do." There is a whole indirect language which people use to say "yes" or "no."   (Gagnon, 208)

Because of their "taboos" regarding a discussion of sexual behavior, many couples rely solely on their nonverbal communication to gain mutual satisfaction. For some this may be acceptable but for others the unclear messages result in frustration, as partners misinterpret the degree or kind of sexual expression desired by the other. Certain partners report a fear of using any affectionate gesture because the other spouse always sees it as an invitation to intercourse; others say that their partners never initiate any sexual activity while the partners report being ignored or rebuffed at such attempts. Mutual satisfaction at any level of sexual involvement depends upon open communication between spouses, yet intercourse, according to Lederer and Jackson is special ". . . in that it requires a higher degree of collaborative communication than any other kind of behavior exchanged between the spouses" (117).

Sexuality and Communication Breakdowns • Finally, we need to note that although sex as a form of communication has the potential for conveying messages of love and affection, many spouses use their sexual encounters to carry messages of anger, domination, disappointment, or self-rejection. Often nonsexual conflicts are played out in the bedroom because one partner believes it is the only way to wage a war. Unexpressed anger may reappear as a "headache," or great "tiredness," roughness, or violence during a sexual encounter.

From his work on sexual communication, Scoresby has devised the following chart (see Table 5-1, p. 105) indicating possible areas of breakdown in sexual communication and possible solutions.

Finally Scoresby also provides advantages for thinking of sex as communication. They are:

1. We become more aware of its complexities and intricacies as opposed to focusing on physical or mechanical procedures.
2. We conclude we'll never utilize all its potential, and leads us to more fully explore its possibilities . . .
3. We view the sexual relationship as a continuous process instead of as a series of isolated events. (46)

Thus for couples engaged in an intimate relationship, often communication about sexuality may deepen the intimacy and provide tremendous pleasure to both spouses.

BARRIERS TO INTIMACY

We have suggested that marital or familial intimacy involves confirmation and affection, self-disclosure, and sexual relations for couples, yet because of the risks and effort involved in intimate communication, such behavior frightens numerous people. Although most persons would declare a desire for intimacy, many actually experience a strong fear of becoming extremely close to another person. Feldman suggests that people fear intimacy for the following five reasons: (1) People may fear a merger with the loved one resulting in the loss of personal boundaries or identity. When the "sense of self" is poorly developed or insecure, merger with another (while sought after in many ways) is experienced as a danger situation and stimulates intense (conscious or unconscious) anxiety" (71); (2) Persons may fear interpersonal exposure since individuals with low self-esteem or low self-acceptance may be threatened by being revealed as weak, inadequate, undesirable; (3) Persons may fear attack if their basic sense of trust in themselves and the world remains underdeveloped. When development is impaired, unresolved conflicts "exert a powerful negative effect on current life experiences, particularly those involving interpersonal intimacy" (72); (4) Persons fear abandonment, the feeling of being overwhelmed and helpless when the love object is gone. For those who have experienced excessive traumatic separations, one way to defend against anxiety is to reduce intimacy; (5) Persons fear their own destructive impulses. "When depressed anxiety has not been resolved during the course of childhood development, it becomes a powerful potential stimulus for defensive behavior in adult intimate relationships" (72). Once one has taken the risk to be intimate, rejection can be devastating resulting in reluctance to be hurt again.

After our separation the hardest thing we faced was regaining our sense of intimacy. We had hurt each other so badly that we had to rebuild a whole new sense of trust and sharing. It was an effort to say personal things, to touch each other lovingly, to discuss our feelings. We have been back together for over a year and only now is our sexual life coming around. It had been so important to us before and we were scared of allowing ourselves to be free, truly free, in that area. Each small risk has been a victory but it has been a very painful slow process.

Table 5-1 Signs of Difficulty and Suggested Solutions

Elements of Sexual Communication	Common Symptoms	Possible Solutions
Emotional Bond and Communicating Desire	1. Failure to talk openly with each other. 2. Repeated lack of orgasm by female. 3. Tension and lack of relaxation. 4. One demanding the other to perform. 5. Excessive shyness or embarrassment. 6. Hurried and ungentle performance. 7. Absence of frequent touching, embracing, and exchanges of intimacy.	1. Increase each person's ability to self-disclose feelings. 2. Spend increased positive time alone together. 3. Avoid threatening to dissolve the marriage. 4. Check for angry conflict and reduce if possible.
Sexual Responsibility	1. Only one person initiating. 2. Excessive modesty that restricts full expression. 3. Failure to freely consent or refuse invitations. 4. Blaming each other for sexual failure. 5. Double standard for males or for females. 6. Existence of beliefs that males and females differ sharply about feelings. 7. Insistence by one on exceeding the desired sexual limits of the other. 8. Feeling of pressure to perform by either or both.	1. Review training and education about sex to see if cultural training has disparaged positive sexual expression. 2. Discuss how previous experience and early training may affect each person. 3. Examine current relationship to see if excessive dominance is present. 4. Reduce criticism each may have for the other. 5. Seek professional help for the purpose of helping each feel accepting of sexual desires and asserting personal responsibility.
Optimal Variation	1. Repeatedly feeling that sex has become monotonous. 2. Feeling bored by having to participate in intercourse. 3. Excessive experimentation that violates the preferences of one or both. 4. Hurried and mechanical intercourse. 5. Lack of a set of sexual preferences.	1. Discuss what each prefers, why and when. 2. Stay within the sense of propriety felt by each person unless excessively restrictive. 3. Focus on varied feeling states as opposed to variations in techniques. 4. Acquire additional information about sexual techniques.

Table 5-1 (Continued)

Elements of Sexual Communication	Common Symptoms	Possible Solutions
Physical Performance	1. Existence of physical dysfunction: (a) impotence, (b) premature ejaculation, (c) retarded ejaculation, (d) failure to be orgastic, (e) vaginismus, (f) sensation of pain.	1. Seek competent professional help. 2. Examine each person's individual life or relationship for sources of tension and stress and reduce if possible. 3. Increase the amount of care, warmth, and nurturance rather than criticizing or ridiculing. 4. Evaluate and improve all elements of the sexual relationship.

(A. Lynn Scoresby, *The Marriage Dialogue,* © 1977, Addison-Wesley Publishing Co., Inc., Chapter 4, pages 45-46; Table 2, pages 64-65. Reprinted with permission.)

Sometimes intimacy becomes confused with an unhealthy togetherness or extreme cohesion resulting in a loss of personal boundaries and identity. As you remember, boundaries serve as regulatory factors to help one see differences and similarities within systems and subsystems providing one with certain limits and certain rights. As we saw in Chapter 1, families may range in their distance regulation capacities from very high cohesion to very low cohesion, or as family therapist Minuchin (1974) labels it, from polar dimensions of "enmeshment" to "disengagement" (53–56).

He provides the following diagram suggesting most families fall within the wide normal range (54):

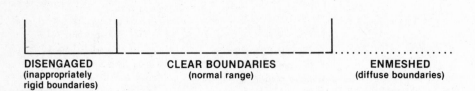

| DISENGAGED
(inappropriately
rigid boundaries) | CLEAR BOUNDARIES
(normal range) | ENMESHED
(diffuse boundaries) |

Typical families, including their interpersonal subsystems, find themselves within the wide normal range but at times experience some degree of enmeshment or disengagement. In a highly cohesive or enmeshed family, ties are so close that boundaries become blurred—each lives the others' lives, reverberating strongly to the slightest shift in the system. One person's business is everyone's business. A great deal of communication occurs across family subsystem boundaries and people may feel obligated to engage in high self-disclosure and even seek disclosure inappropriate to the subsystem or role. A child may feel obligated to discuss all of his or her dating behavior with a parent. A mother may discuss marital problems with a teenage son. Yet the enmeshed person requires the other to ". . . be like me; be one with me." He or she suggests, "You are bad if you disagree with me. Reality and your differentness are unimportant" (Satir, 1967, 13), demonstrating the difficulty of negative self-disclosure. Members may require, or sense a demand for, constant confirmation to serve as reassurance that they are cared for. Yet, intimacy becomes smothering if people are fused.

When I was still living at home, my mother would often say to me, "Louise, I'm cold. Go put on a sweater." A child is more apt to listen to her mother without really thinking about the words, but one day I said, "Mom, I'm not cold." This was only a small moment in our relationship but it typified my struggle to move away from such a tightly bonded relationship that it was hard to tell who was who.

On the other hand, within disengaged or very low cohesive families, individuals do not get through the rigid boundaries to reach each other so the members may not receive necessary affection or support. Each person remains as a psychological subsystem with few links to the surrounding family members. Intimacy remains undeveloped or at a low intensity level in households where each family member concerns himself or herself solely with personal affairs, remains constantly busy, and spends time away from the home. Yet, even if persons spend time together, unless their communication goes beyond the task-oriented type, they may remain generally disengaged. Both types of families set up barriers to true intimacy by smothering or ignoring individual family members.

CONCLUSION

Within this chapter we have explored the close relationship between intimacy and communication. After detailing the concept of intimacy, we examined specific communication behaviors that encourage intimacy within marital and family systems: confirmation, self-disclosure, and sexual communication. Confirmation behaviors give value to another as a person and may be found in recognition, dialogue, acceptance, and personal treatment. Self-disclosure which involves communication about self provides a vehicle for deep sharing and personal growth within a relationship characterized by self-esteem, confirmation, and commitment. Healthy self-disclosure is critical to the development of intimacy within family relationships. We presented our view of sexual behavior as a form of marital communication and a contributing factor to overall marital satisfaction. Each family socializes its members into certain sexual beliefs and attitudes within the context of the family rules. We asserted that sexual encounters have the potential for conveying messages of intimacy or of conflict.

When you look at the families around you, what kind of interactions do you see? Is most of their communication strictly functional? Do you see attempts at intimacy—through confirmation or self-disclosure? Are these people able to demonstrate an ability to touch each other comfortably? If you think back to Gilbert's model of the curvilinear versus the linear development of self-disclosure (p. 97) you can imagine the model applied to all relationships, knowing that only a few are likely to have the mutual acceptance risk-taking capacity and commitment to move toward true intimacy.

Achieving intimacy involves great effort and risk; maintaining intimacy over time involves the same. Some people never experience an intimate relationship during a lifetime; others experience a number of such relationships. No matter how many intimate relationships you may experience, you will find communication at the core of such relationship development.

Communication and Family Roles and Types

I grew up in a very traditional family and held all the beliefs about wives as dependent persons who maintain the home and provide emotional support. By strange fate I married a man who was raised by a single-parent mother and he saw women as more independent than I did. Over time he has influenced me to be more of my own person, to have a career, to be independent in many ways. If I had married a man with the same original conception of husband and wife that I had, my life would have been very different.

Each of us grows up with images of how persons in certain positions in a family should act. As a child you have expectations for how to be a husband, wife, parent, or step-parent while you are functioning as a child, sister, or stepson. As an adult you may be actively involved as a parent, spouse, step-parent, interacting with spouses, ex-spouses, children. Collectively the members of your family system may develop certain patterns which are characterized by predictable behaviors. In this chapter we will examine the positions or family roles, and predictable patterns or family types as they relate to communication.

ROLE ISSUES

The area of role theory is fraught with controversy, and it is not our purpose to try to detail the many approaches to this concept. We will use Heiss' role description (1968) "prescriptions for interpersonal behavior which are associated with particular, socially recognized, categories of persons" (3). These categories may be viewed as statuses or positions. Heiss suggests that role theorists also share two basic assumptions: (1) they assume that "roles are learned in the process of social interaction" and (2) they believe that "when people interact with others they see themselves and these others as occupants of particular statuses, and are given guides for action by what they know or learn, are the expectations associated with these statuses" (3–4).

Definition of Roles

Traditionally roles have been tied to status or position within some group leading to a general definition of roles as a "collection of rights, duties, attitudes, and values that constitute norms defining behavior appropriate to performing a given function in a given group" (Muchmore, 1974, 38). In keeping with this perspective, family roles would include the "attitudes, beliefs, values, and behavior expected by society of any family member in a given position" (Linton, 1945, 77). Such views present a static or unchanging image of roles since, according to this view, one holds certain expectations toward the occupant of a given social position and these expectations carry with them beliefs about how a role can and should be enacted no matter what the circumstances. At the furthest extreme you can imagine a script for being in a family. Thus the role of child, or wife, or father entails particular behaviors. Such beliefs lead to statements such as—fathers do X, wives do Y, children do Z—with the assumption that these statements are applicable to all persons with such labels under all conditions.

A less static approach may be found within an interactive perspective. This perspective emphasizes the emerging aspects of roles and the behavioral regularities that develop out of social interaction. Thus this approach takes into account the transactional nature of the interpersonal encounters experienced by persons with labels such as father, son, wife, or husband and reflects the reciprocal nature of roles. Those in other roles evaluate, react, and convey expectations at the same time you are doing the equivalent to them. In accordance with this interactive philosophy, you cannot be a stepfather without a stepchild, a wife without a husband; in fact, you cannot be a loving stepfather to a child who rejects you or a confrontive wife to a man who avoids conflicts. Yet roles do not reflect interaction solely. Part of learning roles occurs by observing and imitating role models, or persons whose behavior serves as a guide for us (Heiss, 13).

From our perspective the interactive role reflects (1) the personality and background of the person who happens to occupy the social position, and (2) the relationships in which the person engages. For example, Sharon Ferrari's behavior in the social position of wife may have been very different in her first than in her second marriage due to her own personal growth and the actions of each husband.

According to one expert on roles, "Instead of playing a part prescribed by norms each individual in a situation assesses the other's role on the basis of the behaviors the other displays. The first individual then reacts according to the behaviors he predicts as a consequence of taking the role of the other" (Aldous, 1974, 231). In this sense role development becomes a transactional process with each family member influenced by others in the family and influencing them by his or her actions. Thus, how you function in a role reflects the members of the system in which the role is assumed.

British sociologist Basil Bernstein (1970) identifies two primary forms of communication that serve to contrast and typify families, the position-oriented type and the person-oriented type. Position-oriented families are more likely to maintain "sharp boundaries between statuses and social identities along the lines of age, sex, and age-related family roles" (Johnson, 1978, 5). Thus the behaviors attached to the roles of grandparent, mother, and son become carefully defined and delineated. In a position-oriented family, aunts do X, mothers do Y, and husbands do Z. Person-oriented families center more on the unique individuals occupying each label and have fewer boundaries or exacting rules for appropriate behavior. Johnson describes the communication differences between these two approaches by discussing a hypothetical child—Allison—as she might develop in either family:

> If she develops in a position-oriented family, she learns that her role as a child is very communalized; she learns that mother and father can direct and prohibit behavior because they are mother and father and as such need only provide general rule statements as directives of behavior: "You're not to leave the table until you drink your milk," "Apologize to your father," "Be quiet, I'm on the phone." If, on the other hand, Allison develops in a person-oriented family, she will probably be asked to drink her milk, apologize to her father, and be quiet, but these directives are less likely to stand on their own. Allison's parents will provide reasons for the desired behaviors that go beyond mother and father's rights to direct. (5–6)

Thus a child raised in a position-oriented family "learns that what can be said and done in relation to others depends on the roles one has relative to others," whereas a child raised in a person-oriented family learns that although role relationships are important, "the desirability or undesirability of certain behaviors depends on reasons that transcend the role relationships and focus on the personal nature of the participants" (6). As we explore the role-related behaviors occurring in families, keep in mind the continuum representing position-oriented and person-oriented approaches to these roles.

Roles are inextricably bound to the communication process. In short, family roles are developed and maintained through communication. One learns how to assume his or her place within a family from the feedback provided by other family members. "Such a good girl, helping Mommy like that." "Well, why don't you stand up for me when your buddies start to put some of my ideas down? Husbands should support their wives." "I don't think either of us should use four-letter words in front of the children. If parents can't be role models then what can we expect?" We talk about what we expect from another as we enter a marital relationship. How many countless hours are spent by young couples dreaming and scheming about their marriage and family and the kind of spouses and parents they intend to be? In-laws may be verbally or nonverbally informed about what is considered appropriate behavior; children are given very direct instructions about being a son or daughter in a particular household. In general adults tend to use their family-of-origin history from which to negotiate particular mutual roles as they form a family system; children develop their communicative roles through "the interplay of cognitive abilities and the social norms and expectations" (Johnson, 2).

Family roles and communication rules are strongly interrelated as each contributes to the maintenance or change of the other. Rules may serve to structure certain role relationships while particular role relationships may foster the development of certain rules. For example, rules such as "Children should not hear about family finances" or "School problems are to be settled with Mother" reinforce a position-oriented role structure; in turn, such a structure contributes to the creation of this type of rule.

COMMUNICATION AND ROLE DEVELOPMENT

Within families roles are established, grown to, grown through, discussed, negotiated, worked on, accepted, or rejected. As family members mature, or outside forces cause change within the family, roles may develop, shift, disappear. The adjustments may be obvious or subtle, but adjustments do occur as families grow and change.

Six months ago I married a woman whose husband died one year ago and who has two children. Between us we now have five children living in the house and although our own relationship is going well, we are having a hard time fulfilling the role of parent to each other's children. Maybe she married too soon after their father's death, but her two boys treat me like a distant acquaintance. If I try to be affectionate they pull away. If I give them orders, they will obey me but they certainly cannot put me in the role of father. On the other hand, my kids have been without a mother for 7 years and are willing to let Karen get into the mothering act but she seems afraid to do so. It's like her kids vs. my kids. Although she is affectionate with her boys, she doesn't really hug or kiss my kids and she seems afraid to even give them orders. With mine, it's always, "Ask your father." I knew it wouldn't be easy to develop a new family of seven people but I didn't think the parenting things would be so difficult.

In order to more fully understand family roles, we need to examine (1) the sources of role expectations, and (2) the determinants of role performance. How many of you remember making comments such as "When I'm a parent, I'll listen to my kids" or "I'd never let my wife go out to work." Probably each of us has spent some time planning how we will fulfill a specific future role based on our expectations of how such a role should be performed. Our role expectations for family roles come from a number of sources.

Role Expectations

The society in which we live provides models and norms for how certain family roles should be assumed. Currently the media stands as one important societal source of family role expectations. Look at any newsstand and you'll see articles on "Being a Successful Single Parent," "The Changing Grandparent," or "The New Young Couples." Books tell us about "Parent Effectiveness Training" or "T.A. for Tots" while television has provided us with years of family role models since the time of "Father Knows Best." Advertising reinforces certain stereotypes of how family members should act.

Daily life within a community serves as a major source of role expectation. Growing up, the neighbors and your friends all knew who were the "good" mothers or the "bad" kids on the block or in the community. Ministers, priests, and rabbis presented exhortations for the prescribed "good family life." School personnel could influence adult expectations for what "good" parents would do with their children. Each of us has grown up with hundreds of expectations thrown at us about how people should function in family roles.

One of the hardest things about being divorced was living with the initial shame. I grew up learning that only "bad" women got divorced and that women had a duty to remain married no matter what. I remained married for longer than I should have because I couldn't deal with what the neighbors or the church or the other people around me would think. I got married with all the traditional expectations and that's a hard mold to break out of.

Particular ethnic or cultural groups may hold beliefs about parenting or spouse roles which are learned by members of that community. For example, in the Jewish tradition the role of mother is associated with the transmission of the culture and as such carries a particular significance and implies certain expectations.

Role expectations also arise from significant and complementary others. People important to you will set some expectations for how you will act in a future role. Your mother may greatly influence your expectations of motherhood or your father of fatherhood. You may have had a grandmother who taught you caring behaviors that parents should exhibit. A young childless couple may carefully watch another couple with small children to learn to deal with a new impending role.

Complementary others, or those people who fulfill related role positions, have expectations for your role. A husband has expectations for a wife, a parent for a child. During early stages of a relationship men and women may spend long periods of time discussing their expectations for what being a husband or wife will be like. "I want my wife to be home with the children until they go to school," "I need a man who will take responsibility for the home and children." As families blend, prospective parents may sit down with their future stepchildren and talk about what they think the relationship should be like. If one partner is more position-oriented and the other more person-oriented in their expectations, they are more likely to clash than if both hold similar orientations.

Additional expectations come from each person's self-understanding in relationship to a future role. A person who expects to fulfill the role of spouse or parent has certain ideas about what such a role entails and how he or she thinks a "fit" between the role and the person can be created. You may find that you relied on a role model or you decided that with your skills or personality you would like to be a certain kind of spouse or parent.

My personal expectations of motherhood came from my grandmother and from certain things I knew about myself. My grandmother was the most generous and loving lady I ever met. I could always call her if I needed anything and I could always go there to eat or sleep if I wanted to. She had seven children and sixteen grandchildren and made everyone feel special. I wanted to be like her. I also knew that I wanted to be an artist so that I could only have one or two children in order to continue to create the way I was trained to. I wanted to make two almost contradictory patterns work.

Although society and others greatly influence our expectations, each of us puts our own special identity into our final expectations of how we will assume a role. And sometimes expectations may lead us to a decision not to assume the role.

This is probably a reversal of expectations but on the basis of what I know about myself I decided not to have children. From all I learned and could see children are a very time-consuming responsibility and although they bring great joy, they limit certain growth potential for their parents. I knew that career advancement and travel were major goals for me and in order to fulfill those goals I realized that I could not also have a goal of raising children.

Although we have been talking about expectations as occurring prior to assuming a role, persons in roles may develop new expectations for that role. For example, a woman may watch her boss take his daughters out to lunch every second Saturday and develop new expectations for how she could develop her parenting role in relation to her son.

Role expectations are influenced by an imaginative view of oneself—the way one likes to think of himself or herself being and acting (McCall & Simmons, 1966, 67). A mother may imagine that she goes back to work; a father may imagine himself telling his child the "facts of life" comfortably. An integral part of these imaginings is the reaction of other people to one's hypothetical performance (68). The wife/mother may picture her friends' looks of envy at her ability to juggle everything. The father may imagine his son's eventual gratitude at learning the facts of life from his father. McCall and Simmons stress that such imaginings are not just daydreams, rather they serve as perhaps the primary source of plans of action or as rehearsal halls for actual performance (69). In keeping with an interactive view of roles, they stress the importance of the imagined reactions of others:

> The imagined reactions of various others to these vicarious performances constitute important criteria for evaluating any possible plans of overt action similar in content to these vicarious performances.   (69)

While role expectations represent the notion about how a role could or should be fulfilled, role performance represents the actual behavior with others which defines how the role is enacted. Roles are reciprocal and until they are enacted with others, all one has are expectations.

Role Performance

As with role expectation, role performance is influenced by similar factors including societal or cultural norms, reactions and role performances of significant and complementary others, and the individual's capacity for enacting the role.

Society's general norms for how a role should be performed may affect how the role is performed. Legal constraints exist for family behavior. Courts enforce laws in areas such as child or spouse abuse or child support and alimony. The media may affect how you enact your role as they influence you to hug a child, provide nutritional snacks, or purchase wine for romantic dinners.

I can't tell you how much pressure women are under to be super-women. Just a few years ago women were criticized if they left home to work while children were small. Now everything you read is about the dual career mother! I got so much pressure about returning to work after Donny was born that I finally gave in and after six months I'm beginning to feel like a walking zombie. I'd really like to stay home but I'm afraid of feeling like a failure.

Churches may influence who their members can marry and how parent and child roles are carried out. School and community organizations may give feedback as to how people are doing in their family roles. The extent to which you respond to this feedback determines its influence on you. You may choose to "keep up with the Joneses" or you may decide the Joneses don't know much about how to live.

The actions of significant or important persons in your life affects role performance. In the network concept of family therapy, a family's relatives and friends are invited to work with the therapist in order to provide support for the family in difficulty. Persons are encouraged to give specific feedback and support to individual family members for their behaviors. Most of us have experienced less dramatic examples of feedback from significant others. Perhaps a friend told you he wouldn't be as disrespectful to his mother as you are and you changed your responses. Or someone told you what a good stepparent you are and you try even harder to be a good father to your stepchildren. The reactions of persons we respect or care about are likely to have a great influence on how we fulfill our family roles. The modeling of these people may also influence our behaviors. The woman who watches her boss lunch with his daughters may start to take her son out to lunch once a week also.

Persons in complementary roles have direct bearing on how we assume our roles. Have you ever tried to reason with a parent who sulks, to pamper an independent grandparent, or to order a willful child? You were probably frustrated in enacting your role, if that was the case. On the other hand, if two complementary persons see things in similar ways, it enhances role performance. A college student who believes that she should no longer have to answer for her evening whereabouts will be reinforced by a mother who no longer asks. An older brother who believes little sisters should be treated specially will be reinforced by a little sister who cuddles and plays with him. Thus the way others assume their roles and comment on our roles affect what we do in our roles.

Additionally, our own individual background influences what we actually do. The range of possible behaviors a person can perform limits what he or she can do. For example, if certain communication behaviors are not part of your background they cannot appear as if by magic in a particular situation. A father may wish he could talk to his son instead of yelling at him or giving orders, but he may not know how to discuss a controversial subject with his child. Self-confidence in attempting to fulfill a role may affect behavior. The shy stepmother may not be able to express affection for her new stepchildren for many months. Our personal needs also get in the picture. If we need to appear secure, we won't admit insecurities, even to a mate. If we need to appear helpless, we won't take charge of even simple household situations. The aspects of the role we emphasize colors how we appear. If you view the major function of fatherhood as providing for your children, you may take a second job before you would take the family on weekend picnics. Some people's attitudes and behaviors are almost synonymous, whereas others experience large gaps between what they would like to do and how they enact their role.

Sometimes individual expectations don't match the realities. A woman who planned to mother many children may find herself uncomfortable with the role of mother to one. A man who expected to dominate his marriage may find pleasure in relating to an independent wife. On occasions people discover they can function well in a role they did not expect or desire.

I was really furious when my husband quit his sales job to go finish his degree. I didn't choose the role of provider and I didn't like being conscripted. But after a while though I got to feeling very professional and adult. Here I was supporting myself and a husband. I didn't know I had it in me.

As we will explore in more detail in Chapters 10 and 11, predictable and unpredictable life crises affect the roles we assume and how we function in them. Thus, although role behavior functions as a result of expectations and interpersonal interactions, unforseen circumstances may alter life in such a way that roles change drastically from those first planned or enacted.

In the next section we will develop a set of eight general functions which adults assume in families. To what extent each adult assumes certain functions affects how roles are enacted and the type of communication that occurs within the family.

COMMUNICATION AND SPECIFIC FAMILY FUNCTIONS

In order to examine more fully the transactional impact or the mutual influence of family roles, we will develop eight adult family functions emphasizing their communication aspects. Nye and Gecas (1976) refer to these eight functions as roles, but since we take an interactive view of roles rather than a static one, we choose to refer to them as functions. Nye and Gecas refer to the roles of provider, housekeeper, child care, recreational, sexual, child socialization, therapeutic, and kinship. We prefer to say that within families adult members may develop behaviors within the following functions: providing, housekeeping, caring for children, recreating, socializing children, developing sexual identity, being therapeutic, and maintaining kinship. Partners without children do not assume all these functions. Within each family system their themes, images, boundaries, and biosocial beliefs interact with how the functions are carried out. As we examine the functions we will place a greater emphasis on those related to sexual identity, child socialization, therapeutic behavior, and kinship since they have stronger implications for communication.

Sexual Identity Function

When you were growing up what were your family's biosocial beliefs about males and females? Did you hear any of the following? "Boys don't play the piano —girls do." "Trumpets and drums are for boys." "Don't be afraid of the ball like a girl!" "Girls aren't engineers!" "Boys don't cry." Or perhaps you heard, "Girls can be anything they want to be." "Boys can cry if they're hurt, just like girls." "Boys and girls both cook and play soccer."

More of you probably heard comments that distinguished between boys and girls because our society traditionally made such distinctions. This process of what it means to be male or female in our society begins with the birth of the child. Even as newborns males and females are handled differently and may be provided with "sex-appropriate toys." Males and females learn expected behaviors at an early age. Studies of kindergarten children show boys keenly aware of what masculine behaviors are expected of them and restricting their interests and activities to avoid what might be judged feminine. Girls continue to develop feminine expectations gradually over five more years (Hartley, 1974, 7). For some people sex-appropriate distinctions remain critical to the future development of society. For them, clearly separate male and female behaviors are necessary for the continuation of the family as they have known it. Some religious and political groups and certain cultural heritages support strong male-female distinctions seeing such practices as necessary for continued family existence and development. For example, in the Mormon Church's Family Home Evenings (1978), the father, "as head of the house" has the responsibility to preside, which is in keeping with the church's male-female role distinctions applied to the family. Although you may believe in open and caring communication, you may believe that men and women should fulfill certain functions in the family on the basis of sex. For others, such sexually bound distinctions appear repressive. This position is well represented in the following statement. "If men cannot play freely, neither can they freely cry, be gentle, nor show weakness—because these are 'feminine,' not 'masculine.' But a fuller concept of humanity recognizes that all men and women are potentially strong and weak, both active and passive, and that these and other human characteristics are not the province of one sex" (Sawyer, 1970).

Part of the patterning of behaviors the child will imitate come from the communication rules in the family that pertain to the sexual distinctions to be made. Sexually bound rules may determine who can perform, or respond to, certain communication behaviors such as crying, swearing, asking for money, hitting, or hugging.

Whatever communication directives you received as a child, based on your sex, come into play when you form your own family system. For example, as we noted in Chapter 5, Jourard (1974) suggests that men are thought to self-disclose less than women and keep more secrets to themselves. Compared to women, men relate more impersonally to others and see themselves as the embodiment of their roles rather than as humans enacting roles. Jourard summarized his findings:

> Man's potential thoughts, feelings, wishes and fantasies know no bounds, save those set by his biological structure and his personal history. But the male role, and the male self-structure will not allow man to acknowledge or to express the entire breadth and depth of his inner experience, to himself or to others. Man seems obliged, rather to hide much of his real self—the ongoing flow of his spontaneous inner experience—from himself and from others.   (21)

As we indicated in Chapter 5, a new concern with "psychological sex" (based on socialization) rather than in "anatomical sex" may reveal different insights into male and female self-disclosure behavior.

Since self-disclosure and openness are critical to communication and sharing love within families, if men accept a very restrictive definition of their nurturing communication, they may deprive themselves and their family members of desired intimacy. Women may suffer when female role prescriptions prohibit spontaneous, assertive, or independent communication. Yet each person's behavior is constantly modified by the other family members with whom he or she interacts.

The recent interest in the concept of androgyny has implications for communication within families. *Androgyny* means "the human capacity for members of both sexes to be masculine and feminine in their behaviors—both dominant and submissive, active and passive, tough and tender" (DeFrain, 1979, 237). Applied to communication this means that in many families sexual expectations and the rules accompanying them would change. Any issue would be evaluated via communication that focused on the merits or demerits of the issue without any reference to sex of the persons involved. Bem (1974) described the androgynous person as flexible, adaptive, and capable of being both instrumental (assertive, competent, forceful, independent) and expressive (nurturing, warm, supportive, compassionate) depending upon the demands of the situation (155). The goal of an androgynous approach would be not to waste energies on creating or maintaining any form of sex stereotype but to concentrate efforts on communication behaviors that provide options for humans to be themselves—their own person.

Another aspect of the sexual identity function relates to engaging in sexual activity. We view sexual behavior as a form of communication which has a powerful effect on the quality of a marital relationship.

If there is anything I would wish for my daughter as she enters marriage, it would be the ability to talk to her husband about sex. I grew up without a vocabulary for doing that and it was unthinkable to me that men and women could really talk about what gave them pleasure in sexual activity. My husband and I spent years in troubled silence. It took an affair, a separation, and counseling for us to be able to begin to talk about our sexual life. I hope I can teach my daughter some of the lessons I learned.

Even in our more "open" society today, many communication breakdowns stem from an inability of couples to share honestly about their sexual relationship. In Carlson's study of 210 couples' sexual behavior in terms of expectations in married couples, he found that 80 percent of both spouses indicated that the husband initiates sexual activity more than the wife, but 45 percent of the husbands feel both should have equal responsibility. Wives respond differently: only 26 percent thought it should be an equal responsibility and another 30 percent saw no duty involved (Carlson, 1976, 103). Over 90 percent of the respondents indicated that the sex role should be defined exclusively within the marriage.

Both spouses in this study disapproved of either refusing sexual relations, but husbands felt more strongly about it. Although most spouses usually granted their partner's request for sex, only 10 percent of the husbands refused or ignored the request compared to 30 percent of the wives who did the same.

Couples thought sexual activity extremely important to them: 73 percent of the wives and 85 percent of the husbands. As to frequency of sex, 37 percent of the husbands indicated they desired sex "much more frequently" than their wives and only 2 percent reported their wives wanted sex more frequently. Over two-thirds of the husbands wanted "somewhat" more sex compared to less than 10 percent for wives. Over half the wives and two-thirds of the husbands reported general satisfaction with their sexual participation.

The differences in the responses of wives and husbands indicate potential communication problems. Couples tend to say little to one another about this most intimate part of their relationship. Whether from fear or family rules that inhibit discussion, couples avoid the topic. Carlson gives another possible explanation: "Wives view sex as being less important to them or something they would prefer to avoid. It is possible that this differential is the cause of many feelings of dissatisfaction between spouses . . ." (105).

For our purposes it is sufficient to note the importance of communication. What can happen in normal relationships between couples is that unsolved problems in other aspects of their lives get carried over into the sexual relationship. A kind of sexual politics game dominates the relationship and one or the other spouse uses power, excuses, pressure, or ignoring tactics instead of direct communication. Some couples reach a stalemate and miss the potential joys and rewards in intimacy that they can derive from sexual encounters. Others learn to communicate about their sexual behavior.

Child Socialization Function

Closely tied to the sexual identity function, the child socialization function requires parents to become involved with the social and psychological processes whereby children, through family experiences, gain a sense of right and wrong. This function incorporates communication since it is the chief process used to transmit values of the parents and community to the children. Through verbal and nonverbal permissions, directives, and answers to questions, children learn what parents and society expect of them. The parent who carries out most of the responsibilities of the child care function has the potential to have a greater socializing influence. In one study although approximately two out of three spouses indicated they shared socialization tasks, observations revealed the wife more involved than the husband. Fathers became more involved with sons than daughters and mothers more with daughters than sons, but overall mothers did more socializing of both sons and daughters (Gecas, 1976, 39–40).

Such socialization has far-reaching implications for adult life. If little girls receive and accept communication about their future housewife functions " . . . by the time they are adults the patterns of behavior are deeply ingrained in them and difficult, if not impossible, to eradicate" (Ericksen, Yancey, and Ericksen, 1979, 302). Even in sexual socialization there can be difficulties about what to teach children.

Somehow it seems easier to raise a girl these days than a boy. Girls can be told they can do anything that was traditionally male or female but that's not the case for boys. I finally ended up telling my five-year-old son that he could cry whenever he wanted at home but that he should try not to cry at school. Although I hate to restrict him in this way, I am afraid of how the other children will make fun of him if he "acts like a girl."

Although socialization relates directly to moral and cultural values, it also can specify acceptable or unacceptable communication behaviors such as yelling, lying, crying, hugging, directness, and silence. We all experience communication socialization and our family-of-origin directly affects our childhood and usually our adult communication competence. For example, children who never engage in making decisions, defending a point of view, or negotiating for something will not automatically develop such communication skills when they leave their childhood home.

Yet in keeping with the interactive nature of roles, children can refuse to accept parts of the socialization process. This frustrates parents, especially those in an extremely rigid family system who cannot be flexible enough to present other options or who may not know other ways to socialize their children.

Therapeutic Function

The therapeutic function implies a willingness to listen and hear the problems of another. The listening must be empathic in order to give the other the understanding needed or the chance to ventilate pent-up feelings of rage, frustration, or exhaustion. Not only should adults do it for one another, but their children require the same kind of listening.

My mother has been an incredible support to me. She never made any judgments about my divorce and has always been around to listen to me or to be a sounding board for the children without taking sides about the divorce. She doesn't tell me what to do with my life but if I'm obviously upset about work or the kids, she will stop whatever she is doing and pay attention to me as if nothing else is going on in her world.

Thus the therapeutic function implies empathy and nonjudgmental understanding of another person. In addition to being available in times of crises or to hear about a problem, a family member needs to know that he or she has someone to give them a sense of belonging—a sense of refuge occasionally from the realities of the world they want to ignore or gain time to cope with. If the communication channels between you and other family members encourage and permit the expression of open feelings, different individuals in the family can carry out the therapeutic role. This could include advice and questioning of motives. For example, one brother can serve as sounding board for another brother.

In his analysis of the therapeutic behavior in couples, Nye (1976) found that over 60 percent of both wives and husbands thought they each had a responsibility for carrying out such behavior. In fact, both sexes expected that problems involving financial matters, sex, problems with children and in-laws would be discussed within the family and not with outsiders. If a spouse responded with criticism to information about a problem and the way the other handled it, 85 percent of each sex judged this to be unfair treatment (121). Nye also found that although this function was not as valued as other ones, it related more highly to satisfaction in marriage than other functions (130).

Parental use of therapeutic behaviors provides children with models of such actions. When children receive emotional reassurance and support from parents, they realize they can bring up problems that originate outside the family and get help or understanding. The therapeutic function may be carried out by friends or extended family members, particularly for single adults or single parent families where only one adult resides. Severe family breakdowns may occur if boundaries keep members from supportive people. In extremely cohesive families certain problems may be avoided since they could threaten the powerful connectedness, while in very low cohesive families members may not feel anyone cares enough to listen. Members of such families may need to go elsewhere for emotional support.

Kinship Function

Kinship involves sharing, participating in, and promoting the family's welfare as contacts are maintained with relations outside the family home. Parents and children, sisters and brothers, uncles, aunts, and cousins, plus step-relatives are all involved in maintaining or not maintaining a family network. Whether or not one is included or excluded from events such as a Bar Mitzvah, wedding, funeral, graduation, or reunion, or whether or not one hears the latest gossip, signifies one's place within the family system.

While fulfilling the kinship function family members may operate within their own rules or rituals and outsiders may not feel welcome or included in the unique family communication patterns. Information about misdeeds of family members (Uncle Mike's divorce, or Brent's involvement with drugs) may be discussed with close relatives, such as the couple's parents or brothers and sisters, but not with cousins, aunts, and uncles.

Holidays become a special communication time in most families. Relatives may travel many miles to share these events. In some families, particularly highly cohesive ones, attendance at get-togethers becomes mandatory and only illness or great distance may be accepted as excuses. Exchange through intimate and economic currencies occurs as part of a ritual. In other households, the holidays cause great pain since certain "cut-off" members may be excluded or members of low cohesive families may feel they are missing something. For most people, the events never match the picture-postcard events pictured in the media and individuals think their family has missed something.

In some families, kinship means sharing family resources and helping out with food, clothing, furniture, or money that other relatives need. It may also involve attitudes of acceptance.

There are people who were informally adopted in my family. My mother and one of my cousins were raised by their grandmother although their mother did not live there. When babies have been born out of wedlock, the grandmother raises them. The baby is treated like anyone else. In my family no one is considered half or step, you are a member of the family and that is that. You have equal access to everything that anyone has and you are included in all family activities.

In his study of kinship behaviors, Bahr (1976) found that women do most of the communication with relatives. Husbands maintained fewer kinship contacts with their relatives and actually had more contact with their wife's kin. According to Bahr, the wife's kinship behavior "cements her family of procreation (including the husband) more firmly to her own parents and siblings than to the husband's family" (78). However, in giving financial aid to kin and in settling disputes with relatives, husbands more often made the decisions, suggesting the husband usually delegates the kinship tasks. Working wives and those with large families gave less attention to the kinship tasks. Ninety percent of interaction with kin was concentrated in three areas: visiting, recreation, and communication by letter and telephone. Bahr summarizes the importance of the woman's future position in the following way: "The consequences of her general stewardship of family communication may be far more important for future family solidarity than the occasional instances when the husband asserts authority, and makes an allocative or administrative decision" (78).

The single-parent system or blended family system encounters special kinship concerns. For example, in divorced families special problems in communication develop depending upon whether the in-laws desire further communication with the ex-wife, husband, and their children. The former husband or wife may refuse to communicate with the "other side of the house"; children may become pawns and resent forced separation from legitimate kinship ties.

Kinship ties can cause communication problems when families-of-origin do not let go of their offspring; even as he or she joins a new system. Frequent meetings or contacts with the family-of-origin reinforces previous role expectancies. According to Longini (1979), an individual still ". . . maintains the part that has been assigned to him by his family. Clan pressure is a hard thing to resist" (9).

Since we believe that persons who consider themselves to be a family constitute a family, kinship ties often include extended family members bound together by caring. Such groups engage in similar kinship behaviors as those previously mentioned.

Since my immediate family is dead and any other relatives on my husband's side or my side live thousands of miles away, we have worked at creating a "local family." Over the years we have developed close friends who serve as honorary aunts and uncles for our children. The highlight of our Christmas is our annual dinner when we all get together to decorate the tree and the children get to see Uncle Bernard or Aunt Lois within a family context. I feel closer to these people than I do to many blood family members.

Such activities represent a special way for this woman to communicate the message to her family that kinship is important. In this mobile age where families often live great distances from all of their kin, or have few relatives, this idea has merit.

When family members feel safe with sharing their problems, joys, and family celebrations, they reap the benefits of the kinship function. The immediate system experiences the extra security, protection, and warmth of the larger unit of relatives. Ideally, communication can flow from kin outside the immediate family, back and forth with members inside the family, and be enriched and deepened by the support and sharing that occurs. The kinship circle can provide a ring of insulation around the family with communication serving as the vehicle for support and comfort.

Other Family Functions

Aside from the functions related to developing sexual identity, socializing children, being therapeutic, and maintaining kinship, adults in families need to engage in providing, housekeeping, caring for children, and recreating. We will examine each of these functions briefly.

Providing Function • Providing deals with satisfying the family's economic needs whereas the housekeeping deals with household maintenance. Overwhelmingly yet today men are expected to be major providers in families (3-1 in most studies) and laws and customs help to carry out these expectations. Studies reveal that both men and women feel that a married woman should work only if she wants to do so. If she does not have a husband and has children and day-care services, then a slight majority of the respondents think the woman should work.

Women have been limited traditionally in terms of the providing function which affects their decision-making and power within the family system. Although there have always been certain women who chose to work and others who headed families as single parents who were forced to work, recent changes have increased the percentage of the women in the work force. Due to inflation, increasing educational and career opportunities for women, improvements in day care and nursery schools, smaller families (2.85 people), greater numbers of female-headed single parent families, and automation in the home, women increasingly have gone to work and today comprise over 50 percent of the work force. Thus the providing function is being shared or assumed by single heads of families. As more men and women assume some type of joint responsibility for family provision, greater potential for shared power and decision making results.

Traditionally, in all classes, married women with more education are more likely to share in providing for the family. Yet, in one large study, over half the working couple's income went into a joint account which either could spend. Another third turned the money over to the wife to manage and disburse (Slocum & Nye, 1976, 85–86). This information about how much women provide and how income is managed will relate to conflicts in communication and to the kinds of functional communication the males and females engage in.

Such a shift in the providing function has modified the traditional housekeeping function. Such changes have a profound effect on everyday communication within the family as well as on male and female familial behavior.

When my father worked, he was the traditional male provider and bill payer. Since his retirement things have changed. My mother returned to work when my father retired. She has taken on responsibilities she never could have attempted before. For example, she pays most bills and even has her own credit cards. Of course, conflicts do happen. My father walks the line between his old position and his decreasing status. Because my father doesn't work he has more energy and free time to devote to housekeeping. My father insists mother doesn't realize how busy he is with shopping, etc., and that it's an all-day job and the work never gets done. Mom laughs and reminds him that she managed all the years he worked.

Housekeeping Function • The housekeeping function traditionally has meant the wife performs the cooking, cleaning, and maintenance of the home. This is changing. Although one survey showed that 70 percent of the men said housekeeping should be shared, they held that it was more the responsibility of the woman. Interestingly only 55 percent of the women thought it should be a shared responsibility (Slocum & Nye, 90). These figures were higher if the woman worked. Men are more likely to see housekeeping as an option whereas more women accept it as a responsibility. Housekeeping is most likely shared when the wife works full time, serving in a providing function, and when the couple has children. In many dual career families children are expected to take on new responsibilities such as babysitting, cooking, or cleaning, and other traditional housekeeping tasks, resulting in greater shared communication about practical issues. Such families face a time-bind and may have to work to find "quality-time" or time for nurturing communication to occur.

Most men strongly identify with the providing function and would be reluctant to give it up, but women do not identify that strongly with housekeeping. Women's days as primary housekeeper may be numbered (Slocum & Nye, 99), resulting in extensive renegotiation within families.

Child-Care Function • The child-care function or keeping the child physically and psychologically safe also is undergoing certain changes in today's society. For the child this means being bathed, dressed, fed, and housed adequately, plus protected from terrifying experiences (Gecas, 33). In our society of smaller families, and more deliberately childless couples, child care has diminished in importance for some families. Yet even in small families the arrival of children requires parents to assume child care and socialization responsibilities for a long period of time.

Especially during children's younger years such responsibilities may become a major communication focus and remain so for many years to come.

Having a baby was a real shock to our system. Although we wanted a child, we just never understood what a change would occur in our whole way of life. Marriage was nothing in terms of adjustment. After Alex was born we had a year in which all we talked about was diapers, formula, baby clothes, thermometers, etc. When we got some time to ourselves, we were too tired to do more than stare at TV or putter around the house. Our communication revolved around the baby and his needs, which was quite a switch for us.

Even when the children leave home, aspects of child care continue. Rossi (1968) sums it up when she declares "We can have ex-spouses and ex-jobs, but not ex-children" (32). Also more unwed mothers are opting to raise their children and more single parents have full responsibility for child care—making it an enormous task in some cases. Parents are under tremendous financial pressure as financial analysts detail the thousands of dollars a year it takes to raise a child. Caring for children involves a continual adaptation to their changes and involves decisions about whether to, and how best to, keep a child physically and psychologically safe.

Recreational Function • Although the last few functions appear very "task oriented," most families make room for recreation. Recreation means those things you do beyond work for relaxation, entertainment, or personal development (Dumazedier, 1967, 13–14). Families vary on whether the mother or father is responsible for carrying out the recreational function, but research indicates both spouses think it important and should be done (Carlson, 137). More husbands carry out recreating functions and feel more strongly about its values. Yet with the rise of two-career families and increased opportunities in sports for woman this may change.

Family recreating can be complicated because individual members have their own interests plus the desire or obligation to participate in family activities. Extremely cohesive families may demand "required fun" whereas families with low cohesion may not encourage much group activity.

Although the recreational function provides opportunities for nurturing communication, in some families people perform the role in isolation or non-familial settings or they bring pressure into the recreational setting. Stereotypically, men have found a recreational niche in tough masculine athletic behaviors whereas women engaged in less aggressive "fun." Parental behavior telegraphs to children what is expected recreational behavior and conflicts may result if a child does not measure up. Most of us have seen parents yelling at the Little League umpire or their eight-year-old batter who struck out. In some families recreation provides a means to escape from the family. Although some of these times may be important, if all recreation is separate, important shared communication experiences may be missed.

Communication may change during recreational activities. Communication between family members often improves when the family travels and leaves behind the usual routines. Discordant families, however, may find the opposite happens with their communication, as they cannot rely strictly on their usual reactions to get them through the day.

To this point we have examined eight functions of adult family roles. Each family will combine the functions in ways unique to how roles are enacted. In the Kondelis family, child rearing and child socialization may no longer be important functions, recreation may be highly valued and organized by the husband/father. Most housekeeping functions may be provided by a cleaning service, whereas providing may be done by husband and wife. In the Rosenthal family, the single-parent mother may engage primarily in the providing and therapeutic functions, delegating child care and socialization functions to the two older children. Recreation may be more individually oriented while kinship functions may receive limited attention.

There are other ways of viewing functions which would place greater emphasis on child-related functions, although as children mature they begin to participate actively in many of the functions. In certain cases children may be inappropriately required to engage in a type or amount of activity usually reserved for a spouse. For example, an older child may assume total child-care responsibilities or housekeeping responsibilities in a busy two-career household. In a single-parent system children may be expected to provide therapeutic listening or empathy that might be expected of a spouse in a two-parent household. Members of highly adaptable families may find themselves fulfilling numerous functions on an unpredictable schedule whereas in highly rigid families specific functions may be associated with the same individual indefinitely.

Thus the way persons in family roles engage in these functions reflects individual personalities and the actions of other system members.

COMMUNICATION AND ENACTMENT OF ROLE FUNCTIONS

I have had a great deal of experience with role conflict in my marriage. I spend most of the time with my in-laws wearing the mask of the "wonderful little woman-wife" who does all the traditional things while they act like guests in my home. The same formality and expectations occur when we visit them. I feel such a sense of relief when our visits are over because we each know this is a big fake but no one will remove the mask. I keep telling my husband that they will have to get used to our way of life but whenever we get together with them he and I fall into these patterns that we know will please them, because it's easier than dealing with their reactions.

As you well know, one doesn't just fall into a role or type comfortably and maintain it happily ever after. Much negotiation occurs as system members attempt to work their own definitions of the role interchange. Both interpersonal and individual conflicts may occur as members try to find what works for them.

Interpersonal Conflicts

Each of you probably can list countless reasons for interpersonal role conflict. In this section we will examine some representative examples including relinquishing expected functions, different expectations and priorities, lack of social acceptance, feelings for role-related others, and inappropriateness of role.

While individuals may know what is expected of them in a family, not all members perform the expected behaviors. For example, a husband may relinquish the provider function for voluntary or involuntary reasons: he may decide to write the Great American novel or he may have suffered a fall that prevents him from returning to work. Consequently, his wife may be thrust into providing for the family with resulting potential conflict.

If persons in complementary positions or significant others have different expectations of the way a person should be performing in a role, conflict may occur. A child may expect far more of a parent in the recreational function and whine or complain about the lack of emphasis on recreation. A wife may expect her husband to assume half the child socialization responsibility and resent his limited attention to what she considers his duty.

My mother always told me that I was too free in raising my children and that they would never grow up to amount to anything unless I disciplined them more. She was always holding up my cousin's parenting behavior to me since my cousin was a real disciplinarian and her kids were "perfect" at all family occasions. Well, my kids have done pretty well and my cousin's kids went crazy as adolescents, I think, because they were fighting for independence. I wish my mother had lived to see the difference.

If the priorities or goals of system members are not congruent with each other, role conflict may occur. If money is critical to one spouse and recreation has a high priority for the other, there may be major fights over how much time either spouse or both should devote to money-making efforts. For many couples the addition of the first baby signals a whole set of role changes which are often accompanied by conflict. One spouse may suddenly devote extensive time to the child-care function, thereby neglecting the therapeutic or kinship functions which the other spouse expects and values highly. If an individual needs approval for performing a function, the lack of it may lead to conflict and eventually the person may alter his or her behavior to reduce the tension. If you marry into a family with an established kinship network with expectations for many shared family get-togethers, you may be faced with rejection if you do not participate whole-heartedly in the family social pattern.

Feelings for the other person may affect the extent to which conflict occurs. A husband who has little feeling for his wife may criticize her performance in various functions and the resulting hostility may erupt into predictable conflicts. A parent may react differently to each child based on the child's behavior. A mother with extensive child-care responsibilities may abuse one child and not another based on differences in the children. In its informational literature on child abuse a state agency explains: ". . . if the child himself is a good baby who doesn't cry much, sleeps all night, eats well, and is generally responsive, he may escape abuse, even when there is significant potential for it" (Van Dyke, 1977, 3). Certain role conflicts may occur when inappropriate expectations develop. Some parents who find themselves suddenly single rely on their older children for support which is more appropriately spousal. A child may be co-opted into the therapeutic role and asked to function as a surrogate spouse to provide emotional support. Usually such actions lead to later conflict as both parties struggle to maintain roles that are not appropriate to the ages or relationship of the persons involved. Other family members often resent the favored status given to the co-opted brother or sister.

As the oldest daughter I ended up with a great deal of responsibility and feel as if I lost part of my own childhood. My mother was an alcoholic and my father and I almost became the "adult partners" in the house. He would spend hours telling me his problems and trying to work out ways to deal with Mom. He also expected me to take care of the younger kids and to fix meals when Mom was "drying out." Although I liked being so close to him, I hated all the work I had to do and all the responsibility. He didn't even want me to get married because he didn't know how he would cope.

Although these and other issues lead to interpersonal role conflict, some people experience role conflict within themselves.

Individual Conflicts

Occasionally people find themselves in roles that do not fit with their self-concepts, and this leads to internal conflict.

Although everyone else seems to accept parenthood well, I have had real problems with seeing myself as a father. I have always had this image of myself as a rising young executive with the "good life" of nice money and freedom. Although the baby has affected us monetarily, through the loss of my wife's salary, the greatest problem is running our lives around another person. I resent giving up all my freedom and wish we had put off having a child until later when I might have been more ready for the responsibilities.

Many people experience difficulty adjusting to child-care functions that might be expected of them. Others find that they did not expect to be breadwinners or do not see themselves as integral members of an extensive kinship network. Such differences between how you see yourself and how you find yourself acting often lead to intense internal conflicts and interpersonal conflicts.

Finally, persons may find themselves in roles that they expected to assume comfortably but which they cannot perform adequately. Although the new "superwoman" is pictured as balancing a career, household duties, and childrearing duties with equanimity, many young women have discovered that there are not enough hours in a day to maintain such a schedule, and they cannot fulfill their ideal wife/mother role. This often leads to disappointment and anger at oneself for not fulfilling expectations.

Such interpersonal and individual role conflicts necessitate sensitive and extensive communication among members of a family system if the system is to be recalibrated to fit the needs of individual members. Such role negotiations may provide opportunities for the communication development of each member involved.

Roles and Communication Competence

Certain role conceptions may constrain or limit the communication competence developed by family members. If, based on her expectations and her husband's responses, a woman perceives she should assume all therapeutic functions, she may continue to develop her listening and empathy skills but may never develop competence in assertion, leadership, and argument. If her husband plays his role as complementary to hers, he may never develop the ability to show caring, concern, or supportiveness since he sees the position of husband as requiring aggressive and strong leadership behaviors. Some children may never experience negotiation, leadership, or persuasion because in their position-oriented family they learn "You know what's expected of you. That's all there is to it."

Particular role conceptions may drastically restrict the topics of conversation which serves to limit competence. For example, men who view the provider function as their sole responsibility may tend to keep job-related concerns out of the family setting excluding wives from experience in discussing such issues. If child care and socialization are considered the wife's domain, fathers may be limited in how they talk to, and about, their children. Position-oriented families provide less communication flexibility and opportunities to try new ways of relating to others.

Roles constitute an important way of regulating family life. Yet if they are viewed as "set in stone" descriptions of how people in certain family positions should act, they will limit personal and system growth. Rather roles should be seen as reflections of the individual and his or her interpersonal encounters, a conception which implies a transactional growth process.

Although role analysis remains a very common way of viewing family systems, increasing attention has been given to the use of family typologies for understanding family interaction. The next section will introduce this concept.

FAMILY AND COUPLE TYPOLOGIES

Although role analysis remains a very common way of viewing family systems, increasing attention has been given to the use of family and marital typologies for understanding family interaction. Family behavior and organization can be conceptualized by classifying the different family systems into typologies or family types depending upon the patterns of their interactions. When these types emerge, with consistency of behavior under certain recognizable conditions, we are able to make some predictions about members' behavior. Varied approaches have been developed; we will introduce some basic concepts from several representative ones in order to understand their communication implications.

Family Types: Kantor and Lehr

Relying on intensive study of nineteen families, including normal and disturbed, researchers Kantor and Lehr (1976) developed a descriptive theory of family process. They identified basic component parts of family process and how these parts affected members' behavior.

As a means of dealing with the basic family issue of separateness and connectedness, or what Kantor and Lehr called "distance regulation," they developed a six-dimensional social space grid on which family communication takes place. All communication represents efforts by family members to gain access to targets, i.e., things or ideas members want or need, according to these researchers. Specifically, family members use two sets of dimensions. One set reaches targets of affect, power, and meaning through the way they regulate the other—the access dimensions of space, time, and energy. Thus families regulate the activities of people, objects, and events.

All family members in carrying out the functions in any role have a target or goal of gaining some degree of affect, power, or meaning. Affect means achieving (e.g., in the kinship or socialization functions) some kind of intimacy or connectedness with the members of the family and receiving some reward in the form of nurturing behavior in their verbal and nonverbal communication. Power implies a member has the independence to select what she or he wants and the ability to get the money, skills, or goods desired. This freedom to choose what an individual wants gives a family member power and the separateness needed to develop autonomy. The third target is meaning. Each family member in the system seeks some philosophical rationale that offers reasons for what happens to them in the family and outside world. The acquisition of meaning by each member develops stronger self-concepts and provides an explanation of why members live as they do. When family members collectively find meaning in their interactions, cohesion develops.

Kantor and Lehr provide descriptions of the access dimensions (space, time, and energy) from an analogical as well as a physical point of view. The spatial dimensions include the way a family handles its physical surroundings (exterior and interior) and the ways in which the members' communication regulates their psychological distance from each other. The time dimension includes a consideration of clock time and calendar time in order to understand a family's basic rhythmic patterns. The energy dimension deals with the storing and expending of physical and psychological energy. Family communication usually involves at least one access dimension and one target dimension. For example, Kathy moves physically closer to Charlie, her husband, in order to gain more affection from him.

Using these six dimensions, the authors create a typology for viewing normal families, consisting of open, closed, and random types, acknowledging that actual families may consist of mixtures of types. The ways in which these three family systems types maintain their boundaries, or regulate distance through access and target dimensions, account for their differences.

Closed-type families tend to regulate functions predictably with fixed boundaries. Such families interact less with the outside world and require members to fulfill their needs, and spend their time and energies within the family. Usually an emphasis on authority occurs and the continuation of family values assumes an important place. Events in closed families tend to be tightly scheduled and predictable. Family members often focus on the preservation of the past or plan for the future. Energy is controlled, used to maintain the system, and dispersed at a steady rate. Moderation, rather than excess, prevails.

In the open-type family, the boundaries tend to remain flexible as members are encouraged to seek experiences in the outside space and return to the family with ideas the family may use if group consensus develops. Open families seldom use censorship, force, or coercion because they believe family goals will change, vary, and be subject to negotiation. They carry these characteristics into intimacy and conflict situations. Members are more likely to concern themselves with the present. Energy in this type of system is quite flexible. Family members do not have total freedom because they cannot cause excess harm or discomfort to other family members by using any method to refuel their energy. For example, a child can't play records at the loudest level after ten o'clock at night when other family members decide to get some sleep.

Unpredictability or "do-your-own-thing" aptly describes the random-type family. The boundaries of space surrounding the family are dispersed. Family members and outsiders join in the living space based on interest or desire, or they voluntarily separate from one another, without censure. Social appropriateness holds little importance for such members. Time is spent on an irregular basis. Each individual functions according to his or her own rhythm resulting in high levels of spontaneity. People may change their minds and their plans at any point.

Energy in the random-type family fluctuates. No one source for refueling has been predetermined by the family. Members may rapidly spend high levels of energy and then need long refueling periods. To refuel, they choose from a wide variety of sources for new energy and direction.

I think we must have been a random family during the first ten years of my life. I am next to last of 11 children and by the time I came along the family was in chaos. The younger kids lived with different relatives off and on until we were almost adolescents. When we did live at home, things were always unpredictable. Every morning my mother would put a big pot of cereal on the stove and people would eat when they wanted. Other meals were usually haphazard, although the food was always there. You never knew exactly who was going to be sleeping where each night, and no one really told me much about what to do. When I was about ten my parents got their own life straightened out and enough older kids were gone so that we could live a more "normal" life, although I found it hard to suddenly have rules that were enforced and times when I had to be places.

Table 6-1 summarizes the characteristics that Kantor and Lehr delineated for each of these family types. Although the descriptions are superficial, each of you may have identified more closely with one of the types, or you may have imagined that your family incorporates two of the types. Also, you may have realized how your family has shifted in typology over the years.

Table 6-1 Characteristics of Family Types

Type of Family	Use of Space	Time	Energy
Closed	Fixed	Regular	Steady
Open	Movable	Variable	Flexible
Random	Dispersed	Irregular	Fluctuating

As I grew up my family could be described as a closed-type family. My parents kept an ever watchful eye over my three sisters' activities by scrutinizing friends, watching phone calls, keeping strict curfews, chaperoning dates, and generally isolating our family from "them," that is, the rest of the South Bronx community. Time in my family was rather regular because, although my mother also worked, each of my sisters knew what her job was and was expected to carry it out. Dad and Mom knew where you were going, who you were with, and told you what time to return. The communication pattern, mostly nonverbal, was also simple: the better you behaved, the more privileges you were allowed, and as soon as you went against the rules set up by my parents, privileges were abolished and punishment was introduced.

Then things changed. When my father died, I found myself closer to my mother and vice versa. My sisters also found themselves closer, not only to my mother, but to each other as well. Thus, since that time, I feel my family has gradually progressed from a more closed to a more open type of family. Affection and support of each other is seen much more readily today than it was ten years ago. A general rule in our current family is that any requests for either joining or separating are viewed as reasonable and legitimate. Conflicts arise, and so do fights, but these are an important part in the decision-making process. Although feelings may be hurt, they are aired out more often now than ever before; and will hopefully lead to constructive criticisms and arrangements.

Couple-Oriented Research: Fitzpatrick Couple Types

Another approach to classifying systems may be found in Fitzpatrick's couple-oriented research. In her early work, Fitzpatrick (1976; 1977) tested a large number of characteristics to find out which made a difference in maintaining couple relationships. She isolated eight significant factors: conflict avoidance, assertiveness, sharing, the ideology of traditionalism, the ideology of uncertainty and change, temporal (time) regularity, undifferentiated space, and autonomy. An individual or a couple fits a type when their answers indicate they share a number of characteristics. From this study Fitzpatrick designated relational definitions of Traditional, Separates, and Independents, plus the combination type, Separate/Traditional. The following is a brief summary of the types.

Independent types accept uncertainty and change; pay limited attention to schedules and traditional values. Independents represent the most autonomous of the types, but do considerable sharing and negotiate autonomy. They do not avoid conflict. Independents are more likely to support an androgynous and flexible sex role.

Separates differ from Independents in greater conflict avoidance, more differentiated space needs, fairly regular schedules, and less sharing. In relationships, Separates maintain a certain distance from people and problems, even their spouses; they experience little sense of togetherness. Separates usually oppose an androgynous sexual orientation. Separates lack a sense of togetherness or autonomy and tend to avoid conflict.

Traditionals uphold a fairly conventional belief system and resist change or uncertainty since it threatens their routines. Physical and psychological sharing characterizes the Traditional type and this leads to a high degree of interdependence and low autonomy. Few boundaries exist in the couples' use of physical and emotional space. They will engage in conflict, but would rather avoid it. Uncertainty and change in values upset them. Traditionals, like Separates, demonstrate strong sex-typed roles and oppose an androgynous orientation.

The final type is the combination Separate-Traditional. In the 40 percent of the couples who were not the same type, most of the husbands labeled themselves as Separates and the wives labeled themselves as Traditionals.

Which relational type experiences the greater satisfaction? Which couples are the most cohesive? In their summary of the research, Fitzpatrick and Best (1979) report Traditional couples significantly higher than the other three types on consensus, cohesion, relational satisfaction, and expressing affection. Independents were definitely lower on consensus, open affection to one another, and dyadic satisfaction; however, their lack of agreement on issues regarding dyadic interactions did not impair their cohesiveness. Separates were the least cohesive but on relational issues appeared high on consensus. Separates demonstrated few expressions of affection toward their spouses and rated lower on dyadic satisfaction. In the Separate (husband)/Traditional (wife) category the couple had low consensus on a number of relational issues but they were moderately cohesive. These couples claimed high satisfaction for their relationship and outwardly expressed much affection for one another.

Further findings indicated that couples who agreed on relational definitions agreed with one another on a greater number of issues in their relationship. Those who agreed were also more cohesive. Interestingly couples who disagreed on typing themselves were as satisfied with their marriages as couples who agreed on their definitions. Enduring relationships were characterized by more variety in the modes of communication used by partners (Fitzpatrick & Best, 167).

In predicting communication you might expect that Traditional families would demonstrate affection and sharing functions in the functions discussed earlier in this chapter with males and females remaining in defined positions. You could expect male dominance in attitudes and values regarding the providing, recreational, housekeeping, sex, and kinship function since the Traditional type resists change. Since Independents are more open to change, they might be more open to dual-career marriages and sharing the providing and housekeeping functions. Because Independents value autonomy and avoid interdependence, individual couple members may be freer in their role functions. This self-reliance might better equip Independents to handle the unknown and accept the inevitable changes that occur in roles and life.

The potential for communication problems over role functions relates especially to the Separates who have not resolved the interdependence/autonomy issue in their marriage. Fitzpatrick uses the label "emotionally divorced" for this type, because Separates are least likely to express their feelings to their partners. Thus if a partner is dissatisfied with the role expectations of the other spouse, yet cannot freely express these feelings, the relationship suffers. This may lead to open conflict which Separates would probably resolve, not by identifying their feelings, but by negotiating some compromise based on values they share. Fitzpatrick's work is ongoing and should provide further insights in these, and potentially other couple types, over time.

Burgess's Marriage Types

Finally we note Burgess's distinction between two types of marriage: "institutional" and "companionship" (1963). In institutional marriages, roles are sex differentiated, meaning males predominantly take charge of the provider, recreation, and sex roles and wives carry out the child care, child socialization, housekeeping, therapeutic, and kinship roles. Husbands are more instrumental and rigid in their roles and wives are more expressive and flexible.

Couples in a companionship-type marriage place an emphasis upon their personalities interacting and the affective aspects of their relationship. Love is openly expressed. Sexual enjoyment, companionship, and communication are expected to follow.

Burgess believes the family is in transition from an institutional to a companionship type of relationship. Within the new companionship, family ". . . unity comes less and less from community pressures and more and more from such interpersonal relations as the mutual affection, sympathetic understanding and comradeship of its members" (Burgess et al., vii).

In his study of graduate student marriages, exploring companionship and institutional couples, Masterson (1977) found that in both types there was a direct positive relationship between a married couple's level of overt talking about their relationship and the couple's level of perceived satisfaction (6). This points up the importance of open expressed communication in the roles in a family. Other studies have proved a strong positive correlation between congruence of role perceptions and satisfaction in those roles. (See Luckey, 1960; Stuckert, 1963; Kotlar, 1965; Taylor, 1967.)

The previous brief presentation of Kantor and Lehr's family types and Fitzpatrick's and Burgess's couple types cannot do justice to the intricacies of their conceptual schemes. Over time this and other related research should continue to provide a fruitful backdrop for analyzing family communication.

CONCLUSION

In this chapter we took a transactional approach to roles, stressing the effect of family interaction on how roles are enacted. We examined the potential effect of position-oriented versus person-oriented role functioning on communication within the family system. After reviewing the various role functions within a family, we presented a typological approach to understanding families and their communication patterns.

A major consideration in examining roles or couple/family types is to view them as dynamic and ever changing, in accordance with the personal developments and unpredictable circumstances faced by the people involved. No matter how straightforward each role or type appears, they are assumed and maintained on the basis of personal choice and adaptation to the overall family system. We hope this examination of roles has given you some insights into how families function in carrying out basic tasks that satisfy physical and emotional needs of each member.

7

Power in Families

In my family-of-origin my father is the power structure. Nearly all decisions rest with him. My mom is capable of making them (and does at times) but Dad usually does. My mom does influence the decisions but Dad announces them. Both parents disciplined us as children but our greatest fear was of our father. His personality and character demanded respect from his children, friends, peers, etc. He hit us when we needed it. In my present family, my wife and I both share power and responsibility. She doesn't make an issue of authority and neither do I. My wife is very capable of decision making and of future planning so I go along with her sometimes and she does the same with me. Each one of us plays our strengths and we try to allow the children some freedom in declaring what they want.

When you think about the power in your family, you may immediately think of one individual who seems to lead or dominate, you may picture shared responsibilities among many people, or you may imagine one or two quiet persons who seem to pull the strings while another appears as a figurehead of power. You may even encounter all these people in one family, demonstrating the complexity of the family power issue.

Any relationship in a family contains a potential power struggle and the members involved continuously define and redefine their relationship. The main goal within "the power dimension of family life is the ability to effect what the system wants, to get done what it wants to get done . . ." (Kantor and Lehr, 1976, 49). This means that any power maneuvers within the family system affect the degree of freedom and restraint for all within the family organization. Picture the chaos if each person in your family did totally what he or she wished; no family goals could ever be achieved.

For many years researchers have been studying power in couples and families, debating over their results. "The topic of power in marital relations is undoubtedly the most controversial issue in family sociology today" (Osmond, 1978b, 58). Research conclusions depend upon what kinds of families were studied, what dimensions of power were isolated for examination, who asked or answered the questions about power, whether children were included or excluded from the study, what vested interest or motivation family members had in the outcome of the power plays within the family, what alternatives for power existed outside the family, and countless other factors. From this controversy there came agreement among the experts that power is an exceedingly complex concept and that no one approach answers all the important questions about power (Cromwell and Olson, 1975, 3–5).

THE CONCEPT OF POWER

Although power may be viewed in many ways, we need to examine it within a systems context. Family researcher Wolfe (1959) stresses that power does not belong to an individual, rather it is a *property of a relationship* between two or more persons. Thus the following definition: "Power, a system property, is the ability (potential or actual) of an individual(s) to change the behavior of other members in a social system" (Cromwell and Olson, 5). In addition, family power is defined as the "ability (potential or actual) of individual members to change the behavior of other family members." We must not think of power in a family as static or fixed. The power dimension in a family system may vary greatly over time, depending upon a host of factors. For example, the age of the children or parents; the amount of predictable and unpredictable stress encountered by the family; the economic, cultural, or intellectual resources and opportunities of the family—these all affect power. Power operates transactionally in a family and any power maneuvers within it have a systemwide effect. One member cannot assert independence or dependence on an issue without other members being affected. As one or more members exert power or acquiesce to power plays of one or more other family members, the whole system may be recalibrated. If you recall our discussion in Chapter 2, you will remember that a human system has properties of interdependence and wholeness. The transactional nature of power within a family creates independence with one another. The total potential power in the family system is greater than the sum of all the individual members' power. Each child or parent has the power to affect the relationship of one or all other people within the family as long as the others allow this to happen.

The system, through its adaptability mechanisms, reacts to all pressures and maintains some kind of balance between the power plays and the players.

> It's hard to really locate the source of power in my family. My mother appears to have the power because she can be so stubborn and demanding, although my father comes in a close second. Power is enforced merely by the threat of household warfare, which none of us can stand except my mother who seems to enjoy it. Yet, I can see that my grandmother has great power to change things in our family by influencing my mother, and thus getting to me. She just says a few things that make my mother feel guilty and everyone has to shape up for a week.

Each of us could relate incidents of power plays or where we think the power lies, but sometimes we may miss a power base or power play because of how we think of "power." In order to examine power in families more carefully, we have to look at the many ways it works by examining (1) family power operations, (2) development of family power, and (3) the communication of power strategies.

FAMILY POWER OPERATIONS

To further clarify the concept of power, we will examine four family power operations: (1) power bases, (2) power exchange, (3) power processes, and (4) power outcomes.

Power Bases

The bases of family power are the resources a family member possesses to increase his or her chances to exert control in a specific situation. No two family members possess exactly the same resources to achieve their ends. You may have power because of your education or your ability to be assertive. Your sister's power may come from her temper while your mother may have the power of vetoing decisions. Yet unless others respond to these power positions, no power actually can be exerted. If your brother does not respond to your assertiveness, you are powerless in relationship to him. In order to understand the sources of power more completely, let us examine six bases of social power that can affect family systems (French and Raven, 1962; Raven, Centers, Rodrigues, 1975, 218–219).

1. Punishment or coercive power serves as a power base when you believe someone can punish you for acting or not acting in a certain way. Such coercive power may be based on Brian's belief that his wife Margaret can and will punish him for refusal of her requests. A child may hold power by "threatening" to punish his parents by repeated screams. Withholding money, food, or favors serves as power punishment.

2. Positive reinforcement or reward power serves as a base when you believe someone can provide you with something you desire. Brian may expect that Margaret will do something nice for him if he cooperates. Messy rooms have

been cleaned, dinners cooked, cars washed for movie money! Reward giving definitely affects power—if you control the rewards some family member wants or needs.

3. Expertise or knowledge serves as a power base when you believe another family member knows more about a subject than you do. Expertise derives from Brian's awareness that Margaret has superior knowledge of a given subject or skill to direct him to the best solution. A teenager may instruct his or her mother on car care and maintenance and she may accept this expertise.

4. Legitimacy or position serves as a power base when you accept that a certain role carries with it certain legitimate responsibilities. Legitimate power occurs when Brian accepts a certain role in their relationship, believing that Margaret has the authority or right to expect compliance and he feels obliged to grant it. A daughter may accept her father's curfew because she understands such regulations as a part of the fathering position.

5. Identification or referent power serves as a base when you see yourself as similar to another and you accept that position. Such identification power occurs when Brian identifies with Margaret, because he feels she possesses attributes he admires and he gets satisfaction from agreeing with her. A 10-year-old girl may identify with her 15-year-old sister and follow her sister's requests in order to feel "grown up" like her.

6. Persuasion or information power serves as a base when you accept the carefully structured arguments of another. Such informational power develops from Margaret's communication ability to carefully and successfully explain to Brian the reasons for a change. A mother may carefully detail the budget problems and persuade her children to keep their winter jackets one more year.

Note that these power terms are defined in the way in which the situation is perceived by others. In a family relationship no member is going to possess all six of these power sources equally or use all of them in a given situation. Some may never be used and others used in combination. It's possible for a husband to use, for example, reward and expertise power extensively in his interactions and simultaneously for his wife to use punishment and identification power in her interactions with husband and children. Children in the same family might use legitimacy and persuasion power, especially if their views are encouraged and respected.

We have six people living in our immediate household and I can see that many different kinds of power are used. My husband used to use a great deal of punishment power with the children and now he seems to use legitimacy as a way to get his own way. I have always tried to use a positive reward type of power and have tried to be knowledge-able about a subject before telling others what to do about it. My daughter-in-law tries to use persuasion most of the time. I can just see her planning her arguments and strategies. My son tries coercion with the children but seems to rely on legitimacy when he and his wife have differences. The baby runs the whole show sometimes since he is able to manipulate us all by crying. His sister, who is "Mommy's little girl" accepts her mother's identification power but I can't put my finger on her power style.

Think about power in your family. Which power bases operate in it that help explain why power functions in your family the way it does? What bases are you most likely to use? Which bases affect you most directly?

Power Exchange

Power moves in families relate to the exchange theory discussed in previous chapters. These remarks indicate uses of exchange theory and relational currencies:

"It's a trade-off. I go along with him and then I get some peace and quiet." "I feel good when I help my in-laws with their tax problems." "My kid brother feels big hanging around me and my friends and we get him to run errands for us."

One way to understand better the underlying basis of family power is to examine it in light of social exchange since power may be said to arise from an imbalance in exchange resources (McCall & Simmons, 1966, 157). The members of the relationship who can provide the greatest rewards may be said to have the greatest power. In their study of marital power, Blood and Wolfe (1960) assert "The balance of power will be on the side of that partner who contributes the greater resources to the marriage." As we saw in Chapter 4, resources consist of whatever is rewarding to an individual or a relationship. "A resource can be anything that one spouse may make available to the other, helping that spouse to satisfy his or her needs or attain his or her goals" (Blood and Wolfe, 68). Any of the previously mentioned sources of power may be tied to rewards. It may be rewarding to avoid punishment to gain positive reinforcement, to learn from an expert, to live within certain defined constraints, to identify with another person, to be persuaded, or most importantly, to be confirmed by others.

In applying exchange theory to power, the assumption is that in long-term relationships individuals behave in a manner to optimize the differences between the rewards and costs they experience (Cromwell and Olson, 10). As Homans (1958) says, "Persons that give much to others try to get much from them, and persons that get much from others are under pressure to give much to them" (606). These pressures can involve all forms of power and become resources to be used for alternative strategies. If this theory were pushed to the extreme it would mean that a family member stays in a relationship as long as the rewards outweigh the costs. However, over a period of time, family members store up relationship debts and credits. The family members who suffer from an abuse of power or an injustice caused by one or more in the family may become upset, yet also remember other experiences that pleased them—times when power uses and resources satisfied their own needs. They balance this current problem against what has happened to them in the past within the family and weigh it in terms of future payoffs.

When the consequences of remaining together overtake the advantages, separation or distancing may happen. Possible extreme consequences are divorce, desertion, suicide, murder, beatings, or running away. The exit act may be an important power play left to a family member, but it can create new problems. Children may be trapped and have to wait to exercise their power to reject a defective family system.

Thus, family members have power over others to the degree that they can control the others' rewards and costs. Family members consciously and unconsciously obtain certain outcomes from the actions they use in a power struggle. In many well-functioning families members attempt to provide rewards for each other in order to maintain a certain level of harmony.

In his review of power in families, Berger (1980) suggests that although Blood and Wolfe found positive relationship between the income, educational level, and occupation prestige of the husband and the extent of his power, ". . . the *absolute* number of resources a person brings to the marriage does not determine his or her power, but rather the *relative* contribution of resources to the relationship" (210). He maintains that most of the studies he reviewed provide support for the resource theory but found notable exceptions particularly in studies of other cultures. Berger concludes that resources have been defined narrowly—mainly as economic contributions and social prestige, and suggests that family research should include an analysis of resources such as interpersonal skills and personality orientations such as dominance, physical attractiveness, and a sense of humor (214).

One alternative way of viewing power in the conjugal dyad involves an examination of the extent to which one spouse loves and needs the other. Safilios-Rothschild (1970), following up on Waller's earlier research on the principle of least interest, suggests that the spouse with the strongest feelings puts himself or herself in a less powerful position because the person with less interest can more easily control the one more involved (548–549). She also suggests that the existence of an alternative relationship provides power to one or another family member.

One of the ways I was able to finally live at home with some degree of peace was to make it clear to my father that I could and would go and live with his sister if he kept hitting me. My mother agreed with my position although she didn't like it and he finally realized I was serious. Once he understood that I had somewhere else to go he began to treat me better.

In discussing alternatives for couples, Berger states, "The mere existence of alternatives does not ensure increased power for the spouse who has them; in addition, the other spouse must have some degree of commitment to the relationship so that the alternatives of the other spouse represent a real threat" (215).

If Roger doesn't care deeply about Susan anymore, he may not become terribly upset by an affair with another man, and Susan may not be able to use this new interest in a power play to win Roger back. According to exchange theory, the continuing costs of Roger remaining in the relationship do not equal the potential rewards. Even though couples may enter a relationship with unequal power, the relationship can balance out over time. One family member may have most of the power in one area and another member in another area. They could perceive their power as balanced. Also the sharing of decisions and tasks causes the balancing principle of the exchange theory to operate successfully. After the establishment of an exchange relationship, spouses "are able to perceive the relative reward outcomes that emerge from the interaction and to judge whether or not such rewards appear equitable or fair" (Osmond, 1978b, 51). Many couples may attempt to develop family themes which stress equality of power for them and some sharing of power with the children. Themes such as "each person is an individual" or "we respect all opinions" may lead to shared power.

Thus the resource theory represents the most commonly accepted basis of power but certainly not the only one you may consider. In the following sections, we will examine more closely ways of observing power at work in a relationship.

Power Processes

The area that reveals how power operates in a family involves power processes or the study of ongoing interaction among family members. These processes are found in the ways power affects interactions in family discussions, arguments, problem solving, decision making, and times of crises. Researchers have examined the number of times people talk, how long they talk, to whom they address their comments, and how long a talk session lasts. They have also analyzed questioning patterns, interrupting patterns, and silence patterns and concluded that "Persons who talk most frequently and for the longest periods of time are assumed to be the most dominant group members. In addition, persons receiving the most communication are assumed to be most powerful" (Berger, 217). In order to get this data, families were asked to hold discussions and make decisions while their comments were recorded for careful analysis.

Yet, as you know from your own experience, the longest or loudest talker may not hold the power in each situation. We may have to distinguish between the power attempts a person makes and the final outcomes. We can look at assertiveness and control maneuvers that attempt to affect family power. Assertiveness means the number of attempts, for example, that Debra makes to change the behavior of her husband or her sister. Control represents the influence or number of effective attempts that Debra made that did change the behavior of her husband or sister (Cromwell and Olson, 6).

When we discussed communication in Chapter 3, we examined the complexities of each message. Bateson and Ruesch (1951) describe how impossible it is for a person to avoid offering definitions of his or her relationship with another. All messages in any family are co-defined by the senders and the receivers. They contain both report and command factors. Thus mixed messages may be sent which become difficult to analyze accurately. In our discussion of mixed messages in Chapter 1, we noted that when an individual says one thing but means and wants something else confusion results. The contradiction often appears in the nonverbal aspects of the message. In analyzing power messages, both the report and command dimensions must be analyzed carefully to understand the communication within a family. According to Haley (1974), "a person who acts helpless attempts to control the behavior in a relationship just as effectively as another who acts authoritarian and insists on a specific behavior" (371). The following example illustrates how mixed messages with conflicting report and command components operate in one family:

My sisters and I refer to it as the "Greek Mother Syndrome" since that's our background, but it's the old "Have a good time and don't worry about your poor old mother" game. My friends think my mother is really neat and flexible because of the things she says in front of them, but only I know what she really means. "Of course Irene can get her own apartment" or "Young women need to get off on their own these days" sounds terrific but I can tell from her tone of voice and her face that she would die if I tried to be that independent.

In this and other families an analysis of power processes involves examining the ongoing interactions of family members in discussions, decision making, resolving conflicts, problem solving, crises interventions, etc., in an attempt to determine who can affect or change the others' behavior.

Power Outcomes

The final area, family power outcomes, focuses upon "issues involving who makes decisions and who wins" (Cromwell and Olson, 6). Power outcomes means that one or more family members gets his or her way or receives rights or privileges of leadership.

It's amazing how getting out of the house can change your power within the family. As a teenager I felt that my stepfather gave me very little freedom and that was one of the reasons I joined the Navy after high school. Now when I go home he asks me what I want to do and he even asks what he should do about my younger sister who is rebelling all over the place. I suggested that he stop giving her such a rough time about her boyfriend and he seems to have taken my advice.

More research has been done on power outcomes, especially on decision-making, than on power bases or power processes (Cromwell and Olson, 6). Some of the findings in this area are reported in the decision-making chapter. Researchers have studied whose ideas are accepted by the family groups, who in the family went along with whom, whose influence counted in which situations. It is easier to measure power outcomes than to measure power processes. Yet in many cases predictions made from the processes are not accurate. The loudest, longest talker may not have his ideas accepted. The most persuasive adult may lose to an angry child.

Each family uses a variety of power sources relevant to its needs and the personalities involved. In some families, traditional roles, including the biosocial issue of male dominance, are clearly defined and since no one challenges them, the family operates as if that were the only way to function. In other families, negotiation has resulted in mutually acceptable compromises on power issues. In the following section we will consider the development of power within the marital and family system.

DEVELOPMENT OF POWER IN THE FAMILY

My grandfather was an immigrant who made it in this country through a construction business he founded with what he saved. He was always the undisputed head of his household and my grandmother went along with his requests or demands. They had four children. My grandfather attempted to run the lives of his sons because he thought they would take over the business. He was very influential in who they married and used his money to help control their lives. My mother and father had huge fights about what my mother called his "interference" in their lives and finally they split because my mother felt my father was married to the business. I think the divorce really shook my father up because he does not allow my grandfather to have any dealings with my stepmother and she seems to run their lives now.

Due to the systemic nature of a marital or family relationship, power occurs in a transactional manner. An alcoholic spouse cannot control the other spouse unless the nonalcoholic permits it. A mother relinquishes her own personal control when she gives a whining child power over her. Probably only the small child who has limited means of resisting power moves must accept certain power outcomes; for example, an abused toddler has few means of resisting punishment. Women have also argued that they have limited means of resisting power because in our culture power outcomes have been largely and sometimes unfairly managed by men. What goes on in society certainly does affect the development of power within families.

Gillespie (1971) claims that as long as the structure of society remains the same, carrying with it the "right" of men to make major decisions about moving, careers, investments, etc., that the majority of women have little chance to gain autonomy regardless of how much good will there was on the part of their husbands.

Blood and Wolfe disagree with Gillespie, presenting a view that although some husbands have extensive power they cannot take for granted the authority held by previous generations of males. Today's husband ". . . must prove his right to power, or win power by virtue of his own skills and accomplishments in competition with his wife" (29).

These thoughts about power between men and women relate family boundaries, themes, and biosocial issues. If a family decides that each member, regardless of sex, should develop his or her potential in order to be self-sufficient, the power process and outcomes will differ from a family which believes men should take care of the women members. This would limit the boundaries and possible future power options of female members.

In the latter family the boundaries of female experience more likely would be limited to contacts and training for homemaking and child rearing rather than banking or financial management of a corporation. If, however, the family cultivates a theme of achievement for every member, like "The Nicholsens rank at the top of their classes" or "The Wayne Jones family will be active in politics and public service," the power dimensions will reflect these goals. Over time the family in its system creates patterns of power that reveal to outsiders how these themes operate.

Types of Power Patterns

Spousal authority may be examined by the number and type of areas over which each spouse exercises authority. The spouse with the greater range of authority has the higher relative authority. Spouses may have shared authority, where there are areas of life jointly managed. According to Wolfe, there are four authority types: wife dominant, husband dominant, syncratic, and autonomic. In the husband or wife dominated families, major areas of activity are influenced and controlled by the dominant one. The following statements may sound familiar to some of you:

Mother decides everything and gets her way by using her temper yelling, screaming and crying if Dad or any of us strongly object.

Father determines when to cut the grass; time for sons to get haircuts; how long my sisters can wear their hair; where to eat or go for entertainment or groceries; when Mom or any of us kids can leave the house after supper.

I wait and wait—until he finally decides he can come home for dinner, get ready to go out, etc. We never go anywhere on time.

This dominance by one spouse or the other permeates all areas of family power: the use of resources, the power processes, and the power outcomes. One spouse demonstrates control of power in the system with the other accepting such control.

In married couples with more equally divided power, the structure can be described as either *syncratic* or *autonomic* (Herbst, 1952, 3–5). A syncratic relationship, characterized by much shared authority and joint decision making, implies that each spouse has a strong say in all important areas.

> When Ed and I married we agreed never to make big decisions alone and we've been able to live with that. This way we share the risks and the joys of whatever happens. It just works out best between us if we wait on deciding all important matters until we sound out the other's opinions. Neither of us wants to force the other to accept something disliked. It's when we decide over the little things that I know that each of us respects the rights of the other and wants equal consideration.

In the autonomic type of power structure the couple divides up the authority, i.e., the husband and wife have relatively equal authority but in different areas of life. Each spouse becomes completely responsible for specific matters. The division of areas usually closely coincides with the roles expectations.

Shared power situations reflect specific agreements or role definition about who controls what situations. The wife might have more power over the budget, vacation plans, and choice of new home and the husband more power over the selection of schools for children, buying anything with a motor in it, and whether the family moves to another state (Raven, Centers, Rodrigues, 218). The following examples typify such sharing:

> In our house I decide long-range programs—repainting the house, remodeling, or landscaping. I also shop for food, liquor, and appliances. My wife selects the nursery schools, arranges for baby sitters when she's at work, chooses the pediatrician, dentist, etc. and makes the social appointments.
>
> Her two children live with us. My three children do not. She makes all decisions regarding her children and her own financial affairs. Together we make all decisions about housing, summer vacation, spending income from our apartment building or reinvesting, and what movies or sports events we see.

Such structures may affect conflict patterns. Allen and Straus (1979) found high violence when the conjugal power structure is either extremely husband-dominant or wife-dominant. A further finding indicated that the lower a husband's economic and prestige resources relative to his wife, the more likely he would use physical violence (coercive power) to maintain a dominant male power position (85). Another study revealed that dissatisfaction in marriage relates closely to coercive power on the part of the spouse (Raven, Centers, and Rodrigues).

If you lived in a two-parent system, how would you classify the type of power exhibited? Would it be father or husband dominated, mother or wife dominated, syncratic, or autonomic? To what extent has this pattern changed over time? If it has changed, what accounts for the change?

Power and Marital Satisfaction

As you might imagine, certain power-arrangements increase marital satisfaction for certain couples. High levels of marital satisfaction occur most frequently among egalitarian couples (using syncratic or autonomic types) followed by husband-dominant couples and least among wife dominant couples (Corrales, 1975, 198). In a study of 776 couples in the Los Angeles area, over two-thirds of husband dominant, syncratic, and autonomic couples reported themselves "very satisfied"; however, only 20 percent of wife dominant couples were "very satisfied" (Raven, Centers, and Rodrigues, 274).

Research by Corrales suggests women do not seem satisfied when dominating a marriage. In a study in which the wives admitted they dominated, they gave themselves low satisfaction scores. This outcome indicates that the wives exercise power by default and do it to compensate for a weak or ignoring husband (Corrales, 211). In this same investigation of 394 couples, one quarter of the sample were wife dominant but according to the Blood and Wolfe decision-making scale, these same wives had only 10.5 percent of the authority indicated by answers to questions regarding final decision making. Corrales explained this discrepancy as follows: "the spouse with little authority may seek less visible ways to make her or his power felt. Interactive control appears to be one such way" (208). Also there appears to be a gap between a couple's perception of their power structure and their actual interactive control. One sidelight is that husbands in wife dominant marriages indicated they were not as dissatisfied as their wives. Kolb and Straus (1974) explain this outcome with their "role incapacity" theory which posits that when a man relinquishes his traditional leadership role, or fails to carry out his part of an egalitarian relationship, the wife becomes dissatisfied because she feels she married a less competent man (761).

In this controversy over who has the most power—male or female—it is well to remember that research indicates men overestimate their power and women underestimate their power in the family. Self-reports further reveal that individuals underestimate their own power and overestimate their spouses' power. However, outside observers in carefully controlled situations found that both spouses report less power for wives than they actually possessed (Olson, 1969, 549). Turk and Bell (1972) substantiated these findings in a later study which covered all three areas of family power (power resources, processes, and outcomes) and included the couples' children. They observed more egalitarian patterns in the families but self-report measures indicated all concerned thought male dominance prevailed (220–222).

As sex-based marital roles continue to change, different uses of power structures may emerge. Women's power should increase. In a study of sex differences in power options, Johnson (1974) demonstrated that men usually use expertise, formal legitimacy, and direct informational power. Women, by comparison, used referent power, helplessness, and indirect information. Ironically he also found that when women did use sources of power more frequently employed by men, they were labeled as being more masculine and less acceptable. Similar future studies may reflect an emphasis on personal instead of positional roles resulting in greater equalization of power between spouses.

The type of power processes used by couples can often be traced to their experience in their respective families-of-origin. A family in which people were physically controlled may result in their child's acceptance of this method, particularly when other alternatives do not appear immediately available. A son who had a dominant father may find it very difficult to see an image of himself in an equal-dominance relationship with his wife.

My German father and my Irish mother both exercised power over us in different ways. My father used to beat us whenever we got out of line and that power move was very obvious. On the other hand, my mother never touched us but she probably exercised greater power through her use of silence. Whenever we did something she did not approve of, she just stopped talking to us—it was as if we did not exist. Most of the time the silent treatment lasted for a few hours but sometimes it would last for a few days. My brother used to say it was so quiet you "could hear a mouse pee on a cotton ball." I hated the silence worse than the beatings.

Families-of-origin serve as the first power base in which a child learns to function and the strategies used there often are repeated later in the child's adult life. Certain types of power moves, such as silence, seem to move from generation to generation because such control was learned at an early age and often not questioned.

Children and Power

As anyone who has been in a family with children knows, they have a great influence on family power situations. Early studies often ignored them, possibly on the assumption that parents controlled decisions and that children essentially had to follow their directions. Traditionally parents are expected to control and be responsible for their children's behavior. Couples are expected to raise "nice children" who know their "manners and place." The law also supports the idea of power in the parents' hands. Children must be off the streets by certain hours, attend school, etc. "Probably in no other relationship does a person in our society have such complete power over another," Hoffman (1960, 27) declares, "as do parents over young children." Wieting and McLaren (1975) stress the importance of including children in any study of power and note their impact on making the family system more than the sum of its parts (99). Parents replying to questionnaires indicated they possessed the power but when trained observers used behavioral methods to measure power, they found children definitely exercised power in a family (Turk and Bell, 220).

A whole new power scheme emerges when two family members become three, or four or more. As we saw earlier, coalitions and alliances can form between and among family members upsetting the original balance of power. The door is open for a two-against-one power play and all other possible combinations.

When I was growing up, I was very close to my father and we usually agreed on things so my mother began to see it as "the two of you against me." I thought it was silly because we enjoyed being together and we did not mean to be against her, but as I've grown older, I can understand that she felt left out. Now I often feel outmatched when my son and my husband agree on things and I do not.

In a study of son-father-mother triads, Strodbeck (1951) concluded that sons had almost as much power as their mothers in solving problems (471). Other studies proved that children influence the interaction and outcomes of power struggles in families by interruptions and other power plays (Turk and Bell, 1972; Mishler and Waxler, 1968).

In many families one spouse consciously or unconsciously co-opts a child into an ally position in order to increase the strength of his or her position. Similarly children become adept at playing one parent against the other. "Daddy said I could do it," "If Mom was here she'd let me" has echoed through most homes as new coalitions are formed. Blended families are especially vulnerable as children cite the ex-spouse's permissions.

Often such alliances will follow a same sex bias. Boys and girls may be expected to be like their respective parents. "My mother and I stick up for each other against the men" represents such a power move.

I couldn't believe it when I heard my four-year-old son announce to his mother and two-year-old sister, "The men will go to the store, the women will stay home." He then turned and followed me out to the car. When I asked him about it he replied, "Men do things together."

Power Coalitions • Coalitions can and do take all sorts of forms within a given family. Parents may form a coalition against the children, establishing an inflexible boundary that prevents negotiation or discussion. The extended family can become a part of the power bloc to be used in both everyday and crisis situations. In-laws, aunts and uncles, older brothers or sisters, and even friends can become involved in coalitions that try to alter the power in a family. Single-parent families display unique power coalitions due to the presence of one adult. One research team points out a potential advantage for a child in a single-parent family because the child may negotiate directly with the parent and get immediate answers and have direct personal power (Wieting and McLaren, 97). In a household headed by a mother, she can't say, "I'll let you know after I talk it over with your father." However, the same child can't form a parent-child coalition to try and change a decision like a child can in a two-parent family. Blended families often contend with children playing one side of the family against the other. "She can't tell me what to do, she's not my real mother" may represent the kind of communication which causes years of pain as new roles are negotiated.

Some coalitions continue in families over a period of time; others exist only for reaching a decision on a given issue. The results of past coalitions can obligate family members to feel they must support another on an issue to repay a debt. For example, "Brad helped me convince Dad to let me buy a new ten-speed bike. Now I ought to help him argue with Dad to get his own car." Wives and husbands can also form coalitions with one another or their children and do much like the example. The drawback of coalitions and returning favors is that issues never get settled on their own merits. Coalitions in some families demand loyalty and "pay-offs" and this affects a fair use of power in the family system. It's also another way members of families adapt to the needs and frustrations of living together in the same system. Coalition members are able to pool their individual assets so as to increase their chances of dominance (Turner, 122).

Independent Power Development • Although young children exercise power (witness the baby who controls a whole family's daily life!), they develop more independent power as they grow older. They go from a state of complete dependence in infancy to a state of independence in adulthood when they leave behind most power constraints of the families.

As children grow and change, they demand and can handle more power within the family structure. Whereas the six-year-old may fight for a later bedtime, the sixteen-year-old fights for his or her independence. Yet a school-age child may begin to have expertise in areas unknown to his or her parents. Each of us has seen a small child explain computer toys, metrics, or a board game to a confused adult. Parents often provide educational opportunities and material advantages to their children they never had. The resulting knowledge and prestige can give children an additional resource advantage over their parents in power struggles.

Adolescence represents a troubled time in certain families as sons and daughters rebel and refuse to accept parental power. Adolescence is also the time when parents can recognize the skills and expertise their children have acquired. In families where power is shared such changes may be welcome whereas they may be threatening in a wife or husband dominated system. Domineering parents could perceive the new skills and knowledge as a threat to their power base. "Oh! You think you are so smart now!" typifies the remarks heard in such families. In a warmer, nurturing family environment, offspring receive positive strokes for their new and expanding talents. The son with expertise in electrical repairs gains a certain kind of power and importance in the family because he can do what no other family member can do.

By now I'm in charge of all the family cars. I decide what needs to be done when and I do a lot of the work myself. My mother lets me decide when she gets new tires or a tune-up. I've worked in a gas station since eighth grade and I'll work there part time even when I start college. I know as much as most of the guys there.

As families grow and change, the power sources and resources are reflected in changes in the family system. The original power relationship of a couple undergoes enormous modification as the family network increases, fragments, or solidifies. In addition to developmental issues, many other forces affect changes in family power. These changes affecting power may be due to separation from family-of-origin, or outside influences that affect the family—varying from inflation and environmental factors to changing cultural norms. The parents' competency in relating first their needs and desires to one another and then to their children affects power. The spouses or children's acceptance or rejection of these requests influences power outcomes. The increasing or decreasing independence or interdependence of the couple alters power in the entire family system. If a spouse falls ill or dies, deserts, or divorces, the remaining parent may return to the family-of-origin seeking everything from shelter and funds to advice. This reestablishes ties in the family network that may have been ignored or not needed previously. The single parent left with children cannot avoid experiencing modifications in power processes in the family. Power structures do not remain static. The power structure in families constantly undergoes changes as the family seeks its goals.

COMMUNICATION OF POWER STRATEGIES

Throughout this chapter we have described the communication of power or power messages. Now we would like to discuss some communication strategies that affect power.

Confirming, Disconfirming, and Rejecting Behaviors

Confirming, disconfirming, and rejecting behaviors become strategies that affect intimacy development and power. These three strategies can become a part of power messages as family members attempt to separate and connect in one-up, one-down subsystems. In a one-up position, one family member attempts to exercise more power control over one or more other family members. The one-down member accepts from the one-up member the control implied in the messages.

Confirming implies acknowledgment or agreement, and may be used to gain power as one tries to get another to identify with him or her, or as one tries to give rewards in order to gain power. The careful nonjudgmental listener may wittingly or unwittingly gain power through the information learned by such behavior. The highly complimentary father may be given power by the child who needs positive support. Such approaches to marital power are found in books such as *Fascinating Womanhood* (Andelin, 1980) or *The Total Woman* (Morgan, 1973) which exhort wives to use positive confirming approaches as a way to gain power in the marital relationship.

Probably the "silent treatment" represents the most powerful and most often used disconfirming behavior—a behavior which does not acknowledge the other person's existence. One family member can put another in a one-down power position through the punishment strategy of disconfirmation. "Ignore him, he'll come around" represents such an effort. On the other hand, disconfirming a power message may serve as an effective method of rejecting power. The child who pretends not to hear the "clean up your room" messages effectively deflects the parental power, at least for a period of time.

Rejecting messages tie directly to punishment messages and are often used as control in family power plays. "I hate you" or "I don't care what you say" may effectively halt control attempts, just as, "If you don't behave, you can't go" may serve to pull a reluctant family member into line. The negative conflict behaviors of displacement, denial, disqualification, disengagement, and sexual withholding also can be used as rejecting power moves.

Self-disclosure serves a major means of gaining intimacy within a relationship, but it can be used as a power strategy as one attempts to control the other through the "information power" gained by self-disclosure. For example, when a self-disclosure is thrown back at a spouse during a fight, that person loses power. "Well, you had an affair, so how can you talk?" Sprey (1971) describes the human bond as a paradox. He observes that moving closer to another person also necessitates moving apart! The more involved the couple becomes, the greater the pressure for one or both to possess the other. He believes that intimacy requires "the awareness and acceptance of the stranger in the other" (724).

Self-disclosure may be used as a means of offering power to a loved one in an intimate relationship.

One of the most meaningful times in my life occurred when my teenage daughter and I had an almost all-night session about love, sex, and growing-up problems. It was the first time I really honestly told her about what I went through growing up and how we faced some of the same things. I had always kept those things to myself but suddenly realized that she shouldn't feel like she was different or bad because of her feelings. It's scary to tell your daughter your faults or fears but it certainly resulted in a closer relationship between the two of us.

The disclosure gives power to the listener in an effort to gain connectedness. Such sharing involves risk and gives the listener "information power" which he or she could use to cause pain or separation in the relationship. In such cases the more knowledgeable person has the capacity to control the relationship.

Transactional Nature of Power

The key issue in power remains the transactional nature of the relationship. Power must be given as well as taken. This transactional quality may be seen in some recent research of Rogers-Millar and Millar (1979) in which they examine the distinction between dominance and domineering behavior. They defined *domineering* as the "transmission of one-up messages—verbal statements which claim the right to dominance" (240). They defined *dominance* "as the transmission of one-up messages that are accepted with one-down messages from the other. Thus, domineeringness is an aspect of individual behavior, dominance an aspect of dyadic relational behavior" (Courtright, Millar, and Rogers-Millar,

1979, 181). Their research focused on the power process domain as they studied the messages exchanged between spouses as they accepted or rejected one another's statements. In this study pure dominance meant the percentage of all one-up remarks made by an individual followed by a one-down response from the other.

Correlating domineering behavior to self-report data, Rogers-Millar and Millar found "higher levels of wife domineeringness related to lower marital and communication satisfaction for both spouses and higher role strain" (244). They found some further important results when they analyzed the interaction data or messages between the spouses. The dominance of one spouse correlated positively to the number of support statements (i.e., agreement, acceptance, approval remarks) and negatively to the number of nonsupport statements made by the other spouse. Nonsupport statements were in the form of rejections, disagreements, or demands. Talk-overs, defined as a verbal interruption or intrusion that succeeds in taking over the communication while another is speaking, occurred more frequently in couples who used the domineering style. In both wife domineering and dominant interactions, the discussions were longer. The reverse was true of husbands (245). A second study provided additional conclusions: The more domineering one spouse was, the more domineering the partner became. This indicated a more defensive or combative style of conversation developed from a domineering style (Courtright, Millar, Rogers-Millar, 1979, 183). Frequent question-asking characterized the wife's style of interaction when the husband dominated (Rogers-Millar and Millar, 184). The more domineering the husband, the less accurate both spouses' predictions about the other's satisfaction with the marriage. The same held true for domineering wives in predicting their mate's satisfaction (187). The researchers suggested that if you did not want to be dominated, you should increase your domineeringness. However, they added that if you do so, be prepared to accept the possibility that you and your partner's satisfaction in the relationship will decrease (191).

Other aspects of one-up, one-down communication have been described by Haley (1974) as dysfunctional communication strategies for many couples or family members. He suggests helplessness will influence the other person's behavior as much as, if not more, than direct authoritarian demands. If one acts helpless, he defines the relationship as one in which he is taken care of (371). This kind of behavior in a relationship can be avoided by using qualifications in part of the message that indicate an individual takes responsibility for her or his decisions. For example, Wayne might say to his brother, "I don't think you should do that, but it's not my duty to tell you so." A husband might say to his wife, "I want your opinion, but I know it's my problem to solve." This approach to communication lessens the likelihood of control of another and leaves persons in possession of their own powers. Thus the communication strategies used to enhance relationships or to increase your intimacy also may be used to gain power.

In order to achieve cohesion, each family has to work out a communication pattern that allows them to gain intimacy without overpowering certain system members. As a result of his research Corrales states: "The data . . . suggests . . . in this culture, behavior that is more conducive to building self and other esteem seems to be more effectively communicated in an equalitarian interaction structure than in either type of dominant structure" (216). The equalitarian structure includes the syncratic and autonomic types of power sharing. In either of these types of families, individuals can deal honestly with their feelings and aspirations. Their more open nature encourages freer communication exchanges than either the husband or wife dominant types.

Steinor (1978) distinguishes between "gentle power" and "control power." He describes communication as a form of gentle power. "I can give you what I feel and think. You can understand it and you can compare and decide. This makes people powerful." To use communication effectively to counteract the negative aspects of power ideally there can be no power plays between the persons involved. Steinor suggests power should not be used to rescue others from solving their own problems. When parents take over their children's problems, they also assume power that is not rightfully theirs. Husbands or wives who through power plays make decisions for the other, reduce that spouse's power potential. An egalitarian family relationship requires that each member have the power to solve the problems they encounter.

CONCLUSION

In this chapter we have discussed power bases, power processes, and power outcomes because they affect cohesion and adaptability in families. The research presented indicated that a rigid power structure, characterized by dominance and little sharing, restricts family flexibility, reduces cohesion, and adversely affects satisfaction in families. Power constantly changes as a family grows and develops within its system. Although power changes may be more obvious in children as they mature and move from a dependent state to an independent one, each of the parents experience equal or greater changes. All power maneuvers take place within the boundaries the family has established, thus all communication and activities take place that either enhance positively or negatively the images, themes, and degree of unity or cohesion the family desires. Remember that all power operates within a dynamic, growing, changing, interdependent, transactional family system. The sum total of the family power will be greater than the individual power of the members. Power struggles may develop when an issue becomes important to one or more family member. When this happens, and the rational exploration of alternatives ceases, various one-up power maneuvers usually follow. This affects family intimacy, a vital element in meaningful relationships. To resolve differences and not become the victim of another's power, in any family, you need to engage in constructive conflict since the ability to clearly and comfortably repudiate another is part of the achievement of intimacy.

8

Decision Making
in Families

In the past whenever there has been a major family decision to be made, we took a family vote. My father, who assumed the role of the ultimate Decision Maker, devised a rule entitling himself to two votes, as opposed to everyone else's single vote. He implied that because he was the "man of the house" he should have the greater decision-making power. His two votes always negated the possibility of us children overruling the parents. At times the females of the family would pool our votes and override his. When this occurred, he would respect our votes unless the issue was crucial to him. In these few cases, his decision was the decision. My mother assumed the role of Advisor of the D.M. She often tried to persuade him about certain issues and often she won him over.

Although you may not have had an ultimate "Decision Maker" in your family, you probably had some process by which decisions were made and you had a specific place in the process.

Decision making involves vital communication skills and relates directly to power. Decisions represent a power outcome. As you might imagine, families are unique decision-making systems because each family has a history of having resolved or not having resolved their past issues effectively. Past successes certainly influence future decisions and affect the processing of current issues. Past failures can bring forth negative skills that impede decision making. Any current decision in a family will also have future effects since individuals within the family unit have to live with or carry out the decision.

Decision making relates to power to the degree that one family member can predict and/or influence the outcome he or she desires. For example, Brent can affect Jeanette's decision making or choices for some behavior Brent wants. The degree of power would be the difference between Jeanette making a certain choice because of Brent's persuasion and the probability of Jeanette doing it anyway. The outcome depends upon the perceptions and intentions of those involved. Thus determining power involves knowing Brent's intentions and the effects he has on Jeanette's decision making (Pollard and Mitchell, 1972, 442).

Your family differs from a small group that comes together for the purpose of doing a task because your family has not only a history of continuous interaction but consists of a combination of interdependent individuals. Even if the decision-making process results in turmoil, all of you remain a unit, although sometimes a factional and unhappy unit. This is not true of outside groups. If the members can't reach a decision, they usually can disband rather easily. Short of death, divorce, or moving out, families tend to remain together even if members disagree.

Decision making is important to families because it enables the family members to meet their needs and realize family goals. Systems develop through a series of decisions as members grow and change and as outside forces affect the system. For example, system members have to decide how rules may be modified as toddlers move on toward their preteen years. If family members work together on decisions that affect one another, they can enhance the operation of their family system. Again the combined energies going into decision making will be greater than the sum of the individual energies resulting in greater rewards for being part of an effective family system. Through decision making families carry out their images, themes, biosocial beliefs and maintain their boundary lines with the outside world.

The place a family falls along the cohesion and adaptability continuums affects their decision-making behavior. Highly enmeshed, rigid families may pressure members to reach predictable and low risk decisions since change or separation would be threatening. Disengaged systems may have trouble sharing enough information to make reasonable decisions while families characterized by chaos probably experience few real decisions that stand.

As we examine the family as a decision-making system, we will discuss: (1) types of family decision making, (2) modes of family governance, (3) steps in decision making, and (4) factors that influence decision making. In the previous chapter we discussed power in families. In this chapter we will extend our study of power to look in greater detail at decision making as an outcome of power: Who influences the decision and how is the influence felt? Who decides what, when, and how certain necessary aspects of family life get resolved? The answers will vary according to how communication is used to maintain the way rules, roles, and power operate within a given family.

TYPES OF DECISION MAKING

> Every Tuesday night is family night and everyone must be present from 7 until 8:30 during which time we find out how everyone is doing, hash out any problems, and spend time playing games or talking about values or concerns. This is also the time when we make certain family decisions that affect all of us. We may make a joint decision about vacations and we try to find a compromise that will please everyone somehow. Sometimes Dad will let us decide on a big item to buy with his bonus. Everyone of the six of us has to finally agree for us to go ahead with the decision.

Each family has its own way of reaching decisions on issues. In his study of family decision-making patterns, Turner (1970) differentiates decision-making outcomes according to the degree of acceptance and commitment of the family members. He identifies three kinds of decision making: (1) consensus, (2) accommodation, and (3) de facto (98–100).

Consensus • In consensus decision making, discussion continues until agreement is reached. This may involve compromise and flexibility but the desired goal is a solution acceptable to all involved. Because each family member has a part in the decision and chance to influence it, they each share the responsibility for carrying it out. In some families all major purchases are decided on the basis of group consensus. This type of decision making doesn't occur as frequently as the ones that follow.

Accommodation • Accommodation occurs when some family members grant their consent to a decision not because they totally agree but because they figure further discussion will be unproductive. They may give their consent with a smile or with bitterness. The accommodation decision may represent a great deal of give and take but no one really achieves what is desired. You may want to go to church family camp and someone else wants to play in three ball games that weekend. Eventually the family may agree on a picnic while the baseball player gets to play one game in the schedule. These wants have not really been satisfied with the decision but merely placated or postponed to some future time. Commitment to the outcome is temporary—until something better comes along. Since not every member achieves his or her wants, this kind of decision making tends to leave certain members disappointed. When decisions are made this way, you may see factions emerge and may feel obligated to repay people who argued for your goals. This type of decision making may occur in families that pressure for high cohesiveness through their themes and boundaries.

> It's just easier to agree with Dad and let him think his ideas are what we all want than to argue with him. He's bound to win anyway since he controls the money. Sometimes when we humor his wishes, Mom,

my sister, and I can then get our way on what we want to do—sort of a trade-off!

Sometimes accommodation results from voting as family members line up on one side of an issue and the majority side wins. The minority views held by the losing family members might have genuine merit but they accept rather than cause trouble. Anyone who loses consistently finds this to be an unacceptable way to make a decision.

One danger of this accommodation is that it encourages dominance behavior. Too often the decisions made favor those who dominate and the less aggressive family members develop a pattern of submitting to their wishes. "An accommodative decision usually accords more with the wishes of some members than of others," Turner warns. He further states, ". . . it is possible to speak of accommodative decision making as the specific process through which dominant and submissive positions in the group are established" (99). Although accommodation may appear to be an approach to decision making that furthers family cohesion and adaptability, such is not the case. The results at best would be temporary because the communication that goes into accommodative decisions represents compromises being made by members through fear or lack of equal power. Decisions of this kind over a period of time would accent separateness and lessen connectedness among family members. This same type of decision making can also enforce negative family themes and images while implementing stereotyped thinking on biosocial issues, especially if male dominance is a problem.

De facto • What happens when the family makes no decision or when the discussion reaches an impasse? Usually some member will go ahead in the absence of a clearcut decision and act. This becomes a de facto decision—one made without direct family approval but nevertheless made to keep the family functioning. A fight over which model of TV to buy while on sale will be continued until the sale nears an end and Dad finally buys one by himself.

Indecision over what the family would do for entertainment ends with no time left to do it. Arguments over what to have for dinner end with Dad or Mother preparing whatever leftovers they can find in the refrigerator. Chaotic families often find themselves in these circumstances. De facto decisions encourage family members to complain about the results since they played either no part or a passive part in the decision. The family member who acts in the vacuum created by no clear cut decision has to endure the harassment or lack of enthusiasm of those who have to accept the decision. Again, dominant type family members can easily emerge victorious in too many decisions—their wishes become accepted and others are unfairly suppressed. In de facto decisions "discussions finish inconclusively and then they are decided by events" (Turner, 99).

We talked about doing something together as a family last Sunday afternoon. I wanted to bowl. Mom wanted to see a movie. My sister wanted to go to the amusement park. Dad thought a ball game or ride in the country would be OK. No one pulled us together. Finally it got too late to do anything. Dad took a nap, Mom read, I went over to Chuck's house, and my sister went swimming with a friend.

The previous example illustrates little cohesion or overall sense of unity in the family system. Frustration levels are high and no one adapts to the other.

Although many families, particularly rigid ones, seem to use only one type of decision making, more flexible ones vary their styles according to the issues. Critical issues may require consensus while less important concerns can be resolved by a vote or a de facto type decision. As we will see later, the family-of-origin style of decision making experienced by each member of a couple has a great effect on the decision-making styles adopted by the couple when they form their own system.

FAMILY GOVERNANCE

One of the greatest rewards from parenthood comes from watching your children grow and pass through different stages until they become young adults who become part of the family community in a new way and contribute sensitively to the family functioning. Right now my youngest daughter is blossoming into a sensitive young woman who can put her needs in perspective according to the other members of the family. She has moved from a self-centered little kid to a person willing to make compromises and to do certain things according to other people's wishes.

Although we can all use different styles or types of decision making, our decisions rest on an underlying approach to power and decision making. In an interesting approach that combines ideas about family power and decision making, Broderick (1975) set up three modes of governance. He based these upon Kohlberg's (1964) study of children in different cultures and the universal steps in reasoning he discovered they go through to reach moral maturity. The lowest level of reasoning for decisions was hedonistic self-interest; the next was based on conventionality and obedience to rules; the third on social contact and principles of conscience (118).

Zero-Sum Decisions

Applied to decision making or conflict situations, the first and most primitive way to reach a decision would be to insist upon your way. Broderick labeled this approach a hedonistic, "zero-sum" power confrontation. This means that in an argument, whenever or whatever it is about, Matthew wins, Katie loses, or vice versa. The sum of all their wins and losses is always zero. You have seen this operate between small children who refuse to share. Instead, they shout, "That's mine, you can't have it." Unfortunately such behavior does not always stop as family members move beyond the toddler stage. In this kind of decision making each family member insists upon his or her way without compromise or hearing the other's views. This approach can lead to threats, yelling, browbeating, and slanting of the truth. When countered with questions and nonacceptance by family members, the discussion can come to a halt. Only after the discussion has survived the pressures from the hedonistic, self-interested family member and reached an impasse, can some sort of compromise be worked out.

Broderick suggests only two circumstances in which families possibly could survive using zero-sum confrontations. For example, if the wife and husband are closely matched with each getting an equal number of wins and losses, the relationship could continue. Also if the consistently losing partner feels there are no alternatives and lacks the emotional or financial resources to leave, he or she may remain in the relationship in spite of the heavy psychological cost of lower self-esteem. Children can definitely be victims in this kind of household because they have no way to escape. Young people caught up in this kind of family make statements like "I can't wait until I graduate and can get out of here," or "I don't like it but it's not worth fighting over." In time the losers either leave the family or define their role as second class (119). [See also Turk, 1974, 43.] In the zero-sum type of governance, the decisions are static and predictable. Whatever Bill wants, Bill gets or else!

The maintenance of a zero-sum relationship would require coercive power or punishment, especially use of fear and threat. One person may declare himself or herself an expert or may claim a particular role gives legitimate sole decision-making powers. Highly enmeshed families may allow someone to do this. Little use would be made of information because too much evidence might weaken the position of the hedonist family member insisting upon her or his views. Even less use would be made of reward power because the "winner" doesn't usually sense the need to give anything in return for the acceptance of the decision. You can imagine how psychologically draining it would be to function in such a family, both for the winners and the losers.

To be a constant winner would require defensive behaviors and putting up with the loser's submissive behaviors; to lose constantly would require a person to live with low self-esteem and to constantly try to subvert the more powerful person. The images maintained in zero-sum family relationships foster separateness and reduce the chance for much cohesion. The pattern of adaptability required to maintain zero-sum relationships does too little to develop positive self-esteem for individual members within the family system. In many families, victories would be hollow because they curb or destroy ideas and limit decision-making skills in others that might lead to better and more meaningful solutions in order to achieve harmony within the family system. The continued chaos and tension in zero-sum type families results in constant overt or covert conflict as the struggle of wills continues.

Decisions Via Rules

A second mode of governance involves the creation and enforcement of rules. A family may live most of its life according to the rules and avoid certain power clashes as well as certain opportunities for growth because the rules dictate life. Rules affect decision making because, over a period of time, they become accepted ways to operate when problems arise. These rules may evolve from repeated family interactions or they may be set by one or more family members. Concerning rules in family decision making, Broderick (1975) distinguished among three types: (1) rules of direct distribution, (2) rules designating authority, and (3) rule-bound negotiation (120–121).

After almost twenty years of working in banking, I decided to return to graduate school to make an eventual career change. Although my family supported this move we did have to make some major financial sacrifices. My wife worked part-time and we used up much of our savings. As part of the process we decided ahead of time how much money could be spent for different necessities and we stuck to it. The children were given a clothing allowance and they had to live within it or use their babysitting money. We set aside a small amount for recreation and had to plan our fun within that budget. Although there was some grumbling, most of us stuck to the rules and we were able to get through a rough period.

Direct Distribution Rules • Rules of direct distribution imply dividing up the family resources directly to members. This could include distribution of family income into the amounts available for food, housing, tuition, vacation, entertainment, etc. Similar distribution can be made of living space—which child gets which room or has to share a bedroom; which shelves belong to each child or parent; where personal items are to be kept from toothbrushes to overshoes and baseball gloves. These rules function to avoid confrontations and reduce power plays in the family through the pre-solution of possible problems. Rules of this kind mean that each family member carries around in his or her head a whole series of predetermined decisions about matters of family living. To violate the expected decision on such matters invites trouble with other family members who accept the prearranged solutions to such problems on the use of facilities and resources. Although you may not have been conscious of them, you probably have lived by certain rules of direct distribution for certain areas of your life.

Designated Authority Rules • Rules of designated authority indicate who has the authority over certain areas. For example, Mother pays the bills and thus collects the checks and does the budgeting. Dad does the painting and refinishing and thus decides on the materials to use. Lois plays in the band and thus doesn't need to explain her absence for practice after school or help with housework on weekends when the band travels. Sometimes rules allocating authority have a series of steps. For example, either Dad or Mom can go out for an evening with friends if the other knows who is going and where they plan to go. Either can veto such a decision if their jobs require them to work overtime and the children will be home alone. This type of rule, dispersing authority, often relates closely to roles in the family. Whoever controls the kitchen and all of the activities that take place there has the authority to make the decisions in that area.

The rule in a particular family might be that Mom doesn't have to accept a cleaning task because her accepted responsibilities entail food gathering and preparation.

As the children grew older we developed a unique system in our house to deal with responsibilities and chores. Ted and I each had two of the children "assigned" to us for a month and those two received orders from one parent and did not have to take orders from the other parent. Each month we switched so the children received supervision from each of us and so they learned to do all kinds of household tasks, not just the outside or the inside type of chore.

The type of rule making involving designated authority tends to set clear boundaries for who may get involved with what. Certain people may have far more decision-making power than others. Yet children can also have areas of decision making assigned to them. For example, if they do their expected tasks, they can make decisions about their free time. If the son likes to bake and does all of the buying and preparation of baked goods from bread to pies, he may be given the authority over the oven when needed and that part of the kitchen. The autonomic family described in the previous chapter quite often operates its decision making in accordance with this rule.

Negotiation Rules • The third type of rules are based on negotiation. Over time families can establish rules that govern the process decision making will follow when conflict occurs. Rules of this type imply greater family input in settling differences. It may mean placing a limit on the amount of force or threat one member can use against another family member. Certain tactics such as yelling and hitting can be outlawed and negotiation done only when all involved agree not to interrupt. This approach implies that the decision reached may require compromise or sacrifice on one or more family member's part. Many of the current marital or family enrichment programs stress how to negotiate differences according to rules that allow all members of the system some input.

As a variation of this approach, Bernhard (1975) stresses that each person has a right to decide what is negotiable and what is non-negotiable for himself or herself. Others intimately involved have a right to know what is non-negotiable and can question or evaluate it, but Bernhard believes the final decision should be up to the individual and should be respected. She defines "an area of autonomy as a statement of power in a relationship—subject to mutual acceptance and negotiation—in which each gives to the other the power of final decision making in defined areas of living" (96).

Ever since the children have grown older, I have declared Saturday as my day to do whatever I desire. It is sacred to me and I only do what I want on that day even if somebody else will be disappointed. I am

wife or mother to four people during six days of the week and I really
need some scheduled time to myself and Saturday's it!

As you think about your family members, could they live according to
this? Could people negotiate areas of autonomy and have these respected by the
other family members? Bernhard attempts to respond to the core issue of separateness and connectedness through this position suggesting that it is self-preserv-
ing. "It sets the boundaries and limitations of togetherness . . . and keeps open
any area of freedom separate from the intimate other." Yet she stresses the
possibility of change since "what is necessary to one's self-esteem today may not
be important tomorrow" (96).

Thus the third type of rule involves negotiation and, potentially, negotiation about what is not negotiable. This approach has the potential to increase
family cohesion and provide a method for adaptability. To be successful, family
members have to communicate directly to all other members their wishes and
take responsibility for their comments. Negotiation implies change and flexibility.
If this expectancy of later possible change is recognized by the family, the members within it realize that negotiation can be another communication skill to use
to gain adaptability within their system. It can help to keep a system open and
flexible.

Decisions by Contract or Principle

Broderick's third mode of governance that affects decision making involves government by contract or principle. As you might imagine, few families
actively operate at this high a level and usually those that do include older
children and adults (121–122). It is based on a belief in the basic human goodness
of each family member and their desire to put the family's welfare above their
own. Individual family members operate on principles of fairness and concern.
For example, if either Dad or Mother works late, they call the other and explain.
The principle operating is that neither partner unnecessarily inconveniences the
other. Both respect the other's right to make overtime decisions but fair play
motivates each of them to inform the other. This prevents one from preparing
food that's not eaten or planning activities to being left waiting. In this family
there is no rule about hours to come and go, but a principle operating that neither
will worry or waste the time of the other. Few rules exist because the principles
preclude exploitation. When rules are used, they are jointly determined and put
into a contract which each family member carries out. Decisions become a part
of the terms of the contract being fulfilled; they are made in terms of what will
be best for the family system.

Governance in families with children works if the parents have taught the
children how to use good judgment and value the rights, strengths, and limitations of one another. It requires harmony and cooperation. Disharmony can be
handled as a temporary condition that will be resolved by fair equitable decisions
that restore the balance to the family system. Children realize that they play an
integral part in the successful operation of the system. A family could have a
contract in which areas of work and play are shared—each has duties assigned

so that time remains for individual activities and for joint family activities. Compromise would certainly be a part of this form of governance so that all members legitimate needs could be met.

We have examined both Turner and Broderick's ways of viewing family decision-making. The former relates to the actual behavior while the latter takes more complex issues into consideration since it involves a level of moral reasoning reached by the members. Turk (1975) offers another way to combine the approaches to decision making when he suggests that choices be divided into either policy-guided or non-policy guided choices (93). If family policy has been established on a given matter, the decision making would then be guided by that policy. This would involve the rules established to deal with similar situations. Non-policy choices could require either accommodation, consensus, or some form of negotiation to reach decisions. The combination of the approaches to viewing the ways families reach decisions provides us with a broad background for understanding our own family and those we encounter.

STEPS IN DECISION MAKING

After my Mom remarried we had ten kids in the family, so we tried to have a series of family meetings in which certain decisions were made about things like curfew, babysitting, household jobs, and use of the cars. Although it didn't always work, we tried to hold a real meeting and to get everyone to say what they wanted. Sometimes we went for hours trying to reach a solution and sometimes people just went away mad.

As you know, most family decisions are made without a formal decision-making meeting but, on occasion, families decide to reach certain decisions in a relatively formal manner. The issue may be very important, the group may be large, or there may be other factors that influence the decision to follow an agenda.

Let's look briefly at the five problem-solving steps in decision making realizing that the process may be short-circuited at any point by a family member or an alliance that doesn't want certain choices made. Or the family group may reach a decision by skipping some steps.

The first step requires the *definition of the problem,* including isolating the parts of it that family members agree need attention. At this stage it's helpful to make sure everyone understands the key terms in the problem the same way. Sometimes differences in meaning cause part of the problem and delay decision making.

The second step includes an *exploration of the problem* and an analysis of the differences. At this stage all pros and cons should be debated with every involved family member having a chance to be heard.

In the third step *criteria* are set up that should meet any solution or decision. Sample criteria might be: that the family can afford the money to do it; that there will be enough time available to do it; that the decision will be equitable and not take advantage of any member; that the advantages will outweigh possible disadvantages. This important step tends to be overlooked, yet it can help clarify the family's goals and lead to better decisions. It becomes a listing of what's needed to be fair and just in making a decision that will solve a problem.

The fourth step focuses on *listing possible solutions* that might solve the problems. In this phase of decision making, alternatives and ways to solve a problem are brought out. If democracy prevails in the discussion, this step gives submissive family members a chance to express their ideas on ways to solve a mutual problem. Each participant should be encouraged to contribute suggestions for solving the problem. In this way, if they have a part in the process, and yet are later outvoted, they can feel their ideas were at least considered.

The last step requires *selecting the best solution* for the problem for this family at this point in time. The decision mode should represent their best combined thinking and meet the criteria agreed upon in the third step.

Finally, a plan of action for implementing the decision needs to be agreed upon—a plan that will enhance the operation of the family system and strengthen it because a problem that reduced the efficiency of the system has been solved. Note the steps followed by the family in this example:

My two brothers and I and our wives actually went through a formal decision-making process as we decided how to take care of my elderly mother after she was unable to live alone. We went through all kinds of hassles on terms such as nursing homes, residential facilities, social security benefits, etc. We had to set a monetary criteria for any solution based on a percentage of our salaries and based on a location that everyone could reach. Mother had to agree to the solution also. We agreed we could not force our solution on her. Each couple investigated different options, specific senior citizen housing options, live-in nurses, nursing homes, and specialized group homes. Then we all sat around and hashed them out. We finally reached two options that we could live with—a particular senior citizen facility or a nursing home that accepted people who were not severely ill. We discussed these with my mother who rejected the nursing home instantly but who agreed to see the senior citizen housing facility. After two visits she agreed that she could have her freedom there and she would have many friends. Since we could afford that solution and she was happy with it, we were very relieved. It took four months to go through the process but it was worth it since everyone was fairly satisfied with the results.

This planned approach to decision making doesn't just happen in families. In fact, left to their own ways, most families do not solve their problems in an organized way. Many families become bogged down and never get beyond the first or second step (O'Flaherty, 1974). The possibility exists that "if incomplete decision-making persists, decision issues will eventually be determined by factors other than decision processes of the participants" (Thomas, 1977, 117).

It's obvious that this approach to decision making requires energy and commitment from all family members but when the issue is critical, certain families decide it's worth the work to go through the steps.

No matter how decision making occurs, whatever style or type of governance is used, the actual process involves many factors. Unfortunately it's not a very predictable and streamlined process. In order to understand the complexity of the process we need to examine a number of factors that affect family decision making.

FACTORS THAT AFFECT FAMILY DECISION MAKING

Over the years each family evolves some patterned ways of solving problems. The decision-making process is more than trial-and-error although that may be a part of it. The family decisions relate to a variety of factors that explain the actions taken. In this section we will discuss (1) how children affect decisions; (2) how male and female role definitions modify outcomes; (3) how the degree of involvement of family members within the system and their individual power resources influence decisions; and (4) how additional influences such as time available and quality of communication skills used determine decisions.

Role of Children in Decision Making

By now you are fully aware that your family-of-origin experiences affect all areas of your life; thus your decision-making experiences as a child will partially determine your approach to adult decision-making situations. On the other hand, your children may have some interesting effects on family decision-making processes. As we noted before, the arrival of the first child opens the door for the formation of triangles or alliances in the family and provides the first opportunity for a chain network by which decisions may be relayed.

Children often influence decisions by forming coalitions with one or the other parent or if all children present a united front to a certain proposed decision. In some families permanent coalitions seem to exist. For example, "Dad, Cindy, and Tom always form an alliance to stick together on issues and that leaves Mom and I often on the other side."

A trite axiom the two of us share is, together we stand, divided we fall. My brother and myself took tremendous advantage of the concept of *joining* throughout our college years. My brother and I marshalled up strategies to combat my parents in order to achieve our ends. At times, we add complexity to the tension-filled situations via pairing one parent off against the other. Sometimes it works, but sometimes we end up by losing.

In certain circumstances children share the leadership in making decisions. Russell (1979) found this happened in a family atmosphere in which a child or spouse felt support from other members. This atmosphere also made it easier for a less assertive member to risk taking charge of a problem and trying to solve it (43). Through observations of family members during problem-solving sessions, Kolb and Straus (1974) found children exercising leadership in directing outcomes but "high child power" was associated with low marital happiness (764). They thought this result might have been caused by the societal expectation of father leadership and when he wasn't the leader, they felt deprived of leadership. On the other hand, certain parents consciously plan to allow their children opportunities to lead or influence decision making as a way of preparing them for future responsibilities. Thus we can see that children do influence family decision-making patterns.

Couple Male/Female Roles

As we mentioned earlier, the ways husbands and wives define these roles and responsibilities directly affect family decision making. In a study of couple allocation of responsibility for 18 family decisions and 13 tasks, Douglas and Wind (1978) selected 240 respondents in six metropolitan areas. The husbands and wives grouped decisions and tasks into areas of responsibility in their families. The findings revealed basic spouse agreement with a group of wife-dominated activities, including washing and drying the dishes, laundry chores, and food budgeting and buying. Other decisions were joint decisions, such as places to go on vacations, who gets invited to dinner, what movie to see, the amount to spend on appliances, what furniture to buy or replace, and if the wife should work.

Couples did differ on other decision areas. Wives made more distinctions than husbands. Certain tasks were perceived as male dominated: getting the car repaired, choosing the liquor, maintaining the yard. The same held true on family financial decisions, such as how much money to invest or save, which credit cards to secure, where the family will bank, the amount of life insurance needed, who pays the bills, the buying of men's toiletries, and clothing for either spouse. Douglas and Wind suggested that wives make these differentiations because of their perceived degree of influence and competence. Wives think of themselves as less qualified to get the car serviced or select liquor. On financial decisions some wives indicated more competence and joint participation and involvement. On clothing decisions wives indicated they often acted as influencer or consultant (39).

It is interesting to note that in this study and several earlier ones, the couples had a harder time identifying who made a decision than who performed a task. For example, a husband couldn't recall who influenced what in their decision to buy a new sofa or whether he or his wife asked friends over for a barbecue, but he knew who did the dishes regularly and who balanced the checkbook!

The second part of this study focused on differences in role patterns and who makes the decisions. Earlier studies indicated that the family's role ideology will determine who carries out certain decisions and tasks. Thus in male dominant households the husband will take over the financial decisions and the wife the household operation. Egalitarian couples will make more joint decisions (Heer, 1963). However, Douglas and Wind found little systematic relationship between couples' role attitudes and responsibility patterns (42). In comparing results with the Blood and Wolfe study (1960) which characterized households based on reported role patterns for certain decisions and tasks, they discovered few areas were husband dominant, wife dominant, or joint across all households. In this study only car and liquor purchases were usual husband duties and household chores for wives. On other matters the conclusions varied from family to family. Brand-choice decisions were usually either husband or jointly made decisions and entertainment decisions were wife or joint decisions. Financial decisions emerged as the area of greatest variation with the results almost equally divided between husband dominant and joint households (43). The previous remarks indicate that responsibility in families for various decision areas and tasks seldom demonstrates a dominant authority pattern. The authors cautioned that even among families, (approximately half of the sample) in which a dominant authority pattern appears to exist, it emerges clearly in relation to the "traditional sex-specialized areas such as financial decisions or housekeeping, rather than new or 'open' areas, such as shopping for furniture, choosing vacations, etc." (45).

Another study of 280 student couples by Price-Bonham (1976) found that resources have a different influence on the decisions of husband and wives. As you remember from the previous chapter, a resource can be anything that one spouse may make available to the other, helping that spouse to satisfy his or her needs or attain his or her goals (Blood and Wolfe, 68). According to this theory, the spouse who contributes the greatest resources to the marriage will have the greater influence and power over decision making. Resources included in this study were age, income, education, number of children (felt to lower power of wife but not proven in this study), father's and mother's occupational status and educational level at time of marriage. Although each individual indicated the degree of importance each decision had to them, the results showed little relationship to resource variables (Price-Bonham, 629). Also, the greater the wife's resources, the greater the input she had in decisions in areas "which could be described as the 'internal domain', i.e. having to do primarily with living arrangements and activities." As the wife's resources increased, her input into decisions relating to the external world decreased relatively (634). This means that husbands exerted more influence over decisions about where to live, how to invest incomes, and contacts for business or political matters.

The results showed variation between the couples with mixed reactions, however "some resource variables do have influence on some decisions" (638). Sprey (1975) also concludes that expertise becomes a major factor in joint decision-making and problem-solving situations since resources and skills in each partner result in a division of labor (70). Thus it appears obvious that the role functions carried out in a family affect the decision-making process. These roles vary greatly from family to family and this means each family's decision making must be studied to see whether they fit the generalizations from the research presented. Although related to male-female roles and decision making, we separated out the use of force since it represents an abuse of role expectations.

Force and Decision Making

In our house you went along with parental decisions or you were punished—it was as simple as that. I had one brother who was a rebel and my father would beat him with regularity. My mother usually went along with whatever my father said because I think she was scared of him, too.

Some family members use force to settle decision making. In an investigation of how family members intimidate one another, Steinmetz (1977) substantiated that violence as a problem-solving method was learned in a family setting which reflected society's attitude toward permitting the use of physical force in intimate relationships. The method the parents used to solve their problems became the method usually employed to solve parent-and-child and child-to-child problems. Thus the parental approach to decision making became the model for other family interactions to follow. When verbal aggression and physical force characterized the parents' attempts to make decisions, the same behavior appeared in the behavior of a parent with his or her children or between the children when they disagreed (Steinmetz, 20–21). [See also Raschke & Raschke, 1979; Straus, 1979.] As unfortunate as it seems, many people use fists rather than words to settle family problems.

Additional Influences

Sometimes I am overwhelmed about all the decisions young people have to make, or are able to make. When Ralph and I decided to marry, we went through all kinds of traumas on whose education should continue and whose job should take precedence. Now that we've been married eight years we have to make decisions about having a child. We have spent hundreds of hours discussing all the implications of having children and how we would raise them and how we would adjust our lifestyles to accommodate them.

Since each family represents one subsystem among many, with permeable boundaries, all sorts of outside factors affect how a family operates. Mom's salary, BJ's friends, and Mary Frances' teacher may all affect how a decision is resolved. Children's peers exert strong influence on decision making. In an interesting report on decision making by ninth and twelfth graders who were asked to select between alternatives approved by parents and by peers, boys in the ninth grade chose the parent-endorsed alternative more than either ninth-grade girls or twelfth-grade boys. Girls' responses tended to remain stable over the same period (Emmerich, 1978, 178).

On a larger scale, "government, business, and industry are deeply and permanently involved in policies that impact upon families" (Hawkins, 1979, 270). Hawkins sees policy decisions by government and industry often as nonfamily oriented, individualistic, and sometimes inhuman and harmful. As evidence of adverse policies, he cites families' lack of adequate health insurance, restrictions on Medicaid and Medicare, extreme dependence upon schools to do what families, churches, and the legal system used to do, factory closing, nonflexible hours of work, and businesses' insistence upon moving plants or personnel (267–268). Decisions forced upon a family by outside agencies restrict the individual family members' choices and require flexibility and adjustments, sometimes for poor reasons, often resulting in more tension in families.

Time • Each family has only so much time to spend on decisions and members compete for the available time. It takes far less time to solve some problems by nondemocratic means. In our earlier discussion of communication networks, we noted how the chain pattern or Y pattern could be used to expedite matters but that the all-channel equal access network required more time for decisions to be decided upon or carried out. The important point is that whatever the network or pattern of decision making followed, the more democratic and egalitarian the communication is, the more likely that additional time has been used. It may well be worth the investment to improve communication in the family system but the many demands upon the family members' time often results in short circuits to decisions. One person can think through his or her own problem more quickly than several family members, but the person is limited to his or her own input and loses the suggested and possibly better alternatives other family members could offer. Too often families in trouble have not taken enough time to make decisions that solve problems. Hastily made decisions may require dominant behavior and power plays by some family members to maintain the outcome. This would lead to less satisfaction for other individuals in the family. Decisions may appear final at one moment and then be reconsidered at a later time. What seemed like the best decision may upon experience be proven otherwise and necessitate a new search for a better decision. In a viable open family system this would be a healthy state—all decisions subject to re-evaluation and study whenever new information or changes seem important to any family member.

Personal Investment • How many times have you dropped out of or avoided a family decision-making session because you didn't care about the result? If you don't see how things affect you, you are not likely to get too involved even though as a system member you will be affected. Not all family members care equally about the outcome of decisions. Antonio's desire to go to college away from home may not affect his younger brothers directly. Mom's desire and need for a new refrigerator will not be perceived as important to a teenager. If money, or any other shared resource is scarce, decision making can become a competitive process for the limited resources. Turk (1974) reminds us that "the decisions may be irrelevant or differentially relevant to some individuals and families; even if relevant, the decisions may not be points of disagreement" (44).

The communication in making decisions changes greatly as the children grow and develop their own sense of self-sufficiency. The same holds true for parents who also go through great changes and growth. Network formations reflect these changes, as do rule adjustments. As parents grow accustomed to problem solving and each year encounter different situations demanding solutions, they can't replicate previous decisions, even if they so desired. The real world doesn't hold that constant. Their personal investment in decisions varies over time with the degree of separateness or connectedness within the family system. The dependence-independence of the members fluctuates and definitely changes as children become adults and leave home. Parents learn from their decision successes and failures with older children and as a result the communication going into decision making with younger children may be quite different than it was with older children. A highly cohesive family will more likely have all members investing time in important decisions that affect all members. However, in decisions that do not jeopardize unity, members may invest little interest and trust the others to be fair.

Since the family is never static, individual members can also be involved in several decision-making matters simultaneously both within and outside the family. These other matters requiring decisions, depending upon their importance, affect the members involved and determine their degree of active or passive commitment to new decisions.

Empathy • Empathy, an important element in effective communication, relates to power and decision making. Olson (1969) defines empathy operationally as the individual's ability to predict the decision of the other spouse on presenting problems. The greater the empathy regarding a particular decision, the greater the agreement between the measures of predicted and actual power (549).

If one member of a family exerts too much power in the form of coercion, control, or suppression over another, decision making falters. According to Filley (1975), problem solving requires an equalization of power. He writes of the necessity of providing a favorable power balance by employing problem-solving methods which insure a balance of power (7).

COMMUNICATION IN DECISION MAKING

Remember our discussion of these family decision-making factors as you read next the results of a comparison of communication and decision making between married and unrelated couples. Note how communication differs in decision making because a couple operates within their own system and the unrelated individuals do not have those systemic ties to consider before deciding. Winter, Ferreira, and Bowers (1973) studied 20 married couples paired for the experiment. They measured spontaneous agreement (the shared values and like preferences among family members that exist prior to the decision-making process); decision time; choice fulfillment (the number of times a positive or negative choice by one agrees with that of the partner); silence (the length of time no one communicated); interruptions by one or the other; explicit information (a definite statement of a liked or disliked choice); and politeness (overall impression of how couples treated one another: tone of voice, asking questions, listening quietly, and being supportive). The results indicated married couples had more spontaneous agreement; were less polite; made more interruptions; and exchanged less explicit information (83). The higher degree of spontaneous agreement would be expected because a married couple has over time learned from the values and wishes of one another and each has a history of arguments or sharing over these values. Married and single couples took about the same amount of time to reach decisions and were almost equally effective in reaching mutually satisfying decisions (88). Unrelated stranger couples listened more respectfully to one another than married couples—a sad commentary on marital communication. Also when married couples interrupted one another the communication was impaired. The authors explain: "Married dyads may be hurt or offended by an intrusion because of what this implies about their relationship with a spouse who can affect them deeply. Unmarried couples are less emotionally involved, more task-oriented" (92).

Throughout all of the materials in this chapter it can be seen that communication used effectively or ineffectively plays a key role in determining the outcomes of family decision making. How family members use communication, both its verbal and nonverbal components reflecting their levels of adaptation/cohesion determines decision-making outcomes. The sending of mixed messages by one or more members affects decisions and may alter the cohesion and balance of the family system. Thomas (1977) listed the following communication difficulties that hinder decision making:

> . . . overtalk, overresponsiveness, quibbling, overgeneralization, presumptive attribution, misrepresentation of fact or evaluation, content avoidance, content shifting, content persistence, poor referent specification, temporal remoteness, opinion surfeit, opinion deficit, excessive agreement, excessive disagreement, too little information, too much information, illogical talk, and negative talk surfeit. There are some others that are potentially less serious, but if extreme, may interfere to some extent, also. These are affective talk, obtrusions, excessive question asking, excessive cueing, and acknowledgement deficit.   (123)

Researchers have argued over whether the dominant authority structure in a family can be determined from the manner in which decision-making responsibilities have been allocated or from studying the decision-outcomes (Douglas & Wind, 1978; Cromwell & Olson, 1975; Safilios-Rothschild, 1970; Sprey, 1975). The conclusion is that family authority and decision making operate as a dynamic, interactive system, requiring give and take among family members. The process remains a complex and involved one which can be streamlined by experiences of a life of shared communication attempts.

For fifty years Lambert and I have always tried to make decisions together. We try to spend our money as we both see fit and discuss what is important to us. We usually shop together: groceries, machinery, cars, etc. Even on buying our tombstone, we looked them over and decided on one we both liked. We've had our differences but we always tried to see things from the other point of view and eventually we'd resolve the problem.

CONCLUSION

In this chapter we discussed consensus, accommodation, and de facto kinds of decision making that families may use. These decisions may occur in families that govern their systems by zero-sum confrontations; by the creation and maintenance of rules of direct distribution of resources; by rules designating authority and rules guiding negotiation; by guiding principles of fairness based on conscience. Thomas (1977) summarized the research findings on items that usually improve decision making:

> (1) a definition of all aspects of the problem in specific, operational terms; (2) a full and comprehensive description of all the problem elements; (3) consideration of all relevant facts; (4) generation of alternatives in a brainstorming, freewheeling fashion in which criticism and judgment are deferred until the point of evaluation; (5) statement of the solution in very specific terms, at the point of decision; (6) selection of the decision response likely to be reasonably successful and satisfactory rather than one that necessarily maximizes given outcomes; (7) inhibition of action until the point of decision has been reached; (8) verification of the adequacy of the solution after the solution response has been carried out.   (114)

We next focused on the steps in decision making that families can use to communicate differences and yet reach decisions on problems. Compromise may be required but the problem-solving approach has the potential to strengthen cohesion in the family. The chapter concluded with a variety of factors from roles to empathy that affect the communication in decision making.

9

Communication and Family Conflict

Communication was poor between my mother and father. Besides not fighting in front of us children, there weren't many signs of affection. What probably happened was by the time I came along, if they were to come in close range to each other, World War III would have broken out—the grievances were so many. Mother told me stories of how she kept hurt feelings and complaints inside her from incidents that occurred years ago. Her favorite role was the family martyr. Her motto was then and still is "See how hard I'm trying."

And my father was a bad fighter if he fought at all. He'd always hit below the belt. Mixed messages were his favorite and he always found it necessary to make a fool out of my mother and call her stupid or dumb. As a result, my mother never trusted my father. Those two could never level with each other.

Conflict happens daily in some families and far less in others. Sometimes the conflicts seem to be predictably tied to times of day, people, past issues, or times of the year. Other times they seem to emerge out of thin air. When you think about your family, you may be able to establish the whys and whens of some conflicts, particularly the predictable ones.

Whenever people in a family unit experience pressure, threats, fear, and insecurity, conflicts can occur. Healthy families engage in some type of conflict. Highly cohesive or enmeshed families may avoid conflict so as not to threaten the system's balance while disengaged systems may not care enough to conflict. The flexible family has a greater chance of resolving conflicts than either a chaotic or a rigid one.

As we examine the conflictual processes within this chapter, we will suggest that conflict is influenced by many factors and may range on a continuum from constructive to destructive with the outcomes varying on that continuum.

THE CONFLICTUAL PROCESS

In the previous example of conflict within a family, the student remarked: "Mother told me stories of how she kept hurt feelings and complaints inside her from incidents that occurred years ago." In this account notice that the conflict developed in a definite, predictable way with each parent demonstrating certain behaviors. Most family systems develop their own fighting styles.

Conflict Defined

Let's start by defining conflict as a process in which two or more members of the family believe that what they desire is incompatible with what the other wants. It may be a matter of perception when Adam believes that the intimacy expected of him is too threatening or requires more of him than he cares to deliver willingly. Conflict may also develop over a difference in attitudes or values. Christine doesn't enjoy cooking and would rather the family went out to eat pizza than expect her to fix dinner. Finally, conflict may emerge when one person's self-esteem is threatened. If each person can reach his or her own goals, there is no conflict. Conflict happens when one person's behavior or desire blocks the goals of another resulting in "a struggle over values, behaviors, powers, and resources in which each opponent seeks to achieve his goals usually at some expense to the other" (Scanzoni, 1980, 31).

The process is very complex. Dan may have had a fight with his boss and because he could not take his anger out at work he came home and exploded about the late dinner. Midge and Ben may seem to have a fight just when things are working really well—when they have really gotten into a pattern of sharing and affection. And sometimes families never experience a real fight—things just seem to go on without much feeling—no fighting and not much loving.

Sociologist Lewis Coser (1967) declares "conflict may be a result just as much as a source of change" (32). His ideas can be applied to family systems. A new family member, the acquiring of a new job or home, the trauma of a divorce, death, or loss of income, will have a differential impact within the family system. Disturbances in equilibrium lead to conditions in which groups or individuals no longer do willingly what they are supposed to do since "change, no matter what its source breeds strain and conflict" (32). Families' systems experience some constant level of friction since they continually change to survive and cope with conflict, either realistically or unrealistically. Coser defines realistic conflicts as those that result "from frustration of specific demands and from estimates of gains of the participants, and which are directed at the presumed frustrating object insofar as their means toward a specific end" (98). Coser distinguishes nonrealistic conflicts as those characterized by the need for tension release of at least one antagonist. Within family systems this would mean that conflict directed toward members for the improvement of conditions and rights would be realistic. Nonrealistic conflicts may result from frustrations caused by family members or outsiders other than those persons against whom the conflict is waged. Such behavior may result in misdirected anger or scapegoating. For the conflict to be realistic the communication must be between the family members directly involved in the matter.

If a couple or family plans to share experiences, and realizes the advantages of family solidarity, conflict will be an inevitable and valuable part of the process. Too often family conflict evolves into a stalemate or bitter fight and no members emerge happily. By exploring the process of conflict and how it can develop realistically or nonrealistically, plus becoming aware of better communication practices to use during conflict, you can better understand the development and management of conflict situations within family life.

Several studies conclude that conflicts are equally present in successfully functioning marriages as well as in dysfunctional marriages (Mudd, Mitchell, & Bullard, 1962; Olson, 1967; Vines, 1979). Although all marriages or relationships have problems, the successful ones have partners who learn how to negotiate conflicts. In addition, conflict outside the home in jobs, social groups, or friendships can cause unrealistic conflicts within the family. No individuals living together in a close and intimate relationship can expect a conflict-free existence. Studies reveal that in certain stages of courtship for some couples there is little conflict but that as the relationship progresses conflicts do develop.

In his work on measuring intrafamily conflict, Straus (1979) states that conflict is an inevitable part of all human association and keeps social units such as nations or families from collapse. "If conflict is suppressed, it can result in stagnation and failure to adapt to changed circumstances and/or erode the bond of group solidarity because of an accumulation of hostility" (75). Most people, especially those in close relationships, fear conflict and seek ways to avoid it. But avoiding conflict can lead to further difficulties because the underlying problems causing it haven't been solved.

Stages of the Conflictual Process

To better understand this complex phenomena, let's examine how conflict develops as a positive or negative human process. Conflict develops in stages with a source, a beginning, middle, end, and aftermath (Filley, 1975, 7–19; Turner, 1970, 137). These stages characterize conflict as a process:

1. Prior Conditions Stage
2. Frustration and Awareness Stage

3. Active Conflict Stage
4. Solution Stage
5. Follow-Up Stage

As these stages are explained, think about a recent conflict in your family. Did each of these stages emerge as a distinct entity or was it difficult to know when one ended and the next happened?

Prior Conditions Stage • Conflict doesn't occur without some prior reason or relation of the present event to the past experiences in the family. It doesn't emerge out of some vacuum, but has a beginning in something in the background of the relationship of the people conflicting. The family system or context establishes a framework out of which conflicts arise. The participants are aware of the family's rules, themes, boundaries, biosocial beliefs, and accepted patterns of communication.

In conflict at least one member perceives that the rules, themes, boundaries, or beliefs have been violated or that they have been threatened by something inside or outside the family. Prior conditions are present in the absence of conflict but under pressure come into play. Such prior conditions which may affect a new conflict situation include: ambiguous limits on each family member's responsibilities and role expectations; competition over scarce resources such as money or affection; unhealthy dependency of one person upon another; negative decision-making experiences shared by those involved in the conflict; necessity for consensus and agreement by all on one decision; and the memory of previously unresolved family conflicts (Filley, 8–12). Thus, past experiences set the groundwork for new tension.

Frustration Awareness Stage • The second conflict stage involves one or more family members becoming frustrated that some person or group is blocking them from satisfying some need or concern. This leads to an awareness of being attacked or threatened by something they have seen or heard. It may be

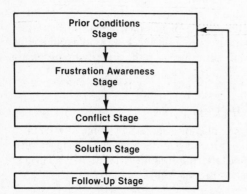

Figure 9-1 Model of Family Conflict

a nonverbal message in the form of a stern look or in avoidance of eye contact. If you closely monitor any developing conflict, usually nonverbal cues of conflict appear before verbal ones. As you become aware of the conflict, you may ask, "What's wrong?" "What's his problem?" "Why am I not being understood?" This awareness depends upon the mutual perceptions of the individuals involved which provides their judgments of the issues in the conflict. Inaccurate perceptions can create conflict where none exists. Perceptions also affect the degree to which the participants feel they will be threatened or lose if the conflict continues. Conflict may end at this stage if one party decides, based on his or her perceptions, that the negative consequences outweigh the possible advantages. In families this happens when one of the parents shows signs of power and expects compliance or else. The "backing off" from the issue ends the conflict but doesn't remove the causes or satisfy the needs that provoked it. This kind of unrealistic conflict may also be avoided through leveling or self-disclosure. "I'm really just upset about the test tomorrow and I'm taking it out on you," or "You're right—I was selfish and I'm sorry."

Active Conflict Stage • In the third stage the conflict manifests itself in a series of verbal and nonverbal messages. This symbolic interchange can either be like a battleground or relatively calm depending upon the rules and style in the family that govern fighting. In some families yelling and screaming signal the fight of the decade whereas others exercise their lungs weekly over minor issues.

An outsider looking in on my family would believe that no one spoke on a normal level, sound wise. Everyone screams including Adrienne who usually screams the loudest and the longest. She can be topped only by my mother who's had a lot of practice refereeing family fights. Someone asked Adrienne once why she screamed so much and she told them that because she was the smallest one, she had to speak louder than anyone else to make sure that she was heard.

Typically conflict escalates from initial statements and queries to some kind of ultimatum or bargaining. More will be said later in this chapter about ways to fight fairly and unfairly in families. In the active conflict stage there is a discernible strategy or game plan as one or more family members try to maneuver and convince others of the merits of the issue. The longer the conflict continues, the more the participants' behavior may create new frustrations, reasons for disliking, and continued resistance. During the conflict sides may be taken and family subsystems and coalitions come into action.

Solution Stage • The active conflict stage evolves into the solution stage when some resolution of the problem takes place. The solution may be creative, constructive, and satisfactory to all involved, or it may be destructive, nonproductive, and disappointing. The solution may represent a compromise or adjustment of previously held positions. In this stage how the conflict is managed or the methods used in solving it determines the outcomes and whether positive or negative results follow.

Follow-Up Stage • The final follow-up stage could also be called aftermath because it includes the later reactions that follow the conflict and affect future interactions such as: re-eruptions of the same conflict, avoidance, or conciliation without acceptance. The grudges, hurt feelings, or physical scars may fester until they lead to the beginning stage of another conflict. The outcomes may be positive, such as increased intimacy and self-esteem, or honest explorations of family values or concerns. This aftermath stage is linked by a feedback chain to the initial stage because each conflict in a family is stored in the prior conditions "bank" of the family computer and comes into operation in determining the pattern of future conflicts.

An Example of the Conflict Model • To demonstrate the operation of this model of conflict in action, let's study an example in the Hanrahan family. The family consists of five members: Dad (45), Mom (45), Chuck (21), Jay (18), and Alice (15). At the Friday evening meal Alice asks her mother to take her to a distant suburban shopping center to look for a new raincoat she needs. Mom responds positively because Alice has been promised the coat and has been most helpful with house chores. Jay assumed he could have the only family car for a date and silently he begins to react. He thinks about other family hassles over the car and recalls other encounters between himself and his sister when Mom took Alice's side. Jay wonders if Dad or Chuck would agree with him that his date was more important than buying a raincoat. In the past the men in the family have banded together. All of these prior conditions are important antecedents to any outcome of this conflict.

Communication shifts into the second stage. Jay clears his throat and nonverbally gains his mother's attention by slightly raising his fork and pointing it toward his mother. He has entered the frustration stage because the planning between Mom and Alice is going too far. There is no way he and his date can walk three miles to the movie they planned to attend. Jay announces, "I was going to use the car tonight." Both his mother and Alice cease talking and nonverbally check Jay out, their eyes asking the question, "Are you serious?" They discover that he is and also that he looks angry enough to fight for the right to the car. The women then look at one another as if to say "Where do we go from here?" This leads to the third stage—active conflict.

"I asked Dad on Wednesday if I could have the car," Jay declares. The women exchange glances again and then each looks at Dad who nods in agreement. "Also I checked with Chuck and he didn't want the car until tomorrow night when his buddy comes into town and he wants to pick him up." Chuck nods to confirm this.

"We never get to use the car," Alice says in a defeated voice. "When all of you (looking at each of the men) get through using the car, there is no time left for what I want to do." Her voice begins to rise as she pushes her chair back and noisily begins to pile up her dishes.

Mom anxiously glances at all the children and then to her husband who catches her eye and then looks toward Alice and toward Jay. His silent message seems to be, "How are we going to solve this?"

This scene of conflict could continue in countless ways. The parents could remain silent and Jay and Alice could escalate the conflict into a series of harsh remarks, including charges of favoritism, or wasting family money, thus repeating unsolved family brawls. The development of the controversy will depend upon what the prior conditions "bank" includes and the family problem-solving style. What rules do they follow in conflict situations? What roles do father or mother assume in such disputes? If Mom is the peacemaker, she will smooth things over. If Father becomes dominant, he will negotiate a settlement—fair or otherwise.

The solution stage of the conflict starts as Dad speaks up: "Wait a minute! Perhaps Mom and I can help this argument." Mom smiles and eye contacts Dad to let him know she likes this idea and smiles at Jay. He still looks concerned. Alice looks at Dad. In this family's conflicts the parents present a unified position and the father usually asserts that "he and Mom" will be the arbitrators. Dad asks, "Is there any way we can go another time?" Alice indicates that won't work by shaking her head. Dad then looks at Jay. His unstated question is to inquire if he has any flexibility and could change his plans. Jay sends back a "no compromise" message. "It's too late to call off a date now," he declares. "Well, what can we do?" Dad asks: "Are there any other options?"

This leads to a series of solutions being offered. "Could Alice and Mom go tomorrow to look for the coat?" Chuck volunteers. "Mom and I could go get the coat now and get back by 8:30 before the second movie starts," Alice suggests.

"Would that work?" Mom asks Jay. Jay shrugs. He doesn't really prefer that solution. "Could you call Carol and ask if she would mind going to the last show?" Dad inquires. "What time had you planned to meet her?" Mom asks Jay. "Around seven." "Could you call and ask to pick her up later?" Jay moves toward the phone.

In this family a compromise solution worked. Jay arranged for a later date and the family had learned something more about how flexibility can maintain unity. This completes the solution stage in which accommodation and conciliation take place if the situation is positively resolved.

The last stage—follow-up or aftermath—continues the conflict process. The family will store in their "prior conditions" computer the positive aspects of this experience as they add this conflict to their family history. Jay may feel Alice owes him a favor and Alice may be more willing in a future encounter to agree because Jay accommodated her. Stored also will be the amount of self-worth and self-confidence each family member received in this conflict. That's why the feedback link is so important from this follow-up stage back to the first stage of conflict. Future conflicts are affected by the positive or negative aspects of current conflict.

FACTORS IN FAMILY CONFLICT

The saddest consequence of my parents' inability to air their grievances was that it spread to the children. Scapegoating was very prevalent with my parents and it spread to the rest of the family who usually used the same people. My parents usually avoided dealing with important issues directly and while we were growing up we would have big battles over everyday stuff but most of the children learned not to deal with the critical stuff. We fell into their pattern and I can see that it is hurting my sisters' marriages.

Although you may find that you fight with your friends or co-workers in a variety of manners, it is likely that you have found a conflict pattern that you seem to fall into when engaging in conflict at home. Over time most families develop their rules for conflictual situations and each member stays within the calibrated levels except for unique situations when he or she may go beyond the acceptable levels of fighting or reconciling behaviors. A tearful embrace may jolt the family pattern far more than a flying frying pan. The family's systemic nature affects the conflictual patterns which emerge and maintain themselves. As the system's architects, the couple sets the stage for the style of conflict developed within the family.

Scanzoni (1972) classified conflicts into two major types: those which concern the basis in the relationship and those which concern less central issues (73). The first happens when basic values and goals held by one family member are ignored or challenged by the other. Conflict over these values can become quite painful or have a dysfunctional effect upon the family system. Unresolved, these conflicts could result in separation or termination of the relationship. These value conflicts might be over religion, having children, or need for education. The second type results in the couple or family members seeking some ways "to change or maintain some part of the distribution of rights and privileges in the relationship" (76). Such conflicts might deal with problems over which bills to pay or where should the family go for vacation.

Patterns of Family Conflict

In their major study of conflict in early marriage, Rausch et al. (1974) found that ". . . whatever the contributions of the specific partners, the marital relationship forms a unit, and the couple can be thought of as a system." Their analysis revealed that the marital unit was the "most powerful source in determining interactive events" (201). Couples developed their own styles of conflict which were unique to them. Soon after marriage the system had its own fight style.

How does a fight style form so quickly? Do yellers marry yellers, apologizers mate with apologizers? Our common sense tells us this is not always the case, yet within a short time, a couple appears to acquire a set of conflictual behaviors which characterizes them. Rausch and his colleagues found similar responses to be one of the major determinants of interaction, i.e., certain conflictual behaviors of one partner were more likely to elicit similar responses from the other partner. The couples they studied exhibited behavioral reciprocity in a way that ". . . cognitive acts by one partner elicit a higher than expected proportion of cognitive responses from the other; approaches to resolution draw similar approaches from the partner; and attempts at emotional reconciliation receive responses in kind . . ." (198). The same reciprocal pattern holds for negative behaviors such as coercive tactics or personal attacks. The only exception occurred when one partner rejected the other. Rejection usually met with either coercion or emotional appeals. If each partner rejected the other, communication would end. Family members' use of appeals, whether to fair fighting, justice, promises, future favors, etc., keeps the communication process going. Thus partners were more likely to send similar messages than they were to shift to a new message style. Such reciprocity is a tendency, not an absolute; conflict does not function as a totally predictable ritual with foregone conclusions. Certain partners may have such different approaches to fighting that reciprocity does not emerge. In the Fitzpatrick typologies discussed in Chapter 6 the Separates, Traditionals, and Independents each displayed particular conflict styles, and when different types marry each other, it may be more difficult to create the reciprocity than when similar types marry. Rosenblatt, Titus, and Cunningham (1979) found that when one or both partners used disrespect, coercion, and other abrasive factors in their communication, conflicts escalated and the couples spent less time together. Before togetherness (or what we call connectedness) could be increased and conflicts settled amicably, the researchers concluded the couples "must first deal with abrasive aspects of the relationship" (54).

As noted, Feldman (1979) views a couple's non-productive conflictual behavior as part of an intimacy-conflict cycle. Couples moved from a state of intimacy as one member became anxious or fearful which led to conflict-provoking behaviors. These behaviors caused conflict and separation between the partners. Eventually one partner or the other would make an attempt to patch up the differences. The desire for intimacy would draw them back together. This need to be touched, reaffirmed, comforted, and nourished is so strong in humans that it serves as a powerful conciliatory force in conflicts. At first one partner might reject attempts to resume more positive communication, but the need for intimacy would provide the motivation for repeated efforts to achieve it (69–70). This research relates to our emphasis upon separateness and connectedness as an issue present in all families.

The couple's coming back together doesn't mean the problem between them has been resolved. Quite often the issue has not been satisfactorily discussed or even fairly treated in the best interests of one or the other. This means that future communications on the same issue take up where the old conflict left off. The intimacy will again evolve into conflict when one or the other partners feels threatened by the issue or feels aggressive enough to challenge. Have you heard people fighting and had the feeling you were hearing a rerun or a rehearsed battle? The communication reaches the conflict stage because some rules in the relationship have been violated; the system tries to recalibrate itself. Important dimensions of a marital system's calibration is the degree and limits of acceptable intimacy and acceptable conflict. When these limits are violated, the intimacy-conflict starts over again. The intimacy-conflict cycle ends when the couple learns how to listen to one another's problems, needs, fears, etc., and finds answers to these demands so that each can return the support and nurturing the other desires.

Costs and Rewards

Part of the systemic function relates to how costs and rewards are negotiated. Conflict may result if a teenager believes the costs of living in a family (rules, obligations, pressures) do not outweigh the rewards (emotional/economic). Partners will stay together as long as the rewards for remaining in the system outweigh the pain or costs of leaving it. Caring for children may be part of a reward and responsibility component in a marriage and hold a family together for a time, but eventually if serious conflicts continue, one of the partners will leave. To avoid constant conflicts there must be sufficient rewards in the family system to justify remaining together. Scanzoni goes so far as to state "if a husband wants certain rewards from his wife then he must provide the rewards that she wants; the same is true for her" (63).

Conflicts may follow when these expectations are not met. When one partner does something special for the other mate or some other family member, a debt is owed. If the family member fails to reciprocate, especially after several requests, conflict will start. Reciprocity becomes, or is a part of, the exchange of costs and rewards in the family. For the family to operate emotionally as a system, this reciprocity doesn't need to be equal either in amount or kind. Most family members don't keep an inventory up to date but they know generally who owes them favors. "This reciprocity," according to Scanzoni, "helps to account for marital stability because it sets up a chain of enduring obligations and repayments within a system of roles in which each role contains both rights and duties" (64). To ignore these obligations and repayments creates conflicts in families.

Extreme differences in communication backgrounds may present a couple with problems as they try to work out their own style.

> My former husband was a fight phobic like his father. He would do just about anything not to confront me with a problem. According to him I was perfect. This was to make it look like I was the one who did all the complaining. I found myself having to gunnysack all my grievances because I could never get them out. Every time I tried to talk with him, he'd avoid the situation by running out, changing the subject, telling me not to yell at him, or making a sexual pass at me which, at the time, I was very vulnerable to. Another one of his famous strategies was to put on a real sorry face and apologize, making some consolatory promise that he most likely had no intention of keeping since he never did.

As couples continue in their relationship, they develop a style ranging from constructive to destructive that tends to characterize most of their conflictual situations.

Family Types and Conflict

Family types and structures may affect their conflict patterns. As a couple evolves into a family, the system develops conflictual behaviors which characterize the group, if not the individuals. Using Kantor and Lehr's (1976) types, we can project how the open, closed, or random families behave in crises or conflict situations. These researchers hypothesized that closed families in conflicts frequently suppress the individual. This type of family operates successfully in conflict if members agree on solutions or accept those handed down to them. However, rebellion results when a member differs and a permanent schism develops if one or more members refuses to comply to a major decision.

Family conflict in open families, using Kantor and Lehr's prediction, is usually resolved via group consensus in a meeting. In this meeting decisions can be reviewed and modified. Conflicts are expected and welcomed if they make family living more meaningful. In the decision making, every family member can reveal his or her feelings about the issue. This openness means that promises made in family conferences would be kept (132). The random type family demonstrates no set way to solve conflicts. No one person's views dominate and ambiguity characterizes the negotiations. Emotional impasses occur when no solutions can be agreed upon. Solutions come spontaneously and creatively. Crises are not taken as seriously as in the other two family types and are viewed more as an interruption of the day-to-day events (137).

Roles and Rules in Family Conflict

How conflict is handled in families relates closely to how roles and rules are carried out. Each of the types of families previously discussed have corresponding roles and rule expectations. Position-oriented parents will require permission, while person-oriented parents may look for consensus and have members in shared leadership roles.

As we indicated earlier, conflict may begin when role demands do not coincide with a family member's desires or abilities. He or she may not be prepared to fulfill certain functions. The expectancy that the individual can fulfill the present role causes anxiety and unhappiness (Aldous, 1974). Young husbands raised in households where men never enter the kitchen to help with household chores will find difficulty in doing so even if they willingly hope to change. In conflict, family rules come into operation and determine who can do what, where, when, and how, and for what length of time (Miller, Corrales, and Wackman, 1975, 147).

Communication rules often provide parameters for conflict. The "what," "how," and "who" develop into multitudinous dictates. To what extent can you disagree with your mother? Where, if anywhere, is swearing allowed? What subjects are too painful to talk about?

I realize that this sounds like I made it up, but at 47 I said something to my mother about my sister's cleft palate and she exploded. My mother had always been very conscious of physical beauty and somehow I learned as a child not to mention Laura's problem. When I brought it up in a conversation, as a middle-aged adult, my mother was furious. She said, "No one has ever talked to me about that and I will not hear a word about it. Don't you ever talk about her like that again." That was the end of the conversation.

Permissions are always tied to rules and role expectations. Permissions mean the freedom to find out information or to take any action to satisfy a want or need you desire. For example, conflicts develop in families when one member, possibly a parent or older child, refuses permission for another member in the system to know something or do something meaningful to them. If you want to check in your family to see if a rule exists or test the strength of it, just break the rule and watch what happens. The feedback will usually come quickly and make you aware of the rules.

Socioeconomic Factors

Finally, socioeconomic factors play their part in affecting family conflict styles. Using the categories autocratic, semi-autocratic, semi-democratic, and democratic, Osmond and Martin (1978) studied 512 normal low-income families and found that where the decision making in conflicts was more egalitarian, or democratic, 72 percent of the respondents remained in intact marriages. Only 27 percent of the marriages were intact where the respondents reported autocratic decision making on the part of the husband. They also found that high self-esteem was positively associated with the intact marriages and was found largely in democratic households. The researchers conclude that the egalitarianism of the decision-making process found in the democratic type families was the single most important variable for explaining why these marriages succeeded over the other types. This is an important conclusion to remember since these economically poor families possibly experience greater stress than other families.

Family Developmental Stages

Conflict also relates to the developmental stages of the family which will be detailed in Chapter 10. The issues to be resolved in families vary greatly over the years.

When we were first married Peter and I had horrible fights because we used to hurt each other so much. People just didn't fight in my house growing up so when I got married I was unprepared for someone who would slam doors or raise his voice. The first time Peter got really upset I locked myself in the bedroom for hours. Eventually I learned to fight back with sarcasm or put-downs, but then we really had problems. It took a long time but fourteen years later I can say it was worth the effort. Most of our battles result in clearing the air. The fights are pretty clean.

During the early years of marriage a couple develops a fight style that may be modified as a family grows. In their developmental analysis of newly married couples who had a child within the first two years of marriage, Raush et al. (1974) identified three stages (Newlywed, Pregnancy, Parenthood) which were characterized by varying conflict behaviors. They compared these "developmental" couples to those couples who did not have a child during those years.

During the Newlywed stage, the developmental couples acted generally like the other couples in the sample although certain trends in establishing distance led the researchers to speculate that this group may have had a somewhat more traditional orientation to marriage and male-female relationships (183).

During the later months of the Pregnancy stage, husbands increased markedly in conciliatory behavior, a finding consistent with other studies of husband concern. So the developmental couples behaved more coercively than the matched couples which may indicate a greater ability to "engage in conflict and resolve it" (193).

Finally, during the Parenthood stage analysis, four months after birth, both members of the couple appeared to handle conflict less emotionally and more cognitively than their matched counterparts. Yet the reconciling behavior of the husbands returned to pre-pregnancy levels.

In summarizing their perceptions, the researchers suggest that as marriage progresses through the three stages "couples tone down the emotional impact of the conflicts by moving from outright rejection of the partner to a more rational argumentative mode" (183).

The early stage of being a "threesome" may lead to difficulties since roles need to be reworked and a new person competes for affection, often causing one or the other adult to feel left out. Although a joyful time in most families, early parenthood provides great stresses which lead to significant conflicts.

In the stage of early childhood, parents often make the decisions and solve conflicts by offering few options. As the ability to reason increases with age the resolution of conflict relates closely to the type of family structure previously outlined. The adolescence period usually presents a greater number of conflicts to a family. The physical changes in adolescent bodies accompany the search for independence and the testing of rules and role expectancies. The intense pressure of peer groups heightens conflicts as family beliefs and practices are questioned. Sibling rivalries increase as older children place more distance between themselves and younger children. Teenagers also make space and privacy demands which may cause conflict. One study of family conflict and children's self-concepts found no significant differences in self-concept scores of children from intact, single parent, reconstituted, or other types of families. However, "self-concept scores were significantly lower for children who reported higher levels of family conflict" (Raschke and Raschke, 1979, 367). Broken homes didn't yield broken lives, but excessive family conflict was definitely detrimental.

The "Empty Nest" stage, defined as the period when the youngest child leaves home, presents fewer problems in flexible families than rigid types. The effects on parents of loneliness, rejection, uncertainty, or worry over capabilities of young adults to care for themselves, largely disappear after two years. In fact the leaving has positive effects upon the psychological well-being of some parents because their child has been successful in making it on his or her own merits. Conflicts develop when the youngest lingers and takes extra years to leave (Harkins, 1975).

Older married couples report significantly less conflict and greater happiness and life satisfaction than do younger couples. Morale increases and older couples evaluate their marriages in a positive manner and the quality of their marriages as improving (Lee, 1978, 131).

DESTRUCTIVE VERSUS CONSTRUCTIVE CONFLICT

Now that all the children in our family are grown and almost all moved out, the seriousness of the conflict that has always been somewhat apparent between my parents has really surfaced. Growing up I became a third member of my parents' marital relationship when each of them would tell me what they thought or felt about the other, especially their hostilities, anger, and pain. Neither of them would ever directly confront the other. Meanwhile, I was caught between two powerful forces that both meant a lot to me. I did not want to chose sides and wanted my parents to be together. By allowing them to vent their anger on me, it lowered the tension between them and I acted as a buffer between them.

Most of you have been involved in a variety of conflict situations, some of which were difficult, but resolved themselves well and others which caused great pain or increased anger. On other occasions you may have discovered that you were upset by something but you couldn't put your finger on the exact cause of the problem. Conflict styles may range from the very overt (pots, words, or fists are flying) to the very covert (the burned dinner, the late appearance, the cutting joke). Although all overt conflict cannot be labeled constructive, it does let you know where you stand. Covert conflict, on the other hand, places you in a guerrilla warfare situation. "Is she really angry?" "Am I reading things into his behavior?" "Are those mixed messages?" In almost all cases covert conflict falls into the destructive category.

Destructive: Covert Conflict

Covert or hidden conflict usually relies on one of the following five communication strategies—denial, disqualification, displacement, disengagement, and pseudomutuality. You experience the denial strategy most directly when you hear words such as "No problem, I'm not upset," "No, you didn't hurt me," or "That's OK, I'm fine," accompanied by the nonverbals which contradict the words.

I have experienced mixed message phenomenons all my life. This communication behavior had its most profound effect on me when I left home for college. At the time I did not want to leave home. I did not feel emotionally ready to "go for good." For years my parents had been sending all of us the message that once you leave home you leave forever. Once at school and when I was supposedly "independent," my parents continued to try to run and control my every action. I was supposed to be independent, yet they forced dependency on me. Since this was what I had desired all along, I readily accepted it. I was caught in this bind between the reality and expectation for a long time, until I finally acted out against the confused communication.

Disqualification occurs when a person expresses anger and then discounts or disqualifies the angry reaction, "I'm sorry, I was upset about the money and got carried away." or "I wouldn't have gotten so upset except that my daughter has been very ill." Admittedly some of these messages have validity in certain settings but they become a disqualification when the person intends to cover the emotion rather than admit to it. Everyone has heard some story about the man whose boss yelled at him but the man could not express his anger at the boss. So when he arrived home he yelled at his wife, who grounded the teenager, who hit the fourth-grader, who tripped the baby, who kicked the dog . . . Only in some families this type of incident is not just a story. When you believe you cannot express anger directly, you may find another route through which to vent the strong emotions. Therefore displacement may occur. One possible type of displacement can happen when a couple who cannot deal emotionally with the differences between themselves and instead create a child into a scapegoat to receive the pent-up anger. Many families tend to single out one person who appears to be the "acting-out" child but who, in many cases, receives covert negative messages with such regularity that he or she finds it necessary to act out to release the feelings. (See Ackerman, 1966; Minuchin, 1974; Gurman and Kniskern, 1981.) Dogs, kids, in-laws, friends, spouses, all may bear the brunt of displaced anger.

The disengaged couple or family lives with the hollow shell of the relationships that used to be.

My wife and I should have separated 10 years before we did because we hardly had any relationship. I was able to arrange my work schedule so that I came home after 11 and slept until Margaret and the kids had left in the morning. That was the only way I could remain in the relationship. We agreed to stay together until Nick graduated from high school. Now I feel as if we both lost 10 years of growthful life and I'm not sure the kids were any better off because we all ate and slept in the same house.

Disengaged family members avoid each other and express their hostility through their lack of interaction. Instead of dealing with conflict they keep it from surfacing, but the below-the-surface anger seethes and adds immeasurably to the already tense situation.

Pseudomutuality represents the other side of the coin to disengagement.

This style of anger characterizes family members who appear to be perfect and delighted with each other because no hint of discord is ever allowed to drop the image of perfection. Often only when one member of the perfect group develops ulcers, nervous disorders, or acts in a bizarre manner does the crack in the armor begin to show. Anger in this situation remains below the surface to the point that the family members lose all ability to deal with it directly. Pretense remains the only possibility.

Finally we need to note the relationship of sexual behavior to these covert strategies. For many couples, sex becomes a weapon in the guerrilla warfare. Demands for, or avoidance of, sexual activity may be the most effective way of covertly expressing hostility. Sexual abuse, put-downs, excuses, and direct rejection serve to wound another without the risk of exposing one's own strong anger. These types of covert anger will suffice to make the point that such expressions of anger destroy rather than strengthen relationships.

Often these covert behaviors reject family themes that discourage conflict or independence. Themes such as "We can only depend on each other" or "United we stand—divided we fall" encourage conflict to occur covertly.

Destructive: Overt Conflict

I think that one of the fundamental guidelines for engaging in conflict is to deal with specific behaviors of the other person. From observing them, I see my mother forever name-calling and assaulting my sister with adjectives that are less than agreeable! This only makes her more defensive and resentful of the needless verbal attack. Also conflicts should be limited to the present. My mother and father bring up instances that happened months ago when dealing with my sister, because they have such a vast storage of unresolved conflict. With these unreleased resentments, nobody can be rational during a time of conflict. Inevitably, either my parents or my sister decides to raise an issue at the most inappropriate and undesirable time for the other person. I cannot recall their ever deciding to discuss something at a time convenient to both of them.

Each of us could list overt forms of destructive conflict that we've participated in or lived through. The following represent some commonly used negative behaviors.

Verbal Attack • In all conflicts the language used by the family members has a great impact on the outcome. Word choice quickly reflects the degree of emotion and reveals the amount of respect the conflicting individuals have for one another. Emotional hate terms ("You idiot!" "Creep," "Sneak," "Liar") quickly escalate conflicts. In some families, swearing becomes an integral part of venting rage. In other families the rules do not permit swearing but name-calling replaces it. Each generation has their own slang terms to be used to put down opponents. Such labeling heightens conflicts and slows down the solution process by selecting words that describe and neutralize bad feelings. These attacks are usually accompanied by screaming or other negative nonverbal cues. Families handle verbal attacks in special ways, such as gunnysacking and game-playing.

Gunnysacking. According to the dictionary, a gunnysack is a burlap bag. But according to some family members, a gunnysack is a deadly weapon since gunnysacking implies storing up grievances against someone and then dumping the whole sack of anger on that person when he or she commits the "last straw." In certain conflicting families, members store resentments instead of dealing with them as they occur. Eventually that person dumps the whole gunnysack out when a spouse or sibling or parent does that "one more thing." The offender usually responds by attacking back and the war escalates.

Game-Playing. In many family conflicts there is a great deal of game-playing. Games are nonproductive ways to solve conflicts. Whether the game is "martyr," "poor me," or "stupid," the interaction played out leaves the problem unsolved. Bach and Wyden (1966) suggest that most couples would love to stop playing games since these players never know where they stand. "The more skillful they are, the less they know, because their objective is to cover up motives and try to trick their partners into doing things" (19). Games end when one player refuses to play and be trapped. An essential test of game players is to ask, "How does this solve the conflict on a more permanent basis?"

My mother used to be really good at the martyr game until we got older and wouldn't let her play it anymore. Christmas was always "I don't need anything—just good children." We would hear about all the clothes she didn't have because she spent the money on us. Yet if we said, "We're fine, you get a new coat" she would never do it. Now we just call her at it and our relationships have improved immensely.

Physical Attack • Hitting, screaming, kicking, grabbing, and throwing objects characterize some family conflicts. One study of persons between the ages of 18–30 in families with more than one child revealed that physical aggression was used in 70 percent of the families to settle conflicts between parents and their children and by the children to settle disputes among themselves. Thirty percent of the husbands and wives used physical means to resolve their conflicts (Steinmetz, 1977, 19). These conclusions supported two earlier studies using larger different samples. (Steinmetz, 1973; 1974. See also Steinmetz and Straus, *Violence in the Family,* 1974.) Instead of solving conflicts, violence led to more violence. This study also confirmed results of previous studies that physical punishment increased rather than decreased aggressive behavior in children. Further evidence indicates that child abusers are likely to have been abused children (Straus, 1974, 16). Aggressive nonverbal abuse causes more harm than good as a way to manage conflicts.

The overall issue of climate may determine the destructiveness of certain communication. Too often the entire setting in which conflict takes place is defensive. As a family member becomes more and more defensive he or she becomes less able to perceive accurately motives, values, and emotions of the sender (Gibb, 1961, 141). Such climates are usually characterized by control and blaming, useless behaviors when viewed from a systems perspective that stresses mutual interaction and discourages trying to assign blame or cause.

Constructive Conflict

Remember back to the example of stages used earlier in this chapter and try to list the constructive behaviors that occurred as Jay, Alice, Mom, and Dad tried to plan the evening. The following characterize successful conflict management: (1) a sequential communication exchange in which each participant has equal time to express his or her point of view; (2) feelings are brought out and not suppressed; (3) people listen to one another with empathy and without constant interruption; (4) the conflict remains focused on the issue and doesn't get sidetracked into other previously unsolved conflict; (5) family members respect differences in opinions, values, and wishes of one another; (6) members believe that solutions are possible and that growth and development will take place; (7) some semblance of rules has evolved from past conflicts; (8) members have experience with problem solving as a process to settle differences; (9) little power or control is exercised by one or more family members over the actions of others. These goals are not achieved in many families because young people are cut off from learning these communication and problem-solving skills because their parents either shield them from conflict or typically make the decisions (Hill and Aldous, 1969, 943–944). In some families better modeling of constructive communication takes place as in the following example involving listening:

One of the things that characterize both my parents is their willingness and ability to listen. They may not always agree with us or let us do the things we want but no one feels like they don't care. At least we feel like they heard us and usually they explain their responses pretty carefully if they don't agree with us. As a teenager I was always testing my limits. I can remember arguing for hours to go on a co-ed camping trip. Mother really understood what I wanted and why I wanted to go but she made it clear that she could not permit such a move at that time. Yet I really felt that she shared my disappointment although she stuck to her guns.

Constructive conflict should be a learning experience for future conflicts. Too often families repeat nonproductive patterns of conflict and fight in predictable ways. As was said earlier, a couple's manner of dealing with conflict probably is established during the first two years of marriage and remains quite consistent (Raush et al., 204). Therefore the partners may create a fight style that characterizes fifty years in the first 24 months of marriage. Raush et al. discovered that harmonious couples were composed of two types of small subgroups—"those who manage to avoid conflict and those who deal with conflict constructively" (204). Those who exhibited constructive conflict showed "even within the space of a single scene, sequential communication exchange, growth, development, and sometimes even creativity" (203–204). Both types of harmonious couples demonstrated the capacity to avoid escalation.

In a comparative study of the communication patterns of couples having problems and seeking counseling with those not doing so, Gottman (1977) found that in conflict situations the happier couples began with remarks that let the partner know that although they disagreed on an issue, the other party was a decent human being. They also avoided negative exchanges and ended discussions with some sort of verbal contract to solve the conflict (476).

How do these wonderful harmonious types pull it off? Families seem to be able to manage conflict creatively by recognizing that they have a twofold responsibility to fulfill—to meet their individual needs and wants and to further enrich the family system. This requires give-and-take resulting in compromise. The attitude behind this view enhances flexibility and helps to avoid conflicts that result from being too rigid and assuming that one family member's views must be followed. A conflict that presents something new to the family system that requires accommodation or assimilation tests the strengths and capacities of the system. If the system is flexible and differentiated, family members can more readily accommodate one another, learn new ideas from members and themselves and change (Raush et al., 48). In this flexible family, new ideas don't threaten the stability of the relationships and members can learn from both outside and within the system.

My sister and her husband deserve a lot of credit. During the first years of their marriage everyone thought they would split up because they had such bad fights. But over time and with the help of a minister, they really learned how to argue without destroying each other. They learned new behaviors so that it's not always that he yells and she cries. Also, they can talk about their fights, something they could never do before.

Although we will devote most of Chapter 13 to specific methods of improving family communication, we will treat some of those constructive conflict behaviors briefly here.

CONSTRUCTIVE STRATEGIES TO RESOLVE CONFLICT

A cornerstone to constructive conflict may be found in good listening behavior. It's an important communication skill to use to defuse conflict and help clarify and keep focus on the issues being debated. Empathic listening requires that you listen without judging and try to hear the feelings behind the remarks. This means accurately hearing what the other is saying and responding to those feelings. Remarks like "You're really angry—I hear that," or "I am hearing you say that you have been misunderstood," indicate to a family member that you have listened, yet not become trapped with your own emotions or thinking about "How can I best turn this complaint off?" Restating what you heard a person say can be most helpful and slow down or stop the escalation of conflict. "Bill, are you saying . . . ?" Asking Bill to repeat his contention is another helpful approach.

Some partners will go so far as to switch roles in a conflict and repeat the conflict scene to check out the accusations. It gives the other person a chance to try out the feelings the other person is having in the conflict.

Thomas Gordon (1975) in his Parent Effectiveness Training program has developed a "no lose" method for solving conflicts that depends on careful listening and involves compromise elements. The Gordon approach asks for those disagreeing to hear each other out, find the areas of agreement, and then zero in on the specific differences. He encourages both sides to seek some reward in the solution of the conflict. "If you let me do X . . . I'll do Y." The philosophy of caring and pleasing one another is basic to its success. Even on difficult family problems the method can work because all parties recognize that no one can totally win or totally lose.

Sometimes flexibility and compromise won't solve conflicts. The consequences outweigh the advantages. An individual's self-worth may be more important than family expectations. Some families permit members to decide what's negotiable and non-negotiable for them.

Stating "This is not negotiable for me at this time" enables one to own his or her position and part of the problem. Being tentative and including the phrase "at this time" leaves the door open for future discussion at some later date. Other items may legitimately be non-negotiable for you on a permanent basis (Bernhard, 1975).

Ever since my stepmother went back to school, certain things have become non-negotiable. She would declare time "off-limits" when no one could expect her to do things for them. At first my Dad found this really hard when he wanted company for a movie or when he wanted to have friends over. I had to learn to tell Elise far ahead of time if I needed her to do certain things with me. Then she tries to plan her time so she'll be free. Sometimes it works and sometimes it doesn't.

Fair Fighting

Bach and Wyden designed a fight element chart (Table 9–1, p. 196) with couples scoring plus, neutral, or minus marks on the following dimensions:

1. **Reality**—meaning a measure of the authenticity of the fight. It is based on justifiable, rational factors that feel real and honest.
2. **Injury**—scored plus or fair (above the belt) if partner can absorb it and minus or dirty (below the belt) if partner is harmed or can't tolerate the aggression.

3. Degree of involvement of the parties; scored active (+) or reciprocal if characterized by give and take and passive (−) if one way or evasive.
4. Assuming of responsibility by the one who began the fight; scored minus when initiator disclaims responsibility or displaces it on others.
5. Humor—plus if it aids tension release and minus if it ends in sarcasm.
6. Expression of aggression—plus if open and leveling, minus if covert and vague.
7. Communication—measure of clarity of both nonverbal and verbal messages. Rated plus if communication is open, transparent, and reciprocal in feedback. Minus if characterized by interruptions, poor listening, redundancy, and misunderstanding.
8. Directness that requires a focus on the here and now.
9. Specificity—scored plus if conflicts limited to specific observable behavior but minus if participants label a specific behavior as part of some larger personality trait. (162–165)

According to their method, each fight/conflict can be analyzed on an effects-of-fight profile. The effects of conflict evaluated include hurt, new information learned, positional moment (fight gained ground if couple end hopeful), power, fear, trust, revenge, reparation or reconciliation, centricity or self-worth, autonomy, catharsis, cohesion, and affection (167–169).

The most bitter conflicts in families result from the use of unfair tactics by various members, such behavior can be changed with a commitment to "fair fighting."

As a marriage counselor, I have seen many couples fight and one of the hardest things is to get people to avoid "red flag" words during a fight. I had one couple where the man would call his wife "crazy like your sister" referring to his wife's sister who had been in a mental institution and his wife finally found that calling him a "faggot" sent him through the roof. It took months to get them to finally agree to drop those words from their vocabularies.

In a fair fight, equal time has to be provided for all participants and name-calling or "below-the-belt" remarks prohibited. In this system, family members agree upon how they will disagree. The procedures are agreed upon with time and topic limitations. They can be used only with the mutual consent of the parties involved and the assurance that receivers will listen.

Jim asks his wife, "I'd like to share a gripe with you." "O.K.," Ann replies. She gives permission for Jim to release his feelings and do so without interruption. "I really felt angry this evening when you told Timmy he didn't have to go to the country with us."

In this approach Jim continues to release his anger and during the time granted by his wife has the right to do it. Another rule of fair fighting is that he only can express his anger verbally—no hitting or furniture throwing. Also Ann

Table 9-1 The Fight Elements Profile

	1 REALITY	2 INJURY	3 INVOLVEMENT	4 RESPONSIBILITY	5 HUMOR	6 EXPRESSION	7 COMMUNICATION	8 DIRECTNESS	9 SPECIFICATION
+	Authentic, Realistic	Fair, Above Belt	Active, Reciprocal	Owning up	Laugh with relief	Open, Leveling	High, Clear, Reciprocal feedback	Direct focus	Specific
0									
−	Imaginary	Dirty, Below the belt	Passive, or One-way	Anonymous or Group	Ridicule, Clowning, or Laugh-at	Hidden or Camouflaged	Static, One-way; No Feedback	Displaced focus	General "Analysis"

The "plus" (+) positions on the profile represent good (or "bonding") styles of aggression.

The "minus" (−) positions represent poor (or "alienating") styles of aggression.

The middle (0) positions indicate styles rated as neutral, irrelevant, or unobservable.

The profile is complete when one line is drawn to connect all nine dimensions, intersecting each dimension at the appropriate level (+ or − or 0). When the line stays predominantly above the "0" level, the fight was fought in a predominantly bonding style. When the line stays predominantly below the "0" level, the fight was fought in predominantly alienating style.

could have asked to postpone hearing the gripe until she had time to really listen. The idea of permission is essential because it implies the obligation of the other party to listen.

Ann can deny Jim's charges. This can lead to a careful recounting of just what was said and with what intended meanings. This often helps to clear the air. She can also ask for a break until later if she becomes angry and cannot listen. Also, if true, she can admit her error in judgment.

Whatever rules or methods couples use in their fighting, the nonverbal aspects of conflict need special attention. Careful monitoring of nonverbal cues often reveals the true nature of conflict. Gestures of threat, harsh squinting stares, refusals to be touched or to look at others indicate the intensity of the conflict. In a study of marital communication, Beier and Sternberg (1977) found the subtle nonverbal cues a couple puts into the messages they send determines the climate in which either conflict or peace reigns. By observing nonverbal cues, they discovered that couples who reported "the least disagreement sat closer together, looked at each other more frequently and for a longer period of time, touched each other more often, touched themselves less often and held their legs in a more open position than couples who reported the most disagreement" (96). This correlates directly with Gottman et al.'s conclusion that "nonverbal behavior thus discriminates distressed from nondistressed couples better than verbal behavior" (469).

When the nonverbal cues contradict the verbal statements, a mixed message has been sent to the receiver who must decide "Do I believe what I hear or what I see?"

It is so frustrating to argue with my son because although he seems to be agreeing, I can tell from his nonverbal responses that he just wants me to stop talking. He'll say "You're right" over and over again but his tone of voice says "I don't believe a word of it." You can't really argue against that.

On the other hand, supportive nonverbals can reduce conflict drastically. For example, a soothing touch or reassuring glance has great healing powers.

Managing the physical environment properly may dampen certain conflicts. Reducing the distance between adversaries may help to reduce the noise level in conflicts. Sitting directly across from someone makes for easy eye contact and less chance for missing important verbal or nonverbal messages. Choosing a quiet and appropriate space lessens distractions or related problems.

One thing I learned about fighting with my teenage son is never to raise an argumentative issue when he is in his bedroom. Whenever we used to fight I would go up to talk to him about school or about his jobs in the house and five minutes after we started arguing I would suddenly get so upset about the state of his messy room that we would fight about that each time also. By now I've learned to ask him to come out or to wait until he is in another part of the apartment to voice a complaint.

Thus conflicting family members need to be aware of all the factors that can escalate a fight.

The rewards of better-managed conflicts in families are numerous. Better use of positive communication practices stops the cumulative aspect of conflict —a series of minor conflicts left unsolved become a major one and can escalate into separation, divorce, or emotionless relationships. Successful resolution of conflict that goes through the five stages of our model of conflict leads to emotional reconciliation and affirmation of the participants. It also decreases fear and anxiety within the family. Future joint enterprises become possible for family members. Knowing how to manage conflicts leads to a greater appreciation for the talents of family members and enjoyment of each of them in the "here and now" of living together.

Unresolved Conflicts

If conflict cannot be solved, what happens in the family? Usually there occurs a loss which affects all members as psychological and/or physical estrangement creates and fosters separation among members. Young family members may remain in the home until they go to school or establish a way to support themselves but they may withdraw from family activities. If circumstances force a continued joint living arrangement, a wall of silence may become part of the family life-style. In some families, members may be cut off from all contacts with the family; the members may be treated as nonexistent.

When I married my husband I was essentially making a choice between my parents and Jim. Jim is black and my parents said they would never speak to me again if we married. Although I knew they were angry, I thought that they would come around when we had a baby. Melissa is two years old now and my parents have never seen her. My brother and sister have been to see me but I am "dead" as far as my parents are concerned.

Many unresolved marital conflicts result in divorce, clearly a rejection strategy. One or both members withdraws from the other and sees the ending of their formal relationship as the only logical solution. Yet, when children are involved, spouses are divorced *to* each other; the system alters itself rather than ending. The original family system evolves into new forms which may include new spouses and children. Legal action does not stop interaction of family members.

Some couples stop their conflicts short of divorce because the cost of the final step may be too great, yet the rewards of living together are too few. For these people, some type of destructive conflict characterizes much of their continued shared existence. Such unresolved conflict adds great tensions to the entire family system.

CONCLUSION

Throughout this chapter we have maintained that unless a family is highly enmeshed or extremely disengaged, conflicts will occur. Conflict can be a creative learning process for all family members. Rather than becoming overwhelmed by conflict in your family, there are ways you can more effectively observe and analyze the conflict. We presented a process model to clarify the stages in the conflictual process and followed with a discussion of how factors such as patterns of behavior, costs versus rewards, and family roles and rules affect conflict. With this material for background, we focused next upon the communication aspects of destructive and constructive conflict with suggestions for improvement.

Today there is more conflict in families. According to Straus, the swing in the pendulum of family roles, the inevitability of conflict in time of change, the glorification of aggression and violence provide reasons for greater conflict. The American family lives under many pressures. "Conflict accordingly develops, because the standards of identity support and agreement are unrealistic" (Turner, 159). Yet families survive. One family realistically faced their problems when they sought outside help—a step that can reward a troubled family system:

When I asked my wife what she wanted for our 25th wedding anniversary, my wife said, "Marriage counseling. The next 25 years have to be better than the first." I knew we had many fights but I never knew she was that unhappy. I agreed to the counseling and we really worked on our differences and ways of resolving them. After a few months we were able to talk rationally about things we always fought over—money, my schedule, our youngest son. Next month we will celebrate our 28th anniversary and I can say, "The last three years were a lot better than the first 25."

In this chapter we have advocated that members in family conflicts understand the value of conflict and attempt to use constructive or fair fighting techniques within a supportive climate. It is hoped that children in such homes will carry those behaviors into their newly-formed system and perpetuate a familial constructive conflict model.

10

Family Communication
and Developmental Stress

Last week I met a friend whom I hadn't seen for almost two years. When I asked how her children were, her eyes filled up and she said, "Mark is in Oregon apprenticing as a baker, Sam is in South America in the Peace Corps, and Rachel went to Israel for a year to discover herself before college." Then she shook her head and continued, "If I hadn't told them they could be whatever they wanted to be, they'd be home for Thanksgiving." I was really touched by her response because, although my children are younger, there will come a time when they, too, will grow up and leave home and I will be very sad.

If you think carefully about all the changes in your family only over the last ten years you may be overwhelmed by what you remember. Families evolve and change with each passing season forcing the system into constant adaptations. Duvall (1971), describing the generation spiral says, "As older family members disappear into death, their family life cycles fade away, but their emotional, intellectual, cultural, biological, material and personal legacies continue on through the generation spiral of which they have been a part in their own family life cycle" (125). Certain interaction patterns, images, and themes may continue through many generations of the system. Families may continue to demonstrate predictable patterns of cohesion and adaptation as members join and leave the system's ranks.

In their work on change in the family life cycle, Carter and McGoldrick (1980) develop a model of stressors that affect the family system. This is indicated in Figure 10-1.

The vertical stressors include patterns of relating and functioning transmitted down generations involving all the family attitudes, expectations, labels, and rules. In other words, "these aspects of our lives are like the hand we are dealt . . ." (Carter, McGoldrick, 9). We have examined many of these communication-related stressors as we discussed the images, themes, myths, rules, boundaries, and expectations that come from our families-of-origin.

The horizontal stressors include both the predictable or developmental issues with which a family has to cope as well as the unpredictable events that disrupt the life cycle. Pressures from these current life events interact with each other and the vertical areas of stress to cause major or minor disruption in the family system.

In this chapter we will look at communication throughout the developmental or predictable changes in family life as the premarital relationship moves on to marriage and parenthood until eventually the cycle begins to repeat itself. We recognize that the specific configuration of each family system means it experiences stages of development slightly differently than the people next door, yet each family does pass through certain similar stages within the birth-death cycle. Chapter 11 to follow will focus on some of the unpredictable external stresses that occur as families develop, such as early death, divorce, economic changes, serious illness, or unforeseen good fortune.

We recognize that many people have spent much of their young lives in single parent, blended, or extended families rather than in the natural family. Yet most people begin life in natural families (mother, father, and children of their

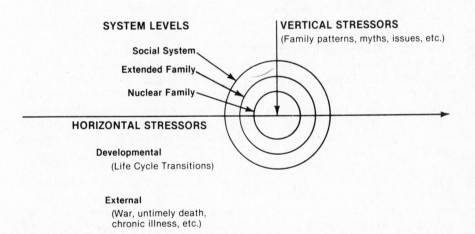

Figure 10-1 Sources of Family Stress

union); as the years go by many of these families evolve into other styles. Some people are born into single families, or blended families where one or both parents have children from previous marriages. Some partners do not have children. This chapter focuses more directly on the predictable changes for a traditional natural family recognizing that this pattern, lived throughout a lifetime, represents only one family form, and is becoming less the norm with each passing year. We will indicate possible variations of the form within this chapter and the following one.

GENERAL ADULT DEVELOPMENT ISSUES

The last decades have witnessed the growth of general interest in adult development, thus refuting one previously held position that adults had "arrived" having passed through childhood and adolescence and that future change or growth was negligible. Although adult changes do not involve the same dramatic events of childhood change, most researchers accept the position that people experience critical periods of change until death. Levinson's (1978) work on the stages of adult male development contained in *Seasons of a Man's Life,* and Sheehy's (1976) popular work *Passages* have brought this mental perspective to the attention of the general public.

Experts differ as to whether or not the developmental focus should be placed on learning theories or stages. Those who stress learning theories maintain that "learning one task or living through one kind of experience makes one ready for the next, presumably more difficult, task, or open to the next order of experience" (Troll, 1975, 5). Thus life is viewed as a series of learning experiences that are not tied to a person's age or position in the life cycle. On the other hand, the stage approach emphasizes sequential changes stressing that all humans at about the same time in their lives experience similar problems or challenges. The stage approach emphasizes sequencing and universality whereas the learning theory approach de-emphasizes universality although some will include sequentiality.

Although we see values to both approaches, we are more likely to accept a stage approach to personal development. You may be familiar with the work of Jung, Erikson, Havighurst, and Levinson who have explored developmental crises or turning points.

Jung views youth and early adult years as a period when the instincts and vital life forces are in ascendance. The late thirties and forties witness a value reorganization as persons become more cultural, spiritual, more introverted, and less impulsive. As a result of this period some persons may fall rigidly into old patterns whereas others experience new growth. Jung also suggests that masculine and feminine features shift into their opposites such that a husband may discover his tender feelings and a wife may find her sharpness of mind (Campbell, 1976, 16).

In his work, *Identity, Youth, and Crisis,* Erikson (1968) details his eight stages of development through which one must pass successfully in order to master the environment, show a certain unity of personality, and perceive the world and self correctly (92). All of the stages lead toward a sense of integrity, of having lived authentically and meaningfully, so that one can accept old age and death with dignity.

Havighurst (1952) describes developmental tasks which must be solved or completed in order to reach life satisfaction within a developmental period. For example, representative tasks of adolescence include developing a sense of self, acquiring an appropriate sex role, and achieving social maturity. Sample tasks of middle age include relating to one's spouse as a person, adjusting to aging parents, and assisting teenage children to become responsible and happy adults.

After intensively studying the lives of 40 men aged 35–45 from four occupations, Levinson entitled his book *The Seasons of a Man's Life.* He chose this since seasons imply that the life course has a certain shape, that it evolves through a series of definable forms. He explains the analogy in the following manner:

> To say that a season is relatively stable, however, does not mean that it is stationary or static. Change goes on within each, and a transition is required for the shift from one season to the next. Every season has its own time; it is important in its own right and needs to be understood in its own terms . . . It is an organic part of the total cycle, linking past and future and containing both within itself.   (7)

You may wonder what all this has to do with families. Just as individuals move through the various seasons of their lives, whole family systems also pass through certain seasons and such passages are reflected in their communication patterns. In the next pages we will examine some perspectives on family development and change and draw some implications for family communication behavior.

FAMILY STAGES: AN OVERVIEW

As you can imagine, we cannot study family change by relying on the different members' stages of development because the complexity would be overwhelming. Instead many family researchers have attempted to apply the stage concept to whole families so that the entire system may be thought of as moving through particular stages. Such analysis has difficulties because families consist of several individuals in different life stages but it becomes more manageable than trying to account for each person.

Hill (1970), a proponent of this approach, emphasizes its developmental nature or the "time dimension neglected by other conceptual frameworks dealing with the family but its focus is on the family as a small group association, the nuclear family occupying a common household" (295). Essentially the system moves through transitions.

Traditionally family stages have been generated through examining the number of positions in the family, or through the age composition of the family, and through changes in the age-role content of the husband-father position. The following sample scheme stresses the age-impact of the children.

    I.   Establishment (newly married, childless)
   II. New Parents (infant–3 years)

III. Preschool Family (child 3–6 years and possibly younger siblings)
IV. School-Age Family (oldest child 6–12 years, possibly younger siblings)
V. Family with Young Adult (oldest 20 until first child leaves home)
VI. Family as Launching Center (from departure of first to last child)
VII. Postparental Family, The Middle Years (after children have left home until father retires
VIII. Aging Family (after retirement of father) (Hill, 1970, 300)

Such a scheme provides simplicity but does not account effectively for families with numerous children or widely spaced children as they go through the middle stages of development. Nor does it focus on adult developmental stages or tasks unrelated to childrearing. More detailed perspectives exist but their complexity limits their use. No matter which framework we adopt, communication emerges as a critical issue at each stage. Hill highlights the complexity of the communication networks and the subsystems as the family enlarges and then contracts, stating:

> This intimate small group has a predictable natural history, designated by stages beginning with the simple husband-wife pair and becoming more and more complex as members are added, with the number of interpersonal relations reaching a peak with the birth of the last child, stabilizing for a brief period, to become less and less complex subsequently with the launching of adult children into jobs, and marriage as the group contracts in size once again to the dyadic interaction of the husband-wife pair. (296)

If we had a book rather than a chapter in which to discuss communication issues relevant to stages of family development, we would try to relate these stages to individual development from childhood through adulthood. These family stages interact with the individual development of each family member but such analysis would be totally unwieldy. Thus, due to our family focus, we have chosen to follow a scheme involving childrearing and child-age impact recognizing that the scheme does not do justice to general adult issues, such as midlife concerns or tasks.

Based on the findings of many family scholars, we have synthesized the following stages for discussion:

1. Forming the System
2. Beginning Marriage
3. Birth of First Child
4. Individuation (preschool children, school-age children, adolescents)
5. Families as Launching Centers
6. Families in Middle Years
7. Families in Older Years (Satir, 1972, 165; Rollins and Feldman, 1973, 381; Hill, 1970, 300; Troll, 1975, 18)

To further complicate our discussion of the developmental process, the cohesion-adaptability axis overlays each system's personal growth. For example, extremely cohesive families may resist certain changes such as children leaving home, whereas low-cohesion families may splinter when children start to leave. As is rather self-evident, the capacity for adaptability aids a family in moving through its stages of development. A rigid family may try to avoid necessary growthful change whereas highly chaotic families may not even place enough significance on life changes and rites of passage. Families characterized by low adaptation and high cohesion may fight the passage of time that carries them through developmental stages. Family themes, boundaries, images, and biosocial beliefs further complicate movement through the developmental stages. In order to understand the entire process more clearly, let us focus briefly on each developmental stage.

SPECIFIC FAMILY DEVELOPMENTAL STAGES

We got married because we couldn't stand being apart.
We got married because she was pregnant.
We got married because of parental pressure.
We got married because we believed we could build a good life together.
We got married because after four years it was either "do it" or split up.

Forming the System

What brought your parents together? Why did you decide to marry your spouse? What happened when your sister or brother decided to marry? You have probably heard the two classic explanations as to why people are attracted to each other—"opposites attract" or "birds of a feather flock together."

Some people support the "theory of complementary needs"—that persons tend to select mates whose needs are complementary rather than similar to their own. (Winch et al., 1954, 245–248), but the evidence for this position appears weak (Berscheid & Walster, 1969, 85).

Often at the beginning of courtship a couple appears to differ on many issues. Sometimes their very oppositeness is what attracted them to one another because each sought in a mate someone quite different either from themselves or their parents. However, most research indicates people select a mate who matches their socioeconomic background, shares similar values, interests, and ways of behaving (Lasswell and Lasswell, 1973, 23). Similar background and similar attitudes often influence the final decision to marry. Although no research has focused directly on the issue, we imagine that similarity in comfortable levels of cohesion and adaptability might make individuals more attractive to each other.

Proximity and similarity play a large role in whom one encounters and eventually with whom one develops close relationships. People are more likely to date others who live nearby or attend the same school, and who share their social background, which makes it likely that a large proportion of their attitudes and values will be in basic agreement from the start. And once a relationship becomes established, the couple's gradual discovery of just how much agreement exists becomes crucial in determining whether or not they decide to marry (Rubin, 1979, 197).

The choice of mate also depends upon the person's needs and his or her self-perception (Murstein, 1973, 248). Later communication will be affected by these needs either being met or frustrated. Each partner in courtship sets out with some image of the person he or she would be happy marrying. High self-esteem persons are more likely to seek partners like themselves and to express greater satisfaction in their marriages. Murstein reports that low self-esteem persons demand less in their relationship with the opposite sex (248). He also suggests that when both partners considered their partners to be close to their ideal spouse, frequently the self-concept of one individual "bore no relationship to the ideal spouse desired by the other." Murstein predicts that after marriage this discrepancy would become apparent and the spouse would experience disappointment. This disappointment emerges in the verbal and nonverbal messages between the couple.

As you probably know, people come together for a complex of reasons, often unknown to themselves. Yet if the relationship is to grow and prosper, it must involve intimacy-producing communication. In Chapter 4 we detailed the stages of relationship development. The system formation period, usually involving courtship/engagement, involves a couple's attempt to move from the facades of the orientation or exploratory affective exchange stage to deeper levels of communication. Through a variety of communication activities, including self-disclosure, touch, questioning, discussion of family rules and backgrounds, and arguments over values and attitudes, two people discover that indeed they are attracted to one another. This period provides the chance for the couple to share and learn about one another and find ways to communicate effectively. The following diagram partially depicts what happens when two people in courtship communicate.

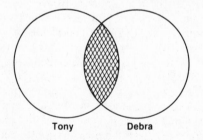

Tony   Debra

Each circle represents the field of experience of each young person. This field includes all the family rules, themes, images, experience in roles, hardships or lack of them in life, success or failure in a previous close relationship, patterns of cohesion and adaptability, and capacities for intimacy and risk-taking. The shaded area represents the overlap in the couple's communication and it means topics, ideas, and feelings that each understands about the other. The couple communicates only when the circles overlap—when one is able to comprehend what the other means with his or her verbal and nonverbal messages. Intimacy increases as they share their meanings.

Both Tony and Debra may also find out through permissions, granted verbally or nonverbally, that there are limits to their communication. Certain topics, feelings, or actions may frighten or offend the other. They create unwritten rules that will govern their communication when they encounter these issues.

As the relationship deepens and marriage appears on the horizon, a series of communication-oriented rituals may occur. The engagement communicates to outsiders the seriousness of the courtship. Prior to the announcement, quite often there have been both verbal and nonverbal signals of the deepening relationship. Significant jewelry may have been exchanged; invitations to attend special family events such as weddings, Bar Mitzvahs, or reunions have been extended.

In my family we always knew when relationships were serious when the annual family reunion time arrived. If you were serious about someone, you were expected to introduce this person to each member of the clan. However, you didn't go through this and take all the teasing that followed unless an engagement followed. Bringing a partner signaled an impending marriage.

Announcing an engagement serves as a type of bonding, a statement to the world that the relationship is formalized. Such an action informs the families and friends involved that a new familial unit will be established. Knapp (1978) suggests that the act of bonding, or institutionalizing the relationship, may in itself change the nature of the relationship. "The contract becomes either explicitly or implicitly, a frequent topic of conversation. Communication strategies can now be based on interpretation and execution of the commitments contained in the contract" (22). This may be a traumatic period since some parents, as well as the young adults, have not prepared for this separation. Mothers especially may feel abandoned (Bart, 1971). If the marriage means moving away, the feelings of loss are stronger. Each family faces the issues of cohesion and adaptability as it responds to the questions: How willing are we to allow a member to separate, physically and psychologically, and how willing are we to accept a new member as an in-law? Some families will struggle for years with these questions.

The premarital period provides the time for testing, dreaming, and communicating. It's the time when all of the "I love you . . . but(s)" should come out for discussion. It's a time when through self-disclosure each can let his or her fears and wants be known. It's a time for planning how roles and role functions will be worked out.

The following issues may need discussion: time to be spent with friends, desires for children, sexual needs, career and educational planning, religious participation, money management, home buying, in-laws, acceptable conflict behaviors. Crucial issues which all couples face need to be talked about and avoiding them sets up the potential for major problems.

The trend today is for shorter engagements; some couples decide to live together during this period. Such living together forces decisions on many of the issues—sometimes before adequate communication has taken place. Couples may discover significant differences between each other after signing the lease and putting a down payment on the furniture. On the other hand, they may get to know one another apart from families and find out they can live together. Because of the high incidence of premarital sexual experience many couples have engaged in serious communication around sexual issues or differences before their marriage. For many couples, the issue remains—can each person risk sharing his or her deepest needs or concerns or is there a fear that such honesty could jeopardize the wedding?

Throughout this period each person may have to deal with a basic fear of giving up his or her independence. This shift from self to mutuality with another requires time and examination. Persons raised in highly cohesive families may need and demand more mutuality than those raised in families with low cohesion. The issue of separation may be difficult for those who are tightly bound to a family-of-origin. For many couples the final part of the engagement period becomes hectic with rituals—wedding plans, bridal showers, apartment hunting, etc. In some families this serves to involve the parents and to keep the focus off the separation issues until the ceremony is over.

In this discussion we are focusing on the young unattached person, yet today many individuals involved in remarriage are planning to blend families so the engagement period becomes fraught with complication as potential step-parents meet potential stepchildren, potential step-siblings eye each other, and former mates anxiously watch the proceedings.

No matter what form the premarriage period takes, its function remains critical. The adjustments made in the engagement period relate directly to the quality of married life that follows. The nature of the future married relationship is formed prior to the wedding "by the way the couple related to one another and how much they knew about each other." (Rapaport, 1973, 231). In the adjustment period there needs to be room for changes and flexibility so that the system remains open and doesn't close out the potential for each spouse's self-actualization through marriage.

Marriage to Birth of First Child

The vows may be repeated before a judge or a minister, before 10 or 300 beaming friends and relatives, as two individuals formally and legally create a new family system. The actual ceremony becomes a communication event—a telegraphing to the outside world that the ultimate formal bonding occurred.

For most couples this stage represents the only period of two-person intimacy for many years to come since this period usually leads to childbearing. For some couples the honeymoon serves as an initial transition from the single life to the married state providing a time for unique physical, sexual, and psychological intimacy, a period to explore further their hopes for the future.

The period following our marriage, before the children began to arrive, served as a critical point in our marriage. If we had not established a really strong trusting relationship in those first two years we would have drifted totally apart in the next 23 years of child-rearing. I didn't realize what a critical period it was until we lost all our time together.

> If I had it to do over, I would have waited five years before having children just to give us that building period for sharing who we really were before we tried to deal with who the four new people in our lives were.

Early marriage involves certain predictable tasks for most couples. It is a time of (1) separating from the families-of-origin, (2) negotiating roles, rules, and relationships, and (3) investing in the new relationship. We have all heard of the young man or woman who "ran home to mother" every time a conflict arose in the new marriage. Although most couples do not experience this exact scene, most young couples and their respective families have to deal with separation issues as the new system emerges. Some young people find it difficult in an "early adult transition" to separate from their parents, establish an adult identity, *and* assume the role of spouse (Vines, 1979, 8–9). Marriage at this time may continue unresolved conflicts with the parents. The new mate becomes the victim of angry projected feelings he or she did little to deserve. This is a period of unconscious or conscious negotiation between the couple and their families-of-origin regarding how the old and new systems will relate to each other.

> I had known my husband since childhood and we dated since our junior year. Our parents knew each other and we attended the same church—yet we had some real difficulties in the first years of our marriage. I had difficulty in the following areas: (1) learning to live with each other's habits, (2) trying to be a full-time employee and a house-wife, (3) deciding which family's house at which to celebrate holidays, (4) telling my husband when I was angry, and (5) dealing with the biggest problem—my husband's mother.

Although not typical of all recently married couples, the above list of problems is quite representative of many issues found in the research as people try to negotiate their rules, roles, and relationships.

As we discussed in Chapter 6, role performance may differ greatly from the original expectations. Being a wife or husband may bring with it a set of pressures from the other spouse of other forces that cause the role to be played out differently than expected. Carl Rogers (1972) in his book *Becoming Partners* records poignant statements about this process from two young people who married after living together for a lengthy period of time:

Dick: "When Gail and I were living together we were sort of equal part-ners in making the living, and if we were broke, nobody really took the blame for it; but when we moved back and came into such close proximity with our respective in-laws, all of a sudden it became *my* fault when we weren't making any money, and *I* was the bum who wasn't going out and looking for work."

Gail: "I sort of had expectations like he did, you fall into a role even if you don't want to . . . of a husband is supposed to be this way and a wife is supposed to be this way . . . So it put me into a big conflict because I'm thinking, 'Well, I've *got* to be like this, I'm married and I'm supposed to do this . . .' " (43)

In this case both personal expectations and family pressure forced the individuals to view their roles differently than they expected.

This period is the time for negotiating rules—usually influenced by those brought from families-of-origin. Will the new couple discuss their sexual life openly? Will open fighting be accepted? Who will be told what about their joys and sorrows? Much negotiation relates to the previous friends and habits. What will be the role of the "old friends"? How much time will the spouses spend apart? How much togetherness will be demanded?

Equally important, but far more subtle, is the verbal and nonverbal negotiation related to cohesion and adaptability. Each person jockeys for the amount of togetherness he or she wishes as well as for the amount of flexibility that can be tolerated. Such moves are rarely dealt with openly but the results have long-lasting effects on communication within the system.

As you may well imagine, the images, themes, boundaries, and biosocial beliefs experienced by each partner in his or her family-of-origin affects the new system's development. A woman whose biosocial beliefs and images create a husband who is strong, unemotional, and powerful puts great pressure on her new husband to deal with such expectations. If one partner has experienced themes of open sharing and very loose boundaries and the other partner has experienced the opposite, much negotiation will be required.

During this period one or the other partner may discover that the person they married doesn't meet the standards they expected in the ideal mate, resulting in "the-honeymoon-is-over" problems. Such remarks as "You changed!" "You were not like this before!" typify this kind of disillusionment.

As we discussed in Chapter 9, couple conflict patterns tend to establish themselves within the first two years of marriage, and demonstrate great stability (Raush et al., 1974, 205). Similarly, the balance of power between a couple is established "early in the marriage by each partner's acceptance or rejection of the other's way of reacting to situations requiring a decision" (Lasswell and Lasswell, 1973, 269). Although it may change over time, many couples set lifetime patterns at this point.

In their study of adjustment in newly married couples, Cutler and Dyer (1973) found communication options varied from open discussion to doing nothing. Husbands, more than wives, adopted a "wait and see" strategy. Wives more often met violation of expectations with open sharing, talking about the problem, or responding negatively. The issues also called forth different behaviors. For example, husbands spoke openly about financial problems but not about their desires for more frequent sex. Wives complained six times more frequently about the amount of time spent at home than husbands. Wives also had more unmet expectations on whose responsibility it was for home care (295).

Many of the previous remarks reflect upon problems that can occur in a new marriage which complicate communication. However, the research definitely indicates that this is a happy stage and differences are often not taken seriously or allowed to develop into crises.

A couple's ability to invest in the new relationship relates directly to the quality of their communication. The extent to which connectedness and adaptation will characterize their life-style finds its roots in this period. Each person's capacity and desire for intimacy will structure the development of these patterns over the relationship's lifetime. This is a time of investing in the system, of taking the risk of self-disclosure, building a pattern of sexual communication, confirming and being confirmed. Time, energy, and risk-taking are needed to nourish the relationship and to establish a range of acceptable intimacy for the system.

For some couples, heterosexual and homosexual, this two-person system will be their permanent form. Partners may not need to add children to their lives or may find it difficult to bear or adopt children. Yet, for most young couples, the two-person system eventually becomes a three-person one, with pregnancy heralding the transition to a new stage. Some of you are parents already and some of you are planning to have children eventually. Others of you haven't reached a final decision. One of the most important choices any couple makes concerns childbearing. Such a decision should, but does not always, involve intense communication—self-disclosure regarding the needs of each partner and how a child could fit into their lives.

Input from all sources affects such a decision. Most women have been conditioned since childhood toward their eventual motherhood although there has been recent counter-conditioning toward meaningful careers that may preclude children. The media, parents, friends, and other relatives often pressure the couple to fulfill parent roles and subtly suggest they are being selfish if they don't. Men may perceive children as a way to prove themselves as mature, responsible males. For both spouses producing a child is partially ego-fulfilling. There may also be the desire to be the kind of parents they never had.

The first pregnancy signals the many changes to come. Rossi (1973) argues that when pregnancy in previous decades followed shortly after marriage, the marriage was the major transition point in a woman's life, but now with children often postponed for several years, the first pregnancy is that point (336). The pregnancy forces choices and may cause far more interruptions in the woman's life than marriage did.

For couples that desire a child and the pregnancy is uncomplicated, pregnancy can be a happy, communicative time with much closeness if each continues openly to share their feelings, fears, and hopes. There is still time to talk and to share without interruptions from outsiders and the third family member. Yet subtle communication changes occur. Raush et al. found some changes in conflict patterns may occur. In the last stages of their wives' pregnancy, "husbands make far more effort at emotional conciliation" than at the newlywed stage (204). Contrary to popular myth, they found no indication that the wives became more emotional in dealing with conflict during pregnancy.

As the wife's body dramatizes the life changes, some couples feel pregnancy has trapped them into a loss of independence. This is a time when the spouses need one another for confirmation of their self-images as individuals and as a couple evolving into parenthood. Women may need extra reassurance as to their continued physical desirability.

As the birth approaches, special communication may take place about naming the child. The naming sessions can be joyful and creative as each suggests names until the couple finds one they both approve. If one spouse dominates and insists upon a certain name, possibly a family "hand-me-down" name, the other may resent it. "Whose grandmother's name will go first?" or "I don't want him to be John the Third!" can promote conflict. Yet names may serve to link family generations.

Additional important communication may center around the role of the father in the birth process. Some husbands or wives are most uncomfortable at the thought of being together in the delivery room while others express a great desire to share the event. Decisions around this issue require careful communication because years later one may feel left out or abandoned by the other at this crucial moment.

I have never felt closer to my wife than at the moment of Carolyn's birth. I had helped her breathe, wiped her forehead, and rubbed her back between contractions. I actually felt a part of the birth process. When Carolyn was finally delivered, Arlene and I cried and laughed and cried again because of the power of the drama we had created. It's indescribable—to share in the birth of your own child.

Many variations of this stage's pattern exist. Although most children are born into two-parent systems, increasing numbers of single women choose to keep their children so they move directly into the parental stages either without a male partner or with a male partner who is not a husband. Also, since about one fifth of all first births in the United States were conceived before marriage (Troll, 1975, 98), many couples do not experience a lengthy period of intimacy before the child arrives.

Initial Parenthood: Birth of the First Child

Those of you who have shared a home with a newborn baby are well aware how one extremely small person can change an entire household. New parents soon discover that they no longer have the leisure for communication that they once had. You can hear comments like these: "The baby woke up every three hours day and night and we're exhausted. Who can talk when you are half asleep?"

At this point when the dyad becomes a triad, alliances and subgroups become possible. As was noted earlier, a more complex network begins to develop and the triangle means that all family members cannot receive undivided attention at the same time. Simply put, all three people cannot relate at one time, cannot experience eye contact or direct speech from each other simultaneously. One person becomes the "odd man out" watching the other two relate. This means that when Dad speaks to Mother, their daughter is left out. When Mother replies to their daughter, Dad loses his line to Mother. New potential challenges for communication result. "The odd man in a triangle always has the choice among breaking the relationship between the other two, withdrawing from it, or supporting it by being an interested observer. His choice is crucial to the functioning of the whole family network" (Satir, 1972, 149). Within this stage the couple must deal with the following communication-related issues: (1) renegotiating roles, (2) transmitting culture, (3) establishing a community of experiences, and (4) developing the child's communication competence. Families with moderate adaptation capacities are more likely to weather this period comfortably than relatively rigid systems.

During the post-birth period each spouse begins to assume his or her parental role while, hopefully, protecting the husband or wife role. In some families the parental roles become so powerful that the spouses may lose sight of each other for a period of time. New parents may feel inept caring for their child. Since the mother traditionally has taken the major responsibility for child care, few future fathers saw much modeling in their families-of-origin of how to share caretaking. Nash (1973), in his summary of research on fathers in a child-care role, concludes that our society is "mother-centered" and suggests that children with little contact or negative experiences with fathers may have identification or self-concept problems. "There is a critical period during which the kind of affectionate relationship with the father necessary to identification can be built up," he writes. "This critical period appears to be early, and . . . lasts from the time of weaning to entering school" (362). When fathers do become involved in child caring, evidence demonstrates they are just as sensitive and responsive to infant cues as mothers. In fact, with newborn babies, fathers were as competent as mothers in providing attention, stimulation, and necessary care (Sawin and Parke, 1979, 509). Due to cultural and economic changes many more families are experiencing some shared parenting responsibilities. Although men's roles are not changing very quickly, Pleck (1974) finds indications that men, especially with working wives, are accepting more family responsibility especially if the system is adaptable (448).

The father's age may affect how he assumes his role. Especially young fathers tend to pay less attention to their wives and children but fathers over 33 are more comfortable in the role while fathers who have their first child around 40 tend to remain involved and concerned longer (Troll, 102).

New mothers may have had greater practice or more expectations regarding their parental role, but the transition still remains critical. Older mothers tend to be even more concerned and anxious than younger ones during the baby's first year. Also, mothers respond differently depending upon the kind of behavior shown by infants. For example, babies who cry are treated differently than those who do not cry. Certain mothers respond more positively to active babies; others to passive babies, underscoring the transactional nature of the parent-child relationship (Troll, 99).

Women must deal with the demands of motherhood and potentially with their loss of a job or profession that held high interest or economic value. If they are returning to work, they must deal with issues of separation from their child. The role adaptations remain countless as husband, wife, and infant communicate to work out their relationships within the context of their roles.

The first child represents the link to posterity and the continuation of the family name and heritage—a heavy burden for some children. Thus parents become involved in transmission of culture and the creation of a community of experiences for their new family.

When you think about your own children, or of having your own children in the future, what parts of your background do you wish to pass on to them? Do you wish they could experience the same type of Passover Seders you did as a child? Do you want them to have a strong African or Italian or Norwegian identity? Are there family traditions, picnics, celebrations, parties, or Christmas customs you want to continue? What type of sexual identity or what type of religious belief should your children develop? Such are the issues of transmission of culture.

The birth of our first child revived many issues that we had fought about in our courtship period and that we finally agreed to disagree about. Sean and I were from very different backgrounds, religiously, culturally, and even economically. As a couple we were able to ignore many of the differences but once Wendy was born we each seemed to want certain things for her that we had experienced growing up. And our families got into the act also. We've dealt with most everything except religion and we are due for a showdown on that soon as she is now five and should begin some religious training soon.

For many people, a child represents a link to the past and the future, a sense of life's flow, and a sense of immortality. Hence children often serve as receptacles for what we consider our best parts, our strengths, and our expectations for the family. Once a couple becomes a triad, certain dormant issues may arise—particularly unresolved ones. A father's unmet personal goals may be transmitted to his son. The couple's differences in values, religious beliefs, importance of traditions, or national/racial/ethnic background may be highlighted by the small member of the next generation. Thus, spousal conflicts may arise over what is "passed down." Clinebell and Clinebell (1970) suggest that the transmission of both the cultural heritage and the family's own unique heritage is a demanding, frightening, and exciting task which depends on marital intimacy. "As personal identity is the foundation of marital intimacy, marital identity and intimacy are the basis for generativity" (117). Simultaneously the three people are forming a community of experiences, a process begun by the couple, but deepened and intensified by the arrival of their offspring.

It was amazing for me to watch my sister and her husband with their first child. After almost 25 years my sister could remember so many of the songs that our mother sang to us as little ones. She and Lee took great pleasure in creating new words and expressions from things that Jonathan did. They set certain patterns for birthday parties, established Friday nights as "family night" and began to take Jonathan to museums, children's theater, and library storybook programs together. They created their own world which now incorporated a little boy.

Through communication new patterns of life are formed and maintained which reflect the uniqueness of the three-person system. In-jokes, camping trips, burned steaks, sing-a-longs, long walks, or Sunday pizza dinners may all contribute to one family's community of experiences.

For some families establishing such a community of experience involves negotiations with relatives and friends, particularly with the families-of-origin. Young marrieds who did not have extensive contact with their parents after the wedding may suddenly feel a need to connect their child to grandparents and other relatives. Other couples may find themselves resisting the over-eager relations who wish to envelop the child. Appropriate boundaries usually require careful consideration and negotiation.

Finally, parents are deeply involved in providing their child with a means to deal with interpersonal relationships. Their relationship serves as the first model for the child and his or her development of communication skills. From the earliest weeks of existence a child learns how much connectedness or separateness is acceptable within the family system and how to attain that level through verbal and nonverbal means.

The moment of birth exposes the child to the world of interpersonal contacts as a powerful parent-child bonding process begins through physical contact.

> It is through body contact with the mother that the child makes its first contact with the world, through which he is enfolded in a new dimension of experience, the experience of the world of the other that provides the essential source of comfort, security, warmth, and increasing aptitude for new experiences. (Montagu, 1978, 75)

Every child explores his or her world nonverbally through touch, sound, and taste since the infant cannot speak or understand verbalizations. Parents can encourage an interpersonal orientation through cuddling and talking with the child, responding to his or her cries, maintaining eye contact, and smiling. They can enrich the communication environment by providing mobiles and some stimulation in the infant's surroundings.

The first few months mark the critical beginning of a child's interpersonal learning. "The basic foundation of a child's personality is being formed in his earliest interchanges with the nurturing adult" (White, 1975, 12). By four to five months a child recognizes mother's voice from among all others and responds with smiles and sounds. Children begin to respond to words at six to seven months; by nine or ten months they can understand five or six words and will begin to use language soon thereafter. Children need supportive communication as they go through cultural processes such as weaning or toilet training. By verbally and nonverbally giving a child the feeling of being loved and cared for, the parents set the stage for positive interpersonal development.

Individuation Stages

After the first few years of great dependency, children develop a sense of themselves and a mastery of skills which allow them to become more independent persons. Such growing independence has a direct bearing on family interaction.

In reviewing the family stages of individuation, the periods of child growth and outward movement, we will examine the following three phases, understanding that each family will experience each phase differently depending on its size and the ages of its members.

1. Family with Preschool Children (3–6 years and possibly younger siblings)
2. Family with School-Age Children (oldest child 6–12 years, possibly younger siblings)
3. Family with Adolescent Children (oldest 13–19 years, possibly younger siblings)

Family with Preschool Children • The preschool family (child 3–6 years) experiences less pressure than in the previous period. Parents have discovered they will survive having learned to cope with the growing child. Barring physical or psychological complications, the former baby now walks, talks, goes to the bathroom alone, and can feed and entertain himself or herself for longer periods of time.

Watching a three- or four-year-old, you may be amazed at his or her language. At this stage a four-year-old may produce well over 2000 different words and probably understands many more (Wood, 1976, 103). Children at this age begin to develop more sophisticated strategies for gaining their ends, such as later bedtimes or specific foods. They also are likely to express their gender role nonverbally.

As children become more independent, parents may directly influence their language acquisition skills through enrichment activities. If they take time to communicate with their children, and teach them to share ideas and feelings, they improve the child's developing self-concept. The parents' own communication behavior in this stage serves as an important model for the child.

As we noted in our discussion of roles, communication with children will differ depending on whether the family is position-oriented or person-oriented. Whereas a child in a position-oriented family is required to rely on accepted roles as communication guides and is not likely to make communication judgments based on the unique factors in the two-person relationship, the child in a person-oriented family is more likely to provide a range of communicative behaviors and to understand their effectiveness in relation to the specific people with whom he or she communicates (Johnson, 1978, 5). In short, positional families require that their children learn rather global rules pertaining to how one communicates with others, while person-oriented families require children to develop more complex strategies for developing roles appropriately suited to the two persons involved (Johnson, 7).

The difference is essentially one of the degree to which the child is provided with verbalized reasons for performing or not performing certain communicative functions at certain times with certain individuals. Persons growing up in a household where things are done "because I told you to" or "because I am your father" do not gain training in adapting to the unique personal relationships of the individuals involved. Children growing up in a person-oriented family are more likely to receive explanations for performing communication behaviors.

all children in a particular action accountable for working things out rather than judging one child as "the cause" (133). He also suggests that children may help each other to understand issues of relationship.

> Brother and sister may "play house," dramatizing their version of mother's and father's life together. This is possible when children have grown up with a clear sense of their status as children in the family, not as substitute adults for the vacuum in mother's or father's life.   (133)

In the 3–6 year stage children begin to communicate on their own with the outside world. Some attend nursery school, and at five years most enroll in kindergarten. Some parents experience difficulty in letting their children go even at this early stage and develop patterns of possessiveness which eventually result in communication problems in the adolescent and early adult stages.

As children move out of infancy they become less helpless and parents gain more control over their own lives, but time alone for the couple remains a problem. Even after they have adjusted to any possible income losses from the new members, husbands and wives are likely to fight over the absence of joint recreation (Troll, 90). Time alone becomes a precious commodity for most couples.

Family with School-Age Children • The school-age family experiences new strains on its communication as the child begins to link further with outside influences. The family system now overlaps on a regular and continuous basis with other systems—the school, the church, the community, and its organizations. Families with very strong boundaries are forced to deal with new influences. Schools provide an introduction to a wider world of ideas and values. New beliefs may be encountered, old beliefs may be challenged.

At this point children may spend many hours away from the home environment and influence. The school offers a variety of activities that often extend the school day. Churches provide special training classes, plus recreational events. Organizations such as the Scouts, YMCA and YWCA, Little League, or 4-H, compete for family members' time.

Parents communicate further rules that set the boundaries in space, time, and energy their children can expend in these new activities. During this period of growth, the child comes under the influence of peer pressures and this can conflict with parents' views. Often at this age conflict develops because the child feels more compelled to please his or her friends than parents.

As a single parent I have been both grateful for, and concerned by, the role school plays in my children's lives. They have a full day kindergarten and provisions for after-school activities. I can see them picking up many new values from their friends and teachers that are hard for me to deal with but I find it hard to compete when I have very little time to spend with them during the week.

"Apologize to your mother because you hurt her feelings." "I need your coop
tion because I don't feel well today."

Children need not only learn to relate to parents or other adults, but
may have to incorporate new siblings into their world. During this period
couples have more children, increasing the complexity of the family's relatior
network. The arrival of second and third children moves the triad to a fou
five-person system and places greater demands on the parents. Each addit
child will limit the amount of time and contact the children have with
parents and the parents with one another. In homes with working parents
dren learn to adjust their communication to other caretakers.

Additional children trigger a birth order effect which combines wi
in affecting parent-child interaction. You may have heard characteristi
tributed to various people because "She is the middle child" or "He is th
of the family." Although all combinations and permutations have no
worked out, there appear to be differences in parent-child communication
on sex and position. Boys may be allowed to ask for more comforting and
more comforting and more praise, particularly if they are firstborn. Mothe
to become intensely involved with their firstborn children and appea
anxious about their performances in other settings. Whereas mothers ar
likely to praise firstborn boys and second-born girls more often, they wil
ally correct firstborn girls and second-born boys. Finally, mothers are moı
to control their daughters more than their sons (Toman, 1976).

The competition of a second child can threaten the firstborn. Comı
tion about the expected child and sharing the planning with the first ch
lessen the concerns.

Angie was three when Gwen was born and it was a very har
for her and therefore for us. Angie changed from being a self-s
happy child to a whining clinger who sucked her thumb and s
wet her pants again. Jimmy and I had to work very hard t
"special" time with her, to praise her, and to let her "help"
baby when she wanted to. Luckily Gwen was an easy bat
could make the time to interact with Angie the way she need

Parents usually find a need for open communication with the c
or children before the next baby's birth or adoption and during the
come. This may include hospital phone calls or visits and time alone a
one is home. Even with the best of communication in a family the child
his or her "nose out of joint" a few days after the second arrives hom
three or more years older are more likely to treat the baby with aff
interest since they are more oriented to children their own age and less
by the new arrival. A sibling close in age may engage in aggressive and
toward the baby (White, 125).

How parents relate to children affects sibling cooperation. In k
the system concept of mutual causality, Bradt (1980) suggests parents

As the children continue their emotional and physical growth their capacities change. Negotiations and priority setting may characterize much child-parent communication as extra-familial demands conflict with traditional patterns. Family role orientations continue to influence behavior. For example, Bearison and Cassel (1975) found first-grade children are more able to accommodate their communication to the perspectives of listeners than are children of the same age who come from position-oriented families. The authors suggest the differences are attributable to the more differentiated role systems of the children from person-oriented families.

Children at this age also prefer peer communication with the same sex and often declare they "hate" the opposite sex. Knowing that this normally characterizes interactions of children between 8–12 helps parents understand the messages they receive from their children.

During this same period additional siblings may be added to the family which greatly complicates the family communication network. Triangles and subgroups multiply. This is the period in which many parents decide to add additional children since it often coincides with the midyears of the woman's child-bearing cycle. Yet "each time a new person is added, the limited time and other resources of the family has to be divided into smaller portions," Satir (1972) states. "But the mother and father still have only two arms and two ears" (153).

During the school years the identity of the family as a unit reaches its strongest form. The family can enjoy all manner of joint activities and these can "add a richness to the intimacy of the marriage relationship, surrounding it with a supportive context of family intimacy" (Clinebell and Clinebell, 120). Due to the intense activity level some partners neglect their own relationship or use the children as an excuse to avoid dealing with marital problems. Yet at this point parents must depend less on satisfactions derived from the child's dependency on them and should be able to gain emotional satisfaction from their spouses. This is not always easy.

My parents believed strongly in giving undivided individual attention to each child so as the family grew larger we developed a pattern of individually talking to our parents about our day. After dinner each of us seemed to take turns going back into the dining room to "report" on what had happened to us. By the time all five of us were done it was time for the bedtime rituals. One night my father came out and stood behind me in the doorway as I waited to go into the dining room because he said "I want a chance to tell your mother about what happened to me today." We all thought it was very funny but suddenly I realized how little time they had to really talk with each other.

This period may be very comfortable for highly cohesive families since joint activities can be enjoyed and children still remain an active part of everyday family life.

Family with Adolescent Children • Eventually those school-age children enter adolescence! "Enjoy the little ones while you can—after this they won't talk to you for six years." Such comments often greet the person about to embark on parenting an adolescent. During the adolescent period, once described by Anna Freud as a "necessary malaise," parents expect weird behavior, locked doors, dramatic mood swings, and despondency over pimples and members of the opposite sex. All of these behaviors certainly can and do influence communication but current research doesn't support the traditional stereotype of adolescence as a rebellious chaotic stage for all young people.

Americans have traditionally viewed adolescence as a more difficult period in the lives of children and their parents than either the middle-childhood or pre-adolescent years. Although a number of recent investigations suggest that the *extent* of adolescent and parental turmoil during this period has frequently been exaggerated, there is general agreement that adolescence, and particularly early adolescence, has traditionally been a challenging and sometimes trying time for both the young and their parents (Conger, 1977).

According to Offer (1979), three major groups of adolescents can be identified. A minority of 21 percent could be characterized as experiencing a tumultuous adolescence, 35 percent moved through the period in spurts emotionally and mentally demonstrating less introspection than other groups, while a third group, representing 21 percent, appeared as models of virtue and confidence. Very few of this final group reported anxiety and depression but they did report receiving affection and encouragement for independence from their parents. Many experts believe that if one does not experience great upheavals during adolescence these turmoils will appear later in life. (Piers, 1966).

Elizabeth Douvan (1966), author of several studies on teenagers, agrees that some teens defer the struggle, particularly girls. "So it comes later in life—the identity crises after the kids have gone to school" (4).

Teenagers do experience internal struggles in coping with sexual changes and the process of individuation or developing a sense of self. This coincides with beginning to separate from the family. The interest in same-sex relationships that characterized the earlier period switches to a growing interest in the opposite sex. "All he does is chase after girls now instead of fly balls." Younger brothers and sisters become boring and bothersome. "Keep Out" signs appear on doors; locks go on diaries; phone calls become private. Young people begin to set their own physical and psychological boundaries which may serve to limit communication with some or all family members.

I grew up in a home where doors were always open and people knew each other's business. I remember going through a terrible period starting at the end of junior high when I hated sharing a room with my sister. I would spend hours alone sitting on my bed listening to music with the door shut and if anyone came in I would have a fit. I even locked my sister out a number of times.

As you probably remember, adolescence was a time of establishing powerful nonfamilial relationships. Media figures, teachers, or other adults may have been important role models you tried to act like. Your friends may have become "the first to know" no matter what the news.

The phone calls, the peer groups, the new models represent a young person's linking network to the world outside of the family system. They become conduits for bringing new messages into the adolescent's life that can result in some painful family moments as the young person moves outward.

Erikson (1968) maintains that adolescents ". . . need above all, a moratorium for the integration of the identity elements ascribed . . . to the childhood stages . . ." (128). In other words, the identity work that a child goes through within the family needs to be similarly repeated with society as the new milieu. Kenniston (1979) speaks of the centrality in adolescence of this process "by which the adolescent relinquishes his of her ties to inner representations of good or bad parents, suffers an inner sense of emptiness and loss, and gradually forms new and more adult bonds" (7). Blos (1979) concurs with Kenniston that all youth reach puberty with intrapsychic tensions that require reworking and transcending in adolescence if a full adulthood follows. From a social-emotional perspective, the adolescent is in the process of slowly moving out of a narcissistic existence, learning to shift from the self-centered to the other-centered position.

During the move toward other-centeredness, a young person begins to develop a true sense of empathy and the ability to take another's perspective. In her work on social perspective-taking ability in adolescents, Ritter (1979) proposes, ". . . adolescent communicative ability can be tied directly to age and the increased capacity to take the perspective of another . . ." (49). Such capacities eventually allow the growing young adult to interact with her or her parents on an adult level.

These changes between 13–19 coincide with Erikson's autonomy and assertive stages. The individuation of the self occurs when the young person becomes self-reliant and insists upon making up his or her own mind. This leads to independence and confidence in decision-making. By asserting his or her developing talents to speak out, work, or perform tasks without constant help and supervision, the adolescent signals parents that past communication directives no longer fit the situation.

Such changes have a profound effect on any family system. Very strong parent-child bonds may be weakened at least temporarily, and other siblings may react to the adolescent's mood or changes. Such actions may have repercussions for the parents themselves. In her summary of the changes in marital conflict patterns over time, Troll states, "They don't report fighting over their children until the children are old enough to get into deliberate trouble (in adolescence)" (90). Additionally parents may turn to each other, as their teenager, engaged in his or her own pursuits, forces the parents to "deal for the first time with such issues as lack of companionship, sexual difficulties, or dominance. The results can be explosive" (Ackerman, 1966, 151).

For many parents their children's sexual awakening has a powerful effect on them. Opposite sex parents and children may find a gulf between them as a response to the power of the "incest taboo" in society. Unfortunately in many families this results in the end of nonverbal affection.

I will never forget being hurt as a teenager when my father totally changed the way he acted toward me. We used to have a real "buddy" relationship—we would spend lots of time together, we would wrestle, fool around, and I adored him. Suddenly he became really distant and I could not understand what I did but I did not feel I could talk about it either. Now that I am older I can see the same pattern happening with the two little girls in the family. Obviously within his head there is a rule that when your daughter starts to develop breasts you have to back off—and for him that means having almost no relationship at all. Now I can understand that it has to hurt him as much as it hurts the girls.

Same-sex parents may face internal conflicts if they perceive a major contrast between their children's budding sexuality and their own sexual identity. Such conflicts are tied to the parents' stage of development and to a negative self-evaluation of themselves. Since such an issue would be uncomfortable, such perceptions may result in conflict around more "acceptable" issues as friends, money, independence, or responsibility. Adolescents are more likely to accept parental guidelines

> . . . when they see that these are shared by other significant adults. When the parents of adolescent peers are in communication with one another, and when all of them expect adolescents to observe certain rules . . . the individual adolescent is less likely to question his or her parents' advocacy of these rules, and the task of the parents is thus made easier.   (Conger, 207)

All adolescents do not radically differ from their parents on issues. Although some parents may openly conflict with teenagers over some issues, many do not. With the exception of alcohol and marijuana, 63 to 85 percent of the youth in a large national study agreed with parental attitudes toward religion, drugs other than marijuana, education, and modern goals for women. Fifty-eight percent agreed with their parents about racial issues and conservation of resources (Phillips, 1979, 4). Communication can improve in this period if parents cultivate empathic listening and provide opportunities for their adolescents to own their own problems; make mistakes and learn from them; and love them even when displeased by their actions (McClelland et al., 1978, 49). Communication that encourages the adolescent to be his or her own person without constant criticism can help the individuation process.

The exploring adolescent often challenges the family's themes, boundaries, and biosocial beliefs. He or she is forever bringing in view people or modes of behavior which may threaten the family, just because it forecasts the eventual departure of the exploring child and because the new input forces the family to reevaluate itself (Ackerman, 151). A relatively flexible family may encounter less difficulty with an acting-out adolescent than a family with rigid rules.

Many families choose or are forced to make adjustments in their interaction patterns. If you recall Kantor and Lehr's closed family type discussed in Chapter 6, you can imagine certain difficulties such a system has in dealing with adolescents. For example Kantor and Lehr suggest "A closed type family may experience a great deal of stress when its offspring become teenagers, so much stress that the system decides to change form by developing a preponderance of open type strategies. Such a decision may produce a curious hybrid such as a family with closed system goals and open system means of attaining these goals" (157). As adolescents mature their families may undergo extensive readjustments. Individuation within families represents the necessary separation moves which are expected, yet painful, as young members move toward adult maturity. Communication which supports gradual separation, rather than that which pushes persons away from each other or holds them rigidly close, serves as an easier transition for all family members.

Families as Launching Centers

The next stage signals the departure of the oldest children as they are "launched" into the world. Yet it is very difficult to generalize about specific predictable events since so many different things may be occurring. There are three competing descriptions of what happens in the post-childrearing stage: "(a) the 'empty nest syndrome,' which posits that there are problems for one or both of the parents; (b) the 'curvilinear model,' which claims increased freedom and independence for the couple; and (c) variations that are minor in nature. All these theoretical premises need further validation" (McCullough, 1980, 176). We do know that decreased parenting and increased parent-child separation usually occur.

Some men, and fewer women, go into the service but many more leave home to go to college or to seek employment, or to start a new home. When young people start living on their own, especially if they totally support themselves, they more readily take on the responsibilities of adulthood or caring for themselves and begin the process of becoming emotionally comfortable living apart from their families-of-origin. This is a time of vacating the bedrooms, sending along the extra coffeepot, and letting go of the predictable daily interactions at breakfast or bedtime that tied parents and siblings into a close interactive system. Tremendous strain may accompany such behaviors if parents attempt to hold on to their emerging adult children.

The summer before my oldest son left for the Air Force, I cried nearly every day. I saw the beginning of the end of our close-knit family. Rob's leaving was the start of the pattern. The first Thanksgiving and Christmas without him were terrible but gradually I learned to adjust. Our last boy will go to school next year and by now I'm resigned to the changes and I've found a job that keeps me busy.

If the separation takes place without conflict or parental strings attached, communication usually remains open and flexible. Frequent contact with parents and siblings via phone calls, letters, visits, etc., maintains the family links and strengthens the bonds. At this time, communication issues may involve handling debt, negotiating living space, dead-end jobs, career decisions, and hours kept.

Some parents react by forcing a separation before their children may feel ready for the break.

Since I've been in college I call home about once a week and sometimes I sense that my mother is upset about something. If I ask about it she will say something like "Oh don't you worry about it. It's not your problem, you don't live here anymore." That upsets me because I still feel I am part of the family.

This often results in hard feelings, conflict, and resentment. Yet many children resist being "on their own" and in some communities or cultures it is expected; in others children may remain home indefinitely.

Certain conflicts may occur when young people remain home during their early twenties since established family rules and regulations tend to be challenged. "You don't need to wait up for me—I'm not seventeen!" "Pay room and board? I can't afford it and make car payments." "I don't have to account for everywhere I go" may typify certain interactions when the new adult-adult roles are not negotiated. If young adults remain longer than expected, some families develop adverse effects (Harkins, 1975). Some parents seize their right to time as a couple and if the children delay leaving, this may create frustrations and negative communication patterns. The failure to leave relates to our earlier discussion in Chapters 1 and 3 of separateness and connectedness. Rather than separate from the family, the young person may remain connected, enjoying the advantages of home and family comforts without working to function as an independent adult.

Major changes occur in the husband-wife relationship as opportunities for increased intimacy present themselves. Troll comments that "Mothers in the launching stage, whose children are getting ready to leave home, are seldom enthusiastic and often bitter about the loss of their husband's affection and companionship. It is only after the children are gone that the second honeymoon occurs—if it is going to" (87). Certain men may be invested more psychologically in their wives (Lewis, Freneau, and Roberts, 1979, 517). Further analysis of these results reveal fathers with fewer children report greater unhappiness over children leaving than fathers with more children. Older fathers reacted more strongly than younger fathers. This finding further related to family communication: The most unhappy fathers also reported they felt most neglected by their wives; received the least amount of understanding; sensed loneliness most; were least enthusiastic about wives' companionship and believed their wives least empathic (517). Ironically Bart's research with women revealed many of the same complaints about men and the same communication barriers. Although we seem to present this as a turbulent time it need not be so. In many families the post-parental period presents little crises and becomes a part of the sequence and rhythms of the life cycle (Schram, 1979, 8). The effects of the empty nest largely disappeared two years following the departure of the last child.

Such times may be very trying for the inflexible and highly cohesive family whose self-definition is being threatened. Several conflicts may result between the young person and the other family members, or between family members who displace their anger onto each other.

It is also a time when the middle or parental generation has to deal with changing relationships with their parents and having to face their retirement, disability, dependency, or death (McCullough, 180). Such issues often result in increased personal and interpersonal conflicts.

Although this period appears tumultuous, it may be followed by an increased couple intimacy, if the partners can come through the child-rearing years together.

Families in the Middle Years

When the children left, I discovered myself living with essentially a mute man. We hadn't realized that for years we had talked little to one another—that most of our communication was with the children or about them. Since we both worked, always took vacations with the kids and kept busy chasing after the kids' activities, we never had time for ourselves. Now I've got time to talk and I have to compete with TV —that's the "other woman" in my house.

In the middle years, after the children have left home until one or both parents retires, communication in the family mainly involves the original dyad. As opposed to earlier days when families were larger and longevity was shorter, the empty nest transition occurs in middle age rather than old age. Thus the "couple alone again" period and its accompanying relationships have not been well researched.

Many contradictory reports about this period appear in family literature. The "second honeymoons" are counterbalanced by the high divorce rate. The decreasing sexuality images are matched by the reports of this as a period of sexual revitalization (Troll et al., 40). In short, we are only now discovering what is happening to the middle-age, post-child-rearing couple as they re-establish themselves as a two-person system. Factors such as health, economics, and social class tend to interact with the couple's development and satisfaction at this stage.

Spouses who allowed their children to become their main focus for so many years may find themselves back at the lower stages of relationship development. Partners may sense a distance between them and feel unable, or unwilling, to try to reconnect. For many couples the readjustment to a viable two-person system requires hard work. Divorces frequently do occur in this midlife transition period. Vines (1979) states:

A man has to make new choices or recommit himself on different terms to old ones. If he is to improve his current marriage, or to enter a new one . . . he must become less illusioned about himself. He has to accept some responsibility for those aspects of his own motivation and character which keep him from forming more adult relationships with women . . . otherwise he will remain in a stagnant marriage destructive to both partners or he will embark on a new kind of relationship with a wife or lover that repeats old hurtful themes. . . . (9)

This also could be said of women who become aware of the limitations in their marriages. When crises develop in this period, you hear remarks like these: "I've changed. I'm a different person with different desires." "I either change or I'm stuck forever."

Certain women face a particularly difficult transition due to the change in their major identifying role of mother. The now empty nest may have been so full for so long that an enormous void occurs. Such feelings need to be sorted out and communicated to a spouse so both can understand and support each other's attempts to cope.

Such couples are dealing with the issue of "constricted versus expanded roles" (Schram). Greater freedom from responsibilities may prompt one member of the couple toward expansion and new exploration while the other spouse attempts to hold on to the marriage and family ties more tightly resulting in dyadic conflict.

Many families have to negotiate the relationship between parents and grown children, who may now be becoming parents. Highly cohesive families may attempt to keep inappropriate ties. In discussing this issue McCullough suggests that "dysfunction seems to occur when the degree and quality of the closeness becomes fixed between two people or when two people triangle in a third one . . ." (190). For example, if a child or grandchild is constantly used as focus for a maturing couple, they are not dealing with their own development.

Contrary to some of our stereotypes about older parents being cut off from the lives of their adult children, Troll et al. suggest that such contact is regular and frequent. Ninety-five percent of those parents under 65 see their children weekly whereas 81 percent of those over age 65 also see their children weekly (7). This does not include letters or phone calls. Such figures raise unanswerable issues. How are such children and parents connected? Are these contacts made out of guilt or need? Do they represent intimate caring relationships? Much of the adult parent-child interaction appears to be carried out through the female networks rather than through the male ones resulting in a potential distancing of the father (Troll et al., 103). Mothers tend to remain in even more constant contact with daughters, especially those with children.

The arrival of grandchildren represents another opportunity for relationship development. Communication between aging parents and children depends upon the style of grandparenting, partially determined by ethnic ties, personalities, and job status of the grandparents. Neugarten and Weinstein (1964) classified five grandparent styles.

1. Formal—Definite boundaries between parents' and grandparents' roles with grandparents interacting infrequently and doing little babysitting.
2. Fun seeker—The grandparents take the children on outings or come over to play with them. They need the play as much as the children.

3. Second parents—Grandmothers often take over while daughter or daughter-in-law works or becomes incapacitated.
4. Family Sage—Grandparents, especially grandfather, serves as reservoir of family wisdom and teacher of special skills.
5. Distant Figure—Benevolent but infrequent visitors who appear for family rituals or holidays. (202–203)

The amount and type of grandparent-grandchild communication reflects the grandparenting style. Formal or distant figures may not attain the same degree of closeness gained by a second parent but the latter may have to act as disciplinarian or ponder which puts an added strain on the relationship.

Walsh (1980) sees grandparenthood as an opportunity for new roles and meaningful interaction since it usually does not entail the responsibilities, obligations, and conflicts of parenthood. Also grandparents and grandchildren may have a "common enemy" (204). Several conflicts can result if grandparents are drawn into parental conflicts; on occasion grandparents act as a refuge for children in a strife-torn family.

Within certain cultural groups grandparents are expected to assume a major role in childrearing; yet if grandparents are coerced into child care they are likely to resent it (Troll; Kahana and Kahana, 1970; Lopata, 1973). Such cross-generational contact provides opportunities for extended transmission of culture and for developing a sense of family history. Grandparents serve as one source of a child's sense of identity and children gain access to their roots and have the opportunity to see the functioning of the two families-of-origin which influenced their parents, and hence themselves.

In spite of the decisions about major changes in midlife, this period can be a happy one for families. Financial worries lessen if money has been managed well over the years. Children become less of an everyday concern and a couple or single parent may have the opportunity to focus on old or new relationships and experiences.

Older Member Families

The final stage in the family begins with retirement and ends with the death of one of the couple. The big communication issue centers around retirement. Some couples experience "reentry" problems when one or both return to the home and remain there twenty-four hours of most days. The increased contact may lead to a deepening of the relationship or may result in friction from the forced closeness. The retired person(s) may undergo severe role adjustments and the loss of certain functions (e.g., providing) that served as self-definition. Without additional support systems this role change may be very difficult to handle. A second issue that affects all communication concerns the health and declining strength of the couple. Ill health creates a need for nurturing communication, plus tapping the resources, physical, mental, and financial, of the couple. Walsh suggests "a disequilibrium in the marital relationship may ensue with the illness of one spouse" (206). Certain spouses may encourage the other's dependency in order to avoid anxiety or vulnerability.

Yet, for more independent persons this may be a time of rejuvenation—

of savoring the time to spend on long-term interests or travel. A study of couples married over fifty years, reports the aging stage as one of the happiest. It means "more time together, travel and activities which they did not previously have sufficient time for" (Sporakowski and Hughston, 1978, 325).

For many older individuals the family takes on additional importance. Troll et al. summarize this position well, saying:

> Older people sometimes disengage from their roles outside their families, but they rarely disengage from their involvements inside their families. They disengage *into* rather than from their families.　　(6)

Interpersonal communication becomes increasingly important at this stage. Many older family members engage in the "elder function," or the sharing of the accumulated wisdom of their lives with younger people, usually family members. There is a need to feel of use to the coming generations and for many older persons such feelings come from revealing information or spinning stories designed to guide the younger listener.

Although older Americans do see their children with some regularity, many older persons are prevented from gaining the interpersonal contacts they desire due to concerns of economics, safety, and health. Rising costs of living restrict the travel and entertainment aspects of older persons' budgets while many urban senior citizens do not feel safe attending evening meetings or social activities.

Health concerns such as decreasing agility, or diminishing hearing and eyesight compounds the problem of maintaining interpersonal relationships. Frustration and low self-esteem may result in a pulling back from initiating such contacts while listeners may decline due to their impatience with the perceived infirmities.

Older couples who do reach their retirement together may turn inward toward each other in order to share intensely their remaining years. Loss becomes a part of aging and this increases when close friends and relatives of the couple die. In order to prevent becoming "the last one out," older couples have to go beyond their age range and establish friendships through communicating with younger adults. This may be difficult if infirmities prevent mobility.

After the death of one spouse the other must face the severe role adjustment inherent in becoming a widow or widower. Working through the grief period, a person may make great demands on younger family members who may be resentful of, or unprepared for, such demands. This is coupled with the younger members' personal grief at a parental loss. The surviving spouse has to renegotiate roles and boundaries as he or she attempts to create or maintain interpersonal contacts.

CONCLUSION

Throughout this chapter we have looked at the effects of developmental stresses on communication within families. As families move through the years each generation faces predictable developmental issues as couples marry, beget children, and the system lives through stages of child development transposed upon individual adult developmental changes. As children leave home to form a new system, the original couple, if still intact, encounters a system readjustment as middle years and adjustment issues are faced. The cohesion-adaptability axis overlays each system's personal growth while themes, images, boundaries, and biosocial beliefs may be challenged and changed as the years pass.

Family communication patterns serve to bring members together or to separate them as the system moves through its developmental stages. Some patterns pass through from generation to generation because they are accepted, or not consciously rejected, whereas others become unworkable and are discarded or cause disruption in the system. Certain communication behaviors and patterns are more predictable at particular periods of life. It is hoped that communication will serve to enhance movement through life's developmental stages making life richer as system members grow closer together.

The entire family developmental process is extremely complex and challenging. Foley (1974) summarizes the adjustments briefly and well:

> The fantasy of the engagement period yields to the reality of daily life. The birth of a child changes the dyadic system into a triad, and presents the possibilities of alliances and splits in the family. The departure of the last child for school brings about a definitive drift into middle age for the couple. The marriage of a child brings still another period of adjustment and initiates the process of the return to the dyadic state. All these situations can be described as normal or developmental, and all of them can cause problems in a marriage if one or another cannot make a transition. (87)

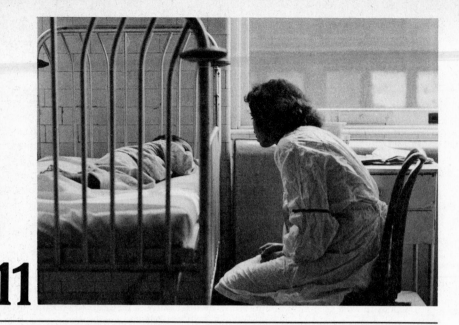

11

Family Communication and Unpredictable Stress

There were nine children in our family and three had muscular dystrophy. I remember how hard it was for Mom to accept their illness. She wouldn't talk about it within the family. Her rule was that it was better not discussed, yet I would find her alone in her room crying. We all learned from Marilyn, Dan, and Virginia. Communication reached a tense stage when Marilyn was the first to die. We knew the fear and panic in Dan and Virginia. It took time to get them to talk about these fears and finally near their own deaths they would joke about who was going next. All of this was strictly with two sisters and myself. Mom, Dad, and the rest couldn't handle any humor on the subject. I feel they would like to have shared these feelings with all of us but some of the living in our family put great distance between themselves and those who were dying.

In addition to all the developmental life changes, each family and family member must cope with negative and positive unpredictable or external stresses which force some significant changes upon the system. Unpredictable stresses mean those events which disrupt the life patterns and are not predictable developmentally. They are the "slings and arrows of outrageous fortune"—the shocks to the system. Such stresses conjure up images of death, divorce, serious illness or injuries, economic reversals, etc. Negative events are the most common, yet positive events, such as a large inheritance, an important job transfer, or the rediscovery of long-lost relatives, also may be classified as stresses for the system. Although we are dealing with unpredictable stresses as distinct from the more predictable developmental changes, there may be certain overlaps. Becoming pregnant or having a child may be considered a developmental event, but an unwanted pregnancy or the birth of a severely handicapped child may also be classified as an unpredictable stress. Death becomes a developmental experience for all persons but the untimely death of a family member serves as a severe crisis for the system. Whether the entire family, or only certain members, are initially affected by the event, the family system will eventually reflect the tension of such stresses in its communication behavior.

In the previous chapter you were introduced to Carter and McGoldrick's model of family stressors (see Figure 10-1, p. 201), and detailed the developmental stresses a family faces. We will now concentrate on the other aspect of the horizontal axis, the external stressors, or as we prefer to call them, the unpredictable stressors. (From our perspective events such as untimely losses are hard to see as external.) In the following pages we will examine (1) the process of dealing with unpredictable stress, (2) communication throughout some of the major events which can cause significant stress on the horizontal axis, and (3) communication in reconstituted families.

In considering factors that contribute to the horizontal stressors we can cite the work of Holmes and Rahe (1967, 215) who studied life stresses. They classified forty-three life events that cause stress. The first twelve cause major role changes particularly within families. Certainly these important crises events affect communication. Holmes and Rahe ranked these crises and placed an impact value on each which is shown in Table 11-1 (see p. 232).

Bain (1978) used this rating scale in his research on a family's ability to cope with transitions. He stressed that the capacity of the family to cope depended upon the psychosocial factors involved in the crises. He noted differences in the effects stress had on families depended upon the nature of the social relationships within which the changes had to be made (675, 685).

In earlier related work Hill (1949) studied stress in families and noted four disruptions to families that caused crises:

1. Dismemberment of the family via the death of husband, wife, child, or grandparents.
2. Accession or additions to the family with unwanted pregnancies; return of deserter; addition of stepmother or stepfather with or without children.
3. Demoralization resulting from nonsupport, infidelity, alcoholism, drug addiction, or anything that disgraces the family.
4. A combination of demoralization, plus dismemberment or accession

Table 11-1 Life Events That Cause Stress

Rank	Event	Mean Value
1	Death of spouse	100
2	Divorce	73
3	Marital separation	65
4	Jail term	63
5	Death of close family member	63
6	Personal injury or illness	53
7	Marriage	50
8	Fired at work	47
9	Marital reconciliation	45
10	Retirement	45
11	Change in health of family member	44
12	Pregnancy	40

as can happen with illegitimacy, desertion, divorce, suicide, imprisonment, homicide or mental illness.   (10)

Another situation in which families may overreact and create crises happens when one or more members disapproves of the life-style and sexual activities of their children or kin. If a young couple lives together prior to marriage, or has no plans to marry, or if a son or daughter reveals a homosexual preference, they may encounter rejection and varied pressures to conform to the family's wishes.

Yet each family demonstrates a particular level of coping. According to Hill, whether an event that happens in a family becomes a crisis depends upon three variables: (a) the hardships caused by the situation or the event itself; (b) the role structure, resources, flexibility, and family's previous history with crises; (c) the definition the family makes of the event, mainly whether they view it as an obstacle to their status and goals (9). Bain suggests the capacity of a family to cope with a transition is related to (1) the amount and type of recent stress which the family has faced, (2) the magnitude of the role changes involved, (3) the type of support from institutions, and (4) the support from the family's social network. The ways in which a family has responded to the functions of establishing a pattern of cohesion and a pattern of adaptability has great bearing on the ability to cope with external stress. From our perspective a family with a high capacity for adaptation and above average cohesion is likely to weather such events more easily than families who are rigid and fragmented. More adaptable families have the capacity to find alternative ways of relating and can adjust their communication behavior to encompass an event. As shown in the opening example, a family that has a rule against discussing debilitating illness has little ability to cope openly with and communicate about the impending death of a member. During a crisis family members often wish to rely on each other for comfort and support, behaviors that cannot suddenly occur if the family has a history of separateness.

Such issues also interrelate with family functions related to boundaries, themes, images, and biosocial issues. Families with rigid boundaries may find themselves unable to cope adequately when severe external stresses occur. By limiting greatly any communication with institutions, such as hospitals, courts, and schools, members deprive themselves of necessary information and possible emotional support. Additionally, boundaries that prevent a social network (friends, extended family) from knowing what is happening within the family eliminates those potential sources of strength and comfort that might help "carry" a family through a critical period.

When my father died suddenly I was almost totally unable to cope with life for many months. Both my mother and I were in shock and we were unable to help each other with our grief; in fact we experienced a great deal of conflict with each other. My major support through that period was an older woman friend who would listen as I would rage, or cry, or question. Unfortunately my mother would not allow herself to use such an "outside" support system and she never fully recovered from losing my father.

Families with themes of total self-sufficiency or images of rocklike members may find support from strong members of the family. Members may find that such themes and images prevent them from turning outward when the pain becomes too great for the family to handle functionally, resulting in severe conflict or separation. The number and magnitude of stresses may determine how functional these themes and images can be.

Finally, families with inflexible beliefs related to biosocial issues, such as sex roles or authority, may find such beliefs aid them through a crisis or may interfere with the resolution of such an event. For example, in a family that sets very distinct male-female roles, the father's loss of a good position may leave the family emotionally and financially devastated since this belief causes the man to feel inadequate and prevents a woman from working to support the family.

Since communication affects and is affected by all these behaviors, it plays a central role in the experiencing and eventual resolution of such stresses and specifically contributes to the family's movement through stages of stress reaction.

Stages of Family Crisis

In any serious crisis situation the family goes through a definite process in handling the grief or chaos that results. Depending upon the event, the stages may last from a few days to several months or years. These stages may be more pronounced in the case of a death, divorce, or news of an incurable illness but in any crisis there will be in family members a progression of feelings ranging from denial to acceptance. Yet, it is important to remember that since no two families accept crisis in the same way, and because family systems are characterized by equifinality, they will reach the final stages of the process in a variety of ways. The following stages, integrated from a variety of sources, approximate the general process of dealing with severe stress. Although the stages usually follow one another, they may overlap and some may be repeated a number of times.

1. Shock resulting in numbness or disbelief, denial;
2. Recoil stage resulting in anger, confusion, blaming, guilt, and bargaining;
3. Depression;
4. Reorganization resulting in acceptance and recovery.
   (Kübler-Ross, 1970; Dunlop, 1978; Parkes, 1972; Feifel, 1977)

The process of going through such stages around a serious life event usually results in some transformation of the system. Persons may find themselves more separated from, or connected to, different members and may find a shift in the patterns of adaptability.

Communication behavior reflects and aids the progress through the stages. Understanding the process allows one to analyze the progress of others through the stages, or to be more understanding of one's own behavior and personal progress.

At the shock stage family members tend to deny the event, or the seriousness of the event. Denying comments such as "It can't be true," "It's a mistake," "It's temporary," are accompanied by nonverbals such as setting a dead person's place at the table, misplaced attempts at smiles and encouragement with a terminally ill person, or spending money lavishly when the paycheck has been cut off.

Most persons quickly move from this stage and exhibit behaviors that indicate the recognition of reality. Principal family members acknowledge their grief and feel the pain of the loss. Crying, or sullen quietness for those who find it hard to cry, characterizes communication. The truth of the crisis news begins to take on fuller meanings such as, "Mom will never get well" or "she has left and never will return." This kind of reasoning sends messages to the self that has a confirming function.

Denial is transformed into an intense desire, especially in the case of a family death, desertion, or severe injury, to recapture what has been lost. This may lead to attempts to recapture memories, for example, "I keep expecting to see her in the kitchen."

After the initial blow, the family may move into the recoil stage of blaming, anger, and bargaining. Blaming often takes place as the grieving family members seek reasons for what has happened. This may include blaming the self: "I was too trusting; I should have watched closer." or "I never should have let her go," or blaming others, "It's his own fault," or "The doctors never told us the truth soon enough." Such behavior may be interspersed with feelings of "It's not fair." "Why did this happen to us?" "We don't deserve this." Anger may be directed at the event or person most directly involved, or may be displaced onto others such as family members, friends, co-workers. Attempts at real or imagined bargains may occur. "If I take a cut in pay they could hire me back." "If you come back I'll stop gambling forever."

Feelings of the unfairness of the world, that God has been cruel to let this happen, that potentials of the members involved had never been realized, and now will never be, flood the intrapersonal communication system of family members and then are released to one another. Again the pain of the loss needs to come out and these feelings need to be met with acceptance.

Family members need to talk about what has happened. In fact, they often retell the crisis news over and over, a normal and healthy response for the family as they feel the intensity of the loss. This is necessary especially for families that will experience a long period of suffering because of death, an incurable illness, permanent injuries, a long jail sentence, or mental breakdown. People outside the family often fail to understand the communication that goes on within such stricken families and may attempt to avoid the people or the subject, not recognizing that support may only be possible from those not as directly affected. Families may allow their boundaries to become more flexible in order to gain this support. Often the confusion and family disorganization may be so great that outsiders tend to take over and guide decision making.

The releasing of genuine hurt feelings leads into the third stage—depression. At the depths of depression the family realizes the old status quo or balance in the family will never return. The death or divorce or injury can't be undone and turning back time is unrealistic. The loss of a good job, especially one that has been held for many years, may not entail the same emotions as death or divorce but the adjustments forced upon the family to cut back its standard of living, for example, can also lead to depression. Some people in this stage speak of having a sinking feeling—a sense of helplessness in not knowing or even caring what to do. Verbally and nonverbally they communicate an overwhelming sadness usually accompanied by a tiredness and slowness of response.

As grief-stricken people pass through this stage, they normally move on to what they describe as a turning point. Usually some decision on their part marks the event. It may be a decision to take a trip, to sell a business that's losing money, to get rid of mementos that serve as daily reminders, to register with a placement bureau, or to join Alcoholics Anonymous.

Nonverbally this decision making signals the individual has moved into the fourth crisis stage—acceptance and reorganization of events in their life to effect a recovery. This stage is characterized by family members taking charge of their lives and making the necessary changes forced upon them by the crisis. They may not like the changes required but they communicate an ability to cope in spite of the loss. Reorganization required by the crisis may mean all sorts of adjustments and the time required varies greatly with the presenting crisis and the individuals involved. It may take six weeks for one family to recover from a job loss, and another family suffering a death or divorce a year to eighteen months to achieve any semblance of balance in the family system.

If emotions in crises could be charted on a linear scale, the line descends to the lowest point with depression. The descent began with the impact of the news and continued the downward spiral with some rises in the recoil stages to descend again as reality returned (see Figure 11-1).

Throughout this process communication serves to link members in sharing their reactions and links one or more to outside sources of support, institutional or social, which can provide acceptance of the emotions which need to be expressed. If a family or a member is cut off from some support the process may not be complete—the family may remain stuck at some point unable to complete

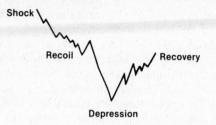

Shock

Recoil

Recovery

Depression

Figure 11-1 Linear Scale of Emotions During Crises

the process and reach some acceptance. In the next section we will consider specifically some common types of family crises and the communication issues involved with each of them.

COMMUNICATION AND SPECIFIC FAMILY CRISES

As was noted earlier, each stage of the coping-mourning process carries with it communication tasks which must be accomplished for the family member or members to move ahead in resolving the crisis. In this section we will briefly examine the specific family crises of death, illness/handicaps, and divorce from a communication perspective. Communication about these crises becomes more difficult when family members fear talking about the issues involved or if they feel discussion makes matters worse. Such silence blocks the natural process described earlier that a family has to go through to reach recovery. We have chosen to focus on these three major crises but recognize that less dramatic events such as moving, losing a job, dealing with alcoholism, or receiving a promotion or large inheritance will disrupt the family system stressfully.

Death

The finality of death closes off relationship options making it an emotionally overwhelming crisis for most families. The system experiences the permanent loss of one member and eventually has to adapt to becoming a system of a different number of people, e.g., a five-person system becomes a four-person system through the death of one member. Family therapist Bowen (1976) describes the impact of death in the following terms: "No life event can stir more emotionally directed thinking in the individual and more emotional reactiveness in those about him" (335). He calls it our chief taboo subject. "A high percentage of people die alone, locked into their own thoughts which they cannot communicate to others. People cannot communicate the thoughts they have lest they upset the family or others" (336). Subgroups may form to keep the subject unmentionable. According to Herz (1980):

It is not uncommon that as the tension increases between any two of the family members around the death issue, the most uncomfortable individual will draw in a third to relieve his tension. Another variant of the same process is that the twosome will collude in avoiding a discussion of the impending death.   (235–236)

Persons who are dying and their family members often resort to silence, new rules, and verbal games to maintain a two-sided pretense that "everything is going to be all right." Family members in their own grief may go into a denial of the information of a terminal illness. They shield the dying from such self-knowledge and begin a series of new communication rules around the dying person. Some families go so far as to forbid any discussion, even by nurses, of the patient's health with the patient. Everyone is to keep fooling the patient at all costs. This can create monumental stress for a rational, articulate human who has the capacity to cope with news of his or her own death since the subterfuges necessary to "keep up the front" often become transparent to the dying. Often the dying family member knows, and then has to play a game of not knowing, to protect the rest of the family.

I will never forget my uncle complaining bitterly two days before he died about his family treating him like a helpless child and insisting he would recover whenever he started to talk about dying or his fear of never leaving the hospital. I was only fourteen and did not fully understand what he was trying to tell me at the time but I never forgot his pain or anger as he tried to explain the feeling of dying without emotional support.

Such rules block dealing with all the interpersonal feelings, the caring, the relationships, as well as dealing with some of the immediate fears and loneliness.

Dunlop (1978) declares that "the dying person has his own grieving to do. We should remember too, that the dying person is not just losing himself (which is a considerable loss that other grievers are not having to deal with), but the dying person is also about to lose everything which is important and everyone who is significant to him and whom he loves" (2). Kübler-Ross (1970) suggests that we should regard death as an "intrinsic part of life" (141) and discuss it openly like other events in family life. The question should change from "Do I tell?" to "How do I share the information?" (28). She discovered almost all terminally ill patients realized they were dying whether they had been told or not (31). If a family confronts the issue openly, they can, according to Kübler-Ross, go through preparatory grief together and this facilitates the later bereavement process (169). Parkes (1972), a British psychiatrist who has made numerous studies of bereaved families, agrees. He recognized that the anticipatory grief in communicating about dying can be quite painful but it had the potential to lead to a kind of tranquility for the family members who share it and left more satisfying memories of the dying person for survivors (131, 154).

Reasons vary on why a family member should not be told he or she has a terminal illness. Dunlop states "Perhaps it is done out of the belief that if the dying person were told he was dying, he would become depressed and despondent, however, in time he will be both, and must be both if his dying is to have some psychological comfort to it" (5). In determining whether to tell a patient, Verwoerdt (1967) lists these criteria: (1) the dying member's emotional and intellectual resources to handle the news; (2) what the dying member already knows or has guessed; (3) the personal meaning the disease has for the dying based on their knowledge of others who had the same terminal illness; (4) the degree to which the dying member wants to know his or her fate (10). The answer to this question in Dunlop's opinion requires considerable skill in assessment of verbal and nonverbal communications from the dying person (121). After careful review of all arguments, Dunlop concludes that a dying person who wants to know has that right. He calls it an absurdity to leave the decision to the physician who "may in fact be the least prepared to make one in which the patient's emotional well-being is at stake" (11). Bowen would concur with Dunlop: "Problems occur when the closed communication system of medicine meets the age-old closed system between the patient and family . . ." (337).

Using Kübler-Ross' five stages, we present one model for the process of dying: (1) denial, (2) anger, (3) bargaining, (4) depression, and (5) acceptance (36). The sequence may vary but eventually the dying person will progress through all of them if he or she lives long enough and does not become arrested or stuck at a particular point, since the length of time one stays in a stage varies according to the individual. Persons will move back and forth through the stages.

Persons preparing for death need to express their denials—to articulate why such cannot be the case, to explore other remedies. They need to vent their anger at themselves, those they love, possibly at God, science, or other institutions. Bargains must be struck or attempted—silently and openly. Finally the loneliness, fears, and practical concerns must be unloaded—ranging from "what is really on the Other Side" to "how will they run the house without me?" Crying, praying, philosophizing, swearing, touching, worrying, and some joking contribute to the conversations.

Regardless of the phase, dying persons need a listener capable of empathic listening who does not insist they will be better if they think about something else. Most dying people welcome an opportunity to talk about their death (Parkes, 131). Bowen, who has counseled dying patients for over thirty years, declares "I have never seen a terminally ill person who was not strengthened by such a talk. This contradicts former beliefs about the ego being too fragile for this in certain situations" (337). Kübler-Ross agrees, "Dying persons will welcome someone who is willing to talk with them about their dying but will allow them to keep their defenses as long as they need them" (37). She further states that those patients who died comfortably had had a chance to rid themselves of guilt and "who have been encouraged to express their rage, to cry in preparatory grief, and to express their fears and fantasies to someone who can sit quietly and listen" (119). For family members this means giving a dying person free expression to let the dying member sort out his or her feelings, even though the other members may be in pain. Family members can create a sense of oneness that facilitates open expression of fears of dying—fears unlike any previously encountered. Although watching a person die can be devastating to the family members ". . . terminal illness of a family member (unlike sudden death) does allow the family, if the system remains open, to resolve relationship issues, reality issues, and to say the final goodbye before death (Herz, 228).

After the death of a family member, the other members of the system go through a bereavement process ranging from numbness to pining to depression to recovery (Parkes, 7). An unexpected death, either by an accident or illness, forces a family into an initial state of shock. Eventually the shock wears off and the bereavement process begins. The actual event traumatizes any family even in cases where members know of an impending death. The survivors will experience times of anger and depression. There may be many regrets about unspoken issues. "If only I had told him how much I loved him." "If I had taken more time to listen to her." They, too, will need supportive listeners.

It's important to recognize the process nature of grief and realize that people will be upset, irrational, and communicate differently. If the death has been caused by a long terminal illness or injury, the bereaved may have been so occupied with the care of the individual, and with maintaining some semblance of order in the family system, that only the death frees them to get in touch with their feelings.

Much also depends upon the place that the deceased filled in the family system. The death of a parent of young children leaves many child-rearing jobs and family responsibilities to the remaining parent. For example, "the loss of a husband, for instance, may or may not mean the loss of a sexual partner, companion, accountant, gardener, baby-minder, audience, bed warmer, and so on depending upon the particular roles normally performed by this husband" (Parkes, 7). The surviving spouse has additional burdens because he or she must learn new role functions and do so without the aid of probably the principal person that had been depended upon. If young children remain in the household, the remaining parent has to help them through the crisis. Herz concludes that the "most influential factor in the child's reaction to the loss of a parent appears to be the ability of the remaining parent to not allow his or her own emotions to create distance from the child (229).

The death of a child carries with it parental images and hopes for the future. Such circumstances usually result in great family pain. From her summary of the literature on childhood death, Herz suggests that family disruption is a common aftereffect, with divorce or separation occurring in a large number of the cases. She states, "the appearance of marital conflict after a filial death is significant" (228).

Thus the death of a family member alters the entire family system, requiring the other members to go through a grieving process with as open communication as possible, in order to reach a new reintegration of the smaller system at a later point.

Illness/Handicap

The family with a permanently handicapped or ill member goes through the crisis process before coming to terms with the problem. Birth defects and diseases require major adjustments in a family's use of time, space, and energy. So do permanent injuries incurred in accidents. The immediate disruption to the family may in no way equal the long-term drain on family resources and energies required to help the injured family member to cope with what may well be a lifelong problem.

In a powerful description of the mourning process that parents of impaired children undergo, psychologist Moses (1978) suggests that parents go through a process identical to the stages described by Kübler-Ross for coping with death. Initially parents may deny the child's impairment by refusing to believe it exists or by denying the true impact of the handicap. Many parents experience guilt directly by believing they caused the handicap or that the handicap is a punishment for something that they must have done in the past. Parents may use depression or self-directed rage to punish themselves for their impotence in helping the child or for not using some omnipotent or "magical" power to prevent the handicap. Eventually such rage may move outward as anger is directed at others, including helping professionals or the children themselves. Parents may bargain with God or science promising, "I will do something for you if you will fix my child." Each of these stages occurs in whatever order is necessary to work through the pain surrounding the shock of losing the fantasied "perfect" child. Some families block this mourning process by preventing the necessary expressions of each stage. This occurs when a subculture or system sets rules like, "You are not supposed to be depressed," "You are *supposed* to keep a stiff upper lip." The system has to support open communication if the family is to move through the necessary stages.

The patients also face similar processes. The person who loses a limb or a vital capacity mourns the leg or the eyesight or the strength by responding with denial strategies, expression of anger, attempts at bargaining, depression, and eventually if the process is not arrested, with some acceptance. Communication must be kept open and the injured or ill member given free rein to emotionally vent his or her anger over not being able to live as other people do. Quite often this forces the afflicted to adopt a completely new interest since they can no longer physically or mentally do what they once were capable of doing. The family system feels the tension until the crisis has been met with some forms of adaptation.

Divorce/Desertion/Separation

Unlike death where the family faces the permanent loss of a system member and its adaptation requires adjustment to a smaller system, the family in a divorce faces adapting to a fragmented state at least temporarily. In most cases, except total desertion, each parent remains somewhat involved with the children thus continuing the parenting aspects of the original system (Weiss, 1975).

Whatever the reasons for the dissolution of the marriage, usually each partner experiences a failure in communication. If you accept a transactional systems perspective, the blame can never be placed on one person in the family —the issues lie with the relationship and not just with one partner. When you think about the issues of mutual influence and punctuation it becomes fruitless to assign blame since the immediate split may have been preceded by months or even years of ineffective communication. At some time in their relationship each failed to meet the needs of the other and a new painful pattern emerged.

The separation and divorce processes essentially follow the pattern described earlier in this chapter. At some point the spouses mourn the loss of the relationship, although one or the other spouse may have mourned the "death" of the marriage years before the divorce became a reality. Initially spouses may deny that anything is really wrong and communicate to children or others that "our problems aren't all that serious" or "Daddy will be back soon so don't tell anyone he's gone." As the reality takes hold, anger, bargaining, and depression all intermingle. There may be attempts at reconciliation. "We had a great thing going once, we can have it again." Such failed attempts may be met with messages such as "After all I've done for you." "What kind of a mother would move out on her children?" which serve to release some of the tensions. Painful accusations and negative conflict are often heightened by the adversary positions required in many legal divorce proceedings. Finally, depression reflects the sense of loss and/or rejection often accompanied with great loneliness.

In terms of communication the couple may experience going back down through the stages of development in the "social penetration model" described in Chapter 4. Thus they would move from whatever stage they had reached, e.g., affective exchange, back down toward the lower stages. Altman and Taylor describe the process as follows:

> A relationship undergoing a process of deterioration should move from more to less intimate and from greater to lesser amounts of interaction— contrary to the forward penetration process. Moreover, the rate and level of dissolution are predicted to be functions of reward/cost properties of the relationship. Thus, as their relationship falls apart, people gradually withdraw affect and intimate contact, and are likely to deal with one another to a lesser extent.   (7)

In other words, as a relationship deteriorates, the high self-disclosure, predictability, uniqueness, openness, and spontaneity that characterize the higher levels of relationship begin to disintegrate. Little effort is invested in the relationship; risk-taking declines.

Eventually communication moves down the continuum toward orientation level behavior. Personal issues are avoided, nonverbals are restrained, little uniqueness and spontaneity remain. Many former spouses relate to each other as casual acquaintances or almost strangers except perhaps around highly-charged issues such as money and children.

According to Knapp (1978), as relationships decline they produce messages which communicate an increasing physical and psychological distance; and an increasing disassociation with the other person (189). Levels of cohesion drop to reflect the distancing; little connectedness remains.

There have been over the years studies showing the adverse effects of divorce on most children (Hetherington, 1973; Wallerstein and Kelley, 1975, 1980; Westman, 1972). Some studies especially indicate problems in the pre-divorce, transition, and early part of the post-divorce periods with children acting out their frustrations and rage. After a year to eighteen months most families have adjusted to the crisis and children may have accepted and may even like the changes. In an interview, this nine-year-old's comment reflects that attitude.

My Dad and Mother divorced last year. I can spend any weekend with him or stay during the week when I am not in school. I didn't think I would like the arrangement but it's better than them fighting all the time. Now I have a house in the suburbs with Mom and an apartment in the city with Dad.

Usually communication improves in the years following divorces. Two months after the divorce, 66 percent of the exchanges between divorced couples involved conflicts over finances, support, visitation, child-rearing, and relating to others in the system (Hetherington, Cox, & Cox, 1976, 423). This same study followed families over a two-year period and noted that conflicts and contact with fathers diminished over time. This statement from the study certainly reflects the changing nature of communication in divorced families:

> The divorced mother tries to control the child by being more restrictive and giving more commands which the child ignores or resists. The divorced father wants his contacts with his children to be as happy as possible. He begins by initially being extremely permissive and indulgent and becoming increasingly restrictive over the two-year period, although he is never as restrictive as fathers in intact homes.   (425)

Although it is impossible in a divorce to remove all the negative aspects of stress upon children and their communication, the parents can certainly reduce the stress. If neither parent uses the child as a go-between, nor encourages "tattle-tale" behavior, they reduce opportunities for conflict.

Throughout any of these crises: death, illness or handicaps, or divorce, the family's capacity for open communication, reflective of its levels of cohesion and adaptation, and its images, themes, boundaries, and biosocial beliefs, will determine how the system will weather the strain. A family with low cohesion may fragment under pressure unless such pressure can serve to connect the unconnected members. A family with limited resources for adaptation faces a painful time since such crises force change upon the system and it must respond with internal changes of its own. A family whose images and themes allow outside involvement into family affairs may use their flexible boundaries to find institutional and social support. A family with rigid biosocial beliefs faces difficult challenges if key family figures are lost or injured and others are not permitted to assume some of the role responsibilities. Throughout this process the communication among the family members serves to facilitate or hinder the accomplishment of revising the system to meet the demands placed on it by the crisis.

As a result of crises in which a family member has died or left the home, the remaining family members undergo a period of adjustment and often need to develop new communication behaviors to function within the altered system. In the next section we will consider these issues.

COMMUNICATION WITHIN FAMILY SYSTEMS

From our perspective death or divorce do not dissolve a system, rather they alter it. After a death the remaining family members are faced with the necessity of restructuring themselves into a smaller system—the hole must be closed—the family cannot continue limping indefinitely due to the "missing" member. After a divorce the members may exist for a long period of time in an altered system of the same size which still functions around issues of the children or monetary considerations. Eventually altered systems may include new spouses and a variety of step-relatives.

Divorced partners may share responsibilities and co-parent their off-spring even if they remarry, thus remaining in a very functional system. A foster child may link two systems together and function as a member of both the foster family, with whom he or she lives temporarily, and the natural family with whom he or she may have intermittent interactions. Such experiences tax the communication competence of all parties involved. The original system undergoes a severe crisis which challenges the previously established levels of cohesion and adaptability tied to the communication patterns. Eventually new balance is found as new subgroups are formed and the system adapts to whatever new arrangements result. This is not an easy task. Particularly when children are involved, lines of communication still exist: divorced spouses must be encountered and communicated with about money and property, children's rights, health, education, special events (birthdays, graduations), and general "growing-up" concerns. Relatives and friends on both sides may also remain involved with both former spouses and the children thus serving as reminders of original ties.

When I divorced I only had one eight-year-old child, and dealing with her became so difficult that I can't imagine what families with three or four children do. First Adrienne had to deal with the tension between her mother and me and the divorce. She had a lot of anger about that and we spent hours talking about why Mommy and I could not remain together. Then she had to adjust to me as a single parent when she visited me and we had to work out our rules for living together. Her mother and I had to communicate often about Adrienne's emotional and economic needs.

In most cases of death or divorce a single-parent system forms, at least for a period of time. If there is a remaining parent, this person will have some effect on that system. Let us look specifically at some varied systems.

Single-Parent Systems

Women head most single-parent families. In fact only 8.4 percent of children of divorced parents live with their father (Hetherington, Cox & Cox, 417). Death, desertion, and unmarried mothers add significant numbers to this type of family structure. The U.S. Census Bureau in its latest report revealed the proportion of family households maintained by a woman with no husband is 8 percent for whites, 16 percent for Hispanics, and 29 percent for blacks. Many young single women are keeping babies and raising them as single parents. In summary, in all families, one in every six children under 18 lives in a one-parent home. Nearly three fourths of these mothers with children 6–17 work along with more than half those with children under 6 (Gaylin, 1977, 94). In addition one third of the two-parent families are remarried systems (Carter and Glick, 1976, 417). This means approximately 46 percent of the children have experienced or are experiencing a single-parent home (Raschke and Raschke, 1979, 367).

A major problem for single-parent families is task overload, most evident in the life cycle of single mothers with young children. Compounding this, social isolation, increased anxiety, depression, and loneliness also affect the single parent. Beal (1980) reports that single parents frequently find themselves emotionally cut off from extended family relationships and social networks (257). Divorced persons find themselves separated from their spouse's extended family as the boundaries are tightened against them. Unmarried women with children may find more support within their extended families, particularly in matriarchical systems.

Shifting subgroups and networks may be a problem. The two-against-one model of the two-parent home may force children to abide by parental wishes; when one parent leaves the system some power may be removed from the parental image. Any troubled parent-child relationship cannot be adequately balanced by the other parent. When one parent leaves the system, the other parent may attempt to place a child in the vacated role to provide emotional support or perform household duties. The child may become the confidant or may share decision making. "You're the man of the house now" typifies this lowering of boundaries between parental and child subsystems and often results in communication breakdowns. This new role may place great pressure on the child, may alienate the child from other siblings, and may eventually interfere with the normal process of separating from the family at the appropriate developmental point.

Numerous researchers have debated the problems of the single-parent family, especially its effects upon children. These studies have importance because they relate to family communication. In measuring self-concept which also includes assessment of social and personal adjustment, Raschke and Raschke (1979) found that children were "not adversely affected by living in single parent families but that family conflict and/or parental unhappiness can be detrimental" (373). In this important study that compared intact families with single-parent families they discovered that in both types there was a high correlation between perceived parental happiness and children's healthy self-concepts. Their work concurs with Burchinal's findings (1964) that adolescents in broken, unbroken, and reconstituted families did not suffer adverse effects in their adjustment or developmental characteristics (50–51). Herzog and Sudia (1971) examined research covering twenty years on the effects of children living in fatherless homes and concluded there was little evidence to support the assumption that households headed by women had a detrimental effect upon children (Raschke and Raschke, 368). However, from his summary of research, Beal (1980) concludes:

> Children in single-parent families exhibit more noncompliant and deviant behavior than children in intact families. Nevertheless, research findings clearly indicate that children reared in conflict-laden intact families may be more poorly adjusted than children in well functioning single-parent homes.   (257)

The type of communication possible within single-parent homes created through death or divorce reflects the ability of the family to adjust to the new systemic arrangement, whether through the permanent or partial loss of a member. As conflicts diminish, increased cohesion may develop among members. Families with high adaptability will be able to create new and functional communication networks. In almost all cases boundaries will be adjusted to reflect the system's need for or desire for outside influence. Themes, images, and biosocial beliefs may also experience adjustment. No matter what, a family with low adaptability will face a more painful time than a family with high adaptability, as evidenced by the following family's inability to adapt to a new identity as a single-parent system.

My father died a slow death of diabetes when my sister and I were eight and six. He had always been the head of the family and my mother depended on his leadership in everything. For ten years we operated as a fractured family. You could say our theme was "We can't be a family without a man." We couldn't get any identity of our own and we hitched ourselves to all kinds of other people and tried to find new families for ourselves. Finally we got some counseling and learned that three women could create a functional family unit. A single-parent family does not have to be a second-class family.

Eventually many single-parent systems become part of a remarried system and experience new adjustments and communication concerns.

Reconstituted Systems

As was noted earlier, one marriage does not end and a totally new system begin. The first marital system continues to influence future relationships. In their discussion of forming a remarried family, McGoldrick and Carter (1980) suggest that the emotions connected with the breakup of the first marriage can be visualized as a "roller coaster" graph with peaks of intensity at the point of:

1. Decision to separate;
2. Actual separation;
3. Legal divorce;
4. Remarriage of either spouse;
5. Death of either ex-spouse;
6. Life cycle transitions of children. (graduations, marriage, illness, etc.) (271)

In a divorce that includes children, each of these points will cause disruption for original system members and must be handled carefully in order to keep a remarriage stabilized. Many counselors consider that a couple is divorced *to* each other rather than *from* each other, especially when children are concerned. Thus a full reconstituted system is formed. For example, a family system may expand to include a woman, two children, her current husband, and her former husband who has remarried and had a stepson. The following diagram (Figure 11-2) will demonstrate how the original marital system of Peggy and Seth has grown and altered.

Although Seth does not live with his children and former wife there are ties, emotional, economic, and practical, which bind all these people to each other. If Maryanne has difficulty in school her mother, her natural father, and her step-parents may all be affected by the problem.

As a remarried system forms, partners bring communication patterns from (1) families-of-origin, (2) the first marriage, and (3) the period between marriages. Children bring patterns from the second and third situations. Forming such a system requires extensive initial adaptation if acceptable cohesion levels are ever to be reached. Family members are cast instantly into multiple roles. A single man may become husband and stepfather. A woman may become a wife, stepmother, or even step-grandmother, with a simple "I do." Knowing some of the results of research on step-parent and children relationships indicate areas where problems in communication can develop. Some evidence indicates that children accept step-parents more readily than they do step-siblings. Relationships also appear more harmonious in mother-stepfather families than in father-stepmother families (Duberman, 1973). In a detailed study of different types of families, the researchers concluded, "There is little evidence suggesting that divorce and/or remarriage causes any lasting intrapsychic damage or major or deviant social behavior in children. There are probably proportionately as many 'normal' children from divorced and reconstructed families as from original intact families" (Baden-Marotz et al., 1979, 10).

Each member of the remarried system must participate in the creation of new family themes, images, boundaries, and biosocial beliefs. Disparate back-

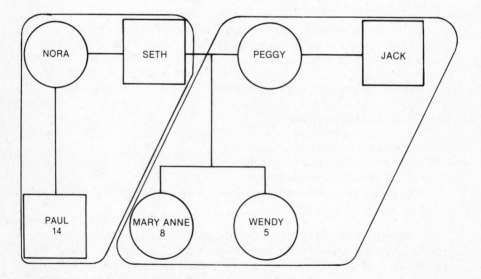

Figure 11-2   Reconstituted Family System

grounds and negative feelings about the remarriage will result in intense periods of conflict, reflected verbally and nonverbally, as family members jockey for position and power. The former oldest child may fight against the role of middle daughter. A child used to great freedom and autonomy may rebel against themes that push for strong cohesion and similarity among family members. Each new system will have to negotiate boundaries issues such as:

1. Membership (Who are the "real" members of the family?)
2. Space (What space is mine? Where do I really belong?)
3. Authority (Who is really in charge? Of discipline? money? decisions? etc.)
4. Time (Who gets how much of my time and how much do I get of theirs?)
(McGoldrick and Carter, 269–270)

Biosocial concerns such as male-female roles or authority positions may need extensive or limited negotiation depending on the previous family positions on such issues.

Communication networks must expand to encompass new members and possibly to maintain ties with first marriage members as children and former spouses and extended family members attempt to maintain necessary contacts. Children may be confused by adjusting to the functioning of two separate households. This may be compounded by pressure, negative remarks, or overt conflict between members of former systems. Children may feel pulled to "side" with one group or another. Each group may establish communication rules to keep information from the other. "Don't tell your mother about my trip to Mexico," "Don't mention that I'm dating anyone." Children may be filled with secrets and resentments which they cannot divulge.

If members of the extended family take sides, the children suffer additional pressures. A spouse may unwisely permit relatives or friends in the children's presence to make derogatory remarks about the other spouse. A grandmother may remind the children of the "no-good" qualities of their father and when the children become boisterous, argue, or get into fights may declare "You're acting just like your father."

What children need to understand in order to communicate openly with both parents is that they did not cause the divorce. Each parent needs to assure children that it's acceptable to love the other parent and that parent-child love in no way diminishes because of the divorce. Nothing positive in communication can be gained by "bad mouthing" one spouse or the other. Often one spouse says little, but children sense the nonverbal communication when the other spouse's name is mentioned. Divorced parents need to remember that as children grieve they may act out their own feelings of loss and alternately blame one parent or the other for the divorce (Luepnitz, 1979, 84) or they may take out their anger on a step-parent.

Eventually most remarried systems stabilize and children and parents report satisfaction. Gilford and Bengtson (1979) analyzed data from 1,056 married members of three-generation families. Their data included once-married versus second or third marriages, as well as generation factors, and concluded that on positive or negative dimensions of marital satisfaction the trends were uniform on such independent variables as chronological age, duration of marriage, and sex. In all types of marriages, the satisfaction resembled a "U-shaped curve"—highest at beginning, declining in child-raising and middle years, and then increasing in old age (394–396).

Reconstituted systems are becoming a common part of the American way of life but the issues of living in such a system remain varied and complex. To date our society's vocabulary has not even developed words to deal with the roles and relationships involved. For example, a child has no names for step-grandparents, no way to easily communicate about his relationship to the son of his father's second former wife, no name for the first stepfather who is now divorced from mother. Such difficulties make contacts with outsiders and institutions more difficult and sometimes more painful. As society becomes more comfortable with these new family forms we will develop more effective ways of communicating about such relationships.

Co-Parenting

Before closing the issue of various family forms, we wish to recognize the growing relational style called co-parenting, or an arrangement whereby divorced parents accept equal responsibility for care and maintenance of children. Co-parenting can take on a variety of forms but it means shared custody with the children living alternately with their parents. Ideally some couples have worked out weekend or every-other-night arrangements or three or four nights with one parent and then an equal number with the other. Instead of separating the child more or less permanently via divorce from one parent, this arrangement enables the child to know, love, and share time with each parent (Galper, 1978). Children seem to readily adapt to the two-home situation and after a short time prefer it. Grote and Weinstein (1977) believe joint custody is "an ideal solution and viable alternative that cries out for acceptance. Joint custody is viable and practical because it maintains the much needed familial structure in our society" (43). The following account describes such a working arrangement:

In the year following the divorce, we continued to fight constantly over raising Mike. At school Mike was constantly in trouble. As a father I wasn't satisfied with an overnight visit on the weekend and I kept running over to the house to see Mike before his mother returned from work. We worked out an every-other-night agreement but this seemed to be too much moving back and forth for Mike. We switched to changing every three days and this suited everyone fine. Every other weekend I am free to date or entertain. Mike has his own room, clothes, and toys at each home, including a dog at mine and a cat at his mother's. Now Mike does well in school—when we settled down, he did, too.

Co-parenting requires cooperation and a commitment to the idea. It necessitates both parents living close to one another although some couples who have moved to different cities alternate school years. Both parents experience the joy and share the tribulations of child raising (Nehls and Morgenbessner, 1980, 117). Both recognize their responsibility and don't dump it on the other. Children may not have to play games to get the support needed. They know they are wanted. Dullea (1980) interviewed Hugh McIsaac, director of the Los Angeles Courts Family Counseling Services, who stated that in joint custody decisions the child wins rather than loses. In the Conciliation Court in Los Angeles one in every five custody cases ends in a plan for joint custody (35).

Co-parenting requires a special skill in communicating between the parents plus their new partners. They have to separate early their marital troubles from their parental roles in order for it to work. If the former spouse's communication remains conflictual, a child will be constantly in the middle of a war. Yet, if the parents can maintain open and supportive communication with each other, the child may experience two supportive environments. Nevertheless the children must have the capacity to adapt to the functions of two different households. In remarried systems step-parents must become heavily involved in the process if it is to succeed. Dullea also interviewed Richard Gardner, clinical professor of child psychiatry at Columbia University, who believes that joint custody "when it works approximates most closely the traditional marital situation in that it gives the child the greatest exposure to both mother and father. Having to make an appointment to see your father can be hard on kids" (35).

CONCLUSION

In this chapter we have looked at communication through unpredictable life stresses. Specifically we focused on (1) the process of dealing with unpredictable stress, (2) communication during certain major stressful life events, such as death, illness, and divorce, and (3) communication in reconstituted families.

Over years every family system will encounter external stress from crisis situations as well as stress from developmental change. The ability of the system to cope effectively with the stress depends on a number of factors: (1) the amount of previous stress sustained, (2) the magnitude of role changes involved, (3) the role of institutions, and (4) the role of support networks. Families which have experienced extensive previous traumas may become dysfunctional under additional pressure and communication may break down. Tremendous role adjustments may also tax the system since appropriate communication would appear to be blocked until roles are renegotiated. Families that are willing to maintain flexible boundaries, communicate with and accept support from institutional sources (Parents without Partners, church groups, medical organization) and social networks (friends and extended family) are more likely to work through their crises and return to functional communication, than are those who block out outside support. Throughout this chapter we have maintained that communication around these issues can serve to facilitate or block the coping process. Open and supportive communication serves to help move families through the stages of denial, recoil, depression, and reintegration.

Death and divorce necessarily alter family systems; these may evolve into remarried systems, with all their communication complexity, over time. In short, communication may serve to facilitate or retard the process of coping with external change but in most cases the resilience of the human system renders it functional eventually.

12

Family Ecology: Spatial and Temporal Dimensions of Communication

Everyone in our family must be home between six and seven-thirty. Dinner is never until seven, and no one goes out before eight. The time before dinner is spent between the family room and the kitchen. This is the social hour. We usually discuss what has gone on during the day and what will go on that evening. We don't necessarily talk as a whole group, but in groups of twos and threes. Mom is usually in the kitchen, Dad is in his chair, and the rest of us flow between the rooms. We all speak to each other at dinner. We have a big table with Dad and Mom at either end and the four of us in our specific seats. Everyone gets a chance to talk and tell what happened to them during the day and relay anything important happening in their life. This conversation continues throughout dinner and the time that it takes us to clean the kitchen. It is not unusual for us to sit in the kitchen and talk until the first people begin to wander off to bed. It is a special time—the time that we're all home and the kitchen seems to be the best place for sharing to take place among all of us.

To more fully understand the communication context we must look at the nonhuman aspects of the environment, as well as the persons involved in the interactions. In this chapter we will view family relationships through the lenses of time and space, demonstrating how these factors affect the process of communication among family members. The following questions may serve to stimulate your initial thinking about family relationships as they are affected by time and space:

1. Where did you go to talk to your parents about personal problems? What time of day was best for this type of discussion?
2. How was dinner organized in your home? Did you all eat at the same time while sitting in specific places or did you eat when you felt like it, while sitting anywhere you chose?
3. Were there rules about places for serious conversation in the house? Were there special chairs that belonged to specific family members? If doors were closed, did you knock first or did you just open them and walk in?
4. Could you shut the door to your room to be alone? How long would you be alone before someone tried to get you back with the rest of the group? Were you sent to your room as punishment?
5. As a small child, what were the safety boundaries around your home which you could not cross? A neighbor's yard? The apartment hallway? A road?
6. What "family times" existed in your home? What happened during these times?

These are some of the topics we will explore further as you view family interactions through spatial and temporal lenses and investigate the interaction between these nonhuman environmental factors and the interpersonal relationship within a family. We will also see how the levels of cohesion and adaptability are affected by and affect these particular environmental forces.

Recent trends in environmental psychology have led architects, designers, and social scientists to focus more directly on the nonhuman environment as a context for, and type of, communication. The nonhuman environment constitutes a system of communication which is learned, socially read, and structured like language (DeLong, 1974). As you will see in the following discussion, we learn to react appropriately within particular dimensions of time and space because of the messages we receive from these dimensions.

Psychologist Albert Scheflen suggests that hierarchical levels of social relationship, including parent/child and family relationships, provide and demand certain traditional patterns of task performance, spacing, speech and body language, and each of these traditions dictates how we are to think and feel about every kind of situation. He maintains that these systems of behavior are organized spatially and temporally, or according to space and time (429–430).

From our perspective, the environmental issues of space and time provide part of the boundaries which limit and define a family's communication behavior. If you analyze the structures within which you relate to people, you will begin to understand how the structural design and the arrangement of furniture and objects within the structure can influence (1) who interacts with whom, (2) where,

(3) when, (4) for how long, and (5) the kinds of things about which they can communicate. In more concrete terms, certain family members are more likely to have greater interactions because they share a room, or they both use the backyard for basketball, or they sit up together for an evening cup of coffee. Whereas the basketball games do not foster intense, deep conversations but do provide shared positive experiences, sitting up in your room or at the kitchen table with one other person may lead to special and deep conversations and greater cohesion; it may encourage the airing of strong conflicts resulting in greater distance, or possibly, greater closeness. Thus, the environment and the people in it combine to form a communication system. Duncan (1964) stresses the interdependence of a way of life and its setting. Failure to respect this intrinsic wholeness is done "at the peril of overlooking the interrelations on which depend the stability of the system as a whole" (69). Communication occurs within a context and that context influences what kinds of interactions can and will take place. Places as well as people form the context for communication events and, although the physical home or time patterns do not *determine* the kinds of family interactions which take place, they do *influence* the kinds of interactions which occur both within and without its walls. Thus, we assume a family ecology viewpoint which recognizes that the total environment has a strong impact on family development. The family and the environment interact and develop a mutual influence pattern; no family remains untouched by its surroundings.

ENVIRONMENTAL FACTORS

In this chapter we will examine the environmental factors of space, territory, privacy, and time and then demonstrate how these interrelate with each other and affect communication within family systems.

Space

Anthropologist Edward Hall (1966) conceptualized the ways in which we use space, including fixed feature space, semi-fixed feature space, and informal space (103–112). *Fixed feature space* refers to that space organized by unmoving boundaries, such as walls in a room (physical) or the unmarked line dividing space that is understood by those who use it. The latter may be called a nonphysical or psychological boundary. Each type serves as a recognizable boundary to which inhabitants must adapt. The actual wall between the kitchen and dining room may keep the cook out of the conversation. Such boundaries are obvious. Yet if you ever shared a room with a brother or sister, you may remember the times that your side of the room and his or her side of the room became separate territories and you did not cross the line, drop things on the other bed, or sit in the other chair.

Semi-fixed feature space refers to flexible space created by the arrangement of furniture and/or other movable objects over which the inhabitants have control. You probably remember rearranging your room according to your moods or having to help rearrange the living room when one of your parents decided to foster conversations or to encourage interaction at a party.

Informal space deals with the way people handle their bodies or the spatial needs they carry with them that vary according to situations. Hall divides the distances at which a person relates into four major levels: intimate space ranging from zero to eighteen inches, personal space ranging from eighteen inches to four feet, social space including four feet to twelve feet, and public space which encompasses interactions at distances over twelve feet.

Intimate space encourages the nonverbal expressions of emotions and supports certain verbal expressions. You can hug, kiss, tickle, engage in intercourse, hit, wrestle, or whisper within this space. This is an ideal situation for the sharing of intimate relational currencies. Infants experience much of the world from this distance as they maintain close physical contact with a parent as a major part of their young existence. As children mature, they learn to rely more heavily on verbal communication and less on extensive physical contact and the sharing of intimate space as a part of developing relationships. Most people voluntarily share intimate space with persons with whom they are emotionally involved. For many of us, the family provides a major source of people with whom to share intimate space.

Personal space provides people with the opportunity to have some positive or negative physical contact and to share important ideas or personal feelings in dyads or small groups without having to shout or be overheard. Important discussions, decision-making, and the sharing of joy or pain can occur at this distance which supports a more verbal style of expressing feelings than does intimate space.

Concerning *social space,* more persons can be involved in a conversation, but only limited nonverbal communication can occur. Eye contact may replace physical touch as a major means of making contact. Fewer very personal topics may be discussed, yet family issues may be reviewed by the whole group. Extensive task-oriented communication related to everyday business and concerns occurs at this distance. "When will you be home?" "Where are my socks?" characterize such transactions.

Public space encourages formal speaking or shorter bursts of communication such as a wave, a greeting, or a short discussion of a pertinent topic. Shouting from room to room, talking across the living room, or calling a child from play typifies interactions at this space. Touch is not possible, but unique communication signals may travel across space such as those at a crowded party or between a "tuned-in" husband and wife or a disruptive child and the child's mother.

Hall's categories may be used as a springboard for looking at spatial relationships, but he cautions that the use of space must be considered as contextually and culturally bound. Appropriateness of spatial distances depends upon circumstances and settings.

Territory

To understand the use of space, we must look at the related factors of territoriality and privacy. A basic concept in the study of animal behavior, territoriality involves "behavior by which an organism characteristically lays claim to an area and defends it against members of his own species" (Hall, 7). It provides a framework for doing things: places to learn, places to play, safe places to hide. Hall relates territoriality to the concepts of fixed feature space when he suggests, "the boundaries of the territories remain reasonably constant, the territory is in every sense of the word an extension of the organism which is marked by visual, vocal, and olfactory signs and, therefore, it is relatively 'fixed' " (9). For our purposes, family territory may be understood as an area that a member of a close-knit group in joint tenancy claims and will "defend." In other words, one stakes out real or imagined space and lays personal claim to it.

Scheflen (1971) maintains that those who own a territory or others who recognize it will behave in particular ways as they approach the boundary even if the boundary is not marked by fences, walls, or other barriers. He suggests that small territories may be marked by postural behavior such as an arm that defends a space or by the placement of possessions. Even unmarked boundaries can be noted by the behavior of people who cross them and "lower their heads, exchange at least a token kinesic greeting, and change their walking posture" (431). People may defend their territory through verbal or nonverbal communication strategies such as aggression or dominance.

Territoriality in a home may be as real as "my parents' room," or as nonphysical as "Mike's part of the yard." Places may come to be recognized as belonging to someone by decrees ("This is my chair"), by tenure ("I always sat there"), by markers ("We left our books here because we were coming back") or agreement ("After I've had the hammock for 15 minutes, it's your turn"). If you think about your own home, you should be able to identify numerous territorial behaviors by which members declare their spatial demands. Some of these behaviors may also indicate a desire for privacy within certain space. Yet, without mutual agreement between those who believe the territory is "theirs" and other potential users, the concept of limited use may eventually disappear or conflicts about the use will arise.

Privacy

Westin (1967) defines privacy as the "claim of individuals, groups, or institutions to determine for themselves when, how, and to what extent information about them is communicated to others" (10). Westin defines four states of individual privacy, two of which relate to physical settings. Solitude is the state in which a person is separated from the group and free from observations of others. Intimacy is a state sought by members of dyads or small groups to achieve maximally personal relationships between or among their members, such as in a family situation. In intimacy, there is an attempt to minimize all sensory input from outside the boundaries of an appropriate physical setting.

Privacy functions to maintain an individual's need for personal autonomy through which he or she can control the environment, including the ability to be alone or to have private communication with another. Some homes encourage such privacy while others cannot or do not provide such possibilities. If you share a home with seven others, and a bedroom with two others, privacy may be a luxury attained only outside the home. Yet, a certain home that can physically support privacy for its members would not permit such behavior.

My mother was fanatical about closed doors. If my door was closed, she would open it and say, "We have no secrets in this house." It drove me crazy. I couldn't even read a book or talk to a friend without leaving the door open. Now I encourage my kids to have private places where they can be alone without someone else bothering them.

Privacy and territory interrelate to serve the function of providing means for protective communication such as the sharing of confidence, problems, and affection.

As with space, territory and privacy are relative within and between cultures. In certain types of homes, personal places and possessions are held in high regard whereas, in others, total sharing is the norm. One gains privacy in some cultures by isolation whereas in other cultures, psychological withdrawal permits privacy while among many people. In his study of urban families, Scheflen asked women, "What do you do when you want to be alone?" and discovered that one half of the Puerto Rican wives " . . . did not comprehend the implication of the question in American middle-class terms. They said they never wanted to be alone . . . the other half said they went home to the family" (437). These women thought the researcher was asking about wanting to be away from neighbors and people in the street.

The interaction of the factors of space, territory, and privacy may be viewed through a discussion of the spatial model provided in *Inside the Family*. Family researchers Kantor and Lehr (1976) discuss certain spatial dimensions as a part of a family's mechanism for maintaining an ongoing system (68). Although their discussion covers physical space and the analogous regulation of ideas and events, we will concentrate only on their physical dimensions. They suggest that a family engages in bounding, linking, and centering as they live within a spatial dimension.

Through *bounding,* a family regulates physical traffic across its borders. A family demarcates a perimeter and defends its territory. It says, "this is ours, we are safe here" (68). It may defend these territorial borders through the use of devices to regulate entrance to the home. Buzzers, doormen, peepholes, bushes, double locks, all provide some privacy and daily control over the domain. Children may experience a designated territory which is permitted for safe exploration. In housing projects, there may be no safety beyond the front door, so the boundary may be synonymous with the apartment. In other areas, a neighbor's yard or the road in front may be the limits.

Linking relates to the regulation of distance within the house. A large dining room table may encourage people to come together and may set up some interaction networks. Or, because an apartment is so small that everyone needs to eat and interact in the living room together, people may be sent to their room to study or to regain a "sunny disposition." At a family party, teenagers may be channeled to the yard and basement while adults maintain their own conversations outside younger ears, everyone may interact together, or a variety of patterns may develop.

Centering provides the guidelines for the regulation of family space. There are family rules for how space is used (when one may go outside, who may be allowed in) and there may be specific ways of using things to keep the family in touch with each other. Blackboards, memo boards, and notes can serve to keep a family in touch. Decorations that keep a family in touch with itself such as crucifixes, travel posters, or trophies may provide reminders of what a family stands for. Highly cohesive families may have stronger rules about family togetherness and how to achieve it within the home, than families characterized by low cohesion.

Time

Time also serves to affect the family environment and again, Kantor and Lehr provide a valuable model for looking at a family's use of time. They believe families are *oriented* toward the past, present, future, or hold a nontemporal orientation. Additionally, families engage in *clocking* behaviors which refer to their daily patterns of time use, and *synchronizing* behaviors, which refer to the regulation of overall time.

"Where a family lives in time is as important as where it lives in space" (Kantor and Lehr, 79). Although we all live in the present, we may experience an orientation toward the past or future which supercedes the emphasis we place on the present. Each person orients himself or herself to the past, present, or future. We all have met people who live in the "good old days" and whose communication reflects a respect for, or delight in, yesterday. Although a total focus in the past limits communication about current issues, such as relationships, some sense of *history,* specifically family history, is important. Jane Howard suggests strong extended families have a switchboard operator who keeps track of what others do and who acts like an archivist, who "feels driven to keep scrapbooks and photograph albums up to date . . . " (241). Some sense of its past helps to keep a family functioning in the present.

The present orientation reflects a concern for the here and now. Current relationships are valued and current joys and sorrows take top priority. In a present-oriented family, less time is spent reminiscing or planning than is spent on day-to-day issues.

A future orientation emphasizes what is to come. Planning, dreaming, or scheming characterize such a mind set and have typified many American families on their way to the "good life."

The future was always the present topic of conversation in our home. My father and mother came from Poland as young people and spent most of their lives running a catering service to earn enough money to send us through college and into a profession. They would spend hours planning, dreaming, and preparing for the time we would graduate. Some of our best interactions occurred around the topic of what would we be when we grew up. Unfortunately, I don't think we enjoyed the everyday parts of life as much as we could have.

Kantor and Lehr suggest that some people experience a nontemporal orientation. Persons engaged in creative work or undergoing severe stress may live according to a nontemporal pattern. Most families strive to integrate the time orientations of their members as a means of fostering communication among them.

While orienting refers to an overall perspective of time, clocking refers to the daily use of time. It regulates the sequence, frequency, duration, and pace of immediate events. Sequencing indicates an ordering pattern for family behaviors. Certain family rules such as who talks first in certain situations, or who gets the last word, may be part of a subtle sequencing pattern. On a more obvious level, some families have to establish functional rituals for moving into a day.

> In our attempt to maintain a two-career family with two small children, we have become very organized and we have very specific morning patterns so we can get out of the house on time and in a good frame of mind. I get up, dress, and start to make coffee. My wife then gets out of bed and dresses and starts to dress our daughter. When they come into the kitchen, I dress while Helen fixes the rest of breakfast. We have to eat and be out by eight. During the week, no one eats breakfast until he or she is fully dressed and ready to go. This way we can have a semi-peaceful breakfast, talk a little and minimize the conflict.

Families also clock how often and for how long things may be done. Growing up, you may have experienced limits on how often you saw certain friends, how long you were allowed to stay with them, or how long you were allowed to argue with them before someone yelled "That's enough." All families need some built-in repetition and guidelines to keep their lives functional. Clocking also refers to the pace or speed with which a day is lived. Do you do fifty-two things and call it a "good day" or do you like to take things easy and maintain a slower pace? Pacing relates to the styles of people characterized by Hall according to their use of time: monochronic and polychronic. *Monochronic* typifies people who compartmentalize time. They schedule one thing at a time and become disoriented if they have to deal with too many things at once. *Polychronic* people tend to keep several activities going at once, perhaps because they are so involved with each other. Hence, one group comfortably separates activities and the other tends to collect activities (Hall, 173). Although these characteristics are more likely to be related to an overall culture, certain points on the continuum between the extremes may be said to characterize one or more family members. Pacing also varies with age, health, and mental state. Large variations in pacing often lead to conflict among family members.

An additional aspect of time involves synchronizing, or the means of maintaining a program for regulating the overall and day-to-day life of a family. Often this is done through discussions or assessments of how things are going and a setting of, or reaffirming of, plans or priorities for the family members.

> As we became teenagers and started to go in every different direction, my parents set down the rule that no one was to talk on the phone-

during dinner. That would last for a while and whoever answered the phone would have the caller leave a message, but after a while Mom would take a business call and Jan would talk to her boyfriend and it would break down. When things got too bad, Mom would reestablish the rule and we would start again.

A family has to integrate its overall way for spending time. A spouse may turn down a position that requires a great deal of travel because it would keep him or her away from the family for too long at that period in their lives. Another couple may agree to a long-term type of separation because the opportunity would set the groundwork for a desirable life-style or professional growth in five years.

Family discontent may lead to a reorganization of original priorities. Some families may establish respect for individual "clocks" whereas others may dictate a "family clock" to which everyone must adhere. Just as the other factors are culture bound, the use of time varies according to culture, e.g., American families may stress punctuality whereas Latin American families may not recognize this as a value.

Time and the issues of space, territory, and privacy are interrelated in most households. There may be appropriate times for being alone and times when it is not permitted. Children may be allowed to play in adult spaces until the adult indicates the space is taken. Holidays may require the presence of all family members in a particular space for a specified time, particularly if their themes stress such togetherness and if the images held by most are of a close-knit group that plays together. Biosocial beliefs interact with how time may be "legitimately" spent in many families. For example, in one household men may not be expected to spend time on household tasks whereas in another all family members, regardless of sex, share household duties. Thus space, territoriality, privacy, and time contribute heavily to the communication context. In order to fully understand the interrelationships of these factors we need to examine the family dwelling as a specific communication context.

THE HOME WORLD: OUTSIDE AND INSIDE

All interaction systems are organized temporally and spatially and important family behaviors occur within the spatial and temporal boundaries of the home. Thus the house influences the interactions that occur within it since its structure and design affect to some extent the development of relationships between and among family members. In his work on environments and interaction, psychologist Harry Osmond (1970) distinguishes between *sociofugal* and *sociopetal* space. The former is that type of space which discourages human interaction; the latter supports such interaction ". . . sociopetality is that quality which encourages, fosters, and even enforces the development of stable interpersonal relationship and which may be found in small face-to-face groups, in homes or circular wards (576). Both the exterior and interior of a home and the way time is used within the home can contribute to the creation of a sociopetal experience for the family.

Exterior Arrangement

A home's exterior may affect the types of interactions family members have with the community at large and with neighbors specifically. Some studies of homogeneous populations indicate that housing planned for easy social interaction (such as doors opening on a common court or homes built around a cul-de-sac) promote neighborliness (Chilman, 1978, 108). A family in a safe territory which desires interaction with the community and which has flexible boundaries may choose to use the openings of a home to invite in the outside world. Neighborhood children may run through unlocked doors, friends may shout at the window or through the screened door, the house may overflow to a porch, steps, or the street below where folding chairs extend the living room to the sidewalk. A less scheduled flexible family can make time for these distractions more easily than a family that runs on a tight clock or has little adaptability. In some cases, visitors may be welcome from dawn through dusk.

Housing Placement • Housing placement influences with whom you interact; therefore, to some extent with whom you develop friendships. Researchers Festinger, Schachter, and Beck (1950) examined the development of friendships in a new housing project for married students. This development consisted of small housing structures arranged in U-shaped courts with the two end houses facing the street. According to Festinger:

> It is a fair summary to say that the two major factors affecting the friendships which developed were (1) sheer distance between houses and (2) the direction in which a house faced. Friendships developed more frequently between next-door neighbors, less frequently between persons who lived in houses that were separated by more than four or five other houses. (156)

The researchers also discovered that those who lived near the stairways, entrances, and exits tended to make more friends in the building as did those who lived near the mailboxes and, therefore, saw more residents regularly. If your front or back door leads into a heavily trafficked area, you have a greater chance of developing neighborhood relationships and becoming a central part of the communication network than if you live off the beaten track. Yet if a family chooses privacy, their home may reflect this. Shrubs, doorbells, peepholes, locks, shades, and signs may discourage casual approach. Architects have offered guidelines for maximizing privacy of the individual and the family in order to encourage concentration, contemplation, and self-reliance. Some suggest achieving this through "careful organization of the plan of the dwelling, placement of windows to avoid surveillance, and the provision of a buffer zone or 'locks' at the entrance to private spaces" (Lennard & Lennard, 1977, 51). A family can create similar buffer zones or boundaries by turning off the phone, establishing rules or hours for visiting, and appearing not to have the time for such interaction. Lack of availability sends a temporal message about the desire for limited interaction.

The Neighborhood • The surrounding territory may partially dictate a family's way of relating to the outside world. A planned community may expect certain social responses from the individual households and those who choose to live another life-style may find themselves ostracized. A particular community may have expectations for coffee klatches in each others' homes or participation in creating the float for the Fourth of July parade—activities that require space and time commitments. As families move from one home to another, the new community will partially influence their interactions.

Certain communities may prevent attempts at socialization or communication because the territory is "unsafe." Scheflen conducted a classic study of 1200 primarily black, Puerto Rican, and Eastern European families living in the East Tremont urban ghetto in upper Manhattan. He reports that within this area:

> A black teenager can often go out for the evening. But the Puerto Rican child may not even be allowed to go out in the apartment let alone the street or to a neighbor's house. The mother may consider any area outside the apartment to be dangerous, and often she is right. (437).

Such living is usually accompanied by many rules about who not to talk to. Yet even if you get to the street in such a territory, you may find that surrounding territories, a gang "turf," or a different ethnic ghetto can limit your movement. Certain territories encourage or permit particular behaviors. For example, a single family home may not encourage romantic behaviors in teenagers due to the presence of other family members but the car or a secluded hallway may provide the environment for such behavior.

I observed a difference in the socialization process in my housing complex and the project building. My peers in the project stayed out much later and had more freedom to go places than those in the housing complex. They began to have sexual intercourse and children at an earlier age. I observed intimate behavior when I visited my friends, while on the elevator, or walking up the stairs. The parents knew what their kids were doing and acknowledged the fact by trying to get them to use some type of birth control. They had boyfriends before my friends and I from the housing complex did and they began kissing early in grammar school.

Each family-of-origin provides such orientations toward developing outside relationships partially depending on the space and time issues within which the family functions. Differences in this type of orientation may cause difficulties for a couple as they establish their spatial/temporal world.

Interior Arrangement

Home interiors are organized spatially and temporally. Once inside the house, the fixed and semi-fixed feature space stands as supports for or as barriers to communication. The interior design influences how much privacy can be attained and how easily members can come together. One way to view a home spatially is to start with the floor plan and determine the possible relationships that may or may not occur based on how space is arranged.

Rooms and Floor Plan • Architect R. W. Kennedy concerns himself with the "livability" of a house and attempts to explain the types of living activities in relation to the public to private zones of a home. Thus the more public zones provide great possibilities for social interaction whereas the more private zones exclude persons from some or all interpersonal contact. Different areas of the home may be associated with specific family functions and hence to the system and subsystem boundaries. Various levels and types of interaction will be acceptable in different spaces, reflected in the range of highly interpersonal to highly private spaces. As you move through a home, the spaces may become more highly private to members and the persons outside the system or subsystem may be excluded from certain spaces. In many homes there are spaces for interpersonal interactions with guests, close friends, and other family members. For example, in one family visitors may have access to the living/dining areas and kitchen areas but may not enter the bedrooms under usual circumstances. In another family there may be a formal living room for socializing or communicating with guests and a family room for relaxing and talking with other members of the family. Some families establish clear spatial boundaries for nonmembers; others do not.

Member boundaries may also vary. If you consider bathing as private, you may go so far as to lock the door when you take a shower. On the other hand, you may come from a family where one person may be showering, the next brushing his teeth, and another urinating in the same small bathroom. Variables such as age, sex, culture, and family size all interact with the spatial dimension.

The actual floor plan can dictate what persons will have the greatest contact and potentially the greatest communication. If you share adjoining territories with your sister, you are more likely to communicate with her than with some other family members. If mother spends large amounts of time in a particular territory (kitchen, study, studio), the people who use that or adjoining territories will have greater access to her. If she spends more time in a central place like the kitchen, she will be more likely to serve as a network hub. If your brother lives in the garage with his souped-up Volkswagen, your communication with him may be limited.

When my mother remarried, she married a widower with eight children which meant that our family suddenly had twelve children, ten of whom lived at home. This led Mom and Grant to remodel the attic where they created bedrooms on the second floor. This really determined the way relationships developed in the family. I didn't see much of the boys who stayed upstairs or who were out playing sports. Because we were on the same floor and always were in and out of each others' rooms, all the girls became really close and some of us would sit up until two in the morning talking about people and things.

Space in some houses may serve to discourage communication among family members. Although in previous generations children shared beds and rooms, many children today have separate rooms equipped for autonomous living. This may lead to a loss of experience in certain types of interpersonal encounters. While one room per child does give everyone privacy and a sense of self, the linkages between them may not occur. If each child has his own room and his own toys or even a television set and stereo, sharing and problem-solving get avoided also. Thus two children don't have to decide together, for example, which television show to watch, rather it's "you watch your show, I'll watch mine." Similarly if a child and parent are at odds, and the child has a nice setup in his own room, he can easily say, "I'm leaving. I'm going to my own room." That room then becomes an escape hatch when personal relationships falter (Kahn in Eshbach, 1976, 3). In certain large homes no one may know if the others are home or what they are doing.

Yet in other cases cramped quarters result in difficulties or pressure. Large families in the East Tremont study lived in small apartments and most of the time everyone functioned in the living room. In the Puerto Rican families all members remained in the living room either bundled together or divided into the TV area or the conversational area. Few secrets or personal conversations occurred within these systems. Black women attempted to keep the living room as a parlor although children usually had to be allowed access to it. If company arrived the children were likely to be sent to play in a bedroom. Conversations were more likely to be separated for "appropriate ears." Often an overlapping of space occurs in these cramped quarters so that space is scheduled according to time of day.

> In one Puerto Rican family breakfast occurred at a fixed time every day. Then father went to work, the children settled down to watch television, and Mother began a highly regular schedule of chores. In the afternoon a single visitor came, sat in a particular chair and talked with the mother. At noon each day the older children were allowed to go out for an hour. (These observations were made in the summer when school was not in session.) Then at a fixed time the mother cooked dinner, and the children ate in the living room. An hour later the father came home from work, sat at a small table in an alcove and had his supper served to him. Then Mother cleaned up, and the family settled down for an evening in the living room before the television set. In this case the same sites were used by the same people each day, according to a regular schedule of household activities.   (Scheflen, 444)

In many homes individuals or subgroups may have to plan for time and space to be alone. Sometimes it may be very structured or sometimes it seems to occur naturally as noted in the following contrasting situations:

Growing up there was rule in our house that no one bothered our parents before 11:00 A.M. on Saturday morning. Their bedroom door was locked and it was understood they were not to be disturbed.

> My parents still manage to have some privacy although I do not know how because their bedroom door has always been open to us day and night and many times it serves as a place to go if you cannot sleep.

In each family rules evolve for locking doors, opening drawers, reading mail, or using another's things. Sometimes status or liking can be understood by watching the access patterns within a household. Parents may have the right to invade privacy, babies may have access to places that are off limits to teenagers or vice-versa, a favorite sibling may be able to borrow clothes, records, money, or use special space. Furniture arrangement may encourage or discourage particular types of interaction. Themes, images, and biosocial beliefs interact with spatial and temporal environments.

For many families mealtime has specific rituals and is a communication event that takes place in a very specified spatial and temporal setting. A study of dinner time in middle-class families with small children revealed that dinner occurred in a dining room, dining area, or kitchen at a dinner table that was almost always rectangular. The formal eating territories were distinct.

> Within families the members sat in the same places at the table every evening. Among families, the only invariable positioning of family members at the dinner table was that the father occupied one side (the head of the table by himself). Mother's position could be either opposite him, or on his right or left. In about half of the families observed, the mother and father sat opposite each other at the table . . . In over two-thirds of our families the mother sat next to the youngest child in the family. (Dreyer & Dreyer, 1973, 294–295)

Yet in a different social/economic setting things are done differently. Scheflen found that the average ghetto kitchen measured 9 by 12 feet and held cabinets, closets, sink, stove, and refrigerator. If a table existed it was small with two or three chairs pushed against the wall. Because there were no dining rooms, whole large families could not physically eat together, resulting in two major adapting patterns. Everyone may have to carry their plates to the living room and eat off their laps or some of the children may be fed from a small children's table in the kitchen. In the middle-class family, mothers may welcome others into their domain, but in cramped quarters a mother usually stakes out the kitchen as her territory and does not welcome "intruders."

Furnishing and Decor • Aside from layout, the furnishings and use of a home influence communication. If you think about some homes you've lived in or visited, you may remember the qualities that made them supportive of interpersonal interaction. There may have been arrangements of chairs or couches in the living room conducive to relaxed conversations. The family room, the kitchen, or a den may have been designed in such a way that you felt comfortable and relaxed enough to really talk. Perhaps you and your best friend were allowed the privacy and time to talk alone for hours in your bedroom. On the other hand, you have probably visited in homes with a cavernous living room that you shouted across, plastic-covered couches which indicated that relaxation was not acceptable, or hard chairs which forced you to limit your stay. Somehow you realized that the environment was working against meaningful communication.

Additionally the quality of communication in a home may be enhanced by the decor that either stimulates conversation or represents an integral part of the family which allows you to understand and relate on appropriate topics. Intriguing pieces of art, collections of rocks, matchbooks, or beer steins, hunting rifles, flower arrangements, or plants may provide the stimulus for good interaction. Certain items may lead you to the "core" of the family.

Music provides the foundation for much of the interaction in our family. My father directs a college jazz band and teaches music while my mother plays the organ in church and plays in the Rockland Orchestra. All three of us play at least two instruments and we sing with varying degrees of ability. Whenever we are together Mom ends up at the piano and the flutes, violins, and clarinet are hauled out while we swap the latest things we've learned and play the "old favorites." Our home is filled with musical decorations—and instruments—which let any outsider know instantly what is important to us.

Religious symbols, such as Bibles, menorahs, crosses, or framed prayers open the door to understanding the persons who live in that home. The Mexican, Norwegian, or Jamaican heritage of a family may be proudly displayed to indicate an identity point for the people who live there. Sports fans, music buffs, and travel fanatics usually let you know who they are through the objects in their homes. Finally, family symbols, grade-school pictures, scrapbooks, third-grade refrigerator art, and assorted Camp Kewanee ashtrays may indicate what is important to the people in that home.

The aesthetic design of a room, lighting, and acoustics play their part in influencing communication. In the often replicated beautiful-ugly room study by Maslow and Mintz, experimenters asked subjects to rate photographs of faces as they sat in a variety of rooms (beautiful, average, ugly) which were alike except for decor. The experimenters and subjects engaged in various escape behaviors to avoid the ugly room. The ugly room was variously described as producing "monotony, fatigue, headaches, discomfort, sleep, irritability, and hostility." In contrast the beautiful room produced feelings of "pleasure, comfort, enjoyment, importance, energy and desire to continue the activity." (Knapp, 1972, 31). This correlates with Mehrabian's finding (1971) that people tend to be more pleasant in pleasant settings rather than in unpleasant settings (75–76). By this we do not mean to imply that you must grow up in beautiful and expensive surroundings in order to have good communication within the family. Pleasant surroundings can enhance relationships if they help people become comfortable and relaxed, but so many other factors intervene that environment cannot be seen as a singular factor. Some researchers will go so far as to say that the quality of relationships are not really affected by the quality of habitat except in extremely adverse conditions but that "high satisfaction with home and community may ameliorate high dissatisfaction with mate or parent-child relationships" (Chilman, 1978, 106).

Family "Fit" and the Environment

Probably one of the more interesting analysis of relationships between people and their home environments may be found in the Lennard and Lennard delineation of the "fit" between the style of family interaction and the home environment: the isomorphic fit, the complementary fit, and the "non"-fit (58).

Isomorphic fit implies congruence between the family and its environment. It occurs when aspects of the environment are clear expressions of the family's identity, of the way the members relate and the way they see the outside world. Let's use the Camerons as an example. The Camerons could be characterized as a generally cohesive and highly adaptable family, with limited intra-family boundaries, who live by themes such as "We work hard and play hard" and "We stick together in the hard times." When the Camerons (mother, father, 4 boys, 1 girl) made a risky move to northern Michigan to open a store, they bought a large old farmhouse and tore out some of the walls on the first floor to create more open space. The Camerons engage in sharing, doing outdoor activities together, and exhibit a rough-and-tumble style of interpersonal interaction. Downstairs there's a large "mudroom" for skis, snowmobile outfits, and assorted sporting equipment. The large family kitchen provides a place where the family can congregate when someone is cooking and a number of people can be involved in some cooking operation at once. The family-living room reflects a rustic decor with a large fireplace (decorated with trophies) and comfortable chairs. It is a place that invites informality and occasional wrestling matches. The house does not have a formal living room. The bedrooms are small but since no one seems to spend time alone it doesn't matter. The Camerons and their home "fit" well together.

A *complementary fit* implies a balance of opposites between aspects of family interaction and home environment. This kind of fit sometimes reflects a pattern of complementarity within the family or it may be consciously selected by a family to balance or counteract a special feature of family life. The Mullers are a blended family with four teenagers (two from each former system) who tried their best to avoid each other as they began life together. At this point in their development, interaction was difficult and the family could be characterized by low cohesion and limited adaptability. Themes at this period reflected the lack of connectedness, e.g., "We are really two families"; "We don't get too involved." In the former family homes each child had a large, well-equipped room to which he or she retreated whenever any discomfort arose. When the homes were sold the parents purposefully invested in an apartment with fewer smaller bedrooms. This forced the two boys to room together and forced all four young people to spend time in common areas such as the attractively furnished family room or the courtyard play area. These parents consciously selected a home-style that was complementary to the life-style that had evolved in their former home.

The *"non"-fit* category applies to those homes which are unsuited to the family's pattern. Quite obviously most lower-income housing falls into this category since many families are trying to "fit" large numbers of people into a few tiny rooms that cannot hold them comfortably. Yet this style need not apply just to those economically unable to afford larger housing. Take the Morris' for example. When the Morris' were married in their early twenties they decided they would not have children. During their early thirties they built their "dream house" in the foothills of the Rockies and created a magnificent wood and glass structure with features such as cathedral ceilings, an open walkway across the top of the living room, a deck that overhangs a gorge, open stairways, and a small kitchen with a breakfast bar for all their eating. At that time their life was characterized by a belief that "We are complete as a couple" and their energies were directed toward cultural and educational pursuits consonant with individual growth. As they approached forty they rethought their decision regarding children, and at age thirty-nine, Sharon Morris brought home a baby girl to the "dream house." During the next years the Morris family and the house entered a non-fit stage. The unrailed walkway across the living room became a dangerous bridge and their daughter could not be left alone on the second floor. She fell off the deck twice and off the stairs numerous times. The lack of a regular dining area became a problem. They are still living there and coping with adjustments but the dream house now has gates, railing, plexiglass panels, and numerous other odd additions.

The concept of "fit" also applies to families and their temporal orientation. Certain life-styles appear more supportive of particular orientations, clocking, or synchronizing behaviors. An isomorphic fit characterizes the family which has set a particular orientation and clocking pattern for itself and can function within the world according to these patterns which reflect the family values. The Breznehan family consists of a father and three children of elementary and high school age. Their world involves, among other things, swimming, baseball, hockey, and soccer along with orthodontist visits, newspaper routes, and jobs at local fast-food stores. Luckily this is a present and future oriented group of people who have a capacity for adapting to tight schedules and fast pacing. Gus Breznehan's schedule is flexible and he can make adjustments relatively easily. Since family priorities include getting ahead and self-improvement, this fast-paced life remains consistent with the group goals.

Grant and Jean Foster could be ads for the two-career up-and-coming couple whose jobs take them to exciting places and whose pace of life never slows down. As an international banker, Jean spends six weeks a year in European cities and Grant does some domestic travel for his computer installation company. They place great priority on their marriage and value a connected interpersonal relationship believing that "together we can cope with whatever life deals us." Yet they were afraid that this hectic work-oriented life-style could destroy their relationship unless they created a retreat for being together. Scorning a high-rise fashionable condominium, they bought a large old farmhouse in a growing suburban area and dedicated themselves to redoing the home in precise historic fashion and to cultivating large flower and vegetable gardens. Except when Jean travels they spend most of their personal time at a slower pace and in a past orientation to consciously counteract the present-oriented hectic pace of their daily lives. To date they have created a complementary style of living with time for their personal hours. Yet they have agreed that if these measures do not ensure enough quality time together each will investigate new job possibilities.

One small baby has thrown the McConnells into a temporary non-fit situation. As a two-career, social couple with good positions they had planned to live a life-style in which each person would take equal responsibility for the baby who they expected to take to many social functions. Five months into parenthood they are totally frustrated trying to share responsibilities because Tim's job requires that he stay late for meetings and Myra's real estate position requires her to drop everything and run when a potential buyer wants to talk, especially on weekends. Although Melissa is a healthy baby, she gets fussy due to colic and seldom sleeps through the night. She cannot be taken easily into adult social situations. Thus each parent needs more ability to live in the present and to live according to the baby's schedule and each needs time to do more around the house.

You can see the need for an integration of the spatial and temporal needs of a family with each other and how some people can integrate these with their levels of cohesion and adaptability for a good fit while others have real difficulty meshing these factors. A past-oriented family may take great pleasure in remodeling a large old home that requires great time and effort. Such people may enjoy investing the effort in order to live in a home that represents another era. Another family who loves to participate in sports may rent an apartment which does not require much maintenance or care, thus freeing the family to engage in their activities.

At other times people have to make some drastic changes in order to alter their temporal and spatial milieu.

My father has been divorced twice and there are six of us kids that he tries to fit into his life. When we visit him in California we end up being squeezed in around his office or court appointments and we really run at a frantic pace. Finally he decided to take off during the time we spend with him in the summer and bring us up to the lake where he has an old fishing cabin. Some of our best times have been spent there since we all slow down and really spend our time relaxing and talking. It's the place where I've gotten to know my half-brothers and where I've re-established my relationship with my father.

Thus we may find "fits" that indicate aspects of our lives are well integrated or we may find ourselves in "fits" which we wish to change.

CONCLUSION

To this point we have demonstrated how the nonhuman family environment creates a context for communication. The environment creates its own communication modality "equal in importance to linguistic, paralinguistic, or kinesic modalities." (Lennard and Lennard, 62). The factors of space, time, territory, and privacy have some effect on who interacts with whom, where, when, for how long, and about what. These may be very functional communication patterns or the mix of environment and intention may result in communication breakdown. These communication patterns may demonstrate a mixed message pattern in which the verbal and nonverbal contradict each other. For example, if space and time are functionally related to behavior, it seems inhumane to ask family members to behave in certain ways within environments that do not support such behaviors. Yet examples of such behavior are easily found: the parent who tells a child to go to the bedroom to study when the room is shared with two other small children and has no space or light for work; the husband who berates his wife for a cluttered kitchen when there's minimal cabinet space; the father who complains bitterly about the time it takes to drive his sons to sports events and only responds to them when they've won trophies. Human messages need to be consistent with the spatial and temporal environment in which they are sent.

A consideration of family ecology leads us to conclude that a relationship exists between family members' communication and the spatial/temporal world in which the family functions. Yet other factors also influence every communication act. A big new home may lessen but will not solve all your family's conflictual problems unless new negotiating behaviors also accompany the move to larger quarters. Slowing down your pace by eliminating activities may have limited effect on your relationships unless the new life-style includes positive interpersonal messages and activities for people to share within the more or less frantic world. Large families in small apartments have the capacity to develop strong nurturing relationships just as a co-parenting situation does not mean that the quality of a mother-daughter relationship needs to be cut in half. Unlimited time together has the potential to enhance a relationship but the quality of the interactions will finally determine the nature of the relationships. Lennard and Lennard explain this issue well as one of control: "To the extent that the interrelationships between a family and its environment are made explicit, the family's area of freedom and control is enlarged" (49–50). Awareness of these factors provides you with the beginnings of the ability to alter or modify the spatial/temporal environment to enhance relationships. The physical and temporal factors can only create an atmosphere conducive to nurturing family communication. After that it's up to the people involved.

13

Improving Family Communication

In my own marriage my wife and I have been using two mechanisms to serve as a kind of check-up on our marital relations. First we have learned to communicate both the negative and the positive feelings we have. Periodically we sit down together with no outside distractions and while maintaining eye contact express our innermost feelings. Another check we use is the presence of a third party (who is a close friend) in a dispute when we are unable to settle it ourselves. This third party has been able to point out to us behavior of which we were unaware.

Up to this point we have presented a primarily descriptive view of issues related to family interaction while stressing the importance of communication in building relationships within the family system. Yet, to what extent do you believe families can change their communication behavior? Can a dysfunctional family develop functional communication patterns? Can new ways to share intimacy develop among family members? To what extent can a family change their ineffective but well-established ways of fighting and making decisions? When you think about yourself, how willing would you be to work, *really* work, on changing some behaviors within your own family systems? Each person must reach his or her own conclusions about how possible it is for people and systems to change.

We believe that since families are human systems they have the potential to grow and change in desired directions, although such growth may require great effort, pain, and risk. We also believe there is no "one right way" for all families to behave—the members of each family have to discover what works well for their system. Because of our own academic communication backgrounds, we view communication as the cornerstone for changing family systems. We hope to see families develop flexible communication patterns which support the growth of the system and its members.

We believe the communication behaviors learned within a family-of-origin will influence greatly a person's future relationships, particularly his or her family and friendship relationships. These communication patterns tend to pass from generation to generation unless they are consciously changed. But, most importantly, we believe firmly that family systems have the ability to change and family members can improve their interaction patterns.

Throughout the book we have focused on healthy or functional families rather than dysfunctional or severely troubled families, recognizing that every healthy or functional family has its low periods as well as its high periods. Yet we must be careful not to dichotomize functional/dysfunctional, or healthy/unhealthy in an either-or manner. We must think of families on a continuum even though in our language we refer to them in ways that sound less flexible. In this chapter we will examine: (1) some of the factors which experts say characterize functional or healthy families, and (2) approaches for developing and maintaining desirable communication within families. These will include personal, educational, and therapeutic approaches.

THE FUNCTIONAL FAMILY

As we noted earlier in this text, equifinality implies no one definition or description of a "normal" family; instead functional families take on various styles with certain similarities. As you have participated in and observed families over the years you have probably found some that looked like they worked well. People in them seemed to "have it all together." Yet each of these functional families probably had differences as well as similarities in the way members related to each other.

General Views

Based on her therapeutic work with dysfunctional families and her enrichment work with functional families, Satir (1972) maintains untroubled and nurturing families demonstrate the following patterns: "self-worth is high; communication is direct, clear, specific, and honest; rules are flexible, human, appropriate, and subject to change; and the linking to society is open and hopeful" (4). In other words, she sees that untroubled families contain people who feel good about themselves, who level with each other, who function within a flexible system of rules, and whose boundaries are flexible enough to permit extensive contact with new people and new ideas. Although we are in agreement with Satir's values we are conscious of Gilbert's curvilinear self-disclosure model (Figure 5-1, p. 95) which suggests totally honest communication can be handled in the unique cases where mutual high self-esteem, risk, commitment, and confirmation exist. These cases may be at the positive end of the functional/dysfunctional continuum.

In his discussion of functional and dysfunctional families, Stachowiak (1975) develops four factors in family effectiveness:

1. Family productivity or efficiency
2. Leadership patterns
3. Expression of conflict
4. Clarity of communication   (70)

Stachowiak values a family's capacity for adaptation noting, "The adaptative families in all our studies reached a significantly greater number of group decisions in the allotted time period than the maladaptive families" (70). Members of adaptative families "tended to emit many short speeches over a given period of time, while members of maladaptive families tended to emit fewer but longer speeches over the same period of time . . ." (70). Within the functional families members employed resources in decision making by balancing task efforts with attention to the social and emotional needs of the family members.

Every member of my family can read body language and we are all capable of determining when a mixed message has been sent and they are usually commented upon. Lines like "now tell me what you really mean" are used whenever the situation calls for it. If you don't want to talk about it, you can say so and unless you are in tears, it is accepted. We were taught to level with each other and there isn't much game-playing. People usually say how they feel and it's usually accepted.

As you might assume from our discussion of decision making, in the adaptive family different members take on the leadership role at various times as opposed to the behavior in dysfunctional families which display an absence of clear leadership. Painful conflict patterns characterized maladaptive families ". . . two or more members of the family are continually at each other's throats and unable to come to any kind of resolution" (72), whereas functional families tend to have the resources to deal with issues and resolve them. Finally Stachowiak finds maladaptive families are more likely to perform behavior that avoids direct communication (turning away, avoiding eye contact, etc.) and maladaptive families had more "general speeches" (conversation not directed at any family member) than did adaptive ones. Thus the patterns described by Satir appear reinforced by this work that indicates functional families are more likely to be characterized by clarity of communication as well as flexibility.

Yet there are other ways of characterizing the functional family. In his comprehensive review of concepts of healthy family functioning, Barnhill (1979) isolates eight dimensions of family mental health that can be grouped according to four major areas. You will see some direct similarities between his conclusions and those of Satir and Stachowiak. According to Barnhill, the eight dimensions of healthy family functioning can be seen to be grouped into the basic family themes.

I. Identity Processes
   1. Individuation vs. isolation
   2. Mutuality vs. isolation
II. Change
   3. Flexibility vs. rigidity
   4. Stability vs. disorganization
III. Information Processing
   5. Clear vs. unclear or distorted perception
   6. Clear vs. unclear or distorted communication
IV. Role Structuring
   7. Role reciprocity vs. unclear roles or role conflict
   8. Clear vs. diffuse or breached generational boundaries (96)

Barnhill stresses the importance of gaining a sense of self through individuation and mutuality. For him, *individuation* refers to ". . . independence of thought, feeling, and judgment of individual family members" which involves ". . . a firm sense of autonomy, personal responsibility, identity and boundaries of the self" (95). In a family where members have a sense of their own competence and believe they can make their own decisions, people are more likely to allow others the freedom to be themselves. Self-worth tends to be high when family members feel they can express their individuality within the system.

Mutuality involves a sense of intimacy or emotional closeness that occurs between two individuals with clearly defined identities. If members become enmeshed, they cannot be separate enough to experience being close because the fusion is too powerful. Likewise if two people are isolated from each other, they will remain disengaged. A daughter drawn into a parent-child conflict to the extent that she feels the conflict as if she were her mother experiences extreme enmeshment. A child totally isolated from her parent's interactions may experience a sense of great disengagement. Think about the difficulties you've seen in families where everyone is expected to be part of everyone else's business; it's hard to grow up in such a system. Likewise in families where members are ignored or abandoned, healthy individual growth remains painful. Thus these criteria relate to a family's capacity for adaptation.

Healthy family members can accept and deal with the inevitability of change yet maintain certain consistencies which provide security and responsibility. Barnhill suggests ". . . both flexibility and stability are necessary in preference to rigid responses which deny the need for (or reality of) change, or disorganized responses to an unstable situation which prevent a clear view of real change" (95).

My grandmother has always sworn that my sister looked just like her daughter, Lorraine, who died at 16. She has tried to replace her daughter with her first granddaughter in the hopes of reviving a communication pattern that once existed but now is gone. Yet my sister Lori has had to fight this distorted perception all her life and her communication with Grandma is very confused.

As a shared phenomenon clear perception refers to "clear joint perceptions and consensual validation of shared events [e.g., conflict, affection]" (Barnhill, 95). Both persons in an interpersonal system have relatively undistorted perceptions of themselves and each other which lead to accurate or clear information.

Such communication may be reflected in members' ability to check out their perceptions and to metacommunicate or talk about their communication. Such clear perceptions and communication permit conflict and intimacy to be dealt with openly and honestly.

Finally, according to Barnhill, role structuring involves: (1) role reciprocity or ". . . mutually agreed upon behavior pattern . . . in which an individual complements the role of a role partner and (2) clear generational boundaries, for appropriate role behavior across generations recognizing appropriate boundaries of marital, parent-child and sibling relationship." People in healthy families tend to make conscious or unconscious agreements about their role relationships. Those in complementary roles appear comfortable with those role definitions that emerge through interactions. Additionally, appropriate generational boundaries are respected. Children are not co-opted into parent roles; in-laws do not become enmeshed with the marital couple. Clarity of generational boundaries contributes to appropriate role development.

When you look at Barnhill's dimensions, you can see that each of these eight factors are interrelated. For example, clear communication facilitates role reciprocity; individuation facilitates clear generational boundaries. According to Barnhill, Satir, and Stachowiak's conceptualization, communication remains a central factor in healthy family functioning. These therapist-scholars stress the need for clear, flexible, and open communication among family members.

In his systemic research on family competence Beavers (1976) views families on a continuum of functioning ranging from severely disturbed, to midrange, to healthy. He details each of these continuum locations in terms of five major areas: power structure, degree of individuation, acceptance of separation and loss, perception of reality, and affect. His data suggest that families with adaptive, well-functioning offspring have ". . . a structure of shared power, a great appreciation and encouragement of individuation, and an ability to accept separation and loss realistically." Additionally he suggests they have a ". . . family mythology consistent with the reality as seen by outside observers, a strong sense of the passage of time and the inevitability of change, and a warm and expressive feeling tone" (80). Beavers describes healthy families as "skillful interpersonally" and with members capable of desirable communication behaviors including: participating in and enjoying negotiation; respecting views of others; sharing openly about themselves; seeing anger as symptomatic of necessary changes; viewing sexual interest as positive; establishing meaningful encounters outside the family system.

We will summarize this academic look at healthy families with a conclusion drawn by Gantman (1980) from the research related to families that "work well." She contends the well-functioning family:

> demonstrates high levels of efficiency in behavior and decision making. Healthy family members are supportive, expressive, and communicate in noisy, discontinuous speech patterns. The power structure of the family

is well defined with father as the most frequent leader. The generational boundaries are clear. Members demonstrate respect for each other's uniqueness. There is an adaptive mechanism to cope with disequilibrium without requiring a rigid hierarchy or return to a status quo.   (118)

Before leaving this area we would like to share with you the perceptions of a different type of family analyst. In her book, *Families,* journalist Howard (1978) presents another conception of functioning families. The author traveled across the country interviewing the members of various types of family systems (natural, blended, single-parent, and extended, including social, racial, and sexual variations) in an attempt to understand what makes them work well. In her conclusion she lists the general characteristics for what she calls "good" families (241–245). We will note her characteristics briefly here.

1. Good families have a chief, or a heroine, or a founder—someone around whom others cluster. Such a person may appear in different generations but somehow this figure or figures sets an achievement level that inspires others.

I grew up in an extended family and my great-grandparents were the dominant figures. Although there was no one living in the base household while I was growing up many of the family members had lived with the dominant figures at one time or another. My great-grandmother, referred to as Mother, babysat all nine of the kids while our parents were at work. Everyone in the family loved and respected her and we would sit for hours listening to how she and/or great-grandfather started their lives together with nothing in a strange city. She has always been someone I looked up to.

---

2. Good families have a switchboard operator—someone who keeps track of what the others are up to. This person also may be the archivist who keeps scrapbooks or albums that document the family's continuity. As we discussed in the section on networks, certain families form into a wheel configuration in which one person serves as the switchboard for information, keeping members abreast of familial events.

3. Good families are much to all of their members but everything to none. Links to the outside are strong and boundaries are not so tight that people cannot become passionately involved in nonfamily activities. Howard suggests that healthy families encourage exploration, "curiosity and passion are contagious" and everyone is busy.

4. Good families are hospitable—there are surrounding rings of relatives and friends who are cared about and supported just as they serve as the family's support system and as extended family members in many cases.

5. Good families deal directly with problems. Problems and pains are faced and not avoided in hopes they will disappear. Communication is open. As Satir and Stachowiak maintain, honest, clear communication undergirds healthy family life. Countless rules do not exist to restrict touchy or painful topics of conversations; people level with each other directly.

6. Good families prize their rituals—these may be the formal traditions of Passover, Christmas, birthdays, funerals, or the informal ones unique to the individual family or clan—the annual Fourth of July picnic or St. Patrick's Day party that becomes a unifying ritual to the people involved.

7. Good families are affectionate, and are willing to demonstrate and share that affection with other family members. The intimate currencies of touch and affect displays demonstrate the depth of affection members have for each other. Children learn this pattern of affection from their first moments if they are in a well-functioning family system.

8. Good families have a sense of place—a sense of belonging that may be tied to a specific geographic location or to the mementos that make a house a home for specific individuals—the old dining room table, the Hummel figures, the photographs that declare "this is home." You may find comfort in being a Bostonian or Iowan or you may carry important pieces of your life with you which symbolize roots and family connectedness.

9. Good families find some way to connect to posterity. For many this involves having children, for others it involves becoming involved in a sense of the generation—connecting to the children in some way.

My husband and I decided that we did not want to have any children of our own, but we realized that we would miss out on a very important area of life through the decision. So we decided to consciously put children in our lives in other capacities. Although our sisters are many states away, we have become "aunt" and "uncle" to some of our friends' children and enjoy the pleasures of spending a good amount of time with them and participate in the usual childhood rituals— birthday parties, confirmation, etc. These children have become a very important part of our lives.

---

10. Good families honor their elders. The wider the age range, the stronger the clan. This may involve biological or "adopted" grandparents and vice versa, but strong families have a sense of generations. Older people are sought out to participate in family life. This may be demonstrated by a recent event in which a 78-year-old Florida man ran a classified ad reading "Grandfather up for adoption." A woman with two children agreed to "adopt" him by taking him into the family. Many mobile nuclear families have attempted to gain contact with the older people through intergenerational church or community groups which encourage the building of three and four generational communities of caring people.

Author Views

Each of you has some strong feelings about what makes a healthy family. You may find yourselves arguing with the "experts." Although we are comfortable with much of what the previously mentioned authors report we would like to close this section by presenting some of our beliefs about the healthy family based on our concern for communication within such systems. In order to do this we return to the issues introduced in the early chapters. We can share our belief that a healthy family recognizes the interdependence of all members of the system and attempts to provide for growth of the system as a whole, and the individual members involved.

Such families develop a capacity for adaptation and cohesion that avoid the extremes of the continuum but which change over time reflecting the course of external and developmental life events. From our perspective the functional families are likely to be found toward the central area of the cohesion/adaptability axis most of the time, while dysfunctional families would be found consistently on the extremes. Members of functional families are joined to the system, yet able to differentiate from their families; changes are incorporated into the system's life. These basically flexible and cohesive families have themes, images, boundaries, and biosocial beliefs consistent with their position on the axis. Such families also work to uncover and understand their themes, images, boundaries, and biosocial beliefs (although they may not use those terms for such characteristics) so as to consciously accept or modify them. Such families value open, clear, and caring communication, understand that they can change their system's communication patterns, and consciously strive to improve their communication so as to promote acceptable levels of intimacy and to modify unhealthy conflict. Such families are willing to take risks in order to grow.

From these descriptions it becomes clear that healthy or functional families may be characterized in a variety of ways, yet it appears that most healthy families' systems give evidence of using clear, honest, open, and flexible communication that permits intimacy and individuation among the family members. For many systems the real question remains "How can we improve communication within our family?" In the following section we will examine approaches for doing just that.

APPROACHES FOR IMPROVING FAMILY COMMUNICATION

My husband and I are team leaders for the Jewish Marriage Encounter and we keep trying to tell our friends that every marriage should have an "annual check-up." People spend millions of dollars on "preventative maintenance" for their cars, their teeth, bodies, homes, etc., but how much do we spend either in dollars, effort, or time to have a marital examination? Too often in attempting to get couples to attend an Encounter weekend I am told "Our marriage is OK" or "We don't need to go on any weekend as we have no problems." I am both angry and sad at such blindness, stupidity, and fear. There is not a marriage existing that does not have some problems and if they are not attended to, they will get bigger.

If you believed that communication in your family could be improved, what would you do about it? Or, if this has already occurred, what did you do? Would you be willing to talk about the difficulties with other family members? Or to participate in a structured improvement program? As we saw in the last chapters a family goes through developmental predictable stresses and external, unpredictable stresses which affect the system's well-being but often members don't know how to help themselves and the system deal with the difficulties.

Concern for family issues appears widespread in all areas of society, resulting in the growth of preventive approaches designed to aid family members before things really fall apart. A walk through a local bookstore will reveal countless books and magazine articles on improving your marital or family life. There are checklists, rules, and prescriptions for family meetings, intimate vacations, and constructive conflict. Most of these prescriptions contain some directives about improving communication between or among family members. Many appear as a panacea or a pill which, once taken, will miraculously transform the withering relationship into a happy, healthy, and functional one. Seen in this light they are doomed to fail. Yet countless numbers of Americans have found relational growth and change through certain marital or family enrichment approaches which are carefully designed and which involve motivation and effort on the parts of the participants.

During the course of your lifetime you may have participated in family meetings, or a marriage enrichment program, or some family therapy sessions. These activities represent the varieties of approaches available to family members who wish to improve communication within the system. We will now examine a continuum of approaches ranging from the more personal to the instructional, and finally, to the therapeutic for families experiencing dysfunctional communication. Most of the individual and instructional approaches are designed for functional couples or families who wish to enrich their relationships.

Personal Approaches

When my own marriage was falling apart I found the most necessary ingredients in turning things around were desire and work—on both our parts. I clearly remember the night I made two decisions. First, I really wanted to keep our marriage, and second, I was willing to do anything to make it work. My wife had seen more value in the marriage all along so when I shared these feelings with her we both committed ourselves to creating a new relationship. The intense part of this struggle took over two years and without this deep desire and belief that we could make it, I never would have been able to continue working over such a long period that was such a painful part of my life.

Do you believe that a couple or family can deal with their communication problems on their own? Have you ever actively participated in such an endeavor?

How did it work for you? Many individuals have consciously set out to change communication with one or more other family members. Many couples or whole family systems have tried consciously to change old dysfunctional communication patterns. Many of these endeavors reflect a personal approach, or one in which system members embark on the process without significant active outside support.

In some homes husbands and wives attempt to identify recurring potentially upsetting "trouble spots" in their relationship and to plan how to avoid them. Although they may never have heard of Feldman's intimacy-conflict cycle (p. 104) they may come to recognize points in their lives when one or the other finds the intimacy or the conflict too threatening and causes shifts in everyday behavior. If they can both understand what happens they may be able to prevent it from occurring as frequently in the future.

Other couples practice their own rules for fair fighting, constructed perhaps through their agreement never to hurt each other so badly again. They may agree to avoid gunnysacking and physical abuse. They may try to refrain from using labels or loaded words. They may struggle to restate the other's position or to find areas of compromise. They may be willing to return to an issue later when some of the emotion has worn off. Parents may force themselves to develop new vocabulary when dealing with children, reflected in the use of "I-" statements rather than the blaming "you" messages, or to share feelings when objective analysis would be more comfortable.

Whole families may agree to try out new decision-making styles, permitting negotiation when previously authority always ruled. Siblings may attempt to discuss space needs to allow each other desired privacy.

Families may consciously attempt to uncover their themes or images in order to recharge or redirect their energies. They may fight out some of the longheld biosocial beliefs in order to develop ones representative of the current members. They may attempt to re-evaluate their boundaries, determining how open they should or could be to new people or ideas.

In-laws may restrain themselves from asking questions that could be considered meddling while children may refrain from "answering back" even though the temptation remains very great. Family members may seek quality time together to eat, sing, ride bikes, or just talk. Couples may attempt a second honeymoon. Father and son may find a mutual hobby, or have a discussion area of joint interest. Although the behaviors vary from family to family, the underlying purpose remains the same—to enhance the relationships. Such attempts involve desire and work if they are to be successful.

You may wonder "How do these things start?" "How do they know what to do?" In some systems one or more members have a nagging feeling or a definite belief that things could be different. They may compare themselves to other families and see something they are lacking. They may encounter new ideas or models for relationships through the media, friends, religious, or educational figures. They may perceive that what is good could get even better. Then they must take the risk to try out new behaviors and evaluate the effectiveness of these approaches. In the next few pages we will note in more detail some examples of personal approaches undertaken by couples or families.

Couple Approaches • "The checkup" stands as an important concept in relational enrichment. In their well-known work *Mirages of Marriage,* Lederer and Jackson (1968) call for marital checkups, saying, "It seems to us that marriages deserve the same care and attention given our bodies, or our automobiles. Marital checkups, we believe, can be useful. First, a checkup enables the husband and wife to identify and appraise marital liabilities . . . and methods of stabilizing or increasing the assets can then be determined" (358–359). Such preventive work can keep couples from destructive relationship patterns and keep spouses in close communication with each other. The authors suggest that checkups can be done by individual appraisal (least desirable), joint evaluation, or through work with a caring third party (nonprofessional). Checkups may also be accomplished with a counselor. The checkup concept has received extensive press from many authors, lecturers, and scholars so countless variations or prescriptions exist. The following questions represent one approach. In his article "Put Marriage on Your Checkup List" Smith (1980) asks couples to review their marriage once a year to "uncover cracks before they become chasms" using questions such as the following:

1. Do you usually settle disagreements with mutual satisfaction and no bitterness?
2. In your relationship is there any game-playing with money, sex, employment, etc.?
3. Is your physical expression of sex mutually satisfying?
4. Do you feel wanted, loved, and appreciated? Even more important, does your mate feel wanted, loved, and appreciated? (1-3)

Lederer and Jackson provide us with another major concept that may be used in conjunction with the checkup—the *quid pro quo.* "*Quid pro quo* literally means 'something for something.' In the marriage process, it means that if you do so-and-so, then I automatically will respond with such-and-such" (178). It implies reciprocal behavior, shared or exchanged behavior which may be unconscious. *Quid pro quo* recognizes the efforts of both partners to be peers and provides a technique enabling both parties to communicate and maintain their self-esteem. Most couples have an unspoken *quid pro quo* which becomes a set of ground rules but which, when broken, result in marital conflict. Lederer and Jackson propose a self-help program which encourages people to recognize their *quid pro quo* and to consciously bargain with each other for individual needs. Hopefully spouses reach a level of negotiation whereby "each has those things which are most important to him and at the same time tries to nourish the well-being of the other to the maximum extent" (286). In short, rewards are gained by both.

The *quid pro quo* approach suggests couples set aside weekly sessions of an hour each devoted solely to the specific bargaining process. The authors provide an outline for the first six sessions. These sessions are designed to help each spouse really hear what the other is saying. Spouses learn to listen, to take directions, to develop effective questioning skills, and finally, to bargain constructively with each other. Eventually a couple reaches the point of exchanging "viewpoints about what each feels is necessary to determine the extent to which these aims are compatible, and to decide what can be done about them" (301).

Such approaches as the "checkup" and the *quid pro quo* represent only two of countless methods for working on a marriage. Books such as *Mirages of Marriage* and *Alive and Aware* provide hundreds of experiential communication approaches for couples to use as they attempt to improve their relationships. Some couples will set aside one time each week or each month to "check in" on how they are doing. They may stay home, or go out for coffee, or meet for lunch—but the topic discussed remains their relationship. Other couples will form or join informal growth groups focused on marital or family issues.

We have belonged to a couples group within our church for four years now and have found it has brought us closer to each other. The group of five couples functions as a support system for the individuals and people are free to bring up their problems in parenting, or in relating to spouses, or to our own parents. By listening to other people's problems and hearing how they dealt with situations we are learning to relate to each other more effectively.

Family Approaches • Just as couple-oriented approaches exist, approaches exit for whole families, the most common of which is the family meeting or family council. Growing up, you may have participated in some variation of this approach. A family council may be defined as "a meeting together, as a group, to attempt to solve democratically problems which affect one or more members, or which affect the group as a whole" (Weaver & Mayhew, 1959, 72–73).

In their early study of the family councils, Weaver and Mayhew found that most families did not meet regularly; half held meetings at the request of the children and half indicated they required attendance. Ninety percent of the parents indicated that they "sometimes" followed through on the decisions made in council; only 8 percent said they always did. Although almost all of them used democratic procedures and two-thirds of them attempted to teach democratic procedures by direct instruction, only a few were willing to be bound by the decision made in the council (73). The families studied reported the council most useful for issues of household duties, allowances, purchases, and vacations. Although many family meetings are rather informal affairs, there have been attempts to establish much more structured family gatherings.

Rudolf Dreikurs (1964) has long been known for his work in family councils—meetings of all members of the family in which problems are discussed and sought. He recommends the councils be established formally as an ongoing part of the family's life. A definite hour on a definite day of the week should be set aside for this purpose; it should become part of family routine. Every member is expected to be present. According to Dreikurs, should one member not wish to come, that person must still abide by the decision of the group. Therefore, it pays for him or her to be present to voice an opinion. The principles of such Family Councils include:

Each member has the right to bring up a problem. Each one has the right to be heard. Together, all seek for a solution to the problem, and the majority opinion is upheld. In the Family Council, the parents' voices are no higher or stronger than that of each child. The decision made at a given meeting holds for a week. After the meeting, the course of action decided upon takes place and *no further discussion* is permitted until the following meeting. If at that time it is discovered that the solution of last week did not work out so well, a new solution is sought, always with the question "What are we going to do about it?" And again, it's up to the whole group to decide!   (301–302)

Such experiences provide children with practice in discussion and decision making which may prove extremely valuable in later family life. Obviously many families attempt to join together for more than solving problems. Members of the insurance industry published a book entitled *Family Time* (Nutt, 1976) which incorporates numerous exercises, games, and suggestions for spending quality time together. The author states "bluntly . . . this book was written solely to help your family talk with and to each other constructively, wisely, compassionately, well and *often . . . even regularly"* (17). The intent was for countless families to take time, usually one or two hours one night a week, to be together and to communicate.

Probably the Mormon's Family Home Evening program is the most well known family night program. Established in the late 1950s, the program requests Mormons to set aside Monday evening for family group meetings or activities. An annual guidebook, *Family Home Evening,* presents a series of lessons that incorporate training in religion with how to practice Christianity in the family. To vary the instruction, the family is encouraged to take one evening a month for recreation (bowling, sports event, picnic, etc.) instead of the lesson. One evening in the program might resemble the following:

The father takes charge of the meeting in what the Mormons call his priesthood role—a role that makes him responsible for instruction in the faith and leadership of the family. All sessions open with a prayer, followed by a hymn, and then discussion of the lesson . . . the instruction ends with members sharing ideas on how they can apply the lesson to their daily life in the family. The meeting concludes with another prayer. Refreshments follow . . .   (Brommel, 1978, 6–7)

Instruction obviously varies greatly from family to family. Some fathers could lecture the content while others share the leadership and participate in the discussion. The guidebook includes questions to ask that will require family members to answer. Special games or approaches are included to meet the comprehension levels of younger children. Adaptations are made for couples, single-parent families, etc.

Although the emphasis is on religious instruction, the guidebook contains materials appropriate for improving interpersonal communication. "Discussion on such topics as 'learning to love each other' or 'organizing yourself' require self-disclosure, risk-taking, sharing. Listening skills are frequently taught and stressed. Each year several of the lessons could be classified or used as communication modules" (8). In an analysis of 44 lessons used in one recent year Brommel found that "sixteen contained either a total focus upon some aspect of communication or over half the content was appropriate and applicable to communication. Entire lessons . . . focused totally upon the importance of families understanding and using effective verbal and nonverbal communication skills" (8). Recently other churches have developed similar programs, such as The Christian Life Home Curriculum of the Christian Church (Disciples of Christ) and the Family Life Program of the Christian Family Movement (Roman Catholic). Countless variations of family evenings are being developed by religious and community groups.

One such approach is known as the Family Cluster, best described as a "group of four or five complete family units which contract to meet together periodically over an extended period of time for shared educational experiences related to being in relationship with their families" (Sawin, 1979, 27). Through Family Cluster families gain mutual support and help in developing skills that enhance family relationships. A Family Cluster may consist of nuclear families, single-parent families, childless couples, single persons, or one or more persons who live together. The designer suggests "when starting a new family cluster, it is usually helpful to begin with a unit of communication . . . communication is a vital force for group building, as well as a crucial element in the family system" (47).

As a single person I have found it very rewarding to belong to a Family Cluster because it provides me with a support system of caring people and it allows me to be of service to some of them in return. I truly enjoy interacting with the children in our Cluster and I'm known as the "game lady" because I usually spend part of my time playing games with the children. I enjoy interacting with young people and their parents are pleased.

The previously discussed approaches represent only a few of the many ways of involving individuals, families, and groups of families in enriching their relationships. Where do you see yourself in relationship to such approaches? Would you be willing to make the effort required to participate fully in a *quid pro quo* bargaining session or in a structured Family Council meeting?

In addition to personal approaches, couples or individuals may attempt to improve family communication through direct instruction.

Instructional Approaches

Both my wife and I had been previously married before we met each other. We were scared that if we got married some of the old patterns would repeat themselves for both of us. Therefore before we got married we attended a Couple Communication program in our town.

Although we had relatively good communication, this program made it easier for us to be honest and for us to hear what the other person was really saying. We took it seriously and did the exercises at home. I believe it really helped us in our first year of marriage when things would get tense.

If a member of your family suggested that you all go on a communication enrichment weekend, how would you react? Would you be willing to attend some sessions on improving parent-child communication with your children or your parents? The past two decades witnessed a tremendous growth in educational, marital, and family enrichment programs designed for individuals and for whole family systems to attend. Their purposes are educational, not therapeutic; they are oriented toward enrichment, not counseling. Koch and Koch (1976) report that couples who attend such marriage enrichment programs are self-referred and self-screened, "only those who perceive their relationships to be 'good' are asked to attend" (33). Most potential applicants receive the message "If your marriage or family life is in trouble, our program is not for you. We are designed to help good relationships become better." Couples contemplating divorce, families experiencing chaos, are referred to therapeutic means of dealing with their problems.

Marital Programs • Although most enrichment/educational programs require or desire the system (couple or family) to attend, some programs will permit individuals to attend with the understanding that an individual can influence what happens within a system. A father's growth in interpersonal awareness and skill may affect the other system members' positively; a sensitive older sibling may develop a strong and supportive relationship with a "lost" nine-year-old within a dysfunctional household. Yet such changes remain more difficult to affect than those changes which involve all members of the system.

Currently most individuals, and private or religious organizations involved in relationship enhancement, strive to work with the whole system of people on the assumption that this is a more effective way of changing the system. For example, if couples can be taught effective interpersonal behavior, they will be most likely to provide a family-of-origin in which children will learn similar communication behavior. If whole families can be instructed in effective communication, the odds are that the system will reflect this influence.

Communication skills appear as the core of most of these marital enrichment programs. According to Wackman (1978), the communication emphasis may be attributed to three factors. First, research on marriage found a consistent, though modest, relationship between "good" communication by members of a married couple and marital satisfaction and happiness, while research with "healthy" families indicates the same moderately positive correlation between "good" communication and satisfaction of family members. Second, theoretical developments in thinking about the family system focused on the crucial role of communication in both marriage and the family. Third, communication training seemed to be an easy, safe, and nonthreatening way to bring about enrichment since communication skills and principles can be taught fairly readily (3-4).

Although there are numerous systems-oriented marital and family enrichment programs which stress communication, we will examine only a few representative ones. The most well-known and frequently attended marital enrichment programs include the religious-based Marriage Enrichment, Marriage Encounter, and Marriage Communication Lab programs and the privately developed Couples Communication Program (Otto, 1975; Koch and Koch, 1976). Each places a heavy emphasis on communication. We will briefly describe how each program functions with the understanding that there may be some variations depending on sponsoring groups and specific leaders.

The Marriage Enrichment Program, sponsored by the Methodist Church, is a weekend small group experience conducted by a leader or a leader-couple who work with four couples through a structured weekend. After having been prepared by leader-modeling, reflecting, and role-playing, each couple engages in a series of interactions within the small group framework. Couples prepare for this through guided rehearsal sessions with nonspouses. Group members also give feedback to each couple. Some of the weekend experiences include: sharing the qualities one admires in his or her spouse, sharing the behaviors that make one feel loved when performed by the spouse, discussing wished-for behaviors from the spouse. Thus intimacy receives great focus. The actual sharing and discussion behavior is constantly monitored and corrected by the team leader who is trying to teach communication skills. The small group functions as a powerful support system for trying new behaviors.

Marriage Encounter is a weekend program conducted by three couples plus a religious leader. The format follows a simple pattern. Each husband and wife "gives" each other the Encounter with the team members merely providing the information and modeling to facilitate each couple's private dialogue. Through a series of nine talks, team members reveal personal and intimate information to encourage participants to do the same when alone. After the talks, each husband and wife separate and write individual responses to the issues raised in each talk. Specific questions to be considered may be provided or the individual may write his or her feelings about the topic. The couple then comes together privately to dialogue using each other's written responses as a departure point. The process of Marriage Encounter involves exposition, reflection, encounter, and mutual understanding. Dialogue topics include understanding of self, relationship to partner, the couple's relationship with God, their children, and the world. Although the program began within the Catholic Church, the past years have witnessed the growth of Jewish and Protestant Marriage Encounters.

The Marriage Communication Lab of the United Methodist Church consists of a couple-led small group weekend experience. The lab experience includes sessions on group building and sharing expectations, communication skills, conflict management, sexuality, trust and values, roles, expectations, and goal setting. Couples perform most of the work within the small group framework using a learning pattern of "do/reflect/draw conclusions" (Hopkins and Hopkins, 1976, 229). Time may be taken during the weekend to allow a couple to work through a real issue, one they are dealing with in front of the other couples, in order to receive feedback.

The Couples Communication program involves a small group experience for five to seven couples meeting one night a week for four consecutive weeks with an instructor. The "couples" may be spouses, friends, or work teams. This program serves as an educational experience in which couples identify, practice, and experiment with communication skills around topics of their choice. Each couple receives feedback on their skills from the leader and other couples. No attempt is made to deal with the content of an interaction: the focus remains solely on skills accomplishment. Practice sessions are held with non-partners but the final demonstration of skills occurs with one's partner.

As you read these four descriptions of marital enrichment programs, it becomes clear that communication assumes a major place within each program. Desirable interpersonal behavior may be taught differently through modeling, role playing, lecture, guided feedback, and readings, but it is incorporated and taught within each program. The unique feature of such programs remains the learning context—you learn and practice communication skills with people with whom you have a relationship. In her summary of the communication instruction contained within these four marital enrichment programs, Galvin concludes:

> All programs give attention to the five skills of empathic communication, recognizing and owning feelings, descriptiveness, self-disclosure, and behavioral flexibility, with descriptiveness receiving the least attention except in Marriage Enrichment. The skills of self-disclosure and recognizing and owning feelings command extensive attention as each program devotes a large proportion of its time to the area of feelings. Marriage Enrichment provides the most predictable structure and uses the most direct approach to teach these skills. Marriage Encounter relies heavily on modeling and direction to teach communication skills.   (26–27)

These programs represent some of the more established approaches. Countless others exist. For example, in his IDEALS program (Institute for the Development of Emotional Life Skills), Bernard Guerney combines behavior modification with techniques from Carl Rogers' client-centered therapy attempt to teach empathy to married couples. IDEALS sets forth rules of talking and listening—knowing when to talk and when to listen. Groups of three or four couples work for six months with a trained leader, learning and practicing these rules until they become automatic. Many other churches and private organizations run their own unique marital communication programs for their own congregations or constituents.

Appraisal of Enrichment Programs • Although these programs may sound very exciting, we need to note some cautions in considering their effectiveness. There may be difficulties in attempting to teach communication principles and skills without a true conjoint contact, or shared desire, on the part of both system members. If such mutual commitment does not exist, the results may be contrary to the expected outcomes. Additionally, the skills must be combined with a desire or spirit of goodwill to motivate system members to use them appropriately (Miller, Corrales, Wackman, 1975, 150).

Additionally the research on these programs does not attribute undisputed success to their efforts. Gurman and Kniskern (1977) summarized 29 studies which purported to examine the impact of marriage enrichment programs. Although positive results were found in a majority of the measures, most studies used self-report measures and administered the questionnaires or interviews immediately after the program. Thus, few real changes in behavior or long-range effects could be documented.

In their admittedly critical appraisal of the Marriage Encounter, Doherty, McCabe, and Ryder (1978) suggest the program could: create illusions through emotional "highs," deny the importance of differences between people, lead to a kind of ritual dependency and guilt if the couple does not engage in the follow-up, plus other possible difficulties. Yet these authors point out the strengths of such a program. Additional critiques of programs note their positive and negative effects (L'Abate, 1981; De Young, 1979; Wampler & Sprenkle, 1979).

Wackman raises three questions about the larger impact of such programs:

1. Do the programs result in changes in communication which last for a reasonable period of time? And if so, do the changes in communication skills result in positive changes in the relationships so that marriages are truly enriched?
2. Do the marriage programs result in changes which generalize to other relationships, particularly relationships with children, thereby enriching family life?
3. What are the major factors in these programs which create the impacts that occur—specific skills taught? format (group vs. individual couple)? degree of structure? pacing of the program (weekend or weekly meetings)? leader characteristics and behavior? or a complex combination of factors?   (6–7)

Family Enrichment Programs • Although programs for families have developed more slowly, many marital programs are creating familial counterparts encouraging entire families to examine and improve their relationships. The Marriage Encounter Program now offers the Family Weekend Experience. As in Marriage Encounter, the family members "give" each other the weekend. Parents and their children of school age spend their waking weekend hours in a local facility engaging in activities, listening to short talks, seeing films, and holding family discussions. Families are encouraged to examine their everyday lives, to discuss nine "blocks" to a family relationship such as fighting, criticism, or indifference and the means to overcoming such blocks, including listening, acceptance, and respect. Family members experience personal reconciliation with each other and plan ways to maintain the feelings of closeness they have achieved. The Marriage Enrichment weekend has spawned a family-oriented weekend and Guerney and his colleagues have developed filial programs for skill training in interpersonal competency between children and parents and adolescents and parents. The founders of the Couple Communication program recently developed a family-oriented program. Numerous other groups have developed educational types of family growth groups focusing on communication (Sawin, 61–68).

One of the most widely accepted family-oriented programs has been PET, Parent Effectiveness Training, through which couples, without their children, attempt to learn more effective parenting skills relying heavily on communication strategies. Designed by psychologist Thomas Gordon, this program requires parents in PET groups to follow a carefully prescribed eight-week, three-hours-per-session, series of lessons. In these 24 hours of instruction parents learn specific ways to handle a variety of family problems. For homework, parents fill out exercises in the PET *Workbook* and read assigned chapters in Gordon's (1975) book, *Parent Effectiveness Training.* This program encourages parents to examine their own self-concepts, to re-evaluate their verbal and nonverbal messages, and to find new approaches to deal with old problems, primarily through communication.

Using lectures, questions and answers, small group discussion, and role-playing, PET stresses effective communication. Listening skills receive the greatest attention within the course. Two of the eight lessons deal totally with developing listening skills and all others incorporate ideas based upon an understanding of what Gordon calls the "active listening method." This method requires learning how to accept whatever the child shares without intervening or judging. Parents are taught to restate to the child what they heard to check out if their listening was accurate and do this without anger or judgment. In this training, the goal of returning feedback is for the parent to check if the child's feelings were accurately understood.

PET also focuses on sending parental "I-messages" and deciding who owns the problem—the child or the parent. This program describes twelve "blocks" or obstacles to effective communication and finally, after intermediate lessons on parental power and conflict of values, presents a "no-lose" method of problem solving. In short, PET serves as a parental communication program.

> Communication instruction permeates each of the eight lessons. The focus in all lessons is to improve the direct interpersonal communication in the family by using strategies that reduce conflict and stimulate shared problem solving.   (Brommel, 2)

As a final instructional example we turn to the Baha'i faith and its approach to family life. In his analysis of the influence of Baha'i faith beliefs on family communication, Ward (1980) describes communication-related behaviors taught within the faith. Members learn a consultation process, which includes identifying the problem, agreeing on the facts and relevant principles, discussing the alternatives fully and frankly, and agreeing on a decision to be put into action (5). Families are expected to use these steps for dealing with any decision they must face. Additionally the faith emphasizes the need to teach children the process of asking questions and to encourage them in such behavior. Stress is placed on "verbal-factual" accord to the extent that "Children are not to be given answers which later have to be denied, but rather, can be elaborated on" (6). Families are encouraged to engage in frequent family study-discussions as a means of teaching the faith and exploring values and personal issues and to seek means of discipline that do not include "striking or vilifying" the child. In addition all members of the faith know that any difficult problem may be brought to the local Assembly for counseling. Ward summarizes his findings stating, "The practice of these teachings interrelate as a communication pattern for the family" (11).

Finally, we wish to note the existence of many self-help groups oriented toward specific topics that also provide formal or informal instruction in family communication for their members. Such groups include: Alcoholics Anonymous,

Parents Anonymous, Families Anonymous, Parents Without Partners, Parents of Gays, Families Who Have Adopted Children of Every Skin, Compassionate Friends, and Candlelighters.

Some of you may have been involved in personal or institutional approaches to marital and family communication; others of you may find yourselves involved sometime in the future. Each year millions of people experience some type of an educational program, a communication course, a weekend through their churches, synagogues, civic groups, or business organizations. As this happens, more couples and families will experience clear, open, honest, and caring communication eventually becoming families-of-origin to a future generation who will be raised with such patterns.

In the next section we will introduce the therapeutic approaches to improving family communication. Because this text concerns itself with communication issues of functional families, we will treat therapeutic approaches only briefly in order to extend the continuum of options for improving relationships. There is a vast body of literature which explores these approaches in detail and we recognize that we will only highlight some relevant issues.

Therapeutic Approaches

Two years ago my family went into therapy because my younger brother was an alcoholic and his treatment center required the entire family to become involved in the treatment program. Over about a year we were able to understand the patterns of family interaction that "fed" Chris' drinking problem. The therapist kept stressing that Chris' drinking was a family problem, not just Chris' problem. The therapy forced my mother and stepfather to deal with some problems in their marriage that they had been ignoring and allowed us to make enough changes that Chris could return to the house and to high school and control his drinking. It was a very difficult year but I think everyone in the family learned something from it.

For those families that live with dysfunctional communication or that experience temporary crises, therapeutic interventions may be warranted. Individual therapy has long been an established approach to dealing with personal problems or illnesses. Many people finding difficulties within themselves and their relationships have been assisted through a one-to-one therapeutic relationship in some type of counseling setting. This one-to-one counselor-client situation represents the traditional therapeutic approach.

Yet starting in the 1950s some therapists began to find success working jointly with a parent and child, or a husband and wife. Eventually some therapists asked to see whole families for a session. These sessions proved so valuable that certain therapists elected to work with husbands and wives, parents and children, or whole family systems on a regular basis, thus forming the basis of systems therapy. Napier and Whitaker (1978) describe the process by which therapists decided to look at whole systems.

> Some therapists discovered the family system by being bruised by it . . . working with an individual and being totally defeated by the family's power over the patient; or seeing the client "recover," only to witness all the progress undermined by the family; or treating the scapegoat child "successfully," only to find another child in the family dragged into the role; or working with an individual patient and feeling the fury of the family's sudden explosion just as the patient improved.   (52–53)

In many cases once therapists examined a whole family system they realized that there would not be a "problem" member, a symptom bearer, without all the rest of the system's dynamics.

Family therapy looks at the family unit as the client to be treated; the focus shifts from the individuals to the entire unit and the relationship among people. Ackerman (1966) describes family therapy as "the therapy of a natural living unit; the sphere of the therapeutic intervention is not a single individual but the whole family unit" (209). Thus the attempt is made to change the system, not just the "problem" person or identified patient since this person may be thought of as acting out the system's problems. For example, from this perspective marital problems cannot be viewed as all "her fault" or all "his fault." The problem belongs to the relationship, to the system. Such therapy requires great commitment on the parts of all persons involved in the system, yet may result in a new, functional interaction pattern for all system members. (Satir, 1967; Gurman & Kniskern, 1981).

Last year my parents seriously considered getting a divorce. I had known about the idea and had talked about it with my mother but I was really upset. As it turned out they decided to work out their differences and began seeing a therapist. This has gotten the whole family involved. Often it hardly seems that we are much happier, discussing all of the little things that bother us, together and apart. I have given much thought to it and have decided that things may not run as smoothly as before, yet under the surface I think we are all more content. I don't know if my parents will divorce, but if they do, we will all be able to cope better with the situation.

As you would think about changing the current communication patterns within your family system, many options are open to you ranging from individual efforts on the part of family members, to participating in organized programs, to seeking counseling for the system. From our perspective the most exciting aspect is the possibility of change. Communication can be improved; families can grow together. We do not deny the effort, time, or pain that might be involved, yet we believe a nurturing family is worth it.

CONCLUSION

In this chapter we have reviewed some of the factors which characterize functional or healthy families and the personal, educational, and therapeutic approaches for developing and maintaining desirable communication within families. We presented our belief that a healthy family system recognizes the interdependence of all members and attempts to provide for system growth as well as individual growth. Such families value open, clear, nurturing communication and take risks in order to grow. So ends our exploration into the area of family communication.

As we indicated in Chapter 1, we have grown from the process of writing this book, and we hope that you have developed new insights about families in general, and your family in particular. We close with our belief, shared with Beavers (1976), that a healthy family may be viewed as a "phoenix." It grows in an atmosphere of flexibility and intimacy; it accepts conflict, change, and loss; it declines—to rise again in another healthy generation which in turn produces healthy family members.

BIBLIOGRAPHY

Abelman, Adrienne. "The Relationship between Family Self-Disclosure, Adolescent Adjustment, Family Satisfaction, and Family Congruence." Unpublished dissertation. Northwestern University, 1975.

Ackerman, Nathan. "Family Therapy." In *American Handbook of Psychiatry.* Silvano Arieti, (ed.). New York: Basic Books, 1966.

Aldous, Joan. "The Making of Family Roles and Family Change." *The Family Coordinator* 23 (1974): 231–235.

Alexander, J. F. "Defensive and Supportive Communications in Family Systems." *Journal of Marriage and the Family* 35 (1973): 613–617.

Allen, Craig M., and Straus, Murray A. "Resources, Power, and Husband-Wife Violence." *The Social Causes of Husband-Wife Violence.* Murray A. Strauss & Gerald T. Hotaling (eds.). Minneapolis: University of Minnesota Press, 1979. Also reference to article in *Journal of Marriage and the Family* 41 (1979): 85.

Altman, Irwin, and Taylor, Dalmas. *Social Penetration.* New York: Holt, Rinehart & Winston, 1973.

Bach, George R., and Wyden, Peter. *The Intimate Enemy.* New York: William Morrow & Co., 1966.

Baden-Marotz, Ramona; Adams, Gerald R.; Bueche, Nancy; Munro, Brenda; and Munro, Gordon. "Family Form or Family Process? Reconsidering the Deficit Family Model Approach." *The Family Coordinator* 28 (1979): 5–14.

Bahr, Howard M. "The Kinship Role." In *Role Structure and Analysis of the Family.* F. Ivan Nye (ed.). Beverly Hills, Calif.: Sage Publications, 1976, 61–80.

Bain, Alastair. "The Capacity of Families to Cope with Transitions: A Theoretical Essay." *Human Relations* 31 (1978): 675–688.

Balswick, Jack, and Averett, Christine. "Differences in Expressiveness: Gender, Interpersonal Orientation, and Perceived Parental Expressiveness as Contributing Factors." *Journal of Marriage and the Family* 39 (1977): 121–127.

Bandler, Richard, and Grinder, John. *The Structure of Magic.* Palo Alto, Calif.: Science and Behavior Books, 1975.

Barbour, Alton, and Goldberg, Alvin. *Interpersonal Communication: Teaching Strategies and Resources.* ERIC/RCS. Speech Communication Association, 1974.

Barnhill, Laurence R. "Healthy Family Systems." *The Family Coordinator* 28 (1979): 94–100.

Bart, Pauline. "Depression in Middle Age Women." In *Women in a Sexist Society.* V. Gornick and B. Moran (eds.). New York: Basic Books, 1971, 163–186.

Bateson, G., and Ruesch, J. *Communication: The Social Matrix of Psychiatry.* New York: Norton, 1951.

Beal, Edward W., M.D. "Separation, Divorce, and Single-Parent Families." In *The Family Life Cycle: A Framework for Family Therapy.* Elizabeth A. Carter and Monica McGoldrick (eds.). New York: Gardner Press, Inc., 1980, 241–264.

Bearison, D. J., and Cassel, T. Z. "Cognitive Decentration and Social Codes: Communication Effectiveness in Young Children from Differing Family Contexts." *Developmental Psychology,* (1975): 29–36.

Beavers, W. R. "Family Variables Related to the Development of a Self." Timberlawn Foundation Report No. 68. Dallas, Texas, 1972.

Beavers, W. Robert. "A Theoretical Basis for Family Evaluation". In *No Single Thread: Psychological Health in Family Systems.* New York: Brunner-Mazel, 1976.

Beier, Ernst G., and Sternberg, Daniel P. "Marital Communication: Subtle Cues Between Newlyweds." *Journal of Communication* 27 (1977): 92–103.

Bem, S. L. "The Measurement of Psychological Androgny." *Journal of Consulting and Clinical Psychology* 47 (1974): 155–162.

Berger, Charles R. "Power and the Family." In *Persuasion: New Direction In Theory and Research.* Michael Roloff and Gerald Miller (eds.). Beverly Hills: Sage Publications, 1980, 197–224.

Bernhard, Yetta. *Self Care.* Millbrae, California: Celestial Arts, 1975.

Bernstein, Basil. "A Sociolinguistic Approach to Socialization: With Some Reference to Educability." In *Language and Poverty.* F. Williams (ed.). Chicago: Markham, 1970.

Berscheid, Ellen, and Walster, Elaine. *Interpersonal Attraction.* Reading, Mass.: Addison-Wesley, 1969.

Bienvenu, Millard. "A Measurement of Premarital Communication." *The Family Coordinator* 24 (1975): 65–68.

Blau, Peter. *Exchange and Power in Social Life.* New York: John Wiley and Sons, 1964.

Blood, Robert O., and Wolfe, Donald M. *Husbands and Wives: The Dynamics of Married Living.* New York: The Free Press, 1960.

Blos, Peter. *The Adolescent Passage.* New York: International Universities Press, 1979.

Bochner, A. P. "Conceptual Frontiers in the Study of Communication in Families." *Human Communication Research* 2 (1976): 381–397.

Book, Cassandra (ed.). *Human Communication.* New York: St. Martin's Press, 1980.

Bowen, Murray A. "Toward the Differentiation of a Self In One's Own Family." In J. L. Framo (ed.), *Family Interaction.* New York: Springer Co., 1972, 190–199.

Bowen, Murray, M.D. "Family Reaction To Death." In *Family Therapy: Theory & Practice.* Phillip J. Guerin (ed.). New York: Halsted Press, 1976, 335–349.

Boyd, Lenore, and Roach, Arthur. "Interpersonal Communication Skills Differentiating More Satisfying From Less Satisfying Marital Relationships." *Journal of Counseling Psychology* 24 (1977): 540–542.

Bradt, Jack. "The Family With Young Children." In *The Family Life Cycle: A Framework for Family Therapy.* Elizabeth Carter and Monica McGoldrick (eds.). New York: Gardner Press, 1980, 121–146.

Broderick, Carlfred. "Power in the Governance of Families." In *Power in Families.* R. E. Cromwell & D. H. Olson (eds.). New York: Halsted Press, 1975, 117–128.

Broderick, Carlfred. "Fathers." *The Family Coordinator* 26 (1977): 269–271.

Brommel, Bernard. "A Critical Analysis of Communication Instruction in Current Family Interaction Improvement Programs." Paper presented at Speech Communication Association Convention, November 1978.

Burchinal, Lee G. "Characteristics of Adolescents from Unbroken, Broken, and Reconstituted Families." *Journal of Marriage and the Family* 26 (1964): 44–51.

Burgess, E. W.; Locke, H. J.; and Thomas, M. M. *The Family: From Institution to Companionship.* New York: American Book Company, 1963.

Burke, Ronald; Weir, Tamara; and Harrison, Denise. "Disclosure of Problems and Tensions Experienced by Marital Partners." *Psychological Reports* 38 (1976): 531–542.

Caine, Lynn. *Widow.* New York: William Morrow and Co., 1974.

Campbell, Joseph. *The Portable Jung.* New York: Penguin Books, 1976.

Carlson, John. "The Recreational Role." In *Role Structure and Analysis of the Family.* F. Ivan Nye. (ed.). Beverly Hills, Calif.: Sage Publications, 1976, 131–148.

Carlson, John. "The Sexual Role." In *Role Structure and Analysis of the Family.* F. Ivan Nye. (ed.). Beverly Hills, Calif.: Sage Publications, 1976, 101–110.

Carter, Elizabeth A., and Monica McGoldrick. "The Family Life Cycle and Family Therapy: An Overview." In *The Family Life Cycle: A Framework for Family Therapy.* Elizabeth A. Carter and Monica McGoldrick (eds.). New York: Gardner Press, Inc., 1980, 3–20.

Carter, H., and Glick, P. C. *Marriage and Divorce: A Social and Economic Study,* rev. ed. Cambridge: Harvard University Press, 1976.

Centers, R.; Raven, B. H.; and Rodrigues, A. "Conjugal Power Structure: A Reexamination." *American Sociological Review* 36 (1971): 264–278.

Chelune, Gordon, and Associates. *Self-Disclosure.* San Francisco: Jossey-Bass, 1979.

Chilman, Catherine. "Habitat and American Families: A Social-Psychological Over-View." *The Family Coordinator* 27, 2 (1978): 105–111.

Clark, Robert A.; Nye, F. Ivan; and Gecas, Viktor. "Husbands Work Involvement and Marital Role Performance." *Journal of Marriage and the Family* 40 (1978): 9–21.

Clinebell, Howard, and Clinebell, Charlotte. *The Intimate Marriage.* New York: Harper and Row, 1970.

Conger, John J. *Adolescence and Youth,* 2nd ed. New York: Harper and Row, 1977.

Corrales, Ramon G. "Power and Satisfaction in Early Marriage." In *Power in Families.* Ronald E. Cromwell and David H. Olson (eds.). New York: John Wiley & Sons, 1975, 197–216.

Coser, Lewis A. *Continuities in the Study of Social Conflict.* New York: The Free Press, 1967.

Courtright, John A.; Millar, Frank E.; and Rogers-Millar, L. Edna. "Domineeringness and Dominance: Replication and Expansion." *Communication Monographs* 46 (1979): 179–192.

Cromwell, R. E.; Klein, D. M.; and Wieting, S. G. "Family Power: A Multitrait-Multimethod Analysis." In *Power in Families.* R. E. Cromwell & D. H. Olson (eds.). New York: Halsted Press, 1975, 151–179.

Cromwell, R. E. and Olson, David H. (eds.). *Power in Families.* New York: Halsted Press, 1975.

Cronen, Vernon; Pearce, W. Barnett; and Harris, Linda. "The Logic of the Coordinated Management of Meaning: A Rules-Based Approach to the First Course in Inter-Personal Communication." *Communication Education* 23 (1979): 22–38.

Cronkhite, Gary. *Communication and Awareness.* Menlo Park, Calif.: Cummings Publishing Co., Inc., 1976.

Cutler, Beverly R., and Dyer, William G. "Initial Adjustment Processes in Young Married Couples." *Love, Marriage, Family: A Developmental Approach.* M. E. Lasswell and T. E. Lasswell (eds.). Glenview, IL: Scott, Foresman, & Co., 1973, 290–296.

Dean, Gillian, and Gurak, Douglas. "Marital Homogamy the Second Time Around." *Journal of Marriage and the Family* 40 (1978): 559–570.

DeFrain, John. "Androgynous Parents Tell Who They Are and What They Need." *Family Coordinator* 28 (1979): 237–243.

DeLong, Alton. "Environments For The Elderly." *Journal of Communication* 24, #4 (1974): 101–112.

Despert, Louise J. *Children of Divorce.* New York: Doubleday and Co., 1962.

DeYoung, Alan J. "Marriage Encounter: A Critical Examination." *Journal of Marital and Family Therapy* 5 (1979): 27–41.

Doherty, William J.; McCabe, Patricia; and Ryder, Robert G. "Marriage Encounter: A Critical Appraisal." *Journal of Marriage and Family Counseling* 4 (1978): 99–106.

Doster, J. A., and Strickland, B. R. "Perceived Childhood Practices and Self-Disclosure Patterns." *Journal of Consulting and Clinical Psychology* 33 (1969): 382.

Douglas, Susan P., and Wind, Yoram. "Examining Family Role and Authority Patterns: Two Methodological Issues." *Journal of Marriage and the Family* 40 (1978): 35–47.

Douvan, Elizabeth Ann Malcolm. *The Adolescent Experience.* New York: John Wiley & Sons, 1966.

Dreikurs, Rudolf. *Children: The Challenge.* New York: Hawthorn Books, 1964.

Dreyer, Cecily, and Dreyer, Albert. "Family Dinner Time As a Unique Behavior Habitat." *Family Process* 12 (1973): 291–302.

Duberman, L. "Step Kin Relationships." *Journal of Marriage and the Family* 35 (1973): 283–292.

Dullea, Georgia. "Is Joint Custody Good For Children?" *The New York Times,* Feb. 3, 1980: 32–46.

Dumazedier, Jafre. *Toward a Society of Leisure.* New York: The Free Press, 1967.

Duncan, O. D. "Social Organization and the Ecosystem." *Handbook of Modern Sociology,* R. Farris & L. Farris (eds.). Chicago: Rand McNally, 1964.

Dunlop, Richard S. *Helping the Bereaved.* Bowie, Maryland: Charles Press Publishers, Inc., 1978.

Duvall, Evelyn Ruth (Millis). *Family Development,* 2nd ed. Philadelphia: J. B. Lippincott, 1962.

Duvall, Evelyn Ruth (Millis). *Family Development,* 4th ed. Philadelphia: J. B. Lippincott, 1971.

D'Zurilla T. J., and Goldfried, M. R. "Problem Solving and Behavior Modification." *Journal of Abnormal Psychology* 78 (1971): 107–126.

Emmerich, H. J. "The Influence of Parents and Peers on Choices Made by Adolescence." *Journal of Youth and Adolescence* 7 (1978): 175–180.

Ericksen, Julia A.; Yancey, William L.; and Ericksen, Eugene P. "The Division of Family Roles." *Journal of Marriage and the Family* 41 (1979): 301–313.

Erikson, Erik H. *Identity, Youth, and Crisis.* New York: W. W. Norton & Co., 1968.

Eshbach, Ellen. "Your Dream House Could Give a Family Nightmares." *Chicago Tribune,* May 16, 1976: Sec. 5, p. 3.

Family Home Evening: Love Makes Our House a Home. Salt Lake City: The Church of Jesus Christ of Latter-Day Saints Press, 1974.

"Father's Priesthood —To Be Used, But Not Abused." *Family Home Evening: Love Makes Our House a Home.* Salt Lake City: The Church of Jesus Christ of Latter Day Saints Press 3 (1974): 224.

Feifel, Herman. *New Meaning of Death.* New York: McGraw-Hill Book Co., 1977.

Feldman, Larry B., M.D. "Goals of Family Therapy." *Journal of Marriage and Family Counseling* 2 (1976): 103–113.

Feldman, Larry B., M.D. "Marital Conflict and Marital Intimacy: An Integrative Psychodynamic-Behavioral Systemic Model." *Family Process* 18 (1979): 69–78.

Festinger, Leon. "Architecture and Group Membership." *Journal of Social Issues* 1 (1951): 152–159.

Festinger, L. S.; Schachter S.; and Beck, K. *Social Pressures in Informal Groups: A Study of Human Factors in Housing.* New York: Harper & Row, 1950.

Filley, Allan C. *Interpersonal Conflict Resolution.* Glenview, IL: Scott, Foresman & Co., 1975.

Fitzpatrick, Mary Ann. "Dyadic Adjustment in Traditional, Independent, and Separate Relationship: A Validation Study." University of Wisconsin-Milwaukee. Paper presented at Speech Communication Association, Dec. 1977a.

Fitzpatrick, Mary Ann. "A Typological Approach to Communication in Relationships." *Communication Yearbook I.* Brent Rubin (ed.). New Brunswick, N.J.: Transaction Press (1977b): 263–275.

Fitzpatrick, Mary Ann, and Best, Patricia. "Dyadic Adjustment in Relational Types: Consensus, Cohesion, Affectional Expression, and Satisfaction in Enduring Relationships." *Communication Monographs* 46 (1979): 165–178.

Foley, Vincent D. *An Introduction to Family Therapy.* New York: Grune & Stratton, Inc., 1974.

Framo, James L. Ph.D. "Family of Origin as a Therapeutic Resource for Adults in Marital and Family Therapy: You Can and Should Go Home Again." *Family Process* 15 (1976): 193–209.

French, J. R. P. Jr., and Raven, B. H. "The Bases of Social Power." In D. Cartwright and A. Zander (eds.), *Group Dynamics.* Evanston, Illinois: Row Peterson, 1962, 607–623.

Gagnon, John. *Human Sexuality.* Glenview, IL: Scott, Foresman and Co., 1977.

Galper, Marian. *Co-Parenting: A Sourcebook for the Separated or Divorced Family.* Philadelphia: Running Press, 1978.

Galvin, Kathleen M. "An Analysis of Communication Instruction in Current Marital Interaction Programs." Paper presented at the Speech Communication Association Convention, 1978.

Gantman, Carol. "A Closer Look at Families That Work Well." *International Journal of Family Therapy* 2 (1980): 106–119.

Gaylin, Jody. "Family Policy—Our Endangered Children: It's A Matter of Money." *Psychology Today* 11 (1977): 94–95.

Gecas, Viktor. "The Socialization and Child Care Roles." In *Structure and Analysis of the Family.* F. Ivan Nye (ed.). Beverly Hills, Calif.: Sage Publications, 1976, 33–60.

Gibb, Jack R. "Defensive Communication." *Journal of Communication* 11 (1961): 141–148.

Gil, D. *Violence Against Children.* Cambridge: Harvard University Press, 1970.

Gilbert, Shirley. "Empirical and Theoretical Extensions of Self-Disclosure." In *Explorations in Interpersonal Communication.* Gerald Miller (ed.). Beverly Hills, Calif.: Sage Publications, 1976b; 197–215.

Gilbert, Shirley. "Self Disclosure, Intimacy, and Communication in Families." *Family Coordinator* 25 (1976a): 221–229.

Gilbert, Shirley, and Whiteneck, Gale. "Toward a Multidimensional Approach To The Study of Self-Disclosure." *Human Communication Research* 2 (1976): 347–355.

Gilford, Rosalie, and Bengtson, Vern. "Measuring Marital Satisfaction in Three Generations: Positive and Negative Dimensions." *Journal of Marriage and the Family* 4 (1979): 387–397.

Gillespie, Dair L. "Who Has The Power? The Marital Struggle." *Journal of Marriage and the Family* 33 (1971): 445–458.

Glenn, Norval, and Weaver, Charles. "A Multivariate, Multi-survey Study of Marital Happiness." *Journal of Marriage and the Family* 40 (1978): 269–282.

Goffman, Erving. "On Cooling the Mark Out: Some Aspects of Adaptation to Failure." *Psychiatry* 15 (1952): 451–463.

Goldstine, Daniel; Zuckerman, Shirley; Goldstine, Hilary; and Larner, Katherine. "The Three Stages of Marriage." *Family Circle* 90 (1977): 10–20. See also *The Dance Away Lover.* New York: William Morrow & Co., 1977.

Goode, William J. "Force and Violence in the Family." *Journal of Marriage and the Family* 33 (1971): 624–635.

Gordon, Thomas. *Parent Effectiveness Training.* New York: New American Library, 1975.

Gottman, John. *Marital Interaction: Experimental Investigations.* New York: Academic Press, 1979.

Gottman, John; Markham, Howard; and Notarius, Cliff. "The Topography of Marital Conflict: A Sequential Analysis of Verbal and Nonverbal Behavior." *Journal of Marriage and the Family* 39 (1977): 461–477.

Greeley, Andrew. "Creativity in the Irish Family: The Cast of Immigration." *Family Therapy* 1 (1979): 295–303.

Greene, Bernard. *A Clinical Approach to Marital Problems.* Springfield, IL: Charles C. Thomas, 1970.

Grote, Douglas F., and Weinstein, Jeffrey P. "Joint Custody: A Viable and Ideal Alternative." *Journal of Divorce* 1 (1977): 43–54.

Guerney, Bernard G. *Relationship Enhancement: Skill Training Programs for Therapy, Problem Prevention, and Enrichment.* San Francisco: Jossey-Bass, 1977.

Gurman, Alan, and Kniskern, David. "Enriching Research on Marital Enrichment Programs." *Journal of Marriage and Family Counseling* 3 (1977): 3–10.

Gurman, Alan, and Kniskern, David. *Handbook of Family Therapy.* New York: Brunner-Mazel, 1981.

Hacker, Helen. "The New Burdens of Masculinity." *Marriage and Family Living* 39 (1957): 227–234.

Haley, Jay. "Establishment of an Interpersonal Relationship." In *Interpersonal Communication: Basic Text and Readings,* B. R. Patton and Kim Giffin (eds.). New York: Harper and Row, 1974, 368–373.

296

Hall, Edward T. *The Hidden Dimension.* Garden City, N.Y.: Doubleday, 1966.

Halpern, Donald. *Cutting Loose: An Adult Guide To Coming To Terms With Your Parents.* New York: Simon & Schuster, 1976.

Harkins, Elizabeth Bates. "Effects of Empty Nest Transition On Self-Report of Psychological and Physical Well Being." *Gerontologist* 15 (1975): 43.

Harry, Joseph. "The 'Marital' Liaisons of Gay Men." *The Family Coordinator* 28 (1979): 622–629.

Hartley, Ruth E. "Sex Role Pressures and the Socialization of the Male Child." In *Men and Masculinity.* Joseph Pleck and Jack Sawyer (eds.). Englewood Cliffs, N.J.: Prentice-Hall, 1974, 7–13.

Havighurst, R. J. *Developmental Tasks and Education.* New York: David McKay, 1952.

Hawkins, James; Weisberg, Carol; and Ray, Dixie. "Marital Communication Style and Social Class." *Journal of Marriage and the Family* 38 (1977): 479–490.

Hawkins, James; Weisberg, Carol; and Ray, Dixie. "Spouse Differences in Communication and Style: Preference, Perception, Behavior." *Journal of Marriage and the Family* 42 (1980): 585–594.

Hawkins, Leo F. "The Impact of Policy Decisions On Families." *Family Coordinator* 28 (1979): 264–272.

Heer, David M. "The Measurement and Bases of Family Power." *Marriage and Family Living* 25 (1963): 133–139.

Heiss, Jerold. "An Introduction to the Elements of Role Theory." In *Family Roles and Interaction.* Jerold Heiss (ed.). Chicago: Rand McNally and Co., 1968, 3–27.

Herbst, P. G. "The Measurement of Family Relationships." *Human Relations* 5 (1952): 3–35.

Herz, Fredda. "The Impact of Death and Serious Illness on the Family Life Cycle." In *The Family Life Cycle: A Framework for Family Therapy.* Elizabeth Carter and Monica McGoldrick (eds.). New York: Gardner Press, 1980.

Hess, Robert, and Handel, Gerald. *Family Worlds.* Chicago: University of Chicago Press, 1959.

Hetherington, E. Mavis. "Girls Without Fathers." *Psychology Today* 7 (1973): 49–52.

Hetherington, E. Mavis; Cox, Martha; and Cox, Roger. "Divorced Fathers." *The Family Coordinator* 25 (1976): 417–428.

Hickok, James E., and Komechak, Marilyn Gilbert. "Behavior Modification in Marital Conflict: A Case Report." *Family Process* 13 (1974): 111–119.

Hicks, Mary, and Platt, Marilyn. "Marital Happiness and Stability: A Review of Research in the Sixties." *Journal of Marriage and the Family* 32 (1970): 553–573.

Hill, Reuben. *Families Under Stress.* New York: Harper & Brothers, 1949.

Hill, Reuben. "Methodological Issues in Family Development Research." *Family Process.* Nathan Akerman. (ed.). New York: Basic Books, Inc., 1970, 294–314.

Hill, R., and Aldous, J. "Socialization From Marriage and Parenthood." In *Handbook of Socialization Theory and Research.* D. A. Goslin (ed.). Chicago: Rand McNally and Co., 1969, 885–950.

Hoffman, Lois W. "Effects of the Employment of Mothers on Parental Power Relations and the Division of Household Tasks." *Marriage and Family Living* 22 (1960): 27–35.

Hoffman, Lynn. "Enmeshment and the Too Richly Cross-Joined System." *Family Process* 14 (1975): 457–468.

Hoffman, Lynn. "The Family Life Cycle and Discontinuous Change." In *The Family Life Cycle: A Framework for Family Therapy.* Elizabeth Carter and Monica McGoldrick (eds.). New York: Gardner Press, 1980, 53–68.

Holmes, T. H., and Rahe, R. H. "The Social Readjustment Rating Scale." *Journal of Psychosomatic Research* 2 (1967): 213–218.

Homans, G. C. "Social Behavior as Exchange." *American Journal of Sociology* 63 (1958): 597–606.

Hopkins, Paul, and Hopkins, La Donna. "Marriage Communication Labs." In *Marriage and Family Enrichment.* Herbert Otto (ed.). Nashville: Abingdon Press, 1976, 229.

Hopper, Robert; Knapp, Mark; and Scott, Lorel. "Couples' Personal Idioms: Exploring Intimate Talk." *Journal of Communication* 31 (1981): 23–33.

Howard, Jane. *Families.* New York: Berkley Books, Simon & Schuster, 1978.

Hunt, Bernice, and Hunt, Morton. "The American Family: Still Alive But Changing." *Chicago Tribune,* September 10, 1978.

Hunt, Morton. *Sexual Behavior in the 1970's.* Chicago: Playboy Press, 1974.

Hurvitz, Nathan, and Komarovsky, Mirra. "Husbands and Wives: Middle Class and Working Class." In Cathy Greenblatt et al. (eds.), *The Marriage Game,* 2nd ed. New York: Random House, 1977.

Ichilov, Orit, and Rubineck, Bracha. "The Relationship Between Girls' Attitudes Concerning the Family and their Perception of the Patterns Existing in the Family of Origin." *Journal of Marriage and the Family* 39 (1977): 417–422.

Jackson, Don D. "The Question of Family Homeostasis." *Psychiatric Quarterly* 31 (1957): 79–90.

Jackson, Don D. "The Study of the Family." *Family Process* 4 (1965): 1–20.

Johnson, Fern. "Communication with Children: Toward a Healthy Construction of Communicative Roles." Paper presented at Central States Speech Association, Chicago, 1978.

Johnson, P. B. "Social Power and Sex Role Stereotyping." Unpublished Dissertation, University of California, Los Angeles, 1974.

Jourard, Sidney. *The Transparent Self.* New York: Van Nostrand Reinhold Co., 1971.

Jourard, Sidney. "Some Lethal Aspects of the Male Role." In *Men and Masculinity.* Joseph Pleck and Jack Sawyer (eds.). Englewood Cliffs, N.J.: Prentice-Hall, 1974, 21–29.

Kahana, F., and Kahana, B. "The Theoretical and Research Perspectives on Grandparenthood." Paper presented at American Psychological Association Meeting, 1970.

Kahn, Malcolm. "Non-Verbal Communication and Marital Satisfaction." *Family Process* 9 (1970): 449–456.

Kantor, David, and Lehr, William. *Inside the Family.* San Francisco: Jossey-Bass, 1976.

Kennedy, Robert W. *The House and the Art of its Design.* New York: Reinhold Publishing Co., 1953.

Kenniston, Kenneth, et al. *All Our Children.* Harcourt Brace Jovanovich, 1977.

Kenniston, Kenneth. "The Search of Adulthood." *New York Times Book Review,* July 8, 1979, 7.

Kimball, Spencer; Farmer, Eldon N.; and Romney, M. G. "Messages from the First Presidency." *Family Home Evening: Love Makes our House a Home.* Salt Lake City, Utah: The Church of Jesus Christ of Latter-Day Saints Press 3 (1974): 2.

Knapp, Mark L. *Nonverbal Communication in Human Interaction.* New York: Holt, Rinehart & Winston, 1972.

Knapp, Mark L. *Social Intercourse.* Boston: Allyn and Bacon, 1978.

Knox, David. "Trends in Marriage and the Family—The 1980's." *Family Relations* 29 (1980): 145–150.

Koch, Joanne, and Koch, Lew. "The Urgent Drive to Make Good Marriages Better." *Psychology Today* 10 (1976): 33–34, 85, 95.

Kohlberg, Lawrence. "Development of Moral Character and Moral Ideology." In M. L. Hoffman and L. W. Hoffman (eds.). *Review of Child Development Research* 1. New York: Russell Sage Foundation, 1964, 383–431.

Kohlberg, Lawrence. "Continuities in Childhood and Adult Moral Development Revisited." In P. Baltes & K. W. Schaie (eds.). *Life-Span Developmental Psychology: Personality and Socialization.* New York: Academic Press, 1973.

Kolb, Trudy M., & Straus, Murray A. "Marital Power & Marital Happiness in Relation to Problem Solving Ability." *Journal of Marriage and the Family* 36 (1974): 756–766.

Komarovsky, Mirra. *Blue Collar Marriage.* New York: Vintage Books, Random House, 1967.

Kotlar, Sally L. "Middle Class Marital Role Perceptions and Marital Adjustment." *Sociological and Social Research* 49 (1965): 283–293.

Kübler-Ross, Elisabeth. *On Death and Dying.* New York: Macmillan, 1970.

Kübler-Ross, Elisabeth (ed.). *Death: The Final Stage of Growth.* New York: Spectrum Books, 1975.

L'Abate, Luciano. "Skill Training Programs for Couples and Families." In Alan Gurman and David Kniskern (eds.), *Handbook of Family Therapy.* New York: Brunner-Mazel, 1981.

Laing, R. D. *The Politics of the Family.* New York: Vintage Books, 1972.

LaRossa, Ralph. *Conflict and Power in Marriage.* Beverly Hills, Calif.: Sage Publications, 1977.

Lasswell, Marcia, and Lasswell, Thomas (eds.). *Love, Marriage, Family: A Developmental Approach.* Glenview, IL: Scott, Foresman and Co., 1973.

Lederer, William, and Jackson, Don. D. *The Mirages of Marriage.* New York: W. W. Norton and Co., 1968.

Lee, Gary. "Marriage and Morale in Later Life." *Journal of Marriage and the Family* 40 (1978): 131–139.

Lennard, Suzanne, and Lennard, Henry. "Architecture: Effect of Territory, Boundary, and Orientation on Family Functioning." *Family Process* 16 (1977): 49–66.

Lenthall, Gerard. "Marital Satisfaction and Marital Stability." *Journal of Marriage and Family Counseling* 3 (1977): 25–32.

Levine, James A. *Raise the Children: New Options for Fathers.* New York: Bantam Books, 1977.

Levinger, G., and Senn, D. J. "Disclosure of Feelings in Marriage." *Merrill Palmer Quarterly* 13 (1967): 237–249.

Levinson, Daniel, et al. *The Seasons of a Man's Life.* New York: Ballantine Books, 1978.

Lewis, Robert A.; Freneau, Phillip, J.; and Roberts, Craig R. "Fathers and the Postparental Tradition." *The Family Coordinator* 28 (1979): 514–520.

Lewis, Robert A., and Pleck, Joseph H. "Men's Roles in the Family." *The Family Coordinator* 29 (1979): 429–432.

Lieberman, Leslie, and Lieberman, Leonard. "The Family in the Tube: Potential Uses of Television." *The Family Coordinator* 26, 3 (1977): 235–242.

Linton, Ralph. *The Cultural Background of Personality.* New York: Appleton-Century-Crofts, 1945.

Littlejohn, Stephen. *Theories of Human Communication.* Columbus, Ohio: Charles Merrill, 1978.

Longini, Muriel. "The Delicate One—Transferring a Childhood Role into Married Life can Cause Problems." *Marriage and Family Living* 61 (1979): 8–9.

Lopata, H. Z. *Widowhood in an American City.* Cambridge, Mass.: Schenkman, 1973.

Lowenthal, Marjorie Fish, and Chiriboga, David. "Transition to Empty Nest: Crisis, Challenge or Relief?" *Archives of General Psychiatry* 26 (1972): 8–14.

Luckey, E. B. "Marital Satisfaction and its Association with Congruence of Perception." *Marriage and Family Living* 22 (1960): 49–54.

Luepnitz, Deborah A. "Which Aspects of Divorce Affect Children?" *Family Coordinator* 28 (1979): 79–85.

Masters, W. H., and Johnson, Virginia. *The Pleasure Bond.* Boston: Little, Brown, 1975.

Masterson, John T. "Speech Communication in Traditional and Contemporary Marriages." Unpublished Ph.D. Dissertation, University of Denver, 1977.

McCall, George, and Simmons, J. L. *Identities and Interactions.* New York: The Free Press, 1966.

McClelland, David; Constantian, Carol A.; Regalado, David; and Stone, Carolyn. "Making it to Maturity." *Psychology Today* 12 (1978): 42–54.

McCullough, Paulina. "Launching Children and Moving On." In *The Family Life Cycle: A Framework for Family Therapy.* Elizabeth Carter and Monica McGoldrick (eds.). New York: Gardner Press, 1980, 171–196.

McGoldrick, Monica, and Carter, Elizabeth A. "Forming a Remarried Family." In *The Family Life Cycle: A Framework For Family Therapy.* Elizabeth A. Carter and Monica McGoldrick (eds.). New York: Gardner Press, 1980, 265–329.

Mehrabian, Albert. *Silent Messages.* Belmont, Calif.: Wadsworth, 1971.

Millar, Frank; Rogers-Millar, L. E.; and Villard, Kenneth. "A Proposed Model of Relational Communication and Family Functioning." Paper presented at the Central States Speech Association Convention, April 1978.

Millar, Frank; Rogers-Millar, L. E.; and Villard, Kenneth. "Relational Communication and Family Functioning: A Second Look." Paper presented at the Eastern Communication Association Convention, May 1979.

Millar, L. Edna Rogers, and Millar, Frank E. III. "Domineeringness and Dominance: A Transactional View." *Human Communication Research* 5 (1979): 238–246.

Miller, Brian. "Gay Fathers and Their Children." *The Family Coordinator* 28 (1979): 544–552.

Miller, Gerald, and Steinberg, Mark. *Between People.* Chicago: Science Research Associates, Inc., 1975.

Miller, Sherod; Corrales, Ramon; and Wackman, Daniel B. "Recent Progress in Understanding and Facilitating Marital Communication." *The Family Coordinator* 24 (1975): 143–151.

Minuchin, Salvador. *Families and Family Therapy.* Cambridge, Mass.: Harvard University Press, 1974.

Minuchin, Salvador, et al. *Families of the Slums.* New York: Basic Books, 1967.

Mishler, E. G., and Waxler, N. E. *Interaction in Families, An Experimental Study of Family Processes in Schizophrenia.* New York: John Wiley & Sons, 1968.

Montagu, Ashley. *Touching: The Human Significance of the Skin.* New York: Harper & Row, 1978.

Morgan, Marabel. *The Total Woman.* Boston: G. K. Hall, 1975.

Morive, Margaret. "Dimensions of Marriage Happiness." *Journal of Marriage and the Family* 38 (1976): 443–447.

Mortensen, C. David. *Communication: The Study of Human Interaction.* New York: McGraw-Hill, 1972.

Moses, Kenneth. "Effects of the Developmental Disability in Parenting the Handicapped Child." In *First and Second Annual Early Childhood Symposia: Patterns of Emotional Growth in the Developmentally Disabled Child.* Margery Rieff (ed.). Morton Grove, IL: Julia S. Malloy Education Center, 1978: 31–62.

Muchmore, John. "Role Context and Speech Communication Education: Approach to Instruction Demonstrated by Application to the Occupational Category of Dental Hygienist. Unpublished Dissertation, Northwestern University, 1974.

Mudd, Emily H.; Mitchell, Howard E.; Bullard, James W. "Areas of Marital Conflict in Successfully Functioning and Unsuccessfully Functioning Families." *Journal of Health and Human Behavior* 3 (1962): 88–93.

Murstein, Bernard I. "Self-Ideal—Self-Discrepancy and the Choice of Marital Partner." In M. E. Lasswell and T. E. Lasswell (eds.), *Love, Marriage, Family: A Developmental Approach.* Glenview, IL: Scott, Foresman & Co., 1973, 246–249.

Napier, Augustus, with Whitaker, Carl. *The Family Crucible.* New York: Harper and Row, 1978.

Nash, John. "The Father in Contemporary Culture." In M. E. Lasswell and T. E. Lasswell (eds.), *Love, Marriage, Family: A Developmental Approach.* Glenview, IL: Scott, Foresman and Co., 1973, 352–362.

Navran, L. "Communication and Adjustment in Marriage." *Family Process* 6 (1967): 173–184.

Nehls, N., and Morgenbesser, S. "Joint Custody: An Exploration of Issues." *Family Process* 19 (1980): 117–124.

Neugarten, B., and Weinstein, K. K. "The Changing American Grandparent." *Journal of Marriage and the Family* 26 (1964): 199–204.

Nutt, Grady. *Family Time: A Revolutionary Old Idea.* Family Communication Committee of Million Dollar Round Table, 1976.

Nye, F. Ivan. *Role Structure and Analysis of the Family.* Beverly Hills, Calif.: Sage Publications, 1976.

Nye, F. Ivan. "Family Mini-Theories as Special Instances of Choice and Exchange Theory." *Journal of Marriage and the Family* 42 (1980): 479–490.

Nye, F. Ivan, and Gecas, Viktor. "The Role Concept: Review and Delineation." In F. Ivan Nye (ed.), *Role Structure and Analysis of the Family.* Beverly Hills, Calif.: Sage Publications, 1976, 3–15.

Offer, Daniel, and Baskin, Judith, with the assistance of Eric Ostrov. *From Teenage to Young Manhood: A Psychological Study.* New York: Basic Books, 1975.

O'Flaherty, K. W. "Evaluation of a Coaching Procedure for Marital Decision Making," Unpublished Dissertation. University of Michigan, 1974.

Olson, D. H. "The Measurement of Family Power by Self-Report and Behavioral Methods." *Journal of Marriage and the Family* 31 (1969): 545–550.

Olson, D. H.; Sprenkle, D. H.; and Russell, C. S. "Circumplex Model of Marital and Family Systems: Cohesion and Adaptability Dimensions, Family Types, and Clinical Applications." *Family Process* 18 (1979): 3–28.

O'Neill, Nena, and O'Neill, George. *Open Marriage.* New York: Avon Books, 1972.

Osmond, Harry. "Function as the Basis of Psychiatric Ward Design." *Environmental Psychology.* H. Proshansky, W. Ittleson, and L. Rivlin (eds.). New York: Holt, Rinehart & Winston, 1970.

Osmond, Marie W. "Reciprocity: A Dynamic Model and a Method to Study Family Power." *Journal of Marriage and the Family* 41 (1978); 49–61.

Osmond, Marie W., and Martin, Patricia. "A Contingency Model of Marital Organization in Low Income Families." *Journal of Marriage and the Family* 41 (1978): 315–329.

Otto, H. A. *More Joy in Marriage: Developing Your Marriage Potential.* New York: Hawthorn, 1969.

Otto, Herbert. "Marriage and Family Enrichment Programs in North America—Report and Analysis." *The Family Coordinator* 24 (1975): 137–142.

Parkes, Collin Murray. *Bereavement.* New York: International Universities Press, 1972.

Pearce, W. Barnett, and Sharp, Stewart M. "Self-Disclosing Communication." *Journal of Communication* 23 (1973): 409–425.

Pearson, Willie, Jr., and Hendrix, Lewellyn. "Divorce and the Status of Women." *Journal of Marriage and the Family* 41 (1979): 375–385.

Phillips, Richard. "Exploding the Myths of Adolescence." *Chicago Tribune,* May 6, 1979, Sec. 12, 1–4.

Piers, Maria W. *Growing up with Children.* Chicago: Quadrangle Books, 1966.

Pincus, Lily, and Dare, Christopher. *Secrets in the Family.* New York: Pantheon Books, 1978.

Pleck, Joseph H., and Sawyer, Jack. *Men and Masculinity.* Englewood Cliffs, N.J.: Prentice-Hall, 1974.

Pollard, W. E., and Mitchell, T. R. "Decision Theory Analysis of Social Power." *Psychological Bulletin* 78 (1972): 433–446.

Price-Bonham, Sharon. "A Comparison of Weighted and Unweighted Decision-Making Scores." *Journal of Marriage and the Family* 38 (1976): 629–640.

Rapoport, Rhona. "The Transition from Engagement to Marriage." In M. E. Lasswell and T. E. Lasswell (eds.), *Love, Marriage, Family: A Developmental Approach.* Glenview, IL: Scott, Foresman & Co., 1973, 250–258.

Raschke, Helen J., and Raschke, Vernon J. "Family Conflict and Children's Self-Concepts: A Comparison of Intact and Single-Parent Families." *Journal of Marriage and the Family* 41 (1979): 367–374.

Raush, H. L.; Barry, W. A.; Hertel, R. K.; and Swain, M. A. *Communication Conflict and Marriage.* San Francisco: Jossey-Bass, 1974.

Raven, B.; Centers, C.; and Rodrigues, A. "The Bases of Conjugal Power." in R. E. Cromwell and D. H. Olson (eds.), *Power in Families.* New York: Halsted Press, 1975, 217–234.

Ritter, Ellen. "Social Perspective-Taking Ability, Cognitive Complexity and Listener-Adopted Communication in Early and Late Adolescence." *Communication Monographs* 46 (1979): 42–50.

Rivenbark, W. H. "Self-Disclosure Patterns Among Adolescents." *Psychological Reports* 28 (1971): 35–42.

Rogers, Carl R. *Becoming Partners: Marriage and its Alternatives.* New York: Delta Books, 1972.

Rogers-Millar, L. Edna, and Millar, Frank E. "Domineeringness and Dominance: A Transactional View." *Human Communication Research* 5 (1979): 238–246.

Rollins, Boyd C., and Bahr, Stephen J. "A Theory of Power Relationships in Marriage." *Journal of Marriage and the Family* 38 (1976): 619–627.

Rollins, Boyd C., and Cannon, K. "Marital Satisfaction over the Family Life Cycle: A Re-evaluation." *Journal of Marriage and the Family* 36 (1974): 271–283.

Rollins, Boyd C., and Feldman, Harold. "Marital Satisfaction over the Family Life Cycle." In M. E. Lasswell and T. E. Lasswell (eds.), *Love, Marriage, Family: A Developmental Approach.* Glenview, IL: Scott, Foresman and Co., 1973, 381–383.

Rollins, Boyd C., and Thomas, Darwin L. "A Theory of Parental Power and Child Compliance." In R. E. Cromwell and D. H. Olson (eds.), *Power in Families.* New York: Halsted Press, 1975, 38–60.

Rosenblatt, Paul C.; Titus, Sandra L.; and Cunningham, Michael R. "Disrespect, Tension, and Togetherness-Apartness in Marriage." *Journal of Marital and Family Therapy* 5 (1979): 47–54.

Rosenfeld, Lawrence; Civikly, Jean; and Herron, Jane. "Anatomical and Psychological Sex Differences." In *Self-Disclosure.* Gordon Chelune and Associates (eds.). San Francisco: Jossey-Bass, 1979, 80–109.

Rossi, Alice. "Transition to Parenthood." *Journal of Marriage and the Family* 30 (1968): 26–39.

Rossi, Alice S. "Transition to Parenthood." In M. E. Lasswell & T. E. Lasswell (eds.), *Love, Marriage, Family: A Developmental Approach.* Glenview, IL: Scott, Foresman & Co., 1973, 334–343.

Rubin, Lillian. *Women of a Certain Age: The Midlife Search for Self.* New York: Harper & Row, 1979.

Russell, Candyce S. "Circumplex Model of Marital and Family Systems." *Family Process* 18 (1979): 29–45.

Safilios-Rothschild, Constantina. "The Study of Family Power Structure: 1960–1969." *Journal of Marriage and The Family* 32 (1970): 539–552.

Satir, Virginia. *Conjoint Family Therapy.* Palo Alto, Calif.: Science & Behavior Books, 1967.

Satir, Virginia. *Peoplemaking.* Palo Alto, Calif.: Science & Behavior Books, 1972.

Satir, Virginia; Stachowiak, James; and Taschman, Harvey. *Helping Families to Change.* New York: Jason Aronson, 1975.

Sawin, Douglas B., and Parke, Ross D. "Fathers' Affectionate Stimulation and Caregiving Behaviors with Newborn Infants." *Family Coordinator* 28 (1979): 509–519.

Sawin, Margaret. *Family Enrichment with Family Clusters.* Valley Forge, Pa.: Judson Press, 1979.

Sawyer, Jack. "On Male Liberation." *Liberation* 15 (1970): 6–8.

Scanzoni, John. *Sexual Bargaining.* Englewood Cliffs, N.J.: Prentice-Hall, 1972.

Scanzoni, John. "Strategies for Changing Male Family Roles: Research and Practice Implications." *Family Coordinator* 28 (1979): 435–444.

Scanzoni, John, and Polonko, Karen. "A Conceptual Approach to Explicit Marital Negotiation." *Journal of Marriage and the Family* 42 (1980): 31–44.

Scheflen, Albert. "Living Space in an Urban Ghetto." *Family Process* 10 (1971): 429–449.

Schram, Rosalyn W. "Marital Satisfaction over the Family Life Cycle: A Critique and Proposal." *Journal of Marriage And The Family* 41 (1979): 7–12.

Schutz, William. "The Postulate of Interpersonal Needs: Description." *Interpersonal Communication: Basic Text and Readings.* Bobby Patton and Kim Giffin (eds.). New York: Harper & Row, 1974, 205–224.

Scoresby, A. Lynn. *The Marriage Dialogue.* Reading, Mass.: Addison-Wesley, 1977.

Sheehy, Gail. *Passages.* New York: Bantam Publishing Co., 1976.

Sieburg, Evelyn. "Interpersonal Confirmation: A Paradigm for Conceptualization and Measurement." Paper presented at International Communication Association, Montreal, Quebec, 1973. ERIC Document No. ED 098 634 1975.

Slocum, Walter L, and Nye, F. Ivan. "Provider and Housekeeper Roles." In F. Ivan Nye (ed.), *Role Structure and Analysis of the Family.* Beverly Hills, Calif.: Sage Publications, 1976, 81–99.

Smith, Reger. "Put Marriage on Your Checkup List." *Marriage Enrichment.* (Newsletter of Association of Couples for Marriage Enrichment), 7, #1 (1980): 1–3.

Snyder, Elise C. "Attitudes: A Study of Homogamy and Marital Selectivity." In M. E. Lasswell and T. E. Lasswell (eds.), *Love, Marriage, Family: A Developmental Approach.* Glenview, IL: Scott, Foresman & Co., 1973, 233–236.

Speck, Ross, and Atneave, Carolyn L. *Family Networks.* New York: Vintage Books, Random House, 1974.

Spector, Bertram I. "Negotiation as a Psychological Process." *Journal of Conflict Resolution* 21 (1977): 607–618.

Spitzer, S. P.; Swanson, R. M.; and Lehr, R. K. "Audience Reactions and Careers of Psychiatric Patients." In Nathan Ackerman (ed.), *Family Process.* New York: Basic Books, 1970, 386–408.

Sporakowski, Michael J., and Hughston, George. "Prescriptions for Happy Marriage: Adjustments and Satisfactions of Couples Married 50 or More Years." *The Family Coordinator* 27 (1978): 321–328.

Sprey, Jetse. "The Family as a System in Conflict." *Journal of Marriage and the Family* 31 (1969): 699–706.

Sprey, Jetse. "On the Management of Conflict in Families." *Journal of Marriage and the Family* 33 (1971): 722–731.

Sprey, Jetse. "Family Power and Process: Toward a Conceptual Integration." In R. E. Cromwell and D. H. Olson (eds.), *Power in Families.* New York: Halsted Press, 1975.

Stachowiak, James. "Functional and Dysfunctional Families." In Satir et al. (eds.), *Helping Families to Change.* New York: Jason Aronson, 1975.

Steinmetz, S. K. "Monkeys See, Monkeys Do: The Learning of Aggressive Behavior." Paper presented at meeting of National Council on Family Relations, 1973.

Steinmetz, S. K. "Intra-Familial Patterns of Conflict Resolution: United States and Canadian Comparisons." Paper presented at meeting of Society for Study of Social Problems, 1974.

Steinmetz, S. K. "The Use of Force For Resolving Family Conflict: The Training Ground For Abuse." *Family Coordinator* 26 (1977): 19–26.

Steinmetz, S. K., and Straus, M. A. *Violence in the Family.* New York: Harper & Row, 1974.

Steinor, Claude. "Problems of Power." Lecture at National Group Leaders Conference, Chicago, March 22, 1978.

Straus, Murray A. "Leveling, Civility, and Violence in the Family." *Journal of Marriage and the Family* 36 (1974): 13–29; and "Addendum" 36 (Aug.): 442–445.

Straus, Murray A. "Measuring Intrafamily Conflict and Violence: The Conflict Tactics (CT) Scales." *Journal of Marriage and the Family* 41 (1979): 75–88.

Strodbeck, F. L. "Husband-Wife Interaction Over Revealed Differences." *American Sociological Review* 16 (1951): 468–473.

Strong, J. R. "A Marital Conflict Resolution Model: Redefining Conflict to Achieve Intimacy." *Journal of Marriage and the Family* 33 (1971): 269–276.

Stuckert, R. P. "Role Perception in Marital Satisfaction—A Configuration Approach." *Marriage and Family Living* 25 (1963): 415–419.

Taylor, A. B. "Role Perception, Empathy, and Marital Adjustment." *Sociology and Social Research* 52 (1967): 22–34.

Terkelsen, Kenneth G. "Toward a Theory of the Family Life Cycle." *The Family Life Cycle: A Framework for Family Therapy.* Elizabeth A. Carter and Monica McGoldrick (eds.). New York: Gardner Press, Inc., 1980, 21–52.

Thibaut, J. W., and Kelley, H. H. *The Social Psychology of Groups.* New York: John Wiley & Sons, 1959.

Thomas, Edwin J. *Marital Communication and Decision Making: Analysis, Assessment, and Change.* New York: The Free Press, 1977.

Toffler, Alvin. *Future Shock.* New York: Bantam Books, 1971.

Toman, Walter. *Family Constellation,* 3rd ed. New York: Springer Publishing Co., 1976.

Troll, Lillian E. *Early and Middle Adulthood.* Monterey, Calif.: Brooks-Cole Publishing Co., 1975.

Troll, Lillian; Miller, Sheila; and Atchley, Robert. *Families in Later Life.* Belmont, Calif.: Wadsworth Publishing Co., 1979.

Turk, James L. "Power as the Achievement of Ends: A Problematic Approach in Family and Small Group Research." *Family Process* 13 (1974): 39–52.

Turk, James L. "Uses and Abuses of Family Power." In R. E. Cromwell and D. H. Olson (eds.), *Power in Families.* New York: John Wiley & Sons, 1975, 80–94.

Turk, James L., and Bell, N. W. "Measuring Power in Families." *Journal of Marriage and the Family* 34 (1972): 215–222.

Turner, Ralph H. "Conflict and Harmony." *Family Interaction.* New York: John Wiley & Sons, 1970, 135–163. See also "Decision Making Process," 97–116; "Determinants of Dominance," 117–135.

"TV's Top Interviewer Phil Donahue." *Chicago Tribune,* February 3, 1980, Sec. 9, p. 12.

Udry, J. R. *Social Context of Marriage.* New York: J. B. Lippincott, 1966.

"Understanding the Irish Culture: Key to Successful Therapy." *Marriage and Divorce Today.* Vol. 5, #34, April 7, 1980, 1–2.

Van Dyke, Vicki. "Understanding Child Abuse." Springfield, IL: Illinois Department of Children and Family Services, 1977.

Verwoerdt, A. "Comments On Communication with the Fatally Ill." *Omega,* 2:1 (1967): 10–11.

Villard, Kenneth, and Whipple, Leland. *Beginnings in Relational Communication.* New York: John Wiley and Sons, 1976.

Vincent, C. "Familia Spongia: The Adaptive Function." *Journal of Marriage and the Family* 28 (1966): 29–36.

Vines, Neville R. "Adult Unfolding and Marital Conflict." *Journal of Marital and Family Therapy* 5 (1979): 5–14.

Wackman, Daniel. "Communication Training in Marriage and Family Living." Paper presented at Speech Communication Association Convention, 1978.

Wallerstein, J. S., and Kelley, J. B. "The Effects of Parental Divorce: Experiences of the Pre-School Child." *Journal of the American Academy of Child Psychiatry* 14 (1975): 600–616.

Wallerstein, J. S., and Kelley, J. B. *Surviving the Breakup: How Children and Parents Cope With Divorce.* New York: Basic Books, Inc., 1980.

Walsh, Froma. "The Family in Later Life". In *The Family Life Cycle: A Framework for Family Therapy.* Elizabeth Carter and Monica McGoldrick (eds.). New York: Gardner Press, 1980, 197–220.

Walters, J., and Stinnett, N. "Parent-Child Relationships: A Decade Review of Research." C. Broderick (ed.), *A Decade of Family Research and Action.* Minneapolis: National Council on Family Relations, 1971.

Wampler, Karen S., and Sprenkle, Douglas H. "The Minnesota Couple Communication Program." *Journal of Marriage and the Family* 42 (1980): 577–584.

Ward, Allan. "The Influence on Family Communication of a Specific Belief System: The Baha'i Faith." Paper presented at Southern Speech Communication Association, Birmingham, 1980.

Waterman, Jill. "Family Patterns of Self-Disclosure." In Gordon Chelune and Associates (eds.), *Self Disclosure.* San Francisco: Jossey-Bass, 1979, 225–242.

Watzlawick, P.; Beavin, J.; and Jackson, D. D. *Pragmatics of Human Communication.* New York: W. W. Norton & Co., 1967.

Weaver, Carl, and Mayhew, Jean. "The Use of the Family Council as a Technique in Reducing a Communication Barrier." *Journal of Communication* 9 (1959): 68–76.

Weiss, Robert S. *Marital Separation.* New York: Basic Books, 1975.

Westin, Alan. *Privacy and Freedom.* New York: Atheneum, 1967.

Westman, J. C. "Effects of Divorce on a Child's Personality Development." *Medical Aspects of Human Sexuality* 6 (1972): 38–55.

White, Burton. *The First Three Years of Life.* Englewood Cliffs, N.J.: Prentice-Hall, 1975.

Wieting, S. G., and McLaren, A. "Power in Various Family Structures." In R. E. Cromwell and D. H. Olson (eds.), *Power in Families.* NY: Halsted Press, 1975, 95–116.

Wilkinson, Charles. "Effective Marital Communication." Lecture given at Winnetka Presbyterian Church, Fall 1979.

Wilmot, William W. *Dyadic Communication: A Transactional Perspective.* Reading, Mass.: Addison-Wesley, 1975. Revised 1979.

Winch, R.; Ktsanes, T.; and Ktsanes, U. "The Theory of Complementary Needs in Mate Selection: An Analytic and Descriptive Study." *American Sociological Review* 19 (1954): 241–249.

Winter, William D.; Ferreira, Antonio J.; and Bowers, Norman. "Decision-Making in Married and Unrelated Couples." *Family Process* 12 (1973): 83–94.

Wolfe, D. M. "Power and Authority in the Family". In D. Cartwright (ed.), *Studies in Social Power.* Ann Arbor: University of Michigan, Institute for Social Research, 1959.

Wood, Barbara. *Children and Communication.* Englewood Cliffs, N.J.: Prentice-Hall, 1976.

Woodward, Kenneth L.; Lord, Mary; Maier, Frank; Foote, Donna M.; and Malamud, Phyllis. "Saving The Family." *Newsweek* 90 (1978): 63.

Zartman, I. William. "Negotiation as a Joint Decision-Making Process." *Journal of Conflict Resolution* 21 (1977): 619–638.

AUTHOR INDEX

SUBJECT INDEX